Melanie Klein
Today

VOLUME 1

THE NEW LIBRARY OF PSYCHOANALYSIS

The New Library of Psychoanalysis, published by Routledge, London and New York, was launched in 1987 in association with the Institute of Psycho-Analysis, London. Its purpose is to provide a forum for increasing mutual understanding between psychoanalysts of different countries and between psychoanalysis and other disciplines. The titles chosen for publication in the series are selected primarily to deepen and develop psychoanalytic thinking and technique; they may contribute to psychoanalysis from other disciplines, or to other disciplines from an analytic perspective; they may also be works in translation which meet any of these criteria.

The Institute, together with the British Psycho-Analytical Society, runs a low-fee psychoanalytic clinic, organizes lectures and scientific events concerned with psychoanalysis, publishes the *International Journal of Psychoanalysis*, and also runs the only training course in the UK in psychoanalysis leading to membership of the International Psychoanalytical Association. Distinguished members of the Institute have included Michael Balint, Wilfred Bion, Ronald Fairbairn, Anna Freud, Ernest Jones, Melanie Klein, John Rickman, and Donald Winnicott. The present editor of the New Library of Psychoanalysis is Elizabeth Bott Spillius, with Donald Campbell, Michael Parsons, Rosine Jozef Perelberg and David Taylor as associate editors.

Other titles in the New Library of Psychoanalysis are listed at the back of this book.

NEW LIBRARY OF PSYCHOANALYSIS

7

General editor: David Tuckett

Melanie Klein Today

DEVELOPMENTS IN THEORY
AND PRACTICE
VOLUME 1: MAINLY THEORY

edited by
ELIZABETH BOTT SPILLIUS

London and New York

First published in 1988 by
Routledge
11 New Fetter Lane, London EC4P 4EE

Simultaneously published in the USA and Canada by
Routledge
29 West 35th Street, New York NY 10001

Reprinted in 1990, 1994, 1996

Routledge is an International Thomson Publishing company

Set by Hope Services (Abingdon) Ltd
Printed in England by Clays Ltd, St Ives plc

British Library Cataloguing in Publication Data
Melanie Klein today: developments in theory and practice./
(The New library of psychoanalysis; 7)
Vol. 1: Mainly theory
1. Klein, Melanie   2. Psychoanalysis
I. Series
150.19'5   BF173

Library of Congress Cataloguing in Publication Data
Melanie Klein today: developments in theory and practice /
edited by Elizabeth Bott Spillius.
p.   cm. – (New library of psychoanalysis: 7)
Bibliography: p.
Includes index.
Contents: v. 1. Mainly theory.
1. Klein, Melanie.   2. Psychoanalysis.
I. Spillius, Elizabeth Bott, 1924– . II. Series.
RC506.K57M45   1988
150.19'–dc19

ISBN 0–415–00675–9 (hbk)
ISBN 0–415–00676–7 (pbk)

Contents

v

Acknowledgements

I want here to thank the Melanie Klein Trust whose generous financial help made possible the preparation of this book, and to thank many colleagues for their help, most particularly Miss Betty Joseph, Dr Hanna Segal, and Mrs Edna O'Shaughnessy who have given painstakingly discriminating advice and assistance.

I also want to thank Ms Jill Duncan and Mrs Jane Temperley who helped with the references, and Miss Jennifer Jeynes and my daughter, Mrs Sisifa Spillius Mitropoulou, who patiently typed the manuscript and references through apparently endless corrections.

I would also like to thank the following for their kind permission to reproduce copyright material: the *International Journal of Psycho-Analysis*, Mrs Francesca Bion, Miss Betty Joseph, Mrs Lottie Rosenfeld, and individual authors for papers published in that journal (Part One: 1, 2, 3; Part Two: 1, 2, 4; Part Three: 2, 3; Part Four: 2, 3, 4, 5, 6, 7, 8); Jason Aronson Inc. and Dr Hanna Segal (Part Three: 1); Jason Aronson Inc. (Part Four: 1); Elsevier Science Publishers/Excerpta Medica and Mrs Lottie Rosenfeld (Part Two: 3). Full details of original publication are given at the head of each paper.

General introduction

The aim of this book is to present and discuss a set of papers which illustrate the development of Melanie Klein's concepts and formulations, written by her colleagues and followers during the past thirty years.

In this general introduction I shall look in a very schematic way at certain main themes in the work of Klein's followers. Several of these themes will then be discussed in greater detail in the succeeding sections of the book. For these more detailed discussions I have picked out themes that have particularly stimulated Klein's colleagues to expand and develop her original formulations through new research.

Volume 1 is concerned with contributions on four topics mainly to do with theory: the analysis of psychotics; work on projective identification; the development of theory about thinking; and new ideas about pathological mental organizations. Volume 2 presents papers that are mainly concerned with practice, clinical and applied: technique, clinical descriptions of adult patients, child analysis, and the application of Kleinian ideas in other fields and disciplines. Although I find it convenient to separate theoretical and clinical papers in this way, such separation is inevitably artificial, especially since it is part of the Kleinian tradition that clinical material should be the focus of discussion even in papers whose primary aim is to make a contribution to theory. I hope that the interplay of ideas and evidence will be abundantly revealed in the papers themselves.

Because I have selected papers according to topic rather than according to author, many important papers and several authors are not included because they have not written on the topics selected. I have further restricted the discussion by confining it almost entirely to developments in Britain, virtually excluding the use made of Kleinian ideas in North and South America and on the Continent. I have focused mainly on work since 1950 because an important collection of papers by Klein's colleagues of that time was published in the notable volume *New Directions in Psycho-Analysis* (edited by Klein and others, 1955). For the most part I take familiarity with Klein's own work for granted. The original texts are to be found in *The Writings of Melanie Klein* (1975) and H. Segal gives a comprehensive introduction to Klein's work (Segal 1964a and 1973).

A crucial experience that informs all Klein's work is that it was initiated in the study and treatment of children. This is the bedrock. It gives her work a peculiar immediacy; it encouraged and made full use of her talent for grasping the meaning of unconscious phantasy. At the same time Klein never lost sight of the child as a whole, as a person struggling with unruly forces rather than the child as a set of phantasies and mental mechanisms. Clinical material from working with children gave her a rich set of facts to explain and led her eventually to develop new theories. Theory building was never an end in itself for Klein, however. It was a means to the end of making better sense of the facts uncovered in the work with patients, adults as well as children.

Klein's colleagues and followers have been inspired by her attitude and have tried to follow her basic orientation. Many lines of work that she initiated have been explored and further developed; others have been refined and filled in. Certain new clinical facts have been uncovered, especially in the treatment of psychotic patients, which have led to new conceptions. But her basic orientation and formulations have been retained.

Indeed, some of Klein's most important concepts have been very little altered or developed by her followers even though the concepts are in constant use. Her particular outlook on unconscious phantasy, on internal objects and the inner world, her orientation on instinct theory and object relationship, her views on the death instinct and envy, and much of her work on defences come into this category. These ideas have been criticized by non-Kleinian analysts but Kleinians have found them valid and useful, and it is perhaps because the ideas have not been much modified in subsequent work that no one has felt a need to write about them extensively. Such papers as have been published by Kleinian analysts specifically on these topics appear to have been written for purposes of expounding Klein's views as they are currently used rather than to extend or develop them.

Klein developed her ideas about unconscious phantasy. for

example, from one of Freud's several usages. She extended it to mean the psychic representative of instinct and the primary content of unconscious mental processes (see Isaacs 1948). Klein developed this view of unconscious phantasy largely from finding that the children she analysed had violently aggressive and loving phantasies that were the source of intense anxiety. She was impressed by the vividness and bodily concreteness of the phantasies and by the intensity of conflict they expressed. Her emphasis on the psychic reality of unconscious phantasy, on conflict between love and hate in the Unconscious, on anxiety as the dominant problem confronting the ego, on emotions as well as ideas as major unconscious contents, on mechanisms of defence being expressed through specific unconscious phantasies – all these ideas about unconscious phantasy have been accepted and used by Klein's followers to the point of being taken for granted. It is noteworthy that since the writing and discussion of Isaacs' original paper (1948) comparatively little has been written specifically on the topic even though the idea is basic to every Kleinian's daily work. (But see especially Segal 1964b and also Joseph 1981.)

Klein's theory is simultaneously an instinct theory and an object-relations theory. Like Freud, she thought of the individual as driven by life and death instincts, but she never speaks of instincts in and of themselves or divorced from objects; they are inherently attached to objects. Kleinians thus view object relationship as fundamental to their orientation, though they have written relatively little about it as an end in itself. (But see Riesenberg-Malcolm 1981b.) It is a source of astonishment to discover that the work of Klein and her followers is sometimes considered not to be an object-relations theory, presumably because of Klein's emphasis on the simultaneous importance of instinct and its expression in phantasy.

Because in Klein's view instincts are inherently attached to objects, relationships with external objects are assumed to become the focus of unconscious phantasy as soon as any form of mental activity is possible. Klein assumes that the individual has a rudimentary ego at birth involving a capacity to feel anxiety and to try to do something psychically to fend it off. Similarly, she assumes that the newborn baby has a rudimentary capacity to relate to objects in external reality and in phantasy, though she makes it clear that the capacity to distinguish internal from external is at first very limited (M. Klein 1942). Through the constant operation in phantasy of projection, introjection, and identification, an inner world of objects and self is built up which is used throughout life to give meaning to events in the external world.

3

Klein makes more use clinically than Freud did of the concept of the death instinct, and posits constitutional envy as the most destructive and intractable form of it, a topic which formed the subject matter of her last major theoretical work, *Envy and Gratitude* (1957). Her idea of constitutional envy has been much criticized by non-Kleinians in the British Psycho-Analytical Society particularly in a symposium on the subject held in 1969, but Klein's followers have continued to find the concept essential to their work. Few papers have been written specifically on the concept (but see Segal 1973, chapter 4, and Joseph 1986) although it is widely used and comes into the discussion of nearly every other major topic.

Klein's major contribution to psychoanalytical theory is her formulation of the paranoid-schizoid and depressive positions (M. Klein 1935, 1940, 1946; see also Segal 1973). It is sometimes said that Klein, in spite of her brilliance as a clinician, was not a theoretician (Meltzer 1978, Mitchell 1986), a view that overlooks the fact that her formulation of the theory of the paranoid-schizoid and depressive positions has fundamentally altered many analysts' views of psychic development and functioning and has influenced the outlook of many others, including many who are not Kleinians. These conceptions have proved to be great seminal formulations that have been the starting point and inspiration of much subsequent work.

Klein conceives of the depressive position as a constellation of characteristic anxieties, defences, and object relationships that normally develops in the second trimester of infancy but continues throughout life, never totally worked through. All Kleinian analysts find this conception basic to their work. In her delineation Klein describes the distinctive features of the depressive position as the integration of part objects to form the whole object and the painful recognition by the individual that his feelings of love and hate are directed to the same, whole object. The theme of concern for the object is central to the idea. These features have been retained by Klein's colleagues, but use of the idea in the study of psychotics, borderline patients, and very envious patients has led to a gradual and increasing emphasis on recognition of the object's separateness and independence as another hallmark of the depressive position. Studies of thinking and artistic endeavour have also showed the very close, indeed intrinsic, relationship that exists between the depressive position, symbolic thought, and creativity (Segal, 1952, 1957, 1974).

One of the most striking features of Klein's work, though perhaps in a sense a superficial feature, is her concentration on anatomical part objects, especially the breast and the penis, as the earliest objects of infantile and unconscious preoccupation. She based this on the importance of such part objects in the thinking and play of small children and their continuing importance in the Unconscious of older children and adults. She assumed that the basis of this importance was that the breast was the focus of the infant's first experiences of the mother and therefore in a sense *is* the mother and is used virtually as a representation of her. For reasons discussed in the section of volume 2 that deals with technique, some Kleinian analysts have begun to be more cautious when formulating interpretations about using the language of anatomical part objects.

But the change is more than terminological. There has been a gradual shift from structure to function, that is, from an idea that we relate to anatomical part objects towards an idea that we relate to psychological part objects (a phrasing of it suggested to me by Edna O'Shaughnessy), to the functions of the part object rather than primarily to its physical structure. It is capacities for seeing, touching, tasting, hearing, smelling, remembering, feeling, judging, and thinking, active as well as passive, that are attributed to and perceived in relation to part objects. In a sense thinking in terms of anatomical part objects, so clearly expressed by small children as soon as they can talk, can be thought of as a relatively advanced conception, one in which various part-functions have been brought together to form an integrated set attributed to physical, anatomical structure. Nowadays it is functions rather than anatomical part objects that Kleinian analysts look out for in their clinical work, and interpretations are likely to be framed, at least initially, in terms of function rather than in the language of anatomical structure; in keeping with Klein's concept of projective identification, these functions are frequently understood as aspects of the self which are projected into the part object.

Klein's conception of the paranoid-schizoid position as a constellation of anxieties, defences, and object relationships characteristic of earliest infancy has been a major source of inspiration to her colleagues. In the 1950s a special interest developed in the application of her ideas about the paranoid-schizoid position to the analysis of psychotic patients, a very fruitful inquiry which led to much further work, especially to Rosenfeld's work on confusional states and narcissism, Segal's theory of symbolism, and Bion's work on thinking. Further work with psychotic patients and the psychotic aspects of normal patients has confirmed Klein's delineation of the anxieties and defences of the paranoid-schizoid position, especially the defences of splitting, projective identification, fragmentation, introjection and idealization. Projective identification has been the focus of much work and writing, though the other defences are equally crucial in Kleinian thinking and work.

In succeeding decades this research has been broadened to include study not only of psychotic but also of narcissistic and borderline patients by many Kleinian analysts, most notably perhaps by Herbert Rosenfeld, Henri Rey, Leslie Sohn, and John Steiner. The study of narcissistic and borderline patients has led to a great deal of interest in what have come to be called 'pathological organizations', meaning relatively stable collusive relationships within the self, suffused with death instinct, and serving to maintain the individual's psychic balance but making maintenance of whole object relationships unstable and acceptance of psychic and external reality unreliable. Through this work with narcissistic and borderline patients several analysts have developed ideas both about sexual perversions and about perversions of character, meaning not exclusively frank sexual malpractice but the distortion and misuse of psychic and external reality. Betty Joseph has been particularly interested in perversions of character and perversion of the transference.

Several analysts have developed or maintained interest in other psychopathological entities and processes that are closely concerned with the anxieties and defences of the paranoid–schizoid position. Psychotics have continued to be studied by Sohn and several others; manic states by S. Klein (1974); hysteria by Brenman (1985b); problems concerning separation and separateness by Brenman (1982); autism by Meltzer and S. Klein (Meltzer *et al*. 1975, S. Klein 1980); eating disorders by Sohn, Scott, Thorner, and Hughes (Sohn 1985b, Scott 1948, Thorner 1970, Hughes, Furgiuele, and Bianco 1985); forensic problems by Hyatt Williams (1960, 1964, 1969, 1978, 1982, and Williams, Hyatt, and Coltart 1975), Sohn (in press), Gallwey (1985 and in press), and S. Klein (1984); psychosomatic disorders especially by Meltzer (1964), S. Klein (1965), Rosenfeld (1978b) and M. Jackson (1978). But the topic that has been studied and discussed repeatedly and has therefore been chosen for detailed discussion in the present volume is the working out of ideas about pathological organizations to interpret the data of narcissistic and borderline states.

Finally, there have been important developments and conceptualizations of Kleinian technique, a central aspect of Klein's approach but one that has only begun to be written about by her followers comparatively recently. Certain analysts, notably Betty Joseph, have developed a particular focus on the analysis of acting in the transference as a means of fostering emotional contact and change. Perhaps in response to Joseph's ideas, other colleagues have begun to state their own ideas about technique more explicitly. Discussion of this work forms a major part of the second volume of this book. The second volume also presents several clinical papers on both adult and child patients which illustrate many of the themes discussed in the first volume. A final section of the second volume discusses the application of Kleinian ideas to other fields of work, especially in the fields of artistic creativity and the understanding of society.

Note
References for the general introduction and the introductions to the four parts of the book will be found at the end of the volume.

PART ONE

The analysis of psychotic patients

Introduction

The 1950s were an important period in the development of Kleinian practice and thinking because Klein's ideas about psychotic anxieties and defences were tested with severely ill patients, mainly schizophrenics. A further aim was to see whether psychotic patients could be analysed without departures from the essentials of psychoanalytic technique. As in the case of Klein's analysis of children, the analysis of psychotic patients threw up new material and led to the development of new ideas and areas of interest.

Rosenfeld, Segal and Bion were the first explorers in this field (see Rosenfeld 1947, 1949, 1950, 1952 (reprinted here), 1954, 1963; Segal 1950 (reprinted in volume 2 of the present work) and 1956 (reprinted here); and Bion 1950, 1954, 1955, 1956, 1957 (reprinted here), 1958a, 1958b, and 1959 (reprinted here in Part Two: Projective identification)). This remarkable series of papers got off to a memorable start with Rosenfeld's 'Analysis of a schizophrenic state with depersonalization' in 1947 which illustrated many of the ideas that Klein had described in her epoch-making paper 'Notes on some schizoid mechanisms' in 1946. Segal's 1950 paper 'Some aspects of the analysis of a schizophrenic', reprinted in volume 2 of the present work, is particularly striking because it is the earliest account of the detailed psychoanalytic treatment of a hospitalized schizophrenic patient without significant modifications of psychoanalytic technique.

Segal, Rosenfeld, and Bion all agree on the viability of the psychoanalytic method in treating psychotic patients, though Rosenfeld discusses it in more detail than Segal and Bion (Rosenfeld, 1952). All report improvement in their patients, though they also make it clear that the patients were exceedingly difficult to understand. All

11

found impressive substantiation of Klein's views on the paranoid-schizoid position as the fixation point of schizophrenia, and all found much confirmation of her views on projective identification, the early and persecuting superego, the pain of depressive anxiety, and retreat from it to the defences of the paranoid-schizoid position.

But none of these authors stopped at confirmation of Klein's ideas. Rosenfeld became interested in failure to differentiate love from hate and self from other in the paranoid-schizoid position, ideas that he developed in papers on confusional states and on narcissism (1950, 1964, 1971b (reprinted below in Part Four: Pathological organizations)). Segal was stimulated to further study of the part played by success or failure in negotiating depressive anxieties in the development of symbolic thinking and in creativity (Segal 1952 and 1957 (reprinted in this volume in Part Three: On thinking)). Bion, probably the most original of Klein's students and colleagues, began to develop ideas about the differences between normal and abnormal experience of the paranoid-schizoid position which led him to make a distinction between projective identification used to evacuate and fragment mental contents and projective identification as a form of communication that could influence the recipient and could in turn be influenced by him. This took him to a study of thinking which, in various forms and developments, remained the major preoccupation of his psychoanalytic life (Bion 1959 (reprinted here in Part Two: Projective identification), 1962a (reprinted here in Part Three: On thinking), 1962b, 1963, 1965, and 1970).

Three papers illustrate the work of this early period. In 'Notes on the psychoanalysis of the superego conflict of an acute schizophrenic patient' (1952) Rosenfeld gives a detailed account of his adherence to a fully psychoanalytic method of treating schizophrenics as contrasted with the introduction of modifications in technique which were being used at that time in the United States. He goes on to describe some details from a brief analysis of a young schizophrenic man who, in common with other schizophrenic patients, had an exceedingly primitive and severe superego. The reader can hardly fail to be struck by the clinical acumen with which Rosenfeld struggled to understand his patient's bizarre but touching communications. He gives detailed illustration of splitting, projective identification, introjection, ego disintegration through massive projective identification, the patient's difficulties in distinguishing self from object; he draws attention to his patient's primitive envy of the breast and the resources of his mother's body.

Segal's 'Depression in the schizophrenic' (1956) gives poignant clinical illustration not only of splitting and projective identification

12

but also of Klein's observation that the schizophrenic cannot stand the pain of the depressive position and regresses to the defences of the paranoid-schizoid position (M. Klein 1946). In one sequence of material the patient, unable to bear the pain of accepting responsibility for or awareness of having had phantasies of attacking her analyst and her father (her father had committed suicide), enacted the role of Ophelia, picking up and scattering imaginary flowers, and thus stirring up sadness (and sanity) in her analyst and claiming the irresponsibility of madness for herself.

Interestingly, Segal gave this paper at almost the same time as Bion's paper 'Differentiation of the psychotic from the non-psychotic personalities' (1957, reprinted here); they had not discussed their respective papers beforehand, but discovered that they were working on very similar lines. Bion's paper focuses on the general theory of pathological projective identification, whereas Segal's paper gives a specific illustration of it. In his paper Bion further develops Klein's view that everyone, however 'normal', suffers from some degree of psychotic anxiety and pathological defences against it and states that all psychotics have some degree of non-psychotic functioning and that it is to this part of the personality that the analyst addresses his interpretations. He describes the minute fragmentation of the psychotic personality, especially of that part of the mind that is aware of reality. Where the non-psychotic part of the personality would use repression, the psychotic part tries to rid itself of the part of the mind that carries out the repression. Projective identification, as carried out by the psychotic part of the personality, involves fragmentation, splitting into many particles, and projection of them which leads to the formation of what Bion calls 'bizarre objects'. The stage is set by the ideas of this paper for the development of his analysis of thinking.

Analysis of psychotic patients was continued after the 1950s by many Kleinian analysts but few papers have been published specifically on the analysability of psychotics or the relevance of Klein's delineation of the paranoid-schizoid position. Interest has shifted to the analysis of narcissistic and borderline patients and to their ways of maintaining their psychic equilibrium.

Notes on the psychoanalysis of the superego conflict of an acute schizophrenic patient

HERBERT ROSENFELD

This article was first published in 1952 in the *International Journal of Psycho-Analysis* 33: 111–31.

In analysing a number of acute and chronic schizophrenic patients during the last ten years, I have become increasingly aware of the importance of the superego in schizophrenia. In this paper I shall present details of the psychoanalysis of one acute catatonic patient in order to throw some light on the structure of the schizophrenic superego and its relation to schizophrenic ego disturbances. I also wish to discuss the controversy about methods of approach to acute schizophrenic patients.

The controversy concerning the approach to schizophrenic patients by psychoanalysis

In discussing the value of the psychoanalytic approach to schizophrenia, we have to remember that psychotherapists with widely different theories and equally different techniques claim success in helping the schizophrenic in the acute states of the disease. The attempt to concentrate on producing a quick therapeutic result in the acute schizophrenic state, irrespective of the method of approach, may be temporarily valuable to the individual patient and gratifying to the therapist; but the more difficult problem is to deal with the chronic mute phase of the disease.[1] The method of approaching the acute schizophrenic patient is important for several reasons. First, we must be sure that we are using a scientific method of investigation and treatment so that we can assess our psychopathological findings correctly. Secondly, our method should be one which can be used in treating a variety of cases, so that it is possible to teach it to our students. Thirdly, our method of approach must also help, not hinder, the treatment of the chronic phase of schizophrenia which follows the acute one. Psychoanalysts have satisfied themselves that psychoanalysis is a method of investigation which serves both treatment and research in neurosis. There is, however, disagreement as to whether psychoanalysis can be used in the treatment of acute schizophrenia. Most American psychoanalytical workers on schizophrenia, for example, Harry Stack Sullivan, Fromm-Reichmann, Federn, Knight, Wexler, Eissler, and Rosen, etc., have changed their method of approach so considerably that it can no longer be called psychoanalysis. They seem all agreed that it is futile to regard the psychoanalytical method as useful for acute psychosis. They all find re-education and reassurance absolutely necessary; some workers like Federn go so far as to think that the positive transference has to be fostered and the negative one avoided altogether. He also warns us against interpreting unconscious material. Rosen seems to interpret unconscious material in the positive and negative transference, but he also uses a great deal of reassurance, a problem which I shall discuss later on in greater detail. A number of English[2] psychoanalysts, stimulated by Melanie Klein's research on the early stages of infantile development, have been successful in treating acute and chronic schizophrenics by a method which retains the essential features of psychoanalysis. Psychoanalysis in this sense can be defined as a method which comprises interpretation of the positive and negative transference without the use of reassurance or educative measures, and the recognition and interpretation of the unconscious material produced by the patient. The experience of child analysts may help us here to define in more detail the psychoanalytic approach to acute schizophrenics, because the technical problems arising in the analysis of acute psychotics are similar to those encountered in the analysis of small children. In discussing the analysis of children from the age of two and three-quarter years onwards, Melanie Klein has found that by interpreting the positive and negative transference from the beginning of the analysis the transference neurosis develops. She regards any attempts to produce a positive transference by non-analytical means, like advice or presents, or reassurance by various means, not only as unnecessary but as positively detrimental to the analysis. She found certain modifications of the adult analysis necessary in analysing children. Children are not expected to lie on the couch, and not only their words but their play is used as analytical material. Co-operation between the child's parents and the analyst is desirable, as the child has to be brought to his sessions and the parents supply the infantile history and keep the analyst informed about real events. In the analysis of children as described by Melanie Klein, however, the fundamental features of psychoanalysis are fully retained.

All these experiences can be used for describing the guiding principles of the analysis of psychotics, particularly acute schizo-phrenic patients. If we avoid attempts to produce a positive transference by direct reassurance or expressions of love, and simply interpret the positive and negative transference, the psychotic manifestations attach themselves to the transference, and, in the same way as a transference neurosis develops in the neurotic, so, in the analysis of psychotics, there develops what may be called a 'transference psychosis'. The success of the analysis depends on our understanding of the psychotic manifestations in the transference situation.

With acute schizophrenic patients we scarcely ever use the analytic couch, and we make use not only of verbal utterances, but also of gestures and play as analytical material. Close co-operation between the analyst and parents or nurses is essential. Another important question is how often and how long at a time the patient should be seen. I have found that acute schizophrenic patients have to be seen at least six times a week, and often the usual 50 minutes' session has seemed to be insufficient. In my own experience it is better not to vary the length of time of the particular sessions, but to give the patient, if necessary, a prolonged session (1 hour 30 minutes) regularly. It is also unwise to interrupt the treatment for more than a few days while the patient is still in the acute state, because it may cause a prolonged setback in his clinical condition and in the analysis.

The analysis of schizophrenic patients has many pitfalls and the inexperienced analyst may find himself unable to cope with the problem analytically. It is in my opinion the very nature of the schizophrenic process which not only makes the analytic task a difficult one but is one of the reasons for the controversy about the possibility of an analytic approach. The answer to the controversy can only be found in practice: namely, by showing that a transference analysis of acute schizophrenic patients is possible; and by examining the nature of the schizophrenic transference and other central schizophrenic problems and anxieties.

I have the impression that the need to use controlling and reassuring methods is related to the difficulty of dealing with the schizophrenic superego by psychoanalysis. Milton Wexler (1951) has contributed to the understanding of this point in his paper 'The structural problem in schizophrenia'. In criticizing the view of

Alexander, who denies the existence of a superego in schizophrenics, Wexler says: 'To explain the schizophrenic's conflicts (hallucinations and illusions) wholly as expressions of disorganized instinctual demands that have lost their interconnection, is a travesty of the clinical picture of schizophrenia which often reflects some of the most brutal morality I have ever encountered. Certainly we are not dealing with a superego intact in all its functions, but a primitive, archaic structure in which the primal identification (incorporated figure of the mother) holds forth only the promise of condemnation, abandonment and consequent death. Though this structure may only be the forerunner of the superego which emerges with complete resolution of the Oedipus situation, its outline and dynamic force may be felt both in young children and schizophrenic patients, and if we do not see it (the superego), I suspect it is because we have not yet learned to recognize the most archaic aspects of its development.'

While fully recognizing the importance of the archaic superego, Wexler has, however, deviated considerably from psychoanalysis in his clinical approach. Apparently he did not attempt to analyse the transference situation. He tried to identify himself deliberately with the superego of his patient by agreeing with the patient's most cruel, moral self-accusations. In this way he established contact with his patient which he had failed to do before. The treatment continued while the therapist was taking over the role of a controlling and forbidding person (for example, he forbade the patient any sexual or aggressive provocations which threatened to disturb the therapeutic relationship). Wexler made it quite clear that he also acted in a very friendly, reassuring manner towards his patient.

The patient who had been distinctly helped by Wexler's method was a schizophrenic woman who had been in a mental hospital for five years. The theoretical background of his approach is the attempt of the therapist to identify himself with the superego of the patient. As soon as he has made contact with the patient in this way he feels that he has succeeded in his first task, and he (the therapist) then begins to act as a controlling but friendly superego. He claims that in this manner a satisfactory superego and ego–control is gradually established which brings the acute phase of schizophrenia to an end.

Rosen (1946) described a technique in approaching acute, excited, catatonic patients who felt pursued by frightening figures. He established contact by 'deliberately assuming the identity, or the identities, of the figures which appeared to be threatening the patient and reassured the latter that, far from threatening him, they would love and protect him'. In another case, Rosen (1950) directly assumed the role of a controlling person by telling his woman patient to drop a cigarette which she had grabbed. He also controlled her physically and told her to lie still on the couch and not to move. But towards the end of the session he described, he changed his attitude by saying, 'I am your mother now and I will permit you to do whatever you want.' In Wexler's and Rosen's case it is clear that the particular approach aims at a modification of the schizophrenic superego by direct control and reassurance. Wexler suggests that Knight's and Hayward's success in the treatment of their schizophrenic patients must have been also due to their taking over superego control. It seems likely that all these methods which use friendly reassurance have a similar aim, i.e. the modification of the superego.

Indeed, from this critical survey, it would seem that all these psychotherapeutic methods are aimed at a direct modification of the superego. But I should add that none of the workers I have quoted have so far made clear whether they tried to approach the acute schizophrenic patient by psychoanalysis and if so, why they failed.

Some psychoanalytic views about the superego in schizophrenia

Freud (1924) said: A transference neurosis corresponds to a conflict between ego and id, a narcissistic neurosis to that between ego and supergo, and a psychosis to that between ego and outer world.' This formula seems to suggest that he did not think the superego could play any role in schizophrenia. But earlier, in 1914, he pointed to a parallel between delusions of observation and the hearing of voices in paranoid diseases, and the manifestations of conscience. He suggested that 'the delusion of being watched presents the conscience in a regressive form, thereby revealing the genesis of this function'. He then proceeded to link the ego-ideal with homosexuality and the influence of parental criticism. Later on in the same paper (1914) he said that in paranoid diseases the origin or 'evolution of the conscience is regressively reproduced'. These statements of Freud (1914) imply that he did appreciate the importance of the superego in schizophrenia. He seems also to hint that the analysis of regressed schizophrenics suffering from auditory hallucinations might help to explain the origin of the superego. E. Pichon Rivieré (1947) stressed the importance of the superego in schizophrenia. He suggested that the psychoses (including schizophrenia) as well as the neuroses, are the outcome of a conflict between the id on the one hand and the ego at the service of the superego, on the other. He says: 'In the process of regression there arises a dissociation of the instincts and that of aggression is channelled both by the ego and the superego, thus determining the masochistic attitude of the former and the sadistic attitude of the latter. Tension between the two instances originates anxiety, guilt feelings and the need for punishment . . .'

Pious (1949) stated that he 'became convinced that the fundamental structural pathology in schizophrenia most probably lies in the formation of the supergo'. He believes in the early development of the superego, but only stresses its positive aspects. He says: 'The superego develops from several loci, the earliest of which is the introjection of the loving and protecting mother image. I believe that the development is jeopardized by prolonged privation and by hostility in the mother.' In his opinion the schizophrenic has a defective superego, but the structure of this defective superego is not explained.

Numberg expressed his views on the superego in schizophrenia in 1920. His patient who suffered from an extremely severe feeling of guilt, claimed that he had destroyed the world; and it became clear that he believed he had done so by eating. Numberg says: 'In his cannibalistic fantasies the patient identified the beloved persons with the food and with himself. To the infant the mother's breast is the only loved object, and this love, at that stage, bears a predominantly oral and cannibalistic character. There cannot yet exist a feeling of guilt.' Numberg, however, suggests that certain feelings and sensations of the oral and anal zone, which cannot yet find expression in speech, 'form the emotional basis for the development of that ideational complex known as the guilt feeling'.

Reading Numberg's description of his patient, we are surprised at his statement that 'there cannot yet exist a feeling of guilt' at the oral stage. For his case suggests that guilt feelings and a superego exist at a pre-verbal period and seems to show that the sensations of the oral tract to which he refers are related to phantasies of consuming or introjecting objects.

Melanie Klein[3] has contributed most to our understanding of the early origins of the superego. She has found that, by projecting his libidinal and aggressive impulses on to external objects, which at first are his mother's breasts, the infant creates images of a good and a bad breast. These two images are introjected and contribute both to the ego and the superego. She also described two early developmental stages corresponding to two predominant early anxieties of the infant; 'the paranoid-schizoid position', which extends over the first three to four months of life, and 'the depressive position', which follows and extends over most of the remaining months of the first year. If during the paranoid-phase, aggression and therefore paranoid anxieties become increased through internal and external causes, phantasies of persecutory objects predominate and disturb the ability to maintain good objects inside on which normal ego and superego development depend. In such cases the core of the primitive superego will have a persecutory character. Another point should be considered. It is characteristic for the paranoid phase that objects are split into good and bad ones. There is an inter-relationship between these good and bad objects in that if the bad objects are extremely bad and persecutory the good objects will become extremely good and therefore idealized. The idealized objects make their contribution to the superego, and in many chronic and borderline schizophrenic patients both the idealized and the persecutory objects seem to have some superego functions. The highly idealized good object increases the severity of the superego, and because of its impossible and exacting demands it is often felt to be persecuting. In the analysis of *acute* schizophrenic patients we can often only observe the persecutory objects functioning as superego. This may be due to the extreme demands of the idealized objects, which make it so difficult to differentiate them from the demands of the persecutory objects. The contribution of the good and the idealized objects to the superego of the acute schizophrenic can only be detected by the analyst at a time when the persecutory anxieties diminish, which coincides with the appearance of depressive anxieties. As the infant during his normal development moves towards the depressive position, the persecutory anxiety and the splitting of objects diminishes, and the anxiety begins to centre round the fear of losing the good object outside and inside. After the first three or four months of life, the emphasis changes from the fear that the self will be destroyed by a persecuting object, to the fear that the good object will be destroyed. Concurrently there is a greater wish to preserve it inside. The anxiety and guilt about the inability to restore this object inside, and secondly outside, then come more to the fore and constitute the superego conflict of the depressive position. The normal outcome of the depressive position is the strengthening of the capacity to love and repair the good object inside and outside. But if there is a failure in the normal working through of the depressive position, regression to the schizoid-paranoid position becomes reinforced.[4]

This may explain why one often observes in an acutely regressed schizophrenic patient a superego which contains a mixture of persecutory and depressive features. At any time one might clinically see a 'struggle' with a predominantly persecutory superego changing into a struggle with one containing more depressive characteristics,[5]

20

and, after a failure to deal with the internal conflict at a depressive level, one would observe a return of the earlier persecutory struggle.

The investigation of the psychopathology of schizophrenia has also shown the importance of certain mechanisms, which were named by Melanie Klein 'schizoid mechanisms'. They involve splitting of both the ego and its objects. Melanie Klein described the splitting of the ego caused by aggression turning against the self and by the projection of the whole or parts of the self into external and internal objects – a process which she called 'projective identification'.[6]

In the clinical material I am presenting I wish to show that a primitive superego exists in an acute schizophrenic patient, that the origin of the superego goes back to the first year of life, and that this early superego is of a particularly severe character, which is due to the predominance of persecutory features.

I cannot discuss in this paper all the mechanisms of ego splitting, but I will draw attention to some of the relations of the superego to *ego splitting*.

Discussion of certain aspects from the psychoanalysis of an acute schizophrenic patient

DIAGNOSIS

When I saw the patient for the first time he had been suffering from acute schizophrenia for about three years. He had always responded for a short time to electric shock or insulin comas, of which he had had at least ninety. There was a query whether the patient was hebephrenic, because of his frequent silly giggling, but, in spite of some hebephrenic features, practically all the psychiatrists who saw him diagnosed a catatonic type of schizophrenia of bad prognosis. Leucotomy was suggested to diminish his violence and to help the nursing problem, but at the last minute his father decided to try psychoanalysis.

HISTORY OF PATIENT

The patient was born abroad in 1929, after a difficult forceps delivery. He was the eldest child (a brother was born four years later). He did not do well at the breast and after four weeks was changed over to the bottle. Difficulties over taking food were present throughout childhood and the latency period. A change occurred

21

several years before the beginning of his illness when he suddenly developed an enormous appetite. He cried for hours as a baby because the parents were advised not to pick him up. He had frequent attacks of nervous vomiting from childhood onwards. Other symptoms were disturbing sensations like deadness and stiffness in his arms and legs, and a feeling in his tongue that it got twisted. He could never stand being hurt, and when he had pain he often tried to pinch his mother as if he were angry with her about it. He was popular at school and had a number of friends. There was a period of exhibitionism between nine and eleven years of age. When he was about sixteen, a disturbing incident occurred during the holidays when he and his brother occupied a bedroom next door to that of his parents. His mother saw him standing on the parapet of the balcony, which was on the fourth floor, and thought he was about to commit suicide by throwing himself to the ground below. She managed to stop him and he 'broke down' and accused his father of not telling him the facts of life. Apparently the patient had had an intense period of masturbation before this episode. At seventeen he fell in love with a ballet dancer. She jilted him and soon afterwards he had his first schizophrenic breakdown.

PARENTS OF THE PATIENT

His mother had not felt well during her pregnancy, and, after her confinement, developed asthma and could not look after the baby, who was handed over to a nurse. It is very difficult to assess clearly the relationship of the mother[7] to the patient; but it seems that she preferred the younger boy. When the patient grew up he frequently quarrelled with his mother, and got on much better with his father. When he fell ill, his mother would not have him at home, and it was clear later on that she was strongly opposed to his having psycho-analytic treatment. His father was an emotional man, very fond of his eldest boy, but undecided and unreliable.

THE TREATMENT

At the time when I first saw the patient he was socially withdrawn, suffered from hallucinations and was almost mute, and sometimes he was impulsive. The first fortnight he was brought by car from a mental nursing home where he was looked after. Later on I saw him there and he had two private male nurses. For the first four to five weeks of the treatment he was at times dangerously violent. From then on the violence lessened a good deal and he became much easier to handle until the time when the nurses and I, and so, indirectly, the patient himself, began to realize that his parents, particularly his mother, intended to stop the treatment. From that moment he became progressively more violent, but till then he co-operated with me in negative and positive states, and never attempted to attack me.

TECHNIQUE

I saw him regularly for about one hour and twenty minutes every day, with the exception of Sundays. When he spoke he rarely used whole sentences. He nearly always said only a few words, expecting me to understand. He frequently acknowledged interpretations which he felt were correct, and he could show clearly how pleased he was to understand. When he felt resistance against interpretations, or when they aroused anxiety, he very often said 'No', and 'Yes' afterwards, expressing both rejection and acceptance. Sometimes he showed his understanding by the clarity and coherence of the material he produced after an interpretation. At times he had great difficulty in formulating words and he showed what he meant by gestures. At other times, in connection with certain anxieties, he altogether lost his capacity to speak (for example, when he felt that everything had turned into faeces inside him), but this capacity improved in response to relevant interpretations. Later on in the course of treatment he began to play in a dramatic way, illustrating in this manner his phantasies, particularly about his internal world.

The problem of case presentation

In presenting certain aspects of an analysis like this, it is impossible to reproduce all the material given by the patient and all the interpretations. It has also to be remembered that, with such a severely ill patient, the analyst cannot understand everything the patient says or tries to say.

However, I hope that I shall be able to show that this deeply regressed patient, who had great difficulty in verbalizing his experiences, conveyed his problems to me not only clearly enough to make a continuous relationship possible, but also in a manner which gave a fairly detailed picture of his guilt conflict in the transference situation, and the ways and means by which he was trying to *deal with it*.

As I am mainly concerned with describing my verbal contact with the patient, it is necessary to discuss the significance of verbal interpretations, as there are some analysts, such as Eissler, who deny the importance of interpretations in acute schizophrenia. Eissler stressed the schizophrenic's awareness of the primary processes in the analyst's mind, and it is these primary processes on which, in his opinion, the result of treatment depends and not on the interpretations. I understand this to mean that the schizophrenic is extremely intuitive and seems to be able to get help from a therapist who *unconsciously* is in tune with his patient. Eissler seems to regard it as unimportant and leading to self-deception to consider whether or not the psychotherapist consciously understands the schizophrenic patient. He writes: 'I did not get the impression that in instances in which interpretations were used during the acute phase there was a specific relationship between interpretation and clinical recovery. It may be assumed that another set of interpretations might have achieved a similar result.'

In my opinion the unconscious intuitive understanding by the psychoanalyst of what the patient is conveying to him is an essential factor in all analyses, and depends on the analyst's capacity to use his counter-transference[8] as a kind of sensitive 'receiving set'. In treating schizophrenics who have such great verbal difficulties, the unconscious intuitive understanding of the analyst, through the counter-transference, is even more important, for it helps him to determine what really matters.

But the analyst should also be able to formulate consciously what he has unconsciously recognized, and to convey it to the patient in a form that he can understand. This after all is the essence of all psychoanalysis, but it is especially important in the treatment of schizophrenics, who have lost a great deal of their capacity for conscious functioning, so that, without help, they cannot consciously understand their unconscious experiences which are at times so vivid. In presenting the following material, I would therefore ask the reader to remember that I had continuously to watch for the patient's reactions to my interpretations, and often to feel my way until I could be sure of giving them in a form that he could use. For example, I was surprised to find that he could follow without much difficulty the interpretation of complicated mechanisms if I used simple words.

Even so, it was at times obvious that he was unable to understand verbal communication, or at least that he misunderstood what was said. We know from the treatment of neurotics that the analyst's words may become symbols of particular situations, for example, a feeding or a homosexual relationship; and this has to be understood and interpreted. But with the schizophrenic, the difficulty seems to go much further. Sometimes he takes everything the analyst says quite concretely. Hanna Segal (1950) has shown that if we interpret a castration phantasy to the schizophrenic he takes the intepretation itself as a castration. She suggested that he has a difficulty either in forming symbols or in using them, since they become equivalents instead of symbols. In my experience I found that most schizophrenics are only temporarily unable to use symbols, and the analysis of the patient under discussion contributed to my understanding of the deeper causes of this problem. This patient had certainly formed symbols, for instance his symbolic description of internalized objects was striking. But whenever *verbal* contact was disturbed, through the patient's difficulty in understanding words as symbols, I observed that his phantasies of going into me and being inside me had become intensified, which led to his inability to differentiate between himself and me (projective identification). This confusion between self and object, which also led to confusion of reality and phantasy, was accompanied by a difficulty in differentiating between the real object and its symbolic representation. Projections of self and internalized objects were always found to some extent, but did not necessarily disturb verbal communication. For it is the quantity of the self involved in the process of projective identification that determines whether the real object and its symbolic representation can be differentiated. Analysis of the impulses underlying projective identification may also explain why the schizophrenic so often treats phantasies as concrete real situations and real situations as if they were phantasies. Whenever I saw that projective identification had increased and interpreted the impulses of entering inside an object in the transference, the patient's capacity to understand symbols, and therefore words and interpretations, improved.

The progress of treatment

Before describing certain stages of the treatment which gave me some detailed and inter-related material about my patient's superego problem, I will sketch briefly the first four weeks of treatment, during which time he co-operated particularly well. In the first few sessions he showed clear signs of a positive and negative transference. His predominant anxieties were his fear of losing himself and me, and his difficulty in differentiating between himself and me, between reality and phantasy, and also between inside and outside. He talked

25

about his fear of losing and having lost his penis: 'Somebody has taken the fork away'; 'Silly woman.' He was preoccupied with being a woman, and he had a wish to be re-born a girl:[9] '*Prince* Ann.' By analysing material like 'The Virgin Mary was killed', or 'One half was eaten', and 'Bib (penis) was killed', we began to realize that he attributed his dangerous, murderous feelings against his mother, and against women in general, to his male half and his penis. We also understood that his phantasies of being a woman were greatly reinforced by his desire to get rid of his aggression. When he began to understand this method of dealing with his aggression, his wish to be a woman lessened and he became more aggressive.

Sometimes his aggression turned outward and he attacked nurses, but frequently it turned against himself. He then spoke of 'Soul being killed', or 'Soul committing suicide', or 'Soul being dead'; 'Soul' being clearly a good part of himself. Once when we discussed these feelings of deadness, he illustrated this turning of his aggression against himself by saying 'I want to go on – I don't want to go on – vacuum – Soul is dead', and later astonished me by stating clearly 'The problem is – how to prevent disintegration.' I had never used that word in talking to him, and it is interesting that the turning of the aggression against the self has been described as part of the splitting process causing disintegration in schizophrenia (Klein 1946; Rosenfeld 1947). A very predominant anxiety in the analytic situation, which the patient on rare occasions was able to formulate, related to his need for me. My not being with him on Sundays seemed at times unbearable, and once on a Saturday he said, 'What shall I do in the meantime, I'd better find someone in the hospital.' On another occasion he said, 'I don't know what to do without you.' He stated repeatedly that all his problems were related to '*Time*', and when he felt he wanted something from me it had to be given 'instantly'.

Whenever he attacked somebody physically, he reacted with depression, guilt and anxiety; and it gradually became clear that when his aggression did not turn against himself, but against external or internal objects, a guilt and anxiety problem arose which in fact occupied most of the time in the analysis.

I will now give some detailed material which followed an attack on Sister X four weeks after the beginning of his treatment. A few days before the attack, he seemed preoccupied with phantasies of attacking and biting breasts and with fear of women ('witchcraft'). He was inarticulate and difficult to understand. He talked about 'three buns', which probably meant three breasts, but it was not clear at the time why there were three. He attacked Sister X suddenly, while he was having tea with her and his father, hitting her hard on the temple. She was affectionately putting her arms round his shoulders at the time. The attack occurred on a Saturday, and I found him silent and defensive on Monday and Tuesday. On Wednesday he talked a little more. He said that he had destroyed the whole world and later on he said, 'Afraid.' He added, 'Eli' (God) several times. When he spoke he looked very dejected and his head drooped on his chest. I interpreted that when he attacked Sister X he felt he had destroyed the whole world and he felt only Eli could put right what he had done. He remained silent. After continuing my interpretations by saying that he felt not only guilty but afraid of being attacked inside and outside, he became a little more communicative. He said, 'I can't stand it any more.' Then he stared at the table and said, 'It is all broadened out, what are all the men going to feel?'[10] I said that he could no longer stand the guilt and anxiety inside himself and had put his depression, anxiety and feelings, and also himself, into the outer world. As a result of this he felt broadened out, split up into many men, and he wondered what all the different parts of himself were going to feel. He then looked at a finger of his which is bent and said, 'I can't do any more, I can't do it all.' After that he pointed to one of my fingers which is also slightly bent and said, 'I am afraid of this finger.' His own bent finger had often stood for his illness, and had become the representative of his own damaged self, but he also indicated that it represented the destroyed world inside him, about which he felt he could do no more. In saying that he can't do it all, he implies a search for an object outside. But what kind of object relations do we find in the transference situation? I immediately seemed to become like him and was frightening. I interpreted to him that he put himself and the problems he could not deal with inside me, and feared that he had changed me into himself, and also that he was now afraid of what I would give back to him. He expressed an anxiety that I would stop treatment, and also a hope that I would continue seeing him.

I shall now examine this material from the theoretical point of view. After the attack on the Sister, the patient felt depressed and anxious. His behaviour, gestures, and the few sentences and words he uttered showed that he felt he had destroyed the whole world outside, and he also felt the destroyed world inside himself. He makes this clearer later on in the analysis; but it is very important to realize at this stage that he felt he had taken the destroyed object, the world, into his ego. The guilt and depression were related to the task of restoring this inner world, which acted as a superego, but his omnipotence failed him. He also felt persecuted by the destroyed world and was afraid. Under the pressure of both the overwhelming guilt and the persecuting anxiety, which were caused by the superego, his ego began to go to pieces: he could not stand it any more and he projected the inner destroyed world, and himself, outside. After this everything seemed broadened out and his self was split up into many men who all felt his guilt and anxiety. The pressure of the superego is here too great for the ego to bear: the ego tries to deal with the unbearable anxiety by projection, but in this way ego-splitting, and so ego-disintegration, takes place. This is, of course, a very serious process, but if we are able to analyse these mechanisms in the transference situation, it is possible to cope analytically with the disastrous results of the splitting process.

The patient himself gave the clue to the transference situation, and showed that he projected the damaged self containing the destroyed world into me, and changed me in this way. But instead of getting relief through this projection he became more anxious, because he was afraid of what I was going to put back into him, which had the result that his introjection processes became severely disturbed. One would therefore expect a severe deterioration in his condition, and in fact his clinical state during the next ten days became very precarious. He began to get more and more suspicious about food, and finally refused to eat and drink anything. He became violent, and appeared to have visual hallucinations and also hallucinations of taste. In the transference he was suspicious of me, but not violent, and in spite of the fact that he was practically mute we never lost contact entirely. He sometimes said 'Yes' or 'No' to interpretations. In these I made ample use of previous material and related it to his present gestures and behaviour. It seemed to me that the relevant point had been his inability to deal with his guilt and anxiety. After projecting his bad, damaged self into me, he continuously saw himself everywhere outside. At the same time, everything he took inside seemed to him bad, damaged, and poisonous (like faeces), so there was no point in eating anything. We know that projection always leads again to introjection, so that he also felt as if he had inside himself all the destroyed and bad objects which he had projected into the outer world: and through coughing, retching, and movements of his mouth and fingers, he indicated that he was preoccupied with this problem. The first obvious improvement occurred one day when the male nurse had left some orange juice on the table which he (the patient) viewed with great suspicion. I went over previous material and showed him that the present difficult situation had arisen through his attempt to rid himself of guilt and anxiety inside by putting it outside himself. I told him that he was not only afraid of getting something bad inside him, but that he was also afraid of taking good things, the good orange juice and good interpretations, inside as he was afraid that these would make him feel guilty again. When I said this, a kind of shock went right through his body; he gave a groan of understanding, and his facial expression changed. By the end of the hour he had emptied the glass of orange juice, the first food or drink he had taken for two days. There was a distinct general improvement in his taking food from that time, and I felt it was significant that a patient, in this very hallucinated state, was able to benefit by an interpretation which showed him the relationship of the acute hallucinated state to his guilt problem.

The analytical material and the mechanisms I have described here are not just an isolated observation. They seem to be typical of the way an acute schizophrenic state develops. I have stressed that it is the inability of the schizophrenic patient to stand the anxiety and guilt caused by his introjected object or objects, representing the superego, which causes the projection of the self, or parts of the self containing the internalized object, into external objects. This results in ego splitting, loss of the self and loss of feelings.[11] At the same time a new danger and anxiety situation develops which leads to a vicious circle and further disintegration. Through the projection of the bad self and all it contains into an object, this object is perceived by the patient to have changed and becomes bad and persecuting itself, as the clinical material above indicated. The persecution expected after this form of projection is a forceful aggressive re-entry[12] of the object into the ego. During this phase therefore introjection may become inhibited in an attempt to prevent the persecuting object from entering.

The most important defence against the re-entry of the objects into which projection has taken place is negativism, which may show itself as a refusal to have anything to do with the world outside including the refusal of food. Such a defence is, however, rarely successful, as almost simultaneously with the projection of the self into an external object, the external object containing the self is introjected also. This implies that the object exists in phantasy externally and internally at the same time. In the process the ego is in danger of being completely overwhelmed, almost squeezed out of existence. In addition, we have to remember that the whole process is not stationary, because as soon as the object containing parts of the self is re-introjected, there is again the tendency to project which leads to further introjection of a most disturbing and disintegrating nature.

Clinically and theoretically it is important to consider the process from at least two angles: first the projection takes place to safeguard the ego from destruction, and may therefore be considered a defensive process which is unsuccessful and even dangerous because ego splitting, and therefore ego disintegration, takes place; secondly there is also an object relation of an extremely primitive nature connected with the projection, because the introjected objects and parts of the self are projected *onto an object*. This is important to understand because the strength of the persecutory fears about the re-entry of the object depends on the strength of the aggressive impulses pertaining to this primitive object relationship. In a previous paper (1951) I have described this object relationship in greater detail, so I only want to repeat here that there is evidence that, apart from the relation to the breast, the infant from birth onwards has libidinal and aggressive impulses and phantasies of entering into the mother's body with parts of himself.[13] When there are phantasies of the self entering the mother's body aggressively, to overwhelm and to take complete possession, we have to expect anxiety, not only about the mother and the entering self being destroyed, but also about the mother turning into a persecutor who is expected to force herself back into the ego to take possession in a revengeful way. When this persecutory mother figure is introjected, the most primitive super-ego figure arises which represents a terrible overwhelming danger to the ego from within. It is most likely that the inability of the schizophrenic ego to deal with introjected figures depends on the peculiar nature of this early object relationship.

In the clinical material I have described above I have not explained why the patient attacked Sister X. So I want to add here that at a later date I had more material about the incident, and after I interpreted that at the moment when Sister X put her arms around him he feared her possessiveness, and that it aroused a phantasy that she might force herself into him, he shuddered violently and made a movement with his arm as if to ward off an imaginary intruder.

I shall now report material which occurred about a fortnight later. Before I saw the patient on the Monday I learnt from the male nurse that, on the previous Sunday, he seemed tense and had been about to make an attack on him. The attack did not materialize, but the patient turned very pale and said 'Hiroshima'.

When I approached him the following Monday, he received me by saying 'You are too late.' His limbs were trembling and he jumped in fright when the nurse sneezed in the room next door. He later said 'I cannot look', and he repeated several times, 'I can't do anything.' He mentioned death several times and then became silent. He opened his mouth as if to speak but no words came out. I said that he could not speak because he was afraid of what he felt inside and what would come out of him. He replied 'Blood.' In my interpretations I told him that he had missed me over the weekend and had felt very impatient. He felt that he had killed me inside himself, and thought that as an external person I was too late now to do anything to help him and to help myself inside him. He was afraid to look at the destruction inside, and his difficulty in speaking, and his fear that blood might come out of him, showed how real this murderous inner attack had felt to him. On the Tuesday, he said, 'We have to stop, I can't do it any more.' He again showed his bent finger, mentioned death and blood, and shrugged his shoulders. After I had again stressed how real and concrete his inner, killing attack on me had been, and that he could do nothing to make me alive, he pointed to a certain part of the hospital and said, 'I want to have shock treatment.' When I asked him what shock treatment meant to him, he replied without the slightest hesitation, 'Death.' I said that having killed me, he now felt that he ought to be killed as a punishment, to which he agreed. What is significant in these two interviews is that he was more aware of having made an attack on me as an internal object. By greeting me on my arrival with the words: 'You are too late', he was recognizing me as an external object and had to some degree differentiated this external me from the internal murdered me (blood). He was struggling to repair the damage he had done, but felt quite unable to do so. He felt less persecuted and more guilty, and his desire to have shock treatment expressed his need for punishment to relieve his guilt. However, the process did not stop here. As before, under the pressure of guilt, the splitting process temporarily increased. When I saw the patient on Wednesday, he looked very confused. He asked, 'Can I help you?' He looked round all over the floor as if he were searching for something he had lost and he picked up imaginary bits and pieces. I interpreted that he felt himself to be confused with me as a helpful person, that he had put himself inside me for help because he could not deal with his inner problems any more, but that he now felt split and all over the place, and was therefore trying to collect himself. He made a movement with his shoulders as if he wanted to say, 'Of course, what else can I do?' After this he made eating movements and I interpreted that he was eating me up to get something good inside himself, and also to swallow back the self he had put into me. He immediately stopped, and said, 'One can't go on eating. What can I do?'

The patient's response to my interpretation gives the impression that he took my interpretation that he was eating me up as a reproach. This is a very common occurrence in treating psychotic or even pre-psychotic patients. I think that it implies that the interpretation has been taken concretely, and that the patient feels the analyst is saying: 'You are in fact eating me up and you must not do it!' From the technical point of view one may attempt to interpret to the patient that he has taken the interpretation simply as a reproach and that he felt attacked by this interpretation. This may be sometimes helpful but a more effective approach is to understand the deeper causes for the misunderstanding. When I discussed the temporary inability of the schizophrenic to use symbols (on p. 25), I suggested that when projective identification is reinforced the patient loses some of his capacity to understand symbols and therefore words, and he takes interpretations very concretely. I feel that the projection of the internal object (the superego) into me, leading to projective identification, was in this instance the essential factor, on which I concentrated in my interpretations. So I again explained to the patient that he had put himself into me as an external object because he could not deal with his guilt about having killed me inside himself. As a result of this interpretation he now seemed to reverse the process, he said, 'Blood and death', and then he talked about Eli in an attempt to find an omnipotent solution of the conflict which we had previously discussed. Then he looked more relaxed and said, 'My son, my son', in a friendly, loving way, and added, 'Memory.' I showed him that he had been able to revive the memory of a good relationship with his father and so with me, and that he had begun to realize that the good feelings and memories about his father and myself were helping him to deal with his hatred and guilt. During this interview the patient repeated a method of dealing with his guilt by projecting himself into an external object – a process which I have described in discussing earlier sessions (after the attack on Sister X). The projective identification was at both times accompanied by confusion and splitting, but this time, following the interpretation, he was able to reverse the process and attempted other means of dealing with his guilt.

I will attempt to explain some of the differences between these two guilt situations, which both ended in projecting the guilt and parts of the self into an external object. In the first instance the patient did attack an external object, Sister X, and he felt he had destroyed the whole world. It appeared that he felt the destruction outside and inside. After the projection of the guilt situation into me he felt that I had been changed and had become persecuting. In the second instance (when the patient said 'Hiroshima') he must have felt violently aggressive and his description afterwards of what he experienced inside himself emphasized that he felt he had killed an object inside (blood, death), but at the time of the violent anger he managed to control himself and did not attack a real person. Later, when he projected his guilt and his self into me, he did not think that he had changed me into his bad self, but he felt that he had changed into me and so had become the helpful person whom, on this occasion, he felt me to be.

A FEW DAYS LATER

The following interview showed another variation of the patient's attempts to deal with his superego. At the beginning of the interview he touched my hand several times, looking at me anxiously. I interpreted that he wanted to see if I was all right. He then asked me directly, 'Are you all right?' I pointed out that he was afraid of having hurt me, and that he was more able to admit his concern about me as an external person. He then said 'chicken' – 'heat' – 'diarrhoea'. I replied that he liked chicken and that he felt he had eaten me like a chicken and his diarrhoea made him feel that he had destroyed me as an inner object in the process of eating me up. This increased his fear that he had also destroyed or injured me as an external object. He now became more concerned about his inside. At first he said 'movement' and 'breath' which I interpreted as a hope that I was alive inside him. But afterwards he kept his leg rigidly stiff for several minutes and on being asked what this implied, he said 'Dead.' This I interpreted as a phantasy and a sensation that I was dead inside him. He then said, 'Impossible' – 'God' – 'Direct', which I interpreted as meaning that he felt that I should be all-powerful like God and do something directly to make this impossible inner situation better. He then said, several times, 'frightened', and he looked very frightened indeed. Suddenly he said 'No war'. He got up and shook hands with me in the most amiable manner, but while he was doing so he said 'Bluff.' I said that he felt at war with me inside after having had the phantasy of eating me up and killing me, and that he was now afraid of my revenge from inside and outside. He wanted to be at peace with me outside and inside, but he felt no real peace was possible, that it was only 'bluff'. I related this to his past life, to his feeling that his good relationship with people outside had been built on bluff, but also that he had felt that his coming to terms with his guilt and anxiety had often been based on bluff and deception.

In considering this session I suggest that my patient tried to make it clear that his guilt and fear were related to an introjected object which he believed he had killed by devouring. He showed that his relationship to this internalized object was a mixture of concern and persecution; when the fear of the persecution by the dead internal object increased, the only solution, apart from an omnipotent one, seemed to be to appease the persecutors, which also represented his superego. This he felt to be bluff.

In the following sessions the patient discovered a different method of helping me to understand his inner relationship to me, and so his superego conflict. When I approached him he was sitting very quietly on a chair, looking intently at his hand, at first examining it from the outside. Afterwards he stared fixedly at the inside; it looked as if he imagined that he was holding something there. I asked him what he saw, and he replied 'Crater'. I then asked whether there was anything inside the crater. He replied, as if to put me off, 'Nothing – empty'. I now interpreted that he was afraid that I was in the crater, and that I was dead. Later he closed his hand and squeezed it tightly. I interpreted that he phantasied that he imprisoned me inside his hand and that he was crushing me. He continued squeezing his hand for some time, looking withdrawn. Suddenly he got up, looked round in a frightened way, and escaped from the treatment room, which was not locked. The nurses brought him back, and he sat down again without any struggle. I pointed out to him that, while he was phantasying holding and squeezing me inside himself, the room had suddenly turned, for him, into a dangerous prison from which he tried to escape. I interpreted also that he had identified himself with me, because he felt guilty about what he was doing to me inside him. While I was interpreting the fear of the room, his anxiety seemed to lessen, and he returned to squeezing his hand.

This hour had an interesting sequel. The next day the nurses reported that the patient had become very frightened during a walk. He had suddenly stopped, staring at the ground. He would not go any further. On questioning him the nurses found that he heard voices threatening to punish him with death. He stopped walking because he saw an abyss in front of him. After some time he calmed down. Later on he had what seemed to be two cataleptic attacks in which he suddenly fell forward as if dead. The nurses were sure that he was not unconscious during this attack. I used this information next day with the patient, as he made no reference to it himself, and I explained this frightening experience as a continuation of what we had been discussing during the previous session. I related the abyss to the crater and interpreted that not only did he feel that he had killed and destroyed me in the crater, but also that he felt he had changed me into a retaliating object which was threatening him with punishment and death. The cataleptic fits represented both his own and my death. The striking feature about this experience is the distinct connection between the threatening superego voices and his own aggressive phantasies against me. The superego is here again persecuting and threatening him on the talion principle.

So far we have seen that the patient was mainly preoccupied with me as an internal object, which he had killed. Once he felt he killed me by devouring; another time he attacked me inside himself when he was longing to be with me as an external object. In surveying these sessions it seems that he felt guilty and persecuted by this internal object which, particularly in its persecutory form, had a superego function.

He showed various methods of dealing with this frightening superego. He attempted to expel it by projecting it into an external object. But this did not lead to a clinical improvement, because in projecting the superego he also projected parts of his self. In the first instance (after the attack on Sister X), where there was a stress on projecting the bad self into an external object in an aggressive manner, not only the splitting but also the persecution from without increased. In the second instance of projection (Can I help you?), the superego was also projected, but the emphasis was on projecting the good self into an external object. This also produced splitting but not external persecution. The projection of goodness led to a depletion of goodness in the self, and therefore to an increased oral greed in an attempt to recapture the good self and a good object by eating it up in phantasy.

These two instances illustrate the relation of the superego to ego splitting, and I suggest that, as methods of dealing with the superego, they commonly occur in acute schizophrenic states with confusion.

The other methods shown by the patient in this material are the desire for punishment and the appeasement of persecutors: the two cataleptic fits[14] seem to imply a complete masochistic[15] submission to the killing superego, and the same explanation applies to the need for punishment in asking for electric shock (death) treatment. In the latter case the masochistic submission, however, was not to the internal superego, but to an external object. This, incidentally, throws some light on the psychological importance of electric shock treatment,[16] which subjects a patient to the experience of death without actually killing him. The appeasement of the persecutory superego by bluff, as illustrated by my patient, is a very common mechanism, particularly in chronic schizophrenics. It also plays a considerable part as a defence against an acute schizophrenic state.

Moreover, the strengthening of the appeasement mechanisms may bring about a remission of an acute attack; but from the standpoint of the psychoanalytical approach, recovery by this means is unsatisfactory, because it completely stifles any development of personality.

THE 'HELPFUL' SUPEREGO

In the following session (which I shall refer to as (a)) we learnt to understand more of the positive relationship of the patient to his superego. In the beginning of the session he was looking for something in his pocket. He could not find it and it turned out that it was his handkerchief he wanted. I interpreted that he was not looking for his handkerchief but also for the part of himself which helped him to control himself, but which he could not find. I pointed out to him that he had frequently lost himself and his inner control because he felt he could not stand the anxiety and guilt inside himself. He then looked at me very rationally and said 'The problem is how to feel the fear'. I interpreted that he wanted to feel the fear which meant anxiety and guilt inside because he realized his need of control. He then looked out of the window where a man was trimming the hedges.[17] He was watching him in a fascinated way, without apparent fear. I pointed out that this man was trimming the hedges, and was in this way keeping them in shape, and in control, without damaging them. That was the relationship he wanted to feel with me inside himself; a helpful control without feeling damaged. The patient's remark 'The problem is how to feel the fear' is significant because it implies his realization that he had always avoided the experience of guilt and anxiety and so was without an inner means of control. The nurses reported that after this session he was rational for the first time since he had been in hospital. He was able to converse with doctors and nurses. This state lasted for several hours, and recurred almost every day for about three weeks. The improvement coincided with a greater capacity to acknowledge the need for an internal object as a helpful, controlling figure, and a lessening of his persecutory anxiety. During the next session (b) he became more able to verbalize his superego conflict. I found him sitting in a rigid position. It took more than twenty minutes before the rigidity lessened. He then said, 'No energy' – 'Struggle', and later on 'I am wrong'. He sighed and continued, 'Worn out', 'Hercules'. Later during the session he said 'I can only do my best, I cannot do any more.' (He was looking very tired.) He also referred to religion but without explaining details. I interpreted that I realized that he was trying to face his sense of guilt which was a struggle, that the demands of his conscience were so enormous that he felt quite worn out, and that he thought he would have to be a Hercules to do all that he felt he ought to do. At the end of the session he opened a black box which stood in a corner of the room where I was treating him. This box contained human bones, used for teaching students and nurses.[18] Almost every time from now on he opened the box once or twice during or at the end of a session, until, at a later date, he gave a full illustration of what this skeleton in the box (his superego) seemed to be like.

The development of the analysis ought to be assessed here from various angles: The patient became more willing to accept and face his superego. He did not regard it, during this hour, as something threatening to kill him, but he feared its overwhelming exhausting demands. Clinically, this progress was accompanied by greater depression. The opening of the box emphasized the patient's greater willingness to look at his inner object, his superego; but the fact that it was represented by dead bones showed that it was still a dead object with which he was preoccupied. The main problem which the analyst had to have in mind, and which varies and changes a great deal all the time, is whether the dead internal object, the superego, is persecuting, or whether there is an attempt to deal with it on the depressive level, that is, whether the patient can face the guilt at having destroyed a good object and the exhausting demands for reparation.

PRIMARY ENVY

During the next session (c) the patient was preoccupied with envy and how to get rid of it. In the session after that (d) he sat silently on a chair, looking anxiously at the outside and inside of his hand. I asked, 'What are you afraid of?' He replied, 'I am afraid of everything.' I then said he was afraid of the world outside and inside, and of himself. He replied 'Let's go back,' which I took to mean that he wanted to understand the early infantile situation in the transference. He stretched out his hand towards me on the table, and I pointed out that he was trying to direct his feelings towards me. He then touched the table tentatively, withdrew his hands and put them into his pockets, and leaned back in his chair. I said that he was afraid of his contact with me, who represented the external world, and that, out of fear, he withdrew from the outer world. He listened carefully to what I said and again took his hands out of his pockets.

He then said, 'The world is round', and continued clearly and deliberately, 'I hate it because it makes me feel burnt up inside'. And later he added, as if to explain this further, 'Yellow' – 'envy'. I interpreted to him that the round world represented me felt as a good breast, and that he hated the external me for arousing his envy because his envy made him feel he wanted to kill and burn me inside himself. So he could not keep me good and alive inside himself, and felt he had a bad and burning inside. This increased his envy and his wish to be inside me, because he felt I had a good inside. At the end of the session (d) he touched the burning hot radiators in the treatment room and the wooden shelf over them.

This session (d) is particularly significant because it throws some light on the patient's fundamental conflict with the world, and his deep-seated envy of the good mother and breast.

In the analyses of neurotic and pre-psychotic patients this early envy has frequently been described. It is, however, interesting that this inarticulate, regressed patient should so stress his envy and jealousy in his earliest infantile object relationship with his mother. Sometimes he referred to the beginning of life, repeatedly stressing birth and envy, and it was clear that the jealousy of his brother, which was also frequently discussed, was not the problem he had most in his mind. It seems that some of the earliest aggression, starting from the separation of the infant from his mother at birth, is experienced as envy, because everything that makes the infant feel comfortable seems to belong to the outer world – the mother.

This conflict became manifest in the transference situation when I was equated with the good mother and the good breast. Historically the patient had had a short, unsatisfactory time at the breast, and his mother was unable to look after him because of her asthma. Previously he had shown that he hated me when I was absent, but in this session (d) it is his envy of me which makes it difficult for him to take good things from me.

The envy of the good mother and her good inside also increases the impulses to force the self inside the mother, because, if the mother has all the goodness, the child wants to be inside her. But the envy and jealousy with which the child enters in phantasy the mother's body creates images of a destroyed mother. At the end of the hour, the patient touched the hot radiators which burned his hand, and afterwards he touched the wooden shelf, which would imply that he feared that by entering me he changed me, so that my inside was as burning as his own.

Another interesting feature is the way the patient, through the gestures of his hands, showed whether his cathexes were directed to external or internal objects. If he turned his instinctual impulses towards an external object, he took his hands out of his pockets, and indicated by the movement of his fingers that he was trying to make contact with the external world. When he withdrew the cathexis from the outer world, and directed it towards what was going on inside him, he put both his hands back into his pockets. When his feelings were directed outside and inside simultaneously, he kept one hand in his pocket and laid the other one on the table.[19]

During the following session (e) he looked inside the box with the bones and again touched the radiators. Then he took some crumpled-up paper out of his pocket and tried to straighten it out, but soon he looked frightened again. He walked past me and looked out of the window. At the next session (f) he emphatically said, 'My own birth.' He kept looking inside his hand and repeated several times, 'Birth-Time and Jealousy.'

I suggest that the patient was trying to indicate the connection of birth and envy. It is the birth situation which starts the envy of the mother and her good inside. The patient's looking out of the window was probably an expression of his being inside me.[20] I pointed out before that when an object is introjected, which through projective identification has been identified with parts of the ego, a particularly complicated situation arises: here the patient was trying to deal with an internal object but he also felt himself to be inside this object.

During this period he again seemed to have difficulties in understanding my interpretations correctly, because he took everything I said very concretely. For example: When I interpreted to him during session (g) that he felt jealous of me, he suddenly got up and moved away from me. He then went to the box and took a bone from it, showed it to me and put it back again. After this he seemed to get more frightened of me, and tried to get out of the room, but again the nurses brought him back. Then he sat on the radiator, at a distance, and laughed at me in an aggressive and challenging manner. Afterward he walked about the room, ignoring me, and looking contemptuous; he made movements with his legs as if he were dancing. His attitude to me had changed after my interpretation of his jealousy. It seemed that he felt that by my interpretation I had made an attack on him, blaming him for his impulse. His taking a bone from the box here emphasized the concreteness of his experiences: namely that he identified me with whatever the bone meant to him; probably a threatening superego. His dancing suggested that he had killed me and that he felt triumph and contempt. He was treating me like dirt. His concreteness of the patient's experiences continued after the session. The nurses reported that after I had left he had a large bowel motion, and used at least five times as much toilet paper as usual to cover it up. When I arrived the next time (session h), he sat in his usual chair. In front of him on the table were two little heaps: one little heap of half-burnt cigarette tobacco and cigarette paper was on one side, next to it there was a little heap of grey ashes. The tobacco and the paper looked like a miniature faecal mess and paper. The patient kept his eyes fixed on the heaps for some time. He came very close to it with his mouth, then he moved away again. He repeated this several times. He did not show that he noticed my presence. I interpreted that the heap which looked like a bowel motion represented me. I added that he felt he had changed me into a motion last time. The little heap of ashes seemed to represent those parts of himself mixed up with me, which he also felt were burnt up and destroyed. He continued staring at the heaps, making eating movements. I interpreted that he felt he had both burnt up and destroyed me and himself, and that he wanted to take me and himself back again by eating. He was now picking up different bits and pieces and trying to sort them out, but they all dropped again into the mess. After the looking and mouthing, the touching and playing with the heap became much more intense. His playing with the mess seemed to be an unsuccessful attempt both to differentiate himself and me and to restore us. After the play he looked first at his hands, which were dirty, and then, for a little time at a whitish spot on the table. I pointed out that he seemed to get mixed up between playing with his faeces and playing with his penis, because the glistening spot on the table seemed to be connected with masturbation (emission). When his confused look lessened I gave him a more detailed interpretation, showing him in detail how the present situation had arisen. I also linked it with the past, particularly with the earliest relations to his mother.

From the material presented, it may be difficult to see why I referred here to my patient's masturbation phantasies, but as I explained before, it is not always possible in an analysis such as this to show all the reasons for giving an interpretation. My patient had never during his breakdown really played with faeces, or eaten faeces, but he masturbated a great deal. He seemed to me confused, and he probably felt as if he were quite concretely in the muddle which he showed me in his play. So the interpretations had to be given in a way that helped him to recognize that his impulses differed from one another, and also to differentiate between himself and the object with which he felt confused.

These last two sessions (g and h) are related to the earlier sessions ('after the attack on Sister X' and 'Can I help you?') in which the patient had projected his self and his superego into me as the representative of the external world. In the earlier instance he had refused food, and he probably at that time had phantasies that he was forced to eat faeces – poison – representing his own bad self and persecuting objects. In the later one he had tried to recapture himself and me, as a lost good object through eating. In the present instance (g and h) he illustrated his experience in play, and made it clear that the faeces represented me as the accusing superego which he tried to expel and destroy. The mix-up, or the confusion, of his self with his object was clear to me as an observer. At this stage of the analysis he was by no means able to keep his superego inside: he still expelled it when persecutory anxiety increased; but his phantasy of eating the heap of faeces, and his playing with and sorting out the heap, seemed to indicate an attempt to deal with his conflict on the depressive level.

I would like to refer here to Abraham's (1924) observation on coprophagic phantasies in melancholia. Abraham suggested that the coprophagic phantasies of his patient turned out to be the expression of a desire to take back into his body the love object which he had expelled from it in the form of excrement. Abraham thought that 'the tendency to coprophagia seems to contain a symbolism which is typical for melancholia'. He continued describing impulses of expelling (in an anal sense) and of destroying (murdering): 'The product of such a murder – the dead body – became identified with the product of expulsion – with excrement.'

My experience with this schizophrenic patient would seem to confirm the view that the coprophagic phantasy can represent a depressive mechanism of reincorporating a lost object identified with faeces. But then the question has still to be answered: Why is coprophagia and playing with faeces in the adult typical of schizophrenia? I would like to suggest a tentative answer: The schizophrenic is trying to take back not only the object he has lost but also the parts of his ego which are mixed up with the object. Moreover, the actual eating of faeces is a sign not only of regression but also of having lost the capacity for symbolic representation. It depends on the concreteness of his experience whether the schizophrenic can differentiate between phantasies of faeces as a destroyed object and faeces themselves.

In his inner experience during this session the patient comes dangerously near to losing his ability to differentiate between symbol and actual object, because of the intensification of the projective identification process, which I had not sufficiently interpreted in the first (session g) of the two sessions (g and h). In the session (h) where he played with the heap, I took care to help him to differentiate again.

During the same session (h) the patient had difficulty in talking, but the nures reported that afterwards he talked rationally and did not seem confused. But it must be remembered that his rational periods never lasted more than a few hours.

In the next session (i) he began by looking away from me and remaining silent, but he looked eager and rational so I decided to go over the last sessions with him, showing him in detail in what way he was repeating experiences and phantasies of his early relationship with his mother and her breasts. I connected his silence with his anger and with the jealousy of the breast. I spoke of the roundness which at first represented the world to him, and of his difficulties in feeding from the breast because of his anger and his feelings of being burnt up inside. I reminded him of his feelings that the breast inside him had turned into faeces, and was threatening him; that, as we had seen last time, he wanted to free himself from this inner persecution, but that he could not bear to lose this internal breast even if it had turned into faeces, and that he was preoccupied with taking it back as he wanted an object he could love. I said he refused to have anything to do with me because of his fear of attacking me as an external object representing the breast, and that he was so angry and jealous because I was separate from him and not his own possession, his own self. After this interpretation he held his head in his hands. I interpreted to him that he wanted to hold me and have a good relationship with me outside and inside himself. He agreed, but very soon withdrew his hands into his pockets, which seemed here to indicate a withdrawal of libidinal cathexis from the outside. I interpreted that the aggressive feelings had become stirred up in him against me as an external object representing the breast, and that he was afraid of his aggressive, biting, mouth. That was the reason why he had turned away from me. He at first said, 'I can't do anything.' Then he got up and went slowly to the black box and looked into it intently. He then took out a lower jaw bone (mandible). I asked him whether he knew what kind of bone this was. He did not answer but turned to me and held the bone in the position of his lower jaw to show me that he knew. He then put the bone back into the box and repeated the behaviour of session (g), only this time he showed more clearly that he was frightened of me, and he walked quickly away from me. I interpreted that he was afraid that I would attack and bite him, because he thought that I had changed into an attacking mouth. Then he came towards me and gave me a very slight punch (which obviously was not meant to hurt but was part of the dramatization of the situation). After this he walked up and down the very large room in a most peculiar manner, with hunched-up shoulders, and a fierce expression. He moved his legs as if he had hallucinations that bodies were lying on the floor and that he had to step over them. He looked so much like a wolf, who was running up and down in a cage, that I called out to him, 'You behave like a wolf in a cage.' He agreed under loud laughter, and went on running up and down, and twice he tried to get out of the room.

During the next session (k) he was much more rational. He asked me how all this related to the past, to fears at night, and to me, which was discussed in detail. Then he said again, 'I am wrong', which suggested to me that he felt that all we had been working over together during the last sessions (g to k) was related to his guilt feelings. He said, 'Lupus', 'Brown cow', 'Yellow cow'. After this he took a match out of his pocket which he broke in three pieces. He asked, 'How are there three pieces?' I said that he showed me that at present he felt his conscience was divided into three pieces: 'Lupus', 'Brown cow' and 'Yellow cow'. And I explained to him that he had shown this to me during the last few days. He had dramatized 'Lupus', the wolf, last time, after taking the lower jaw bone from the black box. The jaw bone represented the internalized breast which he had attacked like an aggressive, hungry wolf, and which in his phantasies had turned into an aggressive, biting mouth. The Brown Cow seemed to be the breast he felt he had destroyed and changed into faeces; while the Yellow Cow seemed to be a breast which he had changed through envious and urinary attacks, and which had also become bad and threatening. The superego was here divided into three different objects, and seemed to correspond to the match divided by him into three bits. The number three had previously appeared when he talked about three buns, which seemed to represent three breasts. But he also sometimes talked about the third penis, and at a later date he referred to the third man. So it appears that the three also represented the Oedipus situation, but at the time when the analysis was stopped the later Oedipal conflict had not clearly appeared in the transference situation.

It is, of course, impossible to clarify all these details, but I thought it was clear enough that the patient used the box containing the bones to illustrate phantasies and sensations of internal objects representing his superego. In particular, these were dramatically represented by 'brown cow', the destroyed breast which had turned into faeces, and 'lupus' representing the persecuting, internalized, attacking mouth (the biting conscience). 'Yellow cow' referred to the times when he talked about envy, birth and yellow, which I had linked with phantasies of entering the mother. But these phantasies were probably more difficult to represent in a dramatic way.

During the next few weeks the patient was more depressed, and seemed less hilariously excited or persecuted. He was eager during the session, showed in words and actions that he was trying to bring things together inside, and felt he wanted to give the good things up to God and me. There was sometimes a distinct desire to be guided by me, but there was also a fear of giving everything back to me lest he should have nothing left himself. To guard against this he played a game in which he kept something hidden from me. For example, he held something in one hand while he allowed me to see only the other one. During this period he once said to the nurse that he had a great deal to worry about, but he felt it would be all right in the end. At times he still projected his depression, with parts of himself, into me; and at such times he was again more occupied with being inside an object rather than with the objects inside himself. For example, he expressed this by smoking a cigarette, dropping ashes on the ground while walking, and running back to search for the ashes; or by saying, 'How can I get out of the tomb?' In projecting a part of himself and his depression into me, I became the tomb, and he also lost a part of himself which he then tried to recapture. But at other times, when in his depressed state, he seemed entirely preoccupied with attempts to restore a good, idealized object inside. He sat quietly and thoughtfully, and when I asked him what he was doing, he replied that he was 'rebuilding Heaven'. During this period the depressions lasted longer, and the periods of excitement were shorter. Since the early stages of his analysis when he had been acutely excited and refused food altogether, there had been a steady clinical progress which was clearly noticed by the nurses and the hospital doctors.

About the time of the arrival in England of the patient's mother, he ceased to co-operate so well as he had done hitherto, and it was obvious that there were still considerable difficulties to overcome. It is very hard to assess how far the expected arrival of the mother was related to the worsening in the patient's co-operation, which might be considered a temporary difficulty. But it is quite clear that when she did arrive, and showed her disapproval of psychoanalysis, asked for further opinions, and considered leucotomy, he became rapidly violent and uncontrollable.

However, before this problem arose, he had co-operated with me so well, in spite of the severity of his condition, that I felt the progress of the analysis, and the understanding derived from it, could be considered in its own right. We have to remember that, in treating acute psychotic patients, we are in the same position as the child analyst treating a young child. There is no way of preventing parents from interfering with, or stopping the treatment, should they so wish.

The improvement, which was as yet not stable, was gradual. It seems to me, however, that the analysis, incomplete as it had been, had distinctly diminished the patient's persecutory anxiety and that the processes of splitting the ego had also decreased. As a resut of this, depression was more clearly coming to the surface, which coincided with a lessening of the persecutory character of the superego.

I wish here to stress that in severe schizophrenic patients fluctuations in their condition have to be expected, even if the psychoanalysis is making good progress. But nevertheless the points which I have discussed just now can be considered as criteria by which the progress in the psychoanalysis of a schizophrenic patient may be judged over *prolonged* periods: stable improvement depends on a gradual lessening of persecutory anxiety and ego splitting, and greater capacity to deal with conflicts on the depressive level, which would imply a greater capacity to maintain good objects outside and inside. These changes also affect the superego so that positive features of the superego become more noticeable.

Conclusion

In this paper I have approached the problem of the superego in schizophrenia by illustrations from the analysis of one acute schizophrenic patient. This is, however, no isolated case, and in all the schizophrenics I have treated, I encountered a particularly severe superego of a persecutory nature.

Usually it takes a long and deep analysis to follow the development of a superego of this kind to its source in early infancy. In treating an acute regressed schizophrenic patient, however, we get a direct glimpse of early infantile processes near the beginning of the analysis, which may give us a certain amount of confirmation of the theories and concepts which have gradually been built up from the deep analysis of neurotic and psychotic adults and children. I found Melanie Klein's concepts most valuable because they enabled me to understand the varying and difficult problems which one meets in such cases, and my experience fully confirmed her views.

Analysts who are anxious to treat schizophrenics must remember that they will be faced with a great number of difficulties which at first appear insurmountable, but which yield to deeper psychoanalytical understanding. If we abandon the psychoanalytical approach, because of these difficulties, we give up the hope of further psychoanalytical insight. In watching the development of the superego conflict during an analysis such as I have described, one may often be tempted to change one's approach. Some American workers may argue: Why not cut right across the superego death-theme by saying to the patient, 'I am not dead, I am not going to kill you, I love and protect and control you'? Rosen has shown that such an approach often works. We do not know why it does, and we cannot answer this question until we have had the opportunity to analyse a schizophrenic patient who has had this kind of psychotherapy. Nevertheless, I should like to refer to the session where my patient said 'No war' and where he most amicably shook hands with me, saying 'Bluff'. Was his previous adjustment based on successful bluff? If so, a forceful reassurance may again build up a more stable bluff situation. I have had the opportunity of analysing a chronic schizophrenic who had an acute schizophrenia many years ago. During the acute state and afterwards for about twelve years, he was treated by a great deal of reassurance and friendliness by a therapist who was very interested in him. The patient had made a better adjustment, but had developed other very disturbing symptoms. When we analysed the superstructure of his illness, it became clear that his improvement and co-operation was due to a terror of the outer world, and that he was continually appeasing phantasied persecutors. The friendly doctor was a persecuting figure to him, and the previous treatment, and the first part of the treatment with me, was dominated by continuous appeasement and bluffing. It took several years to break through this attitude which had been reinforced by reassurance. This patient is practically a normal person now after a long analysis and has remained well since the treatment ended in 1947.

I do not think there is a central bluff situation in all schizophrenics, but I think it is very common. In judging the success of reassurance methods one has also to remember that every schizophrenic patient repeatedly projects himself and his superego into the therapist. The fact that the therapist does not alter, and remains friendly, is important both for the psychoanalytic and the psychotherapeutic situation. The psychotherapist who uses reassurance relieves the patient's anxiety temporarily about his dangerous superego and his dangerous self. When the therapist says: 'I love you and will look after you', he implies: 'You are not bad and I will not retaliate', and also: 'You can put all your badness into me; I will deal with it for you.' This may work, and the therapist's unconscious understanding and acceptance of the feelings of his patient is necessary for the reassurance to be effective, but it is doubtful whether such a patient can ever become independent of the therapist, and whether he can ever develop his personality. In the psychoanalysis of schizophrenia, we have also to accept the fact that the schizophrenic patient has to put his superego and himself continuously into the analyst, but the analyst interprets this situation and the problems connected with it, until the patient is gradually able to accept both his love and hate and his superego as belonging to himself. Only then can we consider that the analysis of a schizophrenic has been successful.

Summary

I have recorded a part of the analysis of this severely ill patient, not to claim a therapeutic success, but to help and encourage all those analysts who aim at treating schizophrenics by analysis, and who want to understand more about the psychopathology of schizophrenia. A detailed conscious understanding of the psychopathology of schizophrenics is, in my opinion, so important as this enables one to make full use of ones's unconscious understanding of their utterances and behaviour in a transference analysis.

The problem of the superego and its development and origins is not only important for schizophrenia, but for the neuroses as a whole. Melanie Klein's research on the early origins of the superego, and the earliest anxieties, has been accepted by many but by no means all analysts. Some of the doubts they have about her view that these origins are to be found in earliest infancy arise from their difficulties in assessing the developmental period to which certain material belongs. It has frequently been suggested that the analysis of very young children, and of severely regressed schizophrenics, may help to throw further light on this problem.

I have tried to show that a transference analysis of a deeply regressed schizophrenic is possible, and that it can throw light on the earliest introjected objects and on their superego functions.

Notes

1 Eissler (1951) suggested the terms: 'acute or (first) and mute or (second) phase of schizophrenia'. He pointed out that the acute phase may last many years and the illness may take its course entirely either in the first

47

or in the second phase. Eissler's contention is that the whole question of the psychoanalysis of schizophrenia can be decided only in the second phase.

2 There may be a number of workers in the USA and South America such as Kaufmann and Pichon Rivieré who have treated schizophrenic patients by psychoanalysis. They have, however, not described their clinical approach. (Pichon Rivieré's papers on schizophrenia are only theoretical.)

3 I do not attempt to present here a detailed description of Melanie Klein's views, I only try to concentrate on those points which are relevant to the theme of my paper.

4 Melanie Klein: 'Notes on Schizoid Mechanisms', p. 105.

5 According to Melanie Klein's views, the superego of the depressive position among other features, accuses, complains, suffers and makes demands for reparation, and, while still persecutory, is less harsh than the superego of the paranoid position.

6 For the more detailed study of these mechanisms I refer to Melanie Klein (1946) and Rosenfeld (1947).

7 In some papers on schizophrenia particularly by American writers like Pious and Fromm-Reichmann the mother's hostile and 'schizophreno-genic' attitude has been stressed. The mother in this case seems to have been unconsciously hostile to the patient and the patient's illness increased her guilt feelings. But we ought not to forget that in all mental disturbances there is a close interrelationship between external factors acting as trauma and internal ones which are determined mostly by heredity. In our analytic approach we know that it is futile and even harmful to the progress of an analysis to allow a patient to *blame* the external environment. We generally find that there exists a great deal of distortion of external factors through projection and we have to help the patient to understand his phantasies and reactions to external situations until he becomes able to differentiate between his phantasies and external reality.

8 Compare Paula Heimann (1950): 'On counter-transference.' She writes: 'My thesis is that the analyst's emotional response to his patient within the analytic situation represents one of the most important tools for his work. The analyst's counter-transference is an instrument of research into the patient's unconscious.'

9 Compare Rosen who described the frequent re-birth phantasies of schizophrenic women wanting to be reborn as boys.

10 'It is all broadened out' refers also to the world which is destroyed; but his ego is included in the destroyed world and this seemed to be the relevant factor to recognize.

11 In my paper 'Analysis of a schizophrenic state with depersonalization' I

have dealt in greater detail with the problem of ego splitting, loss of self and loss of feelings.

12 This process has been described by Melanie Klein in: 'Notes on Some Schizoid Mechanisms' (1946).

13 These impulses and mechanisms have been described by Melanie Klein in her paper 'Notes on Some Schizoid Mechanisms' (1946).

14 These attacks resembled a catatonic stupor. The psychopathology suggested here may also contribute to our understanding of the catatonic stupor.

15 Compare here H. Garmes (1931) and Pichon Riviere's (1946) theory of the masochistic ego and the sadistic superego in schizophrenia.

16 In submitting the patient to electric shock treatment at the time when he asked for it, his guilt conflict would have been temporarily alleviated, and very likely he might have had a remission of the acute state which still persisted, but this would have meant abandoning further psycho-analytical understanding of his conflict.

17 One might of course think that the man with the shears aroused his castration anxiety. But I think this was only indirectly important at the moment, because only through the lessening of the persecution by his superego could his castration anxiety become bearable and acceptable.

18 The hospital unfortunately had no proper consulting rooms. I had several times to change the room where I treated the patient, and in the end the superintendent thought that I would be least disturbed in the lecture room. One day the patient discovered the black box with the bones. I had no knowledge of its presence beforehand. I decided not to have the box removed but to analyse the patient's interest in it. But I want to stress that I was in this room only by force of external circumstances, not by my own choice.

19 I do not want the reader to think that I would always interpret the play with hands in this way, but this interpretation seemed true for this patient at this particular stage of the analysis.

20 In my experience with other schizophrenic patients the looking out of the window frequently meant that the patient felt he was inside the analyst.

References

Abraham, K. (1924) 'A short study of the development of the libido viewed in the light of mental disorders', *Selected Papers*, London: Hogarth Press (1942).

Alexander, F. (1951) 'Schizophrenic psychoses: critical considerations of the psycho-analytic treatment', *Archives of Neurology and Psychiatry*, 26.

Eissler, K. R. (1951) 'Remarks on the psycho-analysis of schizophrenia', *International Journal of Psycho-Analysis*, 32, 139.

Federn, P. (1943) 'Psycho-analysis of psychoses', *Psychiatric Quarterly*, 17, 3–19, 246–57, 470–87.

Freud, S. (1914) 'On narcissism: an introduction', *SE* 14.

Freud, S. (1924) 'Neurosis and psychosis', *SE* 19, 152.

Fromm-Reichmann, F. (1943) 'Psycho-analytic psychotherapy with psychotics', *Psychiatry*, 6, 277–9.

Hayward, M. L. (1949) 'Direct interpretation in the treatment of a case of schizophrenia', *Psychiatric Quarterly*, 23, no. 4.

Heimann, P. (1950) 'On counter-transference', *International Journal of Psycho-Analysis*, 31, 81–4.

Katan, M. (1939) 'A contribution to the understanding of schizophrenic speech', *International Journal of Psycho-Analysis*, 20, 353.

Kaufmann, M. (1932) 'Some clinical data on ideas of reference', *Psycho-Analytic Quarterly*, 1.

——(1939) 'Religious delusions in schizophrenia', *International Journal of Psycho-Analysis*, 20, 363.

Klein, M. (1935) 'A contribution to the psychogenesis of manic depressive states' in *The Writings of Melanie Klein*, vol. 1, London: Hogarth Press (1975).

——(1946) 'Notes on some schizoid mechanisms' in M. Klein, P. Heimann, S. Isaacs, and J. Rivière, J. *Developments in Psycho-Analysis*, London: Hogarth Press (1952), 292–320. (also in *The Writings of Melanie Klein*, (1975), 1–24).

——(1948) 'A contribution to the theory of anxiety and guilt', *International Journal of Psycho-Analysis*, 29, 114.

Knight, R. (1946) 'Psychotherapy of an adolescent catatonic schizophrenic with mutism', *Psychiatry*, 9, no. 4.

Numberg, H. (trans. 1948) *Practice and Theory of Psycho-analysis*, New York: Nervous and Mental Disease Monographs no. 74.

——(1920) *On the Catatonic Attack*.

——(1921) *The Course of the Libidinal Conflict in a Case of Schizophrenia*.

Pichon Rivieré, E. (1946) 'Contribución a la teoria psicoanalitica de la esquizofrenia', *Revista Psicoanálisis*, 4, 1–22.

——(1947) 'Psicoanálisis de la esquizofrenia, *Revista de Psicoanálisis* 5, 293.

Pious, W. L. (1949) 'The pathogenic process in schizophrenia', *Bulletin of the Menninger Clinic*, 13.

Rosen, J. (1946) 'A method of resolving acute catatonic excitement', *Psychiatric Quarterly*, 20, 2, 183.

——(1947) 'The treatment of schizophrenic psychoses by direct analytic therapy', *Psychiatric Quarterly*, 21, 1, 3.

——(1950) 'The survival function of schizophrenia', *Bulletin of the Menninger Clinic*, 4, 3, 81.

Rosenfeld, H. (1947) 'Analysis of a schizophrenic state with depersonalization', *International Journal of Psycho-Analysis*, 28, 130–9; also in *Psychotic States*, London: Hogarth Press (1965), 13–33.

——(1950) 'Note on the psychopathology of confusional states in chronic schizophrenias', *International Journal of Psycho-Analysis*, 31: 132–7; also in *Psychotic States*.

——(1951) 'Transference-phenomena and transference-analysis in an acute schizophrenic patient', *International Journal of Psycho-Analysis*, 33, 3.

Segal, H. (1950) 'Some aspects of the analysis of a schizophrenic', *International Journal of Psycho-Analysis*, 31, 268–78; also in *The Work of Hanna Segal*, New York: Jason Aronson (1981); paperback London: Free Association Books (1986).

Sullivan, H. S. (1931) 'The modified psycho-analytic treatment of schizophrenia', *American Journal of Psychiatry*, ii.

Wexler, M. (1951) 'The structural problem in schizophrenia: therapeutic implications', *International Journal of Psycho-Analysis*, 32, 157.

2

Depression in the schizophrenic[1]

HANNA SEGAL

This article was first published in 1956 in the *International Journal of Psycho-Analysis* 37: 339–43.

The thesis of this paper is that, in the course of development, schizophrenics reach the depressive position and, finding it intolerable, deal with it by projecting their depressive anxieties. This can only be done by projecting a large part of their ego into an object, that is by projective identification. I am speaking here of the depressive position as described by Melanie Klein. Briefly, this is a phase of development in which the infant's ego is integrated enough and the object synthesized enough for the infant to experience a whole object relation involving ambivalence, dread of loss, guilt, and the urge to regain and restore the object. By projective identification I mean that process in which a part of the ego is split off and projected into an object with a consequent loss of that part to the ego, as well as an alteration in the perception of the object.

In the course of psychoanalytic treatment of the schizophrenic, it is of great importance to put him in touch with his depressive feelings and the wish to make reparation which springs from them. As the treatment progresses, and after some analysis of the paranoid anxieties, idealizing and splitting processes, the patient comes more and more frequently to experience, for a short time, depressive anxieties. He usually tries to get rid of these anxieties by projective identification. Very often it will be found that the depressive part of the patient's ego is projected into the analyst, and in order to achieve that projection the patient may resort to careful stage-managing of the analytical situation designed in a way to provoke depressive feelings in the analyst. It is of great importance, then, to find where

52

and in what circumstances the part of his ego capable of experiencing depression has been projected and to interpret this to the patient.

I will illustrate what I mean by two examples taken from the analysis of a 16-year-old schizophrenic girl. She had suffered from hallucinations from the age of 4, or maybe earlier. She was an unusually gifted and intelligent child, and for a long time retained something of her original brilliance, but there had been a progressive withdrawal and a steady though slow deterioration of her personality, and at the time when she started treatment at the age of 16 she had a well-established, chronic hebephrenic schizophrenia.

1st example

This happened in the February of the second year of her treatment. Since the Christmas holiday she had been very silent, speaking at most one or two sentences during the hour and spending most of her time skipping round the room, biting her plaits, her fingers, the cushions, or the couch. She also picked her nose a great deal, eating the pickings, and collected and often ate any odd bit of fluff or dust from the floor. I had interpreted her behaviour mainly in terms of oral greed and aggression in relation to myself, standing for the breast, and in terms of her distress about the good food being changed into bad faeces so that she had to feed on dirt from the floor and faeces. During these hours she had also experienced persecutory hallucinations, which she betrayed by shaking her hands violently as though trying to get rid of something, tearing bits of her skin and clothing and throwing them out, listening in a frightened way to some internal voices, and occasionally shouting. I interpreted this behaviour as evidence of her feeling that the food which had gone bad was attacking her, and that similarly now my interpretations were felt as bad food biting her or soiling her inside.

She had confirmed some of these interpretations verbally and referred to her babyhood, saying that as a baby she did nothing but bite and hate and cry. After some weeks of such behaviour she came in one day, sat on the couch, and said in a composed and rational manner that Mummy took her to the doctor because she was very pale and thin and Mummy was worried. I asked her what she thought was the matter with her. She did not answer, but started biting and again picking her nose and eating the pickings. So I connected her concern about herself with her feeling that she was destroying food, turning it bad, and wasting it. But I obviously

53

missed in this hour the gist of her anxiety, because she came in the next hour and repeated the same behaviour and the same statement as in the hour before. She put great emphasis on the words 'pale and thin', looking at me intently and suspiciously, and then she put her hand to the base of her throat and gave herself two very slight scratches. Now at the beginning of her treatment she used to have phases of being very voluble, and one of the things she talked about a great deal then was vampires and their supposed habits, about which she was very knowledgeable. I knew that vampires are supposed to bite their victims at the base of the neck and invariably to leave two small scratches, supposed to be symptomatic. I said, therefore, when I noticed the two scratches, that she felt she was pale and thin because she was being sucked by a vampire, and I drew her attention to the way she looked at me and said she suspected me of being that vampire.

This interpretation produced a number of associations about vampires and their habits and she directly confirmed my transference interpretation by saying that I could only make interpretations out of what she told me and she felt that I lived on her life and sucked out her brains and her blood. Such a direct verbal admission of feelings about me was most unusual in this patient.

The next day she came extremely late, about ten minutes before the end of the session, and when I suggested that she was afraid to come lest I should suck her blood out, she immediately started complaining of my dragging things out of her, doing it even in her dreams. Then she added that perhaps it was because of this that she had to fly to the 'ideal people' inside herself (we knew by then that she had two kinds of hallucination, one of an extremely persecutory and one of a very ideal character).

In the following hour she came on time and continued to talk about the 'ideal people' inside her. I knew from earlier material that many of her hallucinations were based on characters from books which she used literally to devour in order to create inside herself a hallucinatory world based on the characters from the books, with some of which she also identified. I interpreted to her that she treated me in a manner similar to that in which she treated books, taking in my interpretations and using them to create pleasurable hallucinations inside herself. She said that she knew that, and added that she knew she was draining life out of me. Then she gave me a long look and said that sometimes when vampires were in love they would not kill their victim outright but do so slowly, by degrees, enjoying the sucking enormously.

In the next few sessions we could get at her various feelings about me in the situation of vampires. She had felt that her love for me, like her love for the breast, was as dangerous as hatred in its cruelty and its greed, and that by being silent and making me talk she was sucking my life blood by slow degrees and building something wonderful inside herself that she was not sharing with me. Whereupon I was becoming emptied, and I slowly became the vampire sucking life out of her, taking away her good hallucinations, persecuting her and threatening to kill her. She dreaded cure because cure to her meant being exorcized, and being exorcized meant that it would be discovered that it was *she* who was the vampire to begin with and that she would be made to die. She felt that the situation could only end in death. After some working through of this material, at the end of one of the sessions she was sitting down very quietly on the couch, deep in thought, and she said, 'Do you mean that all that vicious circle happens because I always took and took and ate and ate and did not do anything to rebuild anything good inside myself?' Throughout that session she looked concerned, depressed, thoughtful, and far saner than ever before.

The next day she met me in the waiting room, smiling and greeting me in an unusually open and friendly manner. She looked normal and composed. I also noticed that she wore an open-necked shirt which showed more of her chest than usual. As soon as she came into the consulting room there was an immediate change. She started behaving in an irrational and hallucinated way. She skipped and jumped round the room for a while, flapping her arms, behaving in a manic rather than a persecuted manner. Then she jumped on the couch and lay there muttering to herself and occasionally masturbating. She seemed to ignore me completely. This was a striking change compared with the preceding week when she had associated freely, and particularly compared with the preceding session in which she seemed so well in touch with her feelings. After a time I realized that her behaviour was symptomatic of a negative therapeutic reaction to the great progress in insight which she had gained in the last days. In the previous session my patient had experienced the feeling that she had destroyed the breast that fed her and she was faced with the problem of reparation and rebuilding. This situation had obviously been intolerable to her, and she had acted in a way which would enable her to project these unbearable feelings on to me. To begin with, in the waiting room, she was the mother seducing me by showing me the breast, greeting me in a friendly manner, wanting to arouse my hopes, then in the consulting room she proceeded to frustrate me by ignoring me and exhibited to me the parental intercourse in her masturbation. She was the mother, I was to be the infant experiencing sexual excitement, greed, frustration, rage and guilt. I remembered in this session that this patient's mother often lost her temper with her daughter and then felt absolutely crushed with guilt, and it struck me forcibly how subtly the patient must have managed to make her mother behave like an infant losing her temper and then having to carry the burden of guilt.

I first interpreted to the patient the meaning of her behaviour, the identification with me as the mother who was frustrating her orally and exciting her rage by her intercourse with father. Then I reminded her of the end of the previous session when she had been faced with her own feeling of guilt towards me as the feeding mother. I pointed out to her that she obviously could not bear those feelings inside herself, and therefore she had to become the mother and I had to become the infant, so that she could put that part of herself which she could not bear, the guilty infant, into me. I could also show her that this was often the way she had behaved with her mother, both at present and in her early childhood. She listened to this interpretation carefully and said, with a sigh of relief and with an expression of sanity returning to her face: 'Of course, then I never need to be the child that depends.'

In this series of sessions I have tried to show a sequence of changes in my patient. After weeks of what had seemed wholly irrational and mad behaviour the patient had been enabled to verbalize in the transference her paranoid delusion about me as a vampire. Further analysis enabled her to relate this picture of me to her own sucking impulses and phantasies. Concurrently with that she had become aware that her ideal and persecutory figures were the split-off aspects of one object, the analyst standing for the breast or the feeding mother. At that point her ego became more integrated and her object more synthesized. The persecutory feelings lessened and the patient had to face her responsibility for her own impulses towards the breast and her feeling that she had to restore it, particularly that she had to restore the internal breast. She made it clear when she said 'Is it because I always took and ate and ate and did nothing to rebuild anything good *inside* myself?' At that point she was in touch with her feelings and with reality and she approached sanity. This, however, was unbearable to her and she immediately projected the depressed and saner part of herself into me, thereby getting rid of it and becoming madder.

2nd example

The second sequence that I want to describe happened the same year in October. She had come back from the summer holiday remote and hallucinated. From her behaviour I could gather that she was hallucinating God and the devil; they represented the good and bad aspects of the patient's father, who had committed suicide when she was 15. At times it was clear from her gestures and expressions that she was having intercourse now with God, now with the devil. There was a great deal of screaming, shouting, and attacking; at times she looked terrified. She was also continually picking threads from the cover of the couch and breaking them off angrily. I had interpreted to her mainly her relation to her father in terms of splitting, idealization, and persecution, and related it to the transference, particularly in connection with the long summer holiday. I also paid a great deal of attention to her breaking off the threads from the couch cover, interpreting this behaviour according to the context as breaking the threads of her thoughts, the threads of analysis, the threads connecting her internal world with external reality. Her violence gradually subsided, and although she was still picking off threads and breaking them, and as usual she did a lot of biting, grimacing, and angry shaking, the change in her mood was noticeable. As time went on there was more skipping and dancing, more grace in her movements, less tension, and there was about her a general air of half gaiety, irresponsibility, and remoteness. Then one day as she was dancing round the room, picking some imaginary things from the carpet and making movements as though she was scattering something round the room, it struck me that she must have been imagining that she was dancing in a meadow, picking flowers and scattering them, and it occurred to me that she was behaving exactly like an actress playing the part of Shakespeare's Ophelia. The likeness to Ophelia was all the more remarkable in that in some peculiar way, the more gaily and irresponsibly she was behaving, the sadder was the effect, as though her gaiety itself was designed to produce sadness in her audience, just as Ophelia's pseudo-gay dancing and singing is designed to make the audience in the theatre sad. If she was Ophelia she was scattering her sadness round the room as she was scattering the imaginary flowers, in order to get rid of it and to make me, the audience, sad.[2] As the patient in the past had often identified with characters in books or plays, I felt on fairly secure ground in saying to her: 'It seems to me that you are being Ophelia.' She immediately stopped and said, 'Yes, of course,' as though surprised that I had not noticed it earlier, and then she added, sadly, 'Ophelia was mad, wasn't she?' It was the first time she had admitted that she knew about her own madness.

I then connected her behaviour with the previous material and with my interpretations about her relation to her father and showed her how she had felt guilty about the death of her father-lover whom she wished to kill and whom she thought she had killed for his having rejected her. I also told her how her present Ophelia-like madness was a denial of her feelings about his death and an attempt to put these feelings into me. As I was interpreting, she threw herself on the couch and let her head hang down from it. I said that she was representing Ophelia's suicide and showing me that she could not admit her feelings about her father's death as the guilt and distress about it would drive her, like him, to suicide. But she did not agree with this and said Ophelia's death was not a suicide. 'She was irresponsible, like a child, she did not know the difference. Reality did not exist for her; death did not mean anything.'

I then interpreted to her how putting into me the part of herself capable of appreciating the fact of the death of her father and the reality of her own ambivalent feelings and guilt, resulted in her losing her reality sense, her sanity. She then became a person who 'did not know the difference' any longer.

She came back the next day very hallucinated and persecuted, externally and internally. She was obviously having unpleasant hallucinations, and she also turned away from me in an angry and frightening way. She did a lot of grimacing, muttering, and biting. She again picked up and broke off threads. I reminded her of the previous session and how she was trying to get rid of her painful feelings by putting them into me. I drew her attention to the breaking of the threads and told her that in getting rid of those painful feelings she felt she was trying to break off and get rid of her sanity. At the same time she felt that I had become a persecutor because she put her painful feelings into me and now she felt that in interpreting I was trying to push those feelings back into her and persecuting her with them.

The next day she came looking sad and quiet. She started again picking threads out of the couch, but instead of breaking them off completely she was intertwining them. When I made some reference to her Ophelia-like feelings, she said, 'You know, when Ophelia was picking flowers it was not, as you said, all madness. There was a lot of the other thing as well. What was unbearable was the intertwining.' I said, 'The intertwining of madness and sanity?' She said, 'Yes, that is what is unbearable.' I then told her that my interpretations about how she tried to put her sanity into me made her feel that she had regained the sane part of herself, but she felt it was unbearable because now that sane part of herself could appreciate and feel distress about the disintegration of the rest of herself. In the previous session she had tried to make me into the sane part of herself distressed at her, the patient's, insanity. I pointed out to her how she was intertwining the threads that she was picking up and contrasted this with the earlier session in which she was breaking the threads. I interpreted to her that the breaking of the threads respected her breaking her sanity because she could not bear the distress, sadness, and guilt that sanity seemed to involve for her.

In the next session she looked at me very carefully and said: 'Do you ever smile or laugh? My Mummy says that she cannot imagine you doing either.' I pointed out to her how much laughing and giggling she had done during the last weeks and said that she felt that she had stolen all my smiles and laughter and put into me all her depression and guilt, thereby making me into the sad part of herself, but in doing that she made me into a persecutor because she felt I was trying to push this unwanted sadness back into her; then she could not experience her guilt or her sadness as her own, but she felt it as something pushed into her by me in revenge and punishment. She felt that I had lost my laughter but she herself had lost the meaning and understanding of sadness.

In the sessions of February one could see the emergence of depression following the analysis of the patient's vampire phantasies. In the sessions now described, in the patient's Ophelia-like behaviour the depression was first observed by me in the projected form: I was obviously meant to be sad and depressed. The patient herself became aware of her depression only after interpretations which put her again in touch with this projected part of herself. There are other important differences in the two series of sessions. In February the patient was mainly preoccupied with the early feeding relation to the breast, and the depression, when it emerged, had a violent and ruthless character. The emotions projected on to the analyst were crude and primitive: oral love and greed, excited jealousy, rage followed by guilt and despair. In the October sessions she was dealing with problems from a later stage of development and more related to the genital Oedipus complex. In keeping with that, the feelings projected were more complex, less primitive and more finely shaded, involving not only rage, guilt, and despair, but also sadness, grief, and pining. The similarities of the two situations, however, are important – whenever the patient could be put in touch with her emerging depression she became communicative in a sane manner, sanity and depressive feelings returning to her ego together. Whenever the depressive feelings became intolerable, re-projection occurred with the corresponding loss of reality sense, the return of mad behaviour and an increase of persecutory feelings.

Conclusion

I have tried to show in these examples the emergence of depressive feelings in a schizophrenic patient and the use she made of projective identification as a defence against depression. The analysis of persecutory anxieties and schizoid defences in the transference leads to a greater integration of the ego and the object. When this begins the patient becomes saner and she begins to face the reality of her impulses, her depressive feelings, guilt and the need for reparation, as well as the fact of her own madness. For the schizophrenic, the guilt and distress in this situation is intolerable, and therefore the steps that the patient has taken towards sanity have to be reversed.[3] The patient immediately projects the depressed part of the ego into the analyst. This constitutes a negative therapeutic reaction. The saner part of the ego is lost and the analyst becomes again the persecutor, since he is felt to contain the depressed part of the patient's ego and as forcing this unwanted depression back into the patient. In order to control this negative therapeutic reaction and to enable the patient to regain, retain, and strengthen the sane part of the personality, the whole process of the emergence of the depression and the projection of it has to be followed closely in the transference.

Notes

1 Read at the 19th International Psycho-Analytical Congress, Geneva, 24–28 July, 1955.
2 The scattering of her own feelings and the splitting of the analyst into a multitude of people: the audience is an example of the *minute* splitting of parts of the ego and the object described by Wilfred Bion in the paper read at the 1955 Congress, 'Differentiation of the psychotic from the non-psychotic personalities' (reprinted here, pp. 61–78).
3 I do not propose to discuss in this paper why the depressive position is so unbearable to these patients. Some light is thrown on this problem in Herbert Rosenfeld's 'Notes on the psychoanalysis of the superego conflict in an acute schizophrenic patient' *International Journal of Psycho-Analysis*, 33 (1952) and reprinted here on pp. 14–49.

Differentiation of the psychotic from the non-psychotic personalities

W. R. BION

This article was originally a paper read before the British Psycho-Analytical Society on 5 October 1955 and was first published in 1957 in the *International Journal of Psycho-Analysis*, 38: 266–75.

The theme of this paper is that the differentiation of the psychotic from the non-psychotic personalities depends on a minute splitting of all that part of the personality that is concerned with awareness of internal and external reality, and the expulsion of these fragments so that they enter into or engulf their objects. I shall describe this process in some detail and shall then discuss its consequences and how they affect treatment.

The conclusions were arrived at in analytic contact with schizophrenic patients and have been tested by me in practice. I ask your attention for them because they have led to developments in my patients which are analytically significant and not to be confused, either with the remissions familiar to psychiatrists, or with that class of improvement that it is impossible to relate to the interpretations given or to any coherent body of psychoanalytic theory. I believe that the improvements I have seen deserve psychoanalytic investigation.

I owe my clarification of the obscurity that pervades the whole of a psychotic analysis mainly to three pieces of work. As they are crucial for understanding what follows I shall remind you of them. First: Freud's (1911) description, referred to by me in my paper to the London Congress of 1953 (Bion 1954), of the mental apparatus called into activity by the demands of the reality principle and in particular of that part of it which is concerned with the consciousness attached to the sense-organs. Second: Melanie Klein's (1928) description of the phantasied sadistic attacks that the infant makes on the breast during the paranoid-schizoid phase, and third: her discovery of projective identification (Klein 1946). By this mechanism the patient splits off a part of his personality and projects it into the object where it becomes installed, sometimes as a persecutor, leaving the psyche, from which it has been split off, correspondingly impoverished.

Lest it be supposed that I attribute the development of schizophrenia exclusively to certain mechanisms apart from the personality that employs them I shall enumerate now what I think are the preconditions for the mechanisms on which I wish to focus your attention. There is the environment, which I shall not discuss at this time, and the personality, which must display four essential features. These are: a preponderance of destructive impulses so great that even the impulse to love is suffused by them and turned to sadism; a hatred of reality, internal and external, which is extended to all that makes for awareness of it; a dread of imminent annihilation (Klein 1946) and, finally, a premature and precipitate formation of object relations, foremost amongst which is the transference, whose thinness is in marked contrast with the tenacity with which they are maintained. The prematurity, thinness, and tenacity are pathognomonic and have an important derivation, about which I can say nothing today, in the conflict, never in the schizophrenic decided, between the life and death instincts.

Before I consider the mechanisms that spring from these characteristics I must dispose briefly of a few points that concern the transference. The relationship with the analyst is premature, precipitate, and intensely dependent; when under pressure of his life and death instincts, the patient broadens the contact, two concurrent streams of phenomena become manifest. First, splitting of his personality and projection of the fragments into the analyst (i.e. projective identification) becomes overactive, with consequent confusional states such as Rosenfeld (1952) has described. Second, the mental and other activities by which the dominant impulse, be it of life or death instincts, strives to express itself, are at once subjected to mutilation by the temporarily subordinated impulse. Harassed by the mutilations and striving to escape the confusional states, the patient returns to the restricted relationship. Oscillation between the attempt to broaden the contact and the attempt to restrict continues throughout the analysis.

To return now to the characteristics I listed as intrinsic to the schizophrenic personality. These constitute an endowment that makes it certain that the possessor of it will progress through the paranoid-schizoid and depressive positions in a manner markedly different from that of one not so endowed. The difference hinges on the fact that this combination of qualities leads to minute fragmentation of the personality, particularly of the apparatus of awareness of reality which Freud described as coming into operation at the behest of the reality principle, and quite excessive projection of these fragments of personality into external objects.

I described some aspects of these theories in my paper to the International Congress of 1953 (Bion 1954) when I was speaking of the association of the depressive position with the development of verbal thought and the significance of this association for awareness of internal and external reality. In this paper I am taking up the same story only at a much earlier stage, namely at the outset of the patient's life. I am dealing with phenomena in the paranoid–schizoid position which are associated ultimately with the inchoation of verbal thought. How this should be so will, I hope, presently emerge.

The theories of Freud and Melanie Klein to which I referred earlier must now be considered in more detail. Quoting this formulation in his paper on 'Neurosis and psychosis' in 1924, Freud defined one of the features distinguishing the neuroses from the psychoses as: 'in the former the ego, in virtue of its allegiance to reality, suppresses a part of the id (the life of instinct), whereas in the psychoses the same ego in the service of the id, withdraws itself from a part of reality' (Freud 1924). I assume that when Freud speaks of the allegiance of the ego to reality he is speaking of the developments he described as taking place with the institution of the reality principle. He said, 'the new demands made a succession of adaptations necesary in the mental apparatus, which, on account of insufficient or uncertain knowledge, we can only detail very cursorily'. He then lists: the heightened significance of the sense organs directed towards the outer world and of the consciousness attached to them; attention, which he calls a special function which had to search the outer world in order that its data might be already familiar if an urgent inner need should arise; a system of notation whose task was to deposit the results of this periodical activity of consciousness which he describes as a part of that which we call memory; judgement which had to decide whether a particular idea was true or false; the employment of motor discharge in appropriate alteration of reality and not simply in unburdening the mental apparatus of accretions of stimuli; and, finally, thought which he says made it possible to tolerate the frustration which is an inevitable accompaniment of action by virtue of its quality as an experimental way of acting. As will be seen I very much extend the function and importance of thought, but otherwise accept this classification of ego function, which Freud put forward as putative, as giving concreteness to a part of the personality with which this paper is concerned. It accords well with clinical experience and illuminates events which I should have found infinitely more obscure without it.

I would make two modifications in Freud's description to bring it into closer relation with the facts. I do not think, at least as touches those patients likely to be met with in analytic practice, that the ego is ever wholly withdrawn from reality. I would say that its contact with reality is masked by the dominance, in the patient's mind and behaviour, of an omnipotent phantasy that is intended to destroy either reality or the awareness of it, and thus to achieve a state that is neither life nor death. Since contact with reality is never entirely lost, the phenomena which we are accustomed to associate with the neuroses are never absent and serve to complicate the analysis, when sufficient progress has been made, by their presence amidst psychotic material. On this fact, that the ego retains contact with reality, depends the existence of a non-psychotic personality parallel with, but obscured by, the psychotic personality.

My second modification is that the withdrawal from reality is an illusion, not a fact, and arises from the deployment of projective identification against the mental apparatus listed by Freud. Such is the dominance of this phantasy that it is evident that it is no phantasy, but a fact, to the patient, who acts as if his perceptual apparatus could be split into minute fragments and projected into his objects.

As a result of these modifications we reach the conclusion that patients ill enough, say, to be certified as psychotic, contain in their psyche a non-psychotic part of the personality, a prey to the various neurotic mechanisms with which psychoanalysis has made us familiar, and a psychotic part of the personality which is so far dominant that the non-psychotic part of the personality, with which it exists in negative juxtaposition, is obscured.

One concomitant of the hatred of reality that Freud remarked is the psychotic infant's phantasies of sadistic attacks on the breast which Melanie Klein described as a part of the paranoid–schizoid phase (Klein 1946). I wish to emphasize that in this phase the psychotic splits his objects, and contemporaneously all that part of his personality, which would make him aware of the reality he hates, into exceedingly minute fragments, for it is this that contributes materially to the psychotic's feeling that he cannot restore his objects or his ego. As a result of these splitting attacks, all those features of the personality which should one day provide the foundation for

64

intuitive understanding of himself and others are jeopardized at the outset. All the functions which Freud described as being, at a later stage, a developmental response to the reality principle, that is to say, consciousness of sense impressions, attention, memory, judgement, thought, have brought against them, in such inchoate forms as they may possess at the outset of life, the sadistic splitting eviscerating attacks that lead to their being minutely fragmented and then expelled from the personality to penetrate, or encyst, the objects. In the patient's phantasy the expelled particles of ego lead an independent and uncontrolled existence, either contained by or containing the external objects; they continue to exercise their functions as if the ordeal to which they have been subjected had served only to increase their number and provoke their hostility to the psyche that ejected them. In consequence the patient feels himself to be surrounded by bizarre objects whose nature I shall now describe.

Each particle is felt to consist of a real object which is encapsulated in a piece of personality that has engulfed it. The nature of this complete particle will depend partly on the character of the real object, say a gramophone, and partly on the character of the particle of personality that engulfs it. If the piece of personality is concerned with sight, the gramophone when played is felt to be watching the patient; if with hearing, then the gramophone when played is felt to be listening to the patient. The object, angered at being engulfed, swells up, so to speak, and suffuses and controls the piece of personality that engulfs it: to that extent the particle of personality has become a thing. Since these particles are what the patient depends on for use as the prototypes of ideas – later to form the matrix from which words should spring – this suffusion of the piece of personality by the contained but controlling object leads the patient to feel that words are the actual things they name and so adds to the confusions, described by Segal, that arise because the patient equates, but does not symbolize. The fact that the patient uses these bizarre objects for achieving thought leads now to a fresh problem. If we consider that one of the patient's objects in using splitting and projective identification is to rid himself of awareness of reality it is clear that he could achieve the maximum of severance from reality with the greatest economy of effort if he could launch these destructive attacks on the link, whatever it is, that connects sense impressions with consciousness. In my paper to the 1953 International Congress (Bion 1954) I showed that awareness of psychic reality depended on the development of a capacity for verbal thought the foundation of which was linked with the depressive position. It is impossible to go into this now. I refer you to Melanie Klein's 1930 paper on 'The importance of symbol formation in the development of the ego' (Klein 1930) and to the paper given to the British Psychological Society (1955) by H. Segal (Segal 1957). In this, Segal demonstrates the importance of symbol formation and explores its relationship to verbal thought and the reparative drives normally associated with the depressive position. I am concerned with an earlier stage in the same story. It is my belief that the mischief that becomes much more apparent in the depressive position has in fact been initiated in the paranoid–schizoid phase when the foundations for primitive thought should be laid, but are not, because of the overaction of splitting and projective identification.

Freud attributes to thought the function of providing a means of restraint of action. But he goes on to say, 'It is probable that thinking was originally unconscious, in so far as it rose above mere ideation and turned to the relations between the object-impressions, and that it became endowed with further qualities which were perceptible to consciousness only through its connection with the memory traces of words' (Freud 1911). My experiences have led me to suppose that some kind of thought, related to what we should call ideographs and sight rather than to words and hearing exists at the outset. This though depends on a capacity for balanced introjection and projection of objects and, *a fortiori*, on awareness of them. This is within the capacity of the non-psychotic part of the personality, partly because of the splitting and ejection of the apparatus of awareness I have already described and partly for reasons I am coming to now.

Thanks to the operations of the non-psychotic part of the personality the patient is aware that introjection is leading to the formation of the unconscious thought of which Freud speaks as 'turned to the relations between object-impressions'. Now I believe that it is this unconscious thought which Freud describes as turned to the relations between the object-impressions which is responsible for the 'consciousness attached to' the sense impressions. I am fortified in this belief by his statement twelve years later in the paper on 'The ego and the id'. In this he says 'that the question "How does a thing become conscious?" could be put more advantageously thus: "How does a thing become pre-conscious?" And the answer would be: "By coming into connection with the verbal images that correspond to it"' (Freud 1923). In my 1953 paper I said that verbal thought is bound up with awareness of psychic reality (Bion 1954); this I also believe to be true of the early pre-verbal thought of which I am now speaking. In view of what I have already said of the psychotic's attacks on all that mental apparatus that leads to consciousness of external and internal reality, it is to be expected that the deployment of projective identification would be particularly severe against the thought, of whatsoever kind, that turned to the relations between object-impressions, for if this link could be severed, or better still never forged, then at least consciousness of reality would be destroyed even though reality itself could not be. But in fact the work of destruction is already half done as the material from which thought is forged, in the non-psychotic by balanced introjection and projection, is not available to the psychotic part of the personality, because the displacement of projection and introjection by projective identification has left him only with the bizarre objects I have described.

In fact, not only is primitive thought attacked because it links sense-impressions of reality with consciousness but, thanks to the psychotic's over-endowment with destructiveness, the splitting processes are extended to the links within the thought processes themselves. As Freud's phrase regarding thought being turned to the relations between object-impressions implies, this primitive matrix of ideographs from which thought springs contains within itself links between one ideograph and another. All these are now attacked till finally two objects cannot be brought together in a way which leaves each object with its intrinsic qualities intact and yet able, by their conjunction, to produce a new mental object. Consequently the formation of symbols, which depends for its therapeutic effect on the ability to bring together two objects so that their resemblance is made manifest, yet their difference left unimpaired, now becomes difficult. At a still later stage the result of these splitting attacks is seen in the denial of articulation as a principle for the combining of words. This last does not mean that objects cannot be brought together; as I shall show later when speaking of agglomeration, that is by no means true. Further, since that-which-links has been not only minutely fragmented but also projected out into objects to join the other bizarre objects, the patients feels surrounded by minute links which, being impregnated now with cruelty, link objects together cruelly.

To conclude my description of the fragmentation of the ego and its expulsion into and about its objects, I shall say that I believe the process I have described to be the central factor, in so far as such a factor can be isolated without distortion, in the differentiation of the psychotic from the non-psychotic part of the personality. It takes place at the outset of the patient's life. The sadistic attacks on the ego and on the matrix of thought, together with projective identification of the fragments, make it certain that from this point on there is an ever-widening divergence between the psychotic and non-psychotic parts of the personality until at last the gulf between them is felt to be unbridgeable.

The consequences for the patient are that he now moves, not in a world of dreams, but in a world of objects which are ordinarily the furniture of dreams. His sense impressions appear to have suffered mutilation of a kind which would be appropriate had they been attacked as the breast is felt to be attacked in the sadistic phantasies of the infant (Klein 1928). The patient feels imprisoned in the state of mind he has achieved, and unable to escape from it because he feels he lacks the apparatus of awareness of reality which is both the key to escape and the freedom to which he would escape. The sense of imprisonment is intensified by the menacing presence of the expelled fragments within whose planetary movements he is contained. These objects, primitive yet complex, partake of qualities which in the non-psychotic personality are peculiar to matter, anal objects, senses, ideas and superego.

The diversity of such objects, dependent as it is on the sense by which they are suffused, prevents more than the cursory indication of their mode of genesis that I have given. The relation of these objects to material for ideographic thought leads the patient to confound real objects with primitive ideas and therefore to confusion when they obey the laws of natural science and not those of mental functioning. If he wishes to bring back any of these objects in an attempt at restitution of the ego, and in analysis he feels impelled to make the attempt, he has to bring them back by projective identification in reverse and by the route by which they were expelled. Whether he feels he has had one of these objects put into him by the analyst, or whether he feels he has taken it in, he feels the ingress as an assault. The extreme degree to which he has carried the splitting of objects and ego alike makes any attempt at synthesis hazardous. Furthermore, as he has rid himself of that-which-joins, his capacity for articulation, the methods available for synthesis are felt to be macilent; he can compress but cannot join, he can fuse but cannot articulate. The capacity to join is felt, as a result of its ejection, to have become, like all other expelled particles, infinitely worse than they were when ejected. Any joining that takes place is done with a vengeance, that is to say in a manner expressly contrary to the wishes of the patient at the moment. In the course of the analysis this process of compression or agglomeration loses some of its malignancy and then fresh problems arise.

I must now draw your attention to a matter that demands a paper to itself and therefore cannot be more than mentioned here. It is implicit in my description that the psychotic personality or part of the personality has used splitting and projective identification as a substitute for repression. Where the non-psychotic part of the personality resorts to repression as a means of cutting off certain trends in the mind both from consciousness and from other forms of manifestation and activity, the psychotic part of the personality has attempted to rid itself of the apparatus on which the psyche depends to carry out the repressions; the unconscious would seem to be replaced by the world of dream furniture.

I shall now attempt a description of an actual session; it is a clinical experience based on these theories rather than the description of an experience on which the theories are based, but I hope I shall be able to indicate the material from previous sessions which led me to interpret as I did.

The patient at the time of this session, of which I describe a small part, had been coming to me for six years. He had once been as late as forty-five minutes, but had never missed a session; the sessions were never continued over time. On this morning he arrived a quarter of an hour late and lay on the couch. He spent some time turning from one side to another, ostensibly making himself comfortable. At length he said: 'I don't suppose I shall do anything today. I ought to have rung up my mother.' He paused, and then said: 'No; I thought it would be like this.' A more prolonged pause followed; then, 'Nothing but filthy things and smells', he said. 'I think I've lost my sight.' Some twenty-five minutes of our time had now passed, and at this point I made an interpretation, but before I repeat it I must discuss some previous material which will, I hope, make my intervention comprehensible.

When the patient was manoeuvring on the couch I was watching something with which I was familiar. Five years earlier he had explained that his doctor advised an operation for hernia and it was to be assumed that the discomfort caused by the hernia compelled these adjustments. It was, however, evident that more was involved than the hernia and rational activity to increase his physical comfort. I had sometimes asked him what these movements were, and to these questions his reply had been, 'Nothing'. Once he had said, 'I don't know'. I had felt that 'Nothing' was a thinly veiled invitation to me to mind my own business as well as a denial of something very bad. I continued, over the weeks and years, to watch his movements. A handkerchief was disposed near his right pocket; he arched his back – surely a sexual gesture here? A lighter fell out of his pocket. Should he pick it up? Yes. No, perhaps not. Well, yes. It was retrieved from the floor and placed by the handkerchief. Immediately a shower of coins spilled over the couch on to the floor. The patient lay still and waited. Perhaps, his gestures seemed to suggest, he had been unwise to bring back the lighter. It had seemed to lead to the shower of coins. He waited, cautiously, furtively. And finally he made the remark I have reported. It reminded me of his descriptions, not given in any one session but produced over many months of the tortuous manoeuvres through which he had to go before he went to the lavatory, or went down to breakfast, or telephoned to his mother. I was quite used to recalling many of the free associations which might easily be appropriate to the behaviour he displayed on this as on many other mornings. But these were now my associations, and once when I had tried to make use of such material in an interpretation that is exactly the reply he had made. One interpretation I remembered which had met with some success. I had pointed out that he felt much the same about these movements as he had about a dream he had told me – he had no ideas about the dream and he had no ideas about the movements. 'Yes', he had agreed, 'that's so'. 'And yet', I replied, 'you once had an idea about it; you thought it was the hernia.' 'That's nothing', he replied, and had then paused, almost slyly I thought, to see if I had grasped the point. So, 'Nothing is really a hernia', I said. 'No idea', he replied, 'only a hernia.' I had been left feeling that his 'no idea' was very like the 'no ideas' about the dreams or the movements, but for that session at least I could get no further. In this respect the movements and the dreams were very fair instances of mutilated attempts at co-operation, and this too was something to which I had drawn his attention.

It may have occurred to you, as it often had to me, that I was watching a series of miniature dramatic presentations, preparations for a baby's bath or feed, or a change of nappies, or a sexual seduction. More often it would be correct to say that the presentation was a conglomeration of bits out of a number of such scenes, and it was this impression that led me finally to suppose that I was watching an ideomotor activity, that is to say a means of expressing an idea without naming it. From this it was a short step to think of it as the kind of motor activity which Freud had described as characteristic of the supremacy of the pleasure principle (Bion 1954). For, in so far as I was watching psychotic phenomena, the patient could not be acting in response to awareness of external reality; he was exhibiting the kind of motor discharge which Freud said under the supremacy of the pleasure principle 'had served to unburden the mental apparatus of accretions of stimuli, and in carrying out this task had sent innervations into the interior of the body (mien expressions of affect).' It was this impression which returned to me when the patient said, 'I don't expect I shall do anything today.' It was a remark that could refer to the likelihood of his producing any material for interpretation or, equally, to the likelihood that I would produce any interpretations. 'I ought to have rung up my mother' could mean that his failure to do so was being visited upon him by the punishment of not being able to do any analysis. It also meant that his mother would have known what to do about it – she could get associations out of him or interpretations out of me; something depended on what his mother meant to him, but on this point I was really in the dark. She had come in to the analysis as a simple working-class woman who had to go to work for the family; this view was entertained with the same degree of conviction that stamped his statements that the family were extremely wealthy. I was vouchsafed glimpses of her as a woman with such multitudinous social engagements that scant time was left her to satisfy the needs either of the patient, who was her eldest son, her eldest daughter, two years older than the patient, or the remainder of the family. She had been spoken of, if anything so inarticulate could be described as speech, as devoid of common sense or culture, though in the habit of visiting art galleries of international fame. I was left to infer that the bringing up of her children was ignorant and painstaking in the extreme. I may say that at the time of which I write I knew little more of his real mother than would be known by a person who had rid himself of his ego in the way I have described as typical of the psychotic personality. Nevertheless I had these impressions, and others which I omit, and on them I based my interpretations. The patient's responses to these interpretations were outright rejection as either quite inadmissible because wrong, or accurate but improperly arrived at in that I must have been using his mind (really his capacity for contact with reality) without his permission. It will be observed that he thereby expresses a jealous denial of my insight.

When the patient said, after a pause, that he knew it would be like this, I felt on fairly sure ground in assuming that it was I who was unlikely to do anything in that session and that his mother was some person or thing who could have enabled him to deal with me more satisfactorily. This impression was strengthened by the next association.

If the theories I have described are correct, then, in any given situation, the patient who is ill enough, as this one was, to have achieved certification, has two main problems to solve, one appertaining to the non-psychotic part of the personality and one to the psychotic part . With this particular patient, at this particular juncture, the psychotic personality and its problems still obscured the non-psychotic personality and its problems. Nevertheless, as I hope to show, the latter were discernible in the material. The non-psychotic personality was concerned with a neurotic problem, that is to say a problem that centred on the resolution of a conflict of ideas and emotions to which the operation of the ego had given rise. But the psychotic personality was concerned with the problem of repair of the ego, and the clue to this lay in the fear that he had lost his sight. Since it was the psychotic problem that obtruded I dealt with that, taking his last association first. I told him that these filthy things and smells were what he felt he had made me do, and that he felt he had compelled me to defecate them out, including the sight he had put in to me.

The patient jerked convulsively and I saw him cautiously scanning what seemed to be the air around him. I accordingly said that he felt surrounded by bad and smelly bits of himself including his eyes which he felt he had expelled from his anus. He replied: 'I can't see.' I then told him he felt he had lost his sight and his ability to talk to his mother, or to me, when he had got rid of these abilities so as to avoid pain.

In this last interpretation I was making use of a session, many months earlier, in which the patient complained that analysis was torture, memory torture. I showed him then that when he felt pain, as evidenced in this session by the convulsive jerks, he achieved anaesthesia by getting rid of his memory and anything that could make him realize pain.

Patient: 'My head is splitting; may be my dark glasses.'

Now some five months previously I had worn dark glasses; the fact had, as far as I could tell, produced no reaction whatever from that day to this, but that becomes less surprising if we consider that I, wearing dark glasses, was felt by him as one of the objects to which I referred when describing the fate of the expelled particles of ego. I have explained that the psychotic personality seems to have to await the occurrence of an apt event before it feels it is in possession of an ideograph suitable for use in communication with itself or with others. Reciprocally, other events, which might be supposed to have immediate significance for the non-psychotic personality, are passed by because they are felt to be significant only as ideographs serving no immediate need. In the present instance the problem created by my wearing dark glasses, in the non-psychotic part of the personality was obscured because the psychotic part of the personality was dominant; and in that part of the personality the event was merely significant as an ideograph for which it had had no immediate need. When at last the fact obtruded in analysis it had the appearance, superficially, of being perhaps some kind of delayed reaction, but such a view depends on the supposition that the association of the dark glasses was an expression of neurotic conflict in the non-psychotic part of the personality. In fact it was not a delayed expression of a conflict in the non-psychotic part of the personality but, as I shall show, the mobilization of an ideograph needed by the psychotic part of the personality for an immediate repair of an ego damaged by the excessive projective identification that I have described. Such obtrusions of fact, originally passed by in silence, must then be regarded not so much as significant because their appearance is delayed, but because they are evidence of activity in the psychotic part of the personality.

Assuming then that the dark glasses here are a verbal communication of an ideograph it becomes necessary to determine the interpretation of the ideograph. I shall have to compress, almost I fear to the point of risking incomprehensibility, the evidence in my possession. The glasses contained a hint of the baby's bottle. They were two glasses, or bottles, thus resembling the breast. They were dark because frowning and angry. They were of glass to pay him out of trying to see through them when they were breasts. They were dark because he needs darkness to spy on the parents in intercourse. They were dark because he had taken the bottle not to get milk but to see what the parents did. They were dark because he had swallowed them, and not simply the milk they had contained. And they were dark because the clear good objects had been made black and smelly inside him. All these attributes must have been achieved through the operation of the non-psychotic part of the personality. Added to these characteristics were those that I have described as appertaining to them as part of the ego that has been expelled by projective identification, namely their hatred of him as part of himself he had rejected. Making use of these accretions of analytic experience, and still concentrating on the psychotic problem, that is to say, the need to repair the ego to meet the demands of the external situation, I said:

Analyst. Your sight has come back into you but splits your head; you feel it is very bad sight because of what you have done to it.

Patient (moving in pain as if protecting his back passage). Nothing.

Analyst. It seemed to be your back passage.

Patient. Moral strictures.

I told him that his sight, the dark glasses, were felt as a conscience that punished him, partly for getting rid of them to avoid pain, partly because he had used them to spy on me, and on his parents. I could not feel I had done justice to the compactness of the association.

It will be observed that I have not been able to offer any suggestion as to what might be stimulating these reactions in the patient. This is not surprising, for I am dealing with a psychotic problem, and since the psychotic problem as opposed to the non-psychotic problem is precisely related to the destruction of all the mental apparatus that brings awareness of stimuli from reality, the nature and even existence of such stimuli would not be discernible. However, the patient's next remark gave it.

Patient. The week-end; don't know if I can last it.

This is an instance of the way in which the patient felt he had repaired his capacity for contact and could therefore tell me what was going on around him. It was a phenomenon by now familiar to him and I didn't interpret it. Instead I said:

Analyst. You feel that you have to be able to get on without me. But to do that you feel you need to be able to see what happens around you, and even to be able to contact me; to be able to contact me at a distance, as you do your mother when you ring her up; so you tried to get your ability to see and talk back again from me.

Patient. Brilliant interpretation. (*With a sudden convulsion*) O God!

Analyst. You feel you can see and understand now, but what you see is so brilliant that it causes intense pain.

Patient (clenching his fists and showing much tension and anxiety). I hate you.

Analyst. When you see, what you see – the week-end break and the things you use darkness to spy on – fills you with hate of me and admiration.

It is my belief that at this point the restoration of the ego meant that the patient was confronted with the non-psychotic problem, the resolution of neurotic conflicts. This was supported by the reactions in the following weeks, when he would display his inability to tolerate the neurotic conflicts stimulated by reality and his attempt to solve that problem by projective identification. This would be followed by attempts to use me as his ego, anxieties about his insanity, further attempts to repair his ego and return to reality and neurosis; and so the cycle would repeat itself.

I have described this portion of a session in detail because it can be used to illustrate a number of points without burdening the reader with a number of different examples of assocation and interpretation. I have regretfully had to exclude some striking and dramatic material, because to include it without including a quite overwhelming mass of description of day-to-day mundane analysis with its load of sheer incomprehensibility, error, and so forth would produce an entirely misleading picture. At the same time I do not wish to leave any doubt that the approach I am describing is one which in my opinion is producing quite striking results. The change that took place in this patient during the weeks when I was able to demonstrate the interplay I have just described, was of a kind that I believe any analyst would accept as worth the name of psychoanalytic improvement. The patient's demeanour softened; his expression became much less tense. At the beginnings and ends of sessions he met my eyes and did not either evade me or, what with him had been a common event, focus beyond me as if I were the surface of a mirror before which he rehearsed some inner drama, a peculiarity that had often helped me to realize that I was not a real person to him. Unfortunately these phenomena are not easy to describe and I cannot dwell on the attempt; for I wish to draw attention to an improvement which I found, and still find with other patients, both surprising and baffling. As it touches the main theme of this paper I can deal with it by returning to the theoretical discussion that I interrupted to introduce my clinical example.

If verbal thought is that which synthesizes and articulates impressions, and is thus essential to awareness of internal and external reality, it is to be expected that it will be subjected, on and off throughout the analysis, to destructive splitting and projective identification. I described the inception of verbal thought as appertaining to the depressive position; but the depression that is proper to this phase is itself something to which the psychotic personality objects and therefore the development of verbal thought comes under attack, its inchoate elements being expelled from the personality by projective identification whenever depression occurs. In her paper to the International Congress of 1955 Segal (1956) described the manner in which the psyche deals with depression; I would refer you to that description as apposite to that part of the depressive position which I here include in the discussion of the development of verbal thought. But I have said that in the even earlier phase, the paranoid-schizoid position, thought processes that should be developing are in fact being destroyed. At this stage there is no question of verbal thought but only of inchoation of primitive thought of a pre-verbal kind. Excessive projective identification at this early stage prevents smooth introjection and assimilation of sense impressions and so denies the personality a firm base on which the inception of pre-verbal thought can proceed. Furthermore, not only is thought attacked, as itself being a link, but the factors which make for coherence in thought itself are similarly attacked so that in the end the elements of thought, the units, as it were, of which thought is made up, cannot be articulated. The growth of verbal thought is therefore compromised both by the continuing attacks I have described as typical of the depressive position, and by the fact of the long history of attacks on thought of any kind that precedes this.

The attempt to think, which is a central part of the total process of repair of the ego, involves the use of primitive pre-verbal modes which have suffered mutilation and projective identification. This means that the expelled particles of ego, and their accretions, have got to be brought back into control and therefore into the personality. Projective identification is therefore reversed and these objects are brought back by the same route as that by which they were expelled. This was expressed by a patient who said he had to use an intestine, not a brain, to think with, and emphasized the accuracy of his description by correcting me when, on a subsequent occasion, I spoke of his having taken in something by swallowing it; the intestine does not swallow he said. In order to bring them back, these objects have to be compressed. Owing to the hostility of the rejected function of articulation, itself now an object, the objects can only be joined inappropriately, or agglomerated. I suggested in my clinical example that the dark glasses were an instance of this kind of agglomeration of bizarre objects which were the product of projective identification of the ego. Furthermore, that owing to the patient's inability to distinguish between such objects and real objects he frequently had to wait for appropriate events to provide him with the ideograph his impulse to communicate required, and that this case was a reciprocal of this, namely an instance of the storing of an event not on account of its neurotic significance but on account of its value as an ideograph. Now this means that this particular use of dark glasses is fairly advanced. For one thing the storage of such an event for use as an ideograph approximates to Freud's description of a search for data, so that they might be already familiar, if an urgent inner need should arise, as a function of attention as one of the aspects of the ego. But it also shows, albeit in this instance in a somewhat rudimentary form, a skilful agglomeration which is successful in conveying meaning. Now the surprising, and even disconcerting, improvement of which I spoke touches this point of skilful agglomeration. For I have found not only that patients resorted more and more to ordinary verbal thought, thus showing an increased capacity for it and increased consideration for the analyst as an ordinary human being, but also that they seemed to become more and more skilful at this type of agglomerated rather than articulated speech. The whole point about civilized speech is that it greatly simplifies the thinker's or speaker's task. With that tool problems can be solved because at least they can be stated, whereas without it certain questions, no matter how important, cannot even be posed.

The extraordinary thing is the *tour de force* by which primitive modes of thought are used by the patient for the statement of themes of great complexity. And I find it significant that his ability to do this improves concurrently with more welcome advances. I say more welcome because I have not yet satisfied myself that it is right to ignore the content of an association because dealing with it would keep the analyst talking at infinitely greater length than the patient. What, for example, is the correct interpretation of the content of moral strictures? And having decided that, what is the correct procedure? For how long is one to continue the elucidation?

The particles which have to be employed share, as we have seen, the qualities of things. The patient seems to feel this as an additional obstacle to their re-entry. As these objects which are felt to have been expelled by projective identification become infinitely worse after expulsion than they were when originally expelled, the patient feels intruded upon, assaulted, and tortured by this re-entry even if willed by himself. This is shown, in the example I gave, by the convulsive movement of the patient and by his striking reaction to the 'brilliant' interpretation. But this last also shows that the senses, as part of the expelled ego, also become painfully compressed on being taken back, and this is often the explanation of the extremely painful tactile, auditory, and visual hallucinations in the grip of which he seems to labour. Depression and anxiety, being subject to the same mechanism, are similarly intensified until the patient is compelled to deal with them by projective identification, as Segal described.

Conclusion

Experience of these theories in practice has convinced me that they have a real value and lead to improvements which even psycho-analysts may feel to deserve stern testing and scrutiny. Conversely, I do not think real progress with psychotic patients is likely to take place until due weight is given to the nature of the divergence between the psychotic and non-psychotic personality, and in particular the role of projective identification in the psychotic part of the personality as a substitute for repression in the neurotic part of the personality. The patient's destructive attacks on his ego and the substitution of projective identification for repression and introjection must be worked through. Further, I consider that this holds true for the severe neurotic, in whom I believe there is a psychotic personality concealed by neurosis as the neurotic personality is screened by psychosis in the psychotic, that has to be laid bare and dealt with.

References

Bion, W. R. (1954) 'Notes on the theory of schizophrenia', *International Journal of Psycho-Analysis*, 35, 113–18.

Freud, S. (1911) 'Formulations regarding the two principles of mental functioning', *SE* 12.

——(1923) *The Ego and the id*, *SE* 19, 1–66.

——(1924) 'Neurosis and psychosis', *SE* 19, 149–53.

Klein, M. (1928) 'Early stages of the Oedipus conflict', *Contributions to Psycho-Analysis*, 1921–45 (and subsequently in *The Writings of Melanie Klein*, vol. 1, London: Hogarth Press (1975), 186–98).

——(1930) 'The importance of symbol formation in the development of the ego' in *The Writings of Melanie Klein*, vol. 1.

——(1946) 'Notes on some schizoid mechanisms' in M. Klein, P. Heimann, S. Isaacs, and J. Riviere *Developments in Psycho-Analysis*, London: Hogarth Press (1952), 292–320 (also in *The Writings of Melanie Klein*, vol. 3, 1–24).

Rosenfeld, H. (1952) 'Transference-phenomena and transference-analysis in an acute catatonic schizophrenic patient', *International Journal of Psycho-Analysis*, 33, 457–64.

Segal, H. (1957) Paper on symbol-formation read to the Medical Section of the British Psychological Society, and subsequently published as 'Notes on symbol formation'. *International Journal of Psycho-Analysis*, 38, 391–7 and reprinted here on pp. 160–76.

——(1956) 'Depression in the schizophrenic', *International Journal of Psycho-Analysis*, 37, 339–43; also in *The Work of Hanna Segal*, New York: Jason Aronson (1981) 121–9 and reprinted here, pp. 52–60.

PART TWO

Projective identification

Introduction

Klein developed the idea of projective identification in 1946 in the course of describing the paranoid-schizoid position in her paper 'Notes on some schizoid mechanisms'. She used the actual term 'projective identification' in passing towards the end of the 1946 paper, although she did not put in the crucial definitory sentence, 'I suggest for these processes the term "projective identification"' until the 1952 version of the paper published in *Developments in Psycho-Analysis* (M. Klein 1952a). Klein had been talking for a long time about the child having phantasies of getting inside the mother's body, but in 'Notes on some schizoid mechanisms' she gave the familiar idea a different emphasis by relating it to projection. She thought of projective identification as a phantasy in which bad parts of the self were split off from the rest of the self and, together with bad excrements, were projected into the mother or her breast to control and take possession of her in such a fashion that she was felt to *become* the bad self. Good parts of the self were projected too, she thought, leading to the enhancement of the ego and of good object relations, providing the process was not carried to excess.

Although Klein defined the term 'projective identification' almost casually and was apparently always somewhat doubtful about its value because of the ease with which it could be misused (Segal 1982), the term has gradually become the most popular of her concepts, the only one that has been widely accepted and discussed by non-Kleinians, especially in the United States, even though it is often discussed in terms that are incompatible with Klein's conception. Considerable controversy has developed over the definition and use of the concept. Whether there is a difference between projection and projective identification is perhaps the most frequently raised

81

question, but others have been important too. Should the term be used to refer only to the patient's unconscious phantasy, regardless of the effect on the recipient, or should it be used only in cases in which the recipient of the projection is emotionally affected by what is being projected into him? Should the term be used only for projection of aspects of the self, or should it also be used for the projection of aspects of internal objects? What about the many possible motives for projective identification; should all be included? Should the term be used only in cases where the patient has lost conscious awareness of the quality and part of the self he has projected, or does it also apply to cases in which such awareness is retained? What about the projection of good qualities and good parts of the self; should the concept be used for these as well, as Klein so clearly thought, or should it be reserved for the projection of bad qualities, which has been the dominant tendency? Is a specific bodily phantasy always involved in the projection, as Klein thought, or is it clarifying enough to speak of the phantasy in mental terms?

Of these many questions, by far the most discussion has been devoted to the question of whether and how projective identification should be distinguished from projection. According to Segal (1967 and personal communication) Klein's own view on projection as distinct from projective identification was clear; she thought of projection as the mental mechanism and projective identification as the particular phantasy expressing it. This usage, however, has not been closely adhered to even by British Kleinian analysts; their usual view, though rarely explicitly stated, is that it is not clinically useful to make a distinction between projection and projective identification. What Klein's concept of projective identification has done has been to add depth and meaningfulness to Freud's concept of projection by emphasizing that one cannot have a phantasy of projecting impulses without projecting part of the self, which involves splitting, and, further, that impulses and parts of the self do not vanish when projected; they are felt to go into an object. Unconsciously, if not consciously, the individual retains some sort of contact with the projected aspects of himself.

Among analysts in the United States there has been a protracted discussion of the difference between projection and projective identification. (See especially Malin and Grotstein 1966, Ornston 1978, Langs 1978, Ogden 1979 and 1982, Meissner 1980, Grotstein 1981). In these discussions the most usual basis for the distinction between projection and projective identification is held to be whether or not the recipient of the projection is or is not affected emotionally by the projector's phantasy. This emphasis derives from the work of

Bion, although Bion, like Klein, thought of projective identification as a phantasy; indeed I think that most analysts, Kleinian and non-Kleinian, agree that patients do not take thoughts and feelings literally out of their own minds and concretely put them into the analyst's mind (cf. Sandler 1987). Bion shows, however, that in many cases the person doing the projecting acts in such a way as to get the analyst (or other recipient of the projection) to have the feelings appropriate to the projector's phantasy, and sometimes the recipient finds himself feeling pressure to act on the feelings (Bion 1959, reprinted here). But to restrict the term projective identification to such instances greatly diminishes the usefulness of the concept and is in any case totally contrary to what Klein herself meant by it. The English view is that the term is best kept as a general concept broad enough to include both cases in which the recipient is emotionally affected and those in which he is not. It might be useful, however, to have distinguishing adjectives to describe various subtypes of projective identification; 'evocatory' might be used to describe the sort where the recipient is put under pressure to have the feelings appropriate to the projector's phantasy.

Most of the other questions that have developed in the use of the concept are best answered in the same way, that is, by using the concept as a general term within which various subtypes can be differentiated. The many motives for projective identification – to control the object, to acquire its attributes, to evacuate a bad quality, to protect a good quality, to avoid separation – all are most usefully kept under the general umbrella.

Ideas about projective identification have developed our understanding, thanks especially to the work of Bion, of the dynamics of transference and countertransference, a matter which is discussed more fully in volume 2 of the present work. Bion's examinations of various aspects of projective identification are described in several papers in the 1950s (1952, 1955, 1957, 1959 reprinted here). In stressing the patient's capacity through projective identification to arouse emotions in the analyst, he stresses the communicative as well as the defensive aspects of projective identification, although, as Joseph points out, it is the analyst's response that can turn or fail to turn the patient's projective identification into communication and understanding (Joseph 1987, reprinted here). Bion's first explicit description of the communicative effect of projection into himself as analyst comes in his discussion of work with groups (1952):

'The experience of counter-transference appears to me to have quite a distinct quality that should enable the analyst to differentiate the occasion when he is the object of a projective identification from the occasion when he is not. The analyst feels he is being manipulated so as to be playing a part, no matter how difficult to recognize, in somebody else's phantasy.'

(Bion 1952)

Soon afterwards he gives a striking clinical illustration in a session with a psychotic patient in which Bion felt a growing fear that the patient would attack him. He interpreted that the patient was pushing into his (Bion's) insides the patient's fear that he would murder Bion: shortly afterwards, when the tension had lessened but the patient was clenching his fists, Bion said that the patient had taken the fear back into himself and was now himself afraid that he would make a murderous attack (Bion 1955).

Such use by the analyst of his emotional responses to his patient's material is of course susceptible to error and misuse. Discussion about this topic is basically concerned with the same issue as the controversy about whether the term counter-transference should be restricted to the psychopathological responses of the analyst to his patient or widened in the fashion suggested by Paula Heimann (1950) to include all emotional responses to the patient. Do we need, for example, a special term such as 'projective counter-identification' suggested by Grinberg for the responses in the analyst specifically evoked by the patient (Grinberg 1962)? How is the analyst to know whether his feelings about his patient are a product of his own psychopathology, of the patient's projection, or a mixture of the two? As Money-Kyrle puts it:

'How exactly a patient does succeed in imposing a phantasy and its corresponding affect upon his analyst in order to deny it in himself is a most interesting problem . . . A peculiarity of communications of this kind is that, at first sight, they do not seem as if they had been made by the patient at all. The analyst experiences the affect as being his own response to something. The effort involved is in differentiating the patient's contribution from his own.'

(Money-Kyrle, 1956)

As Bion and Money-Kyrle both say, this is a difficult technical problem, one that depends on the analyst's total experience and knowledge of both the patient and himself.

In keeping with her views on the physical concreteness of unconscious phantasy, Klein was punctilious about specifying the exact physical means by which a projection was being effected and into which part of the recipient's body. Even the original definition specifies 'together with these harmful excrements, expelled in hatred, split off parts of the ego are also projected onto the mother, or, as I would rather call it, into the mother' (Klein, 1946), thus making it clear that the excretory organs are the executive agents of the projection. Several of the early papers on psychotic patients continued this practice, drawing attention, for example, to the use of the eyes and ears and other receptor organs for purposes of projection. Gradually, however, many analysts have come to speak and think of projection by the mind of the projector into the mind of the recipient without specifying the physical basis of the phantasy, unless it is particularly obtrusive. It is Segal's view that the degree of bodily concreteness of projective identification depends on the degree of disturbance in the patient; the more the patient uses defences characteristic of the paranoid–schizoid position, the more concrete and bodily his projections will be.

The papers reprinted in this section are landmarks in Kleinian ideas about projective identification. In 'Attacks on linking' (1959) Bion develops his model of projective identification as communication to a recipient/container capable of modifying the projection so that the transformed content can be taken in again by the individual in a less distressing form. This is a fundamental aspect of his model of the development of thoughts and the capacity to think as well as of growth in analysis. It is basic to all his later work.

Meltzer's paper, 'The relation of anal masturbation to projective identification' (1966), describes phantasies of projective identification with internal parents expressed in and accompanied by anal masturbation, leading to denigration of parental functions and to denial of dependence on internal parents, and thus to false independence and 'pseudo-maturity' in the individual.

Rosenfeld's 1971 paper, 'Contribution to the psychopathology of psychotic states: the importance of projective identification in the ego structure and object relations of the psychotic patient' (1971a), further develops the idea of the communicative aspect of projective identification propounded by Bion. His paper is distinguished by a detailed discussion of the motives for projective identification, already described by Klein herself (1964a) and briefly by Segal (1964), but here discussed in detail. In his recent posthumously published book *Impasse and Interpretation* (1987), Rosenfeld expands this exposition and gives many clinical examples.

Joseph's recent paper (1987, reprinted here) is noteworthy for a particularly lucid introduction and for a very convincing exemplification of her use of the concept with less psychotic patients than those described by Bion and Rosenfeld. She contrasts the differing usages of projective identification by patients stuck in the paranoid–schizoid position and those in the depressive position.

Preoccupation with the concept of projective identification continues. In current work, much of it not yet published, several analysts are attempting to define different aspects of projective identification, including their relation to splitting, and to discuss the technical problems that each involves.

2

Attacks on linking[1]

W. R. BION

This article was originally a paper read before the British Psycho-Analytical Society on 20 October 1957 and was first published in 1959 in the *International Journal of Psycho-Analysis*, 40: 308–15.

In previous papers (Bion 1957) I have had occasion, in talking of the psychotic part of the personality, to speak of the destructive attacks which the patient makes on anything which is felt to have the function of linking one object with another. It is my intention in this paper to show the significance of this form of destructive attack in the production of some symptoms met with in borderline psychosis.

The prototype for all the links of which I wish to speak is the primitive breast or penis. The paper presupposes familiarity with Melanie Klein's descriptions of the infant's fantasies of sadistic attacks upon the breast (Klein 1934), of the infant's splitting of its objects, of projective identification, which is the name she gives to the mechanism by which parts of the personality are split off and projected into external objects, and finally her views on early stages of Oedipus complex (Klein 1928). I shall discuss phantasied attacks on the breast as the prototype of all attacks on objects that serve as a link and projective identification as the mechanism employed by the psyche to dispose of the ego fragments produced by its destructiveness.

I shall first describe clinical manifestations in an order dictated not by the chronology of their appearance in the consulting room, but by the need for making the exposition of my thesis as clear as I can. I shall follow this by material selected to demonstrate the order which these mechanisms assume when their relationship to each other is determined by the dynamics of the analytic situation. I shall conclude with theoretical observations on the material presented. The examples are drawn from the analysis of two patients and are taken from an advanced stage of their analyses. To preserve anonymity I shall not distinguish between the patients and shall introduce distortions of fact which I hope do not impair the accuracy of the analytic description.

Observation of the patient's disposition to attack the link between two objects is simplified because the analyst has to establish a link with the patient and does this by verbal communication and his equipment of psychoanalytical experience. Upon this the creative relationship depends and therefore we should be able to see attacks being made upon it.

I am not concerned with typical resistance to interpretations, but with expanding references which I made in my paper on 'The differentiation of the psychotic from the non–psychotic personalities' (Bion 1957) to the destructive attacks on verbal thought itself.

Clinical examples

I shall now describe occasions which afforded me an opportunity to give the patient an interpretation, which at that point he could understand, of conduct designed to destroy whatever it was that linked two objects together.

These are the examples:

(i) I had reason to give the patient an interpretation making explicit his feelings of affection and his expression of them to his mother for her ability to cope with a refractory child. The patient attempted to express his agreement with me, but although he needed to say only a few words his expression of them was interrupted by a very pronounced stammer which had the effect of spreading out his remark over a period of as much as a minute and a half. The actual sounds emitted bore resemblance to gasping for breath; gaspings were interspersed with gurgling sounds as if he were immersed in water. I drew his attention to these sounds and he agreed that they were peculiar and himself suggested the descriptions I have just given.

(ii) The patient complained that he could not sleep. Showing signs of fear, he said, 'It can't go on like this'. Disjointed remarks gave the impression that he felt superficially that some catastrophe would occur, perhaps akin to insanity, if he could not get more sleep. Referring to material in the previous session I suggested that he feared he would dream if he were to sleep. He denied this and said he could not think because he was wet. I reminded him of his use of the term 'wet' as an expression of contempt for somebody he regarded as feeble and sentimental. He disagreed and indicated that the state to which he referred was the exact opposite. From what I knew of this patient I felt that his correction at this point was valid and that somehow the wetness referred to an expression of hatred and envy such as he associated with urinary attacks on an object. I therefore said that in addition to the superficial fear which he had expressed he was afraid of sleep because for him it was the same thing as the oozing away of his mind itself. Further associations showed that he felt that good interpretations from me were so consistently and minutely split up by him that they became mental urine which then seeped uncontrollably away. Sleep was therefore inseparable from unconsciousness, which was itself identical with a state of mindlessness which could not be repaired. He said, 'I am dry now'. I replied that he felt he was awake and capable of thought, but that this good state was only precariously maintained.

(iii) In this session the patient had produced material stimulated by the preceding week-end break. His awareness of such external stimuli had become demonstrable at a comparatively recent stage of the analysis. Previously it was a matter for conjecture how much he was capable of appreciating reality. I knew that he had contact with reality because he came for analysis by himself, but that fact could hardly be deduced from his behaviour in the sessions. When I interpreted some associations as evidence that he felt he had been and still was witnessing an intercourse between two people, he reacted as if he had received a violent blow. I was not then able to say just where he had experienced the assault and even in retrospect I have no clear impression. It would seem logical to suppose that the shock had been administered by my interpretation and that therefore the blow came from without, but my impression is that he felt it as delivered from within; the patient often experienced what he described as a stabbing attack from inside. He sat up and stared intently into space. I said that he seemed to be seeing something. He replied that he could not see what he saw. I was able from previous experience to interpret that he felt he was 'seeing' an invisible object and subsequent experience convinced me that in the two patients on whose analysis I am depending for material for this paper, events occurred in which the patient experienced invisible–visible hallucinations. I shall give my reasons later for supposing that in this and the previous example similar mechanisms were at work.

89

(iv) In the first twenty minutes of the session the patient made three isolated remarks which had no significance for me. He then said that it seemed that a girl he had met was understanding. This was followed at once by a violent, convulsive movement which he affected to ignore. It appeared to be identical with the kind of stabbing attack I mentioned in the last example. I tried to draw his attention to the movement, but he ignored my intervention as he ignored the attack. He then said that the room was filled with a blue haze. A little later he remarked that the haze had gone, but said he was depressed. I interpreted that he felt understood by me. This was an agreeable experience, but the pleasant feeling of being understood had been instantly destroyed and ejected. I reminded him that we had recently witnessed his use of the word 'blue' as a compact description of vituperative sexual conversation. If my interpretation was correct, and subsequent events suggested that it was, it meant that the experience of being understood had been split up, converted into particles of sexual abuse and ejected. Up to this point I felt that the interpretation approximated closely to his experience. Later interpretations, that the disappearance of the haze was due to reintrojection and conversion into depression, seemed to have less reality for the patient, although later events were compatible with its being correct.

(v) The session, like the one in my last example, began with three or four statements of fact such as that it was hot, that his train was crowded, and that it was Wednesday; this occupied thirty minutes. An impression that he was trying to retain contact with reality was confirmed when he followed up by saying that he feared a breakdown. A little later he said I would not understand him. I interpreted that he felt I was bad and would not take in what he wanted to put into me. I interpreted in these terms deliberately because he had shown in the previous session that he felt that my interpretations were an attempt to eject feelings that he wished to deposit in me. His response to my interpretation was to say that he felt there were two probability clouds in the room. I interpreted that he was trying to get rid of the feeling that my badness was a fact. I said it meant that he needed to know whether I was really bad or whether I was some bad thing which had come from inside him. Although the point was not at the moment of central significance I thought the patient was attempting to decide whether he was hallucinated or not. This recurrent anxiety in his analysis was associated with his fear that envy and hatred of a capacity for understanding was leading him to take in a good, understanding object to destroy and eject it – a procedure which had often led to persecution by the destroyed and ejected object. Whether my refusal to understand was a reality or hallucination was important only because it determined what painful experiences were to be expected next.

(vi) Half the session passed in silence; the patient then announced that a piece of iron had fallen on the floor. Thereafter he made a series of convulsive movements in silence as if he felt he was being physically assaulted from within. I said he could not establish contact with me because of his fear of what was going on inside him. He confirmed this by saying that he felt he was being murdered. He did not know what he would do without the analysis as it made him better. I said that he felt so envious of himself and of me for being able to work together to make him feel better that he took the pair of us into him as a dead piece of iron and a dead floor that came together not to give him life but to murder him. He became very anxious and said he could not go on. I said that he felt he could not go on because he was either dead, or alive and so envious that he had to stop good analysis. There was a marked decrease of anxiety, but the remainder of the session was taken up by isolated statements of fact which again seemed to be an attempt to preserve contact with external reality as a method of denial of his phantasies.

Features common to the above illustrations

These episodes have been chosen by me because the dominant theme in each was the destructive attack on a link. In the first the attack was expressed in a stammer which was designed to prevent the patient from using language as a bond between him and me. In the second sleep was felt by him to be identical with projective identification that proceeded unaffected by any possible attempt at control by him. Sleep for him meant that his mind, minutely fragmented, flowed out in an attacking stream of particles.

The examples I give here throw light on schizophrenic dreaming. The psychotic patient appears to have no dreams, or at least not to report any, until comparatively late in the analysis. My impression now is that this apparently dreamless period is a phenomenon analogous to the invisible–visual hallucination. That is to say, that the dreams consist of material so minutely fragmented that they are devoid of any visual component. When dreams are experienced which the patient can report because visual objects have been experienced by him in the course of the dream, he seems to regard these objects as bearing much the same relationship to the invisible objects of the previous phase as faeces seem to him to bear to urine. The objects appearing in experiences which we call dreams are regarded by the patient as solid and are, as such, contrasted with the contents of the dreams which were a continuum of minute, invisible fragments.

At the time of the session the main theme was not an attack on the link but the consequences of such an attack, previously made, in leaving him bereft of a state of mind necessary for the establishment of a satisfying relationship between him and his bed. Though it did not appear in the session I report, uncontrollable projective identification, which was what sleep meant to him, was thought to be a destructive attack on the state of mind of the coupling parents. There was therefore a double anxiety; one arising from his fear that he was being rendered mindless, the other from his fear that he was unable to control his hostile attacks, his mind providing the ammunition, on the state of mind that was the link between the parental pair. Sleep and sleeplessness were alike inacceptable.

In the third example in which I described visual hallucinations of invisible objects, we witness one form in which the actual attack on the sexual pair is delivered. My interpretation, as far as I could judge, was felt by him as if it were his own visual sense of a parental intercourse; this visual impression is minutely fragmented and ejected at once in particles so minute that they are the invisible components of a continuum. The total procedure has served the purpose of forestalling an experience of feelings of envy for the parental state of mind by the instantaneous expression of envy in a destructive act. I shall have more to say of this implicit hatred of emotion and the need to avoid awareness of it.

In my fourth example, the report of the understanding girl and the haze, my understanding and his agreeable state of mind have been felt as a link between us which could give rise to a creative act. The link had been regarded with hate and transformed into a hostile and destructive sexuality rendering the patient–analyst couple sterile.

In my fifth example, of the two probability clouds, a capacity for understanding is the link which is being attacked, but the interest lies in the fact that the object making the destructive attacks is alien to the patient. Furthermore, the destroyer is making an attack on projective identification which is felt by the patient to be a method of communication. In so far as my supposed attack on his methods of communication is felt as possibly secondary to his envious attacks on me, he does not dissociate himself from feelings of guilt and responsibility. A further point is the appearance of judgement, which

Freud regards as an essential feature of the dominance of the reality principle, among the ejected parts of the patient's personality. The fact that there were two probability clouds remained unexplained at the time, but in subsequent sessions I had material which led me to suppose that what had originally been an attempt to separate good from bad survived in the existence of two objects, but they were now similar in that each was a mixture of good and bad. Taking into consideration material from later sessions, I can draw conclusions which were not possible at the time; his capacity for judgement, which had been split up and destroyed with the rest of his ego and then ejected, was felt by him to be similar to other bizarre objects of the kind which I have described in my paper on 'The differentiation of the psychotic from the non-psychotic parts of the personality'. These ejected particles were feared because of the treatment he had accorded them. He felt that the alienated judgement – the probability clouds – indicated that I was probably bad. His suspicion that the probability clouds were persecutory and hostile led him to doubt the value of the guidance they afforded him. They might supply him with a correct assessment or a deliberately false one, such as that a fact was an hallucination or vice versa; or would give rise to what, from a psychiatric point of view, we would call delusions. The probability clouds themselves had some qualities of a primitive breast and were felt to be enigmatic and intimidating.

In my sixth illustration, the report that a piece of iron had fallen on the floor, I had no occasion for interpreting an aspect of the material with which the patient had by this time become familiar. (I should perhaps say that experience had taught me that there were times when I assumed the patient's familiarity with some aspect of a situation with which we were dealing, only to discover that, in spite of the work that had been done upon it, he had forgotten it.) The familiar point that I did not interpret, but which is significant for the understanding of this episode, is that the patient's envy of the parental couple had been evaded by his substitution of himself and myself for the parents. The evasion failed, for the envy and hatred were now directed against him and me. The couple engaged in a creative act are felt to be sharing an enviable, emotional experience; he, being identified also with the excluded party, has a painful, emotional experience as well. On many occasions the patient, partly through experiences of the kind which I describe in this episode, and partly for reasons on which I shall enlarge later, had a hatred of emotion, and therefore, by a short extension, of life itself. This hatred contributes to the murderous attack on that which links the pair, on the pair itself and on the object generated by the pair. In the episode I am describing, the patient is suffering the consequences of his early attacks on the state of mind that forms the link between the creative pair and his identification with both the hateful and creative states of mind.

In this and the preceding illustration there are elements that suggest the formation of a hostile persecutory object, or agglomeration of objects, which expresses its hostility in a manner which is of great importance in producing the predominance of psychotic mechanisms in a patient; the characteristics with which I have already invested the agglomeration of persecutory objects have the quality of a primitive, and even murderous, superego.

Curiosity, arrogance, and stupidity

In the paper I presented at the International Congress of 1957 (Bion 1957) I suggested that Freud's analogy of an archaeological investigation with a psychoanalysis was helpful if it were considered that we were exposing evidence not so much of a primitive civilization as of a primitive disaster. The value of the analogy is lessened because in the analysis we are confronted not so much with a static situation that permits leisurely study, but with a catastrophe that remains at one and the same moment actively vital and yet incapable of resolution into quiescence. This lack of progress in any direction must be attributed in part to the destruction of a capacity for curiosity and the consequent inability to learn, but before I go into this I must say something about a matter that plays hardly any part in the illustrations I have given.

Attacks on the link originate in what Melanie Klein calls the paranoid-schizoid phase. This period is dominated by part-object relationships (Klein 1948). If it is borne in mind that the patient has a part-object relationship with himself as well as with objects not himself, it contributes to the understanding of phrases such as 'it seems' which are commonly employed by the deeply disturbed patient on occasions when a less disturbed patient might say 'I think' or 'I believe'. When he says 'it seems' he is often referring to a feeling – an 'it seems' feeling – which is a part of his psyche and yet is not observed as part of a whole object. The conception of the part-object as analogous to an anatomical structure, encouraged by the patient's employment of concrete images as units of thought, is misleading because the part-object relationship is not with the anatomical structures only but with function, not with anatomy but with physiology, not with the breast but with feeding, poisoning, loving, hating. This contributes to the impression of a disaster that is dynamic and not static. The problem that has to be solved on this early, yet superficial, level must be stated in adult terms by the question, 'What is something?' and not the question 'Why is something?' because 'why' has, through guilt, been split off. Problems, the solution of which depends upon an awareness of causation, cannot therefore be stated, let alone solved. This produces a situation in which the patient appears to have no problems except those posed by the existence of analyst and patient. His preoccupation is with what is this or that function, of which he is aware though unable to grasp the totality of which the function is a part. It follows that there is never any question why the patient or the analyst is there, or why something is said or done or felt, nor can there be any question of attempting to alter the causes of some state of mind. . . . Since 'what?' can never be answered without 'how?' or 'why?' further difficulties arise. I shall leave this on one side to consider the mechanisms employed by the infant to solve the problem 'what?' when it is felt in relation to a part–object relationship with a function.

Denial of normal degrees of projective identification

I employ the term 'link' because I wish to discuss the patient's relationship with a function rather than with the object that subserves a function; my concern is not only with the breast, or penis, or verbal thought, but with their function of providing the link between two objects.

In her 'Notes on Some Schizoid Mechanisms' (1946) Melanie Klein speaks of the importance of an excessive employment of splitting and projective identification in the production of a very disturbed personality. She also speaks of 'the introjection of the good object, first of all the mother's breast' as a 'precondition for normal development'. I shall suppose that there is a normal degree of projective identification, without defining the limits within which normality lies, and that associated with introjective identification this is the foundation on which normal developments rests.

This impression derives partly from a feature in a patient's analysis which was difficult to interpret because it did not appear to be sufficiently obtrusive at any moment for an interpretation to be supported by convincing evidence. Throughout the analysis the patient resorted to projective identification with a persistence suggesting it was a mechanism of which he had never been able sufficiently to avail himself; the analysis afforded him an opportunity for the exercise of a mechanism of which he had been cheated. I did not have to rely on this impression alone. There were sessions which led me to suppose that the patient felt there was some object that denied him the use of projective identification. In the illustrations I have given, particularly in the first, the stammer, and the fourth, the understanding girl and the blue haze, there are elements which indicate that the patient felt that parts of his personality that he wished to repose in me were refused entry by me, but there had been associations prior to this which led me to this view.

When the patient strove to rid himself of fears of death which were felt to be too powerful for his personality to contain he split off his fears and put them into me, the idea apparently being that if they were allowed to repose there long enough they would undergo modification by my psyche and could then be safely reintrojected. On the occasion I have in mind the patient had felt, probably for reasons similar to those I give in my fifth illustration, the probability clouds, that I evacuated them so quickly that the feelings were not modified, but had become more painful.

Associations from a period in the analysis earlier than that from which these illustrations have been drawn showed an increasing intensity of emotions in the patient. This originated in what he felt was my refusal to accept parts of his personality. Consequently he strove to force them into me with increased desperation and violence. His behaviour, isolated from the context of the analysis, might have appeared to be an expression of primary aggression. The more violent his phantasies of projective identification, the more frightened he became of me. There were sessions in which such behaviour expressed unprovoked aggression, but I quote this series because it shows the patient in a different light, his violence a reaction to what he felt was my hostile defensiveness. The analytic situation built up in my mind a sense of witnessing an extremely early scene. I felt that the patient had experienced in infancy a mother who dutifully responded to the infant's emotional displays. The dutiful response had in it an element of impatient 'I don't know what's the matter with the child.' My deduction was that in order to understand what the child wanted the mother should have treated the infant's cry as more than a demand for her presence. From the infant's point of view she should have taken into her, and thus experienced, the fear that the child was dying. It was this fear that the child could not contain. He strove to split it off together with the part of the personality in which it lay and project it into the mother. An understanding mother is able to experience the feeling of dread, that this baby was striving to deal with by projective identification, and yet retain a balanced outlook. This patient had had to deal with a mother who could not tolerate experiencing such feelings and reacted either by denying the ingress, or alternatively by becoming a prey to the anxiety which resulted from the introjection of the infant's feelings. The latter reaction must, I think, have been rare: denial was dominant.

To some this reconstruction will appear to be unduly fanciful; to me it does not seem forced and is the reply to any who may object that too much stress is placed on the transference to the exclusion of a proper elucidation of early memories.

In the analysis a complex situation may be observed. The patient feels he is being allowed an opportunity of which he had hitherto been cheated; the poignancy of his deprivation is thereby rendered the more acute and so are the feelings of resentment at the deprivation. Gratitude for the opportunity coexists with hostility to the analyst as the person who will not understand and refuses the patient the use of the only method of communication by which he feels he can make himself understood. Thus the link between patient and analyst, or infant and breast, is the mechanism of projective identification. The destructive attacks upon this link originate in a source external to the patient or infant, namely the analyst or breast. The result is excessive projective identification by the patient and a deterioration of his developmental processes.

I do not put forward this experience as the cause of the patient's disturbance; that finds its main source in the inborn disposition of the infant as a I described it in my paper on 'The differentiation of the psychotic from the non-psychotic personalities' (Bion 1957). I regard it as a central feature of the environmental factor in the production of the psychotic personality.

Before I discuss this consequence for the patient's development, I must refer to the inborn characteristics and the part that they play in producing attacks by the infant on all that links him to the breast, namely, primary aggression and envy. The seriousness of these attacks is enhanced if the mother displays the kind of unreceptiveness which I have described, and is diminished, but not abolished, if the mother can introject the infant's feelings and remain balanced (Klein 1957); the seriousness remains because the psychotic infant is overwhelmed with hatred and envy of the mother's ability to retain a comfortable state of mind although experiencing the infant's feelings. This was clearly brought out by a patient who insisted that I must go through it with him, but was filled with hate when he felt I was able to do so without a breakdown. Here we have another aspect of destructive attacks upon the link, the link being the capacity of the analyst to introject the patient's projective identifications. Attacks on the link, therefore, are synonymous with attacks on the analyst's, and originally the mother's, peace of mind. The capacity to introject is transformed by the patient's envy and hate into greed devouring the patient's psyche; similarly, peace of mind becomes hostile indifference. At this point analytic problems arise through the patient's employment (to destroy the peace of mind that is so much envied) of acting out, delinquent acts and threats of suicide.

Consequences

To review the main features so far: the origin of the disturbance is twofold. On the one hand there is the patient's inborn disposition to excessive destructiveness, hatred, and envy: on the other the environment which, at its worst, denies to the patient the use of the mechanisms of splitting and projective identification. On some occasions the destructive attacks on the link between patient and environment, or between different aspects of the patient's personality, have their origin in the patient; on others, in the mother, although in the latter instance and in psychotic patients, it can never be in the mother alone. The disturbances commence with life itself. The problem that confronts the patient is: What are the objects of which he is aware? These objects, whether internal or external, are in fact part-objects and predominantly, though not exclusively, what we should call functions and not morphological structures. This is obscured because the patient's thinking is conducted by means of concrete objects and therefore tends to produce, in the sophisticated mind of the analyst, an impression that the patient's concern is with the nature of the concrete object. The nature of the functions which excite the patient's curiosity he explores by projective identification. His own feelings, too powerful to be contained within his personality are amongst these functions. Projective identification makes it possible for him to investigate his own feelings in a personality powerful enough to contain them. Denial of the use of this mechanism, either by the refusal of the mother to serve as a repository for the infant's feelings, or by the hatred and envy of the patient who cannot allow the mother to exercise this function, leads to a destruction of the link between infant and breast and consequently to a severe disorder of the impulse to be curious on which all learning depends. The way is therefore prepared for a severe arrest of development. Furthermore, thanks to a denial of the main method open to the infant for dealing with his too powerful emotions, the conduct of emotional life, in any case a severe problem, becomes intolerable. Feelings of hatred are thereupon directed against all emotions, including hate itself, and against external reality which stimulates them. It is a short step from hatred of the emotions to hatred of life itself. As I said in my paper on the 'The differentiation of the psychotic from the non-psychotic personalities' (Bion 1957), this hatred results in a resort to projective identification of all the perceptual apparatus including the embryonic thought which forms a link between sense impressions and consciousness. The tendency to excessive projective identification when death instincts predominate is thus reinforced.

Superego

The early development of the superego is effected by this kind of mental functioning in a way I must now describe. As I have said, the link between infant and breast depends upon projective identification and a capacity to introject projective identification. Failure to introject makes the external object appear intrinsically hostile to curiosity and to the method, namely projective identification, by which the infant seeks to satisfy it. Should the breast be felt as fundamentally understanding, it has been transformed by the infant's envy and hate into any object whose devouring greed has as its aim the introjection of the infant's projective identifications in order to destroy them. This can show in the patient's belief that the analyst strives, by understanding the patient, to drive him insane. The result is an object which, when installed in the patient, exercises the function of a severe and ego-destructive superego. This description is not accurate applied to any object in the paranoid-schizoid position because it supposes a whole-object. The threat that such a whole-object impends contributes to the inability, described by Melanie Klein and others (Segal 1950), of the psychotic patient to face the depressive position and the developments attendant on it. In the paranoid-schizoid phase the bizarre objects composed partially of elements of a persecutory supergo which I described in my paper on 'The differentiation of the psychotic from the non-psychotic personalities' are predominant.

Arrested development

The disturbance of the impulse of curiosity on which all learning depends, and the denial of the mechanism by which it seeks expression, makes normal development impossible. Another feature obtrudes if the course of the analysis is favourable; problems which in sophisticated language are posed by the question 'Why?' cannot be formulated. The patient appears to have no appreciation of causation and will complain of painful states of mind while persisting in courses of action calculated to produce them. Therefore when the appropriate material presents itself the patient must be shown that he has no interest in why he feels as he does. Elucidation of the limited scope of his curiosity issues in the development of a wider range and an incipient preoccupation with causes. This leads to some modification of conduct which otherwise prolongs his distress.

Conclusions

The main conclusions of this paper relate to that state of mind in which the patient's psyche contains an internal object which is opposed to, and destructive of, all links whatsoever from the most primitive (which I have suggested is a normal degree of projective identification) to the most sophisticated forms of verbal communication and the arts.

In this state of mind emotion is hated; it is felt to be too powerful to be contained by the immature psyche, it is felt to link objects and it gives reality to objects which are not self and therefore inimical to primary narcissism.

The internal object which in its origin was an external breast that refused to introject, harbour, and so modify the baneful force of emotion, is felt, paradoxically, to intensify, relative to the strength of the ego, the emotions against which it initiates the attacks. These attacks on the linking function of emotion lead to an overprominence in the psychotic part of the personality of links which appear to be logical, almost mathematical, but never emotionally reasonable. Consequently the links surviving are perverse, cruel, and sterile.

The external object which is internalized, its nature, and the effect when so established on the methods of communication within the psyche and with the environment, are left for further elaboration later.

References

Bion, W. R. (1954) 'Notes on the theory of schizophrenia', *International Journal of Psycho-Analysis*, 35, 113–18; also in *Second Thoughts*, London:

Heinemann (1967); paperback Maresfield Reprints, London: H. Karnac Books (1984).

——(1956) 'Development of schizophrenic thought', *International Journal of Psycho-Analysis*, 37, 344–6; also in *Second Thoughts*.

——(1957) 'The differentiation of the psychotic from the non-psychotic personalities', *International Journal of Psycho-Analysis*, 266–75; also in *Second Thoughts* and reprinted here on pp. 61–78.

——(1957) 'On arrogance', *International Journal of Psycho-Analysis*, 39: 144–6; also in *Second Thoughts*.

Klein, M. (1928) 'Early stages of the Oedipus conflict' in *The Writings of Melanie Klein*, vol. 1, London, Hogarth Press (1975).

——(1934) 'A contribution to the psycho-genesis of manic-depressive states', 13th International Psycho-Analytical Congress, 1934.

——(1946) 'Notes on some schizoid mechanisms' in M. Klein, P. Heimann, S. Isaacs, and J. Riviere *Developments in Psycho-Analysis*, London, Hogarth Press (1952) 292–320 (also in *The Writings of Melanie Klein*, 1–24).

——(1948) 'A contribution to the theory of anxiety and guilt', *International Journal of Psycho-Analysis*, 29, 114.

——(1957) *Envy and gratitude*, chap. II, in *The Writings of Melanie Klein*, vol. 3, London, Hogarth Press (1975), 176–235.

Rosenfeld, H. (1952) 'Notes on the psychoanalysis of the superego conflict of an acute schizophrenic patient', *International Journal of Psycho-Analysis*, 33, 111–31 and reprinted here on pp. 14–49.

Segal, H. (1950) 'Some aspects of the analysis of a schizophrenic', *International Journal of Psycho-Analysis*, 31, 269–78; also in *The Work of Hanna Segal*, New York: Jason Aronson (1981) and the paperback London: Free Association Books (1986).

——(1956) 'Depression in the schizophrenic', *International Journal of Psycho-Analysis*', 37: 339–43; also in *The Work of Hanna Segal* and reprinted here on pp. 52–60.

—— (1957) 'Notes on symbol formation', *International Journal of Psycho-Analysis*, 38: 391–7; also in *The Work of Hanna Segal* and reprinted here on pp. 160–77.

The relation of anal masturbation
to projective identification

DONALD MELTZER

This article was originally a paper read at the 24th International Psycho-Analytical Congress, Amsterdam, July 1965 and was first published in 1966 in the *International Journal of Psycho-Analysis*, 47, 335–42.

Introduction

When attempting to relate some character traits of the 'Wolf Man' to his intestinal symptoms, Freud (1918) was forced to the conclusion that an anal theory of femininity and an 'identification' with his mother's menorrhagia had antedated the patient's castration theory of femininity. Until Melanie Klein's establishment of the concept of 'projective identification' it was assumed that such a process would have been due solely to introjection. In her original description (1946, p. 300) of projective identification, Klein linked it very closely to anal processes but nowhere else in her written work has this connexion been made more explicit.

Furthermore, the contribution made by anality to character formation, as studied by Freud (1908, 1917), Abraham (1921), Jones (1913, 1918), Heimann (1962), and others, has always been stated in terms of the outcome in character structure of the so-called 'sublimation' of anal fantasies, in which the emphasis has rested on the narcissistic over-evaluation of the faeces on the one hand and the object-relationship consequences of the toilet-training struggle on the other. The present paper intends to demonstrate the contribution to character formation made by the combination of all three factors working in complex relation to one another, namely narcissistic evaluation of the faeces, the confusions surrounding the anal zone (especially anus–vagina and penis–faeces confusions) and the identification aspect of anal habits and fantasies based on projective identification. In studying this problem in the analytic process, in close collaboration with several colleagues, I have been forced also to the recognition that masturbation of the anus is a far more widespread habit than the analytic literature to date would imply. Freud (1905, 187; 1917, 131) recognized its existence in children who employ both fingers and the faecal mass as the masturbatory object. However, Spitz's (1949) study of faecal play and his conclusions, based on observational and not analytic data, have promulgated an implication of severe pathology not substantiated by our own work.

For the sake of presentation, and partly to accord with the Congress theme of the Obsessional States, this paper is also focused on the character constellation of 'pseudo-maturity' which we find to be intimately related to anal erotism, a finding by no means at variance with the descriptions by Winnicott (1965) and by Deutsch (1942) of what they have called the 'false self' and the 'as if' personality type respectively. The relation of 'pseudo-maturity' to obsessional states will be demonstrated and shown to assume an oscillatory system at a certain stage of the analytic process, throwing some light on the background of obsessional character in a manner similar to the description of the cyclothymic background of obsessional neurosis given in my earlier (1963) paper. Clinical material and theoretical discussion will bind together the three concepts: anal masturbation, projective identification, pseudo-maturity.

The characterology

Inadequate splitting-and-idealization (Klein 1957), operative particularly after weaning, in relation to demands for cleanliness and aggravated by the expectation or arrival of younger siblings, contributes to a strong trend to idealize the rectum and its faecal contents. But this idealization is largely based on a confusion of identity due to the operation of projective identification, whereby the baby's bottom and that of the mother are confused one with the other, and both are equated with the mother's breasts.

As we reconstruct the scene from the analytic situation a typical sequence would appear as follows: after a feed, when placed in the cot, as mother walks away, the baby, hostilely equating mother's breasts with her buttocks, begins to explore its own bottom, idealizing its roundness and smoothness and eventually penetrating the anus to reach the retained, withheld faeces. In this process of penetration, a fantasy of secret intrusion into mother's anus (Abraham 1921, 389) to rob her takes shape, whereby the baby's rectal contents become confused with mother's idealized faeces, felt to be withheld by her to feed daddy and the inside-babies.

The consequence of this is twofold, namely an idealization of the rectum as a source of food and the projective (delusional) identification with the internal mother which erases the differentiation between child and adult as regards capacities and prerogatives. The urine and flatus may also come in for their share of idealization.

In the excited and confused state which results from the anal masturbation, a bimanual masturbation of genital (phallus or clitoris) and anus (confused with vagina) tends to ensue, producing a sado-masochistic perverse coital fantasy in which the internal parental couple do great harm to one another. The projective identification with both internal figures which accompanies this bimanual masturbation harms the internal objects both by the violence of intrusion into them and by the sadistic nature of the intercourse it produces between them. Hypochondria as well as claustrophobic anxieties are thus an invariable consequence to some degree.

In childhood this situation encourages a pre-oedipal (ages 2–3) crystallization of character manifest by docility, helpfulness, preference for adult companionship, aloofness or bossiness with other children, intolerance of criticism, and high verbal capacity. When this characterological crust is broken momentarily by frustration or anxiety, outcrops of hair-raising virulence are laid bare – tantrums, faecal smearing, suicidal attempts, vicious assaults on other children, lying to strangers about parental maltreatment, cruelty to animals, etc.

This structure bypasses the Oedipus complex and seems to equip a child reasonably well superficially for academic and social life and may carry through into adulthood relatively unruffled even by the adolescent upheaval. But the 'pseudo' nature of the adjustment is apparent in adult life even where the perverse tendencies have not led to obviously aberrant sexual activities. The feeling of fraudulence as an adult person, the sexual impotence or pseudo-potency (excited by secret perverse fantasies), the inner loneliness and the basic confusion between good and bad, all create a life of tension and lack of satisfaction, bolstered, or rather compensated, only by the smugness and snobbery which are an inevitable accompaniment of the massive projective identification.

Where this organization is less dominant and pervasive, or during analysis when it begins to give way to the therapeutic process, it stands in an oscillatory relation to an obsessional organization. There the internal objects are not penetrated, but are rather omnipotently controlled and separated on a less part-object level of relationship, as the focal difficulties have moved from separation anxieties toward the previously bypassed oedipal conflicts.

The delusional identification with the mother due to projective identification and the confusion between anus and vagina together produce frigidity and a sense of fraudulent femininity in women. In men these dynamics produce either homosexual activities or more frequently an intense dread of becoming homosexual (since the heightened femininity is not distinguished from passive anal homosexuality). Or conversely the secondary projective identification with the father's penis (in the ensuing bimanual masturbation) may produce a leading phallic quality in either male or female patients especially where omnipotent (manic) reparativeness has been mobilized as a defence against the severe underlying depression present in all such cases.

The nature of the transference

When this configuration of massive projective identification with the internal objects, usually on a part-object level as breast or penis, is active the co-operation of an adult sort in the analytic process is replaced by a pseudo-co-operation or 'helpfulness' to the analyst. This acting out shows itself in a somewhat slavish demeanour, a desire to convince, to demonstrate, to assist, or to relieve the analyst of his burdens. Material is therefore often of a predigested variety, sometimes given in 'headline' fashion or a superficial interpretations of mental states. All sense of the patient's wishing to elicit interpretation is absent, replaced by an evident desire for praise, approval, admiration, or even gratitude from the analyst. When these are not forthcoming, the analyst's activities are often felt to evince lack of understanding, envious attacks on the patient's capacities, mere surliness, or frank sadism. This latter reception of interpretation can quickly lead to erotization and cause the interpretation to be experienced as a sexual assault.

Whether the patient is producing dreams, associations, or a factual account of his daily activities, the acting out aspect is so dominant that the interpretation of content is relatively useless unless coupled with a clear demonstration of the nature and the basis of the behaviour. This of course results in sullenness of the nothing-I-ever-do-pleases-you variety. But by the painstaking demonstration of the acting out, by consistent elucidation of the cryptic masturbation, and finally through dream analysis, progress can usually be made.

Acting out of the infantile projective identification with internal figures is such a prominent part of the character that its continual demonstration as a contaminant in the patient's adult life must be undertaken. Even in the face of intense opposition this scrutiny must also include areas of the greatest pride, success, and apparent satisfaction such as work, 'creative' activities, relations to children, siblings, or continued solicitous helpfulness to aging parents. The significance of clothing for the women, cars for the men, and money-in-the-bank for all must be investigated, for they are sure to be found loaded with irrational significance. So skilled is the counterfeiting of maturity in thought, attitude, communication, and action that only the dreams make possible this teasing apart of infantile 'pseudo-mature' items from the adult pattern of life.

The dreams

It is worth mentioning here that sensitivity to the anal masturbatory aspects of the adult patient's dreams is immeasurably increased by experience with child patients and psychotics. Much of what appears below derives its conviction from such sources:

(a) Idealization of the faeces as food – dreams of scavenging and finding are in this category: finding apples among the autumn leaves, food in the empty larder, reaching into places the inside of which cannot be visualized, or underneath structures. Fishing and hunting may also come into this category, though not generally; but gardening, shopping, and stealing of food do, especially if the place is represented as dark, dirty, cheap or foreign.

(b) Idealization of the rectum – dreams in which the rectum is represented as a retreat or refuge generally show it as an eating place (restaurant or café, kitchen or dining room) but with qualities which announce its significance. It may be dirty, dark, smelly, cheap, crowded, smoky, below ground level, noisy, run by foreigners, in a foreign city. The food may be unappetizing, unhygienic, unhealthy, fattening, overcooked, homogeneous (custards, puddings, etc), or catering to infantile greed in quantity or sweetness. Where rectum and breast are confused such configuration as outdoor cafés or market places with the above characteristics may appear.

(c) Idealization of the toilet situation (Abraham 1920, 318) – this often appears in dreams as sitting in lofty or exciting places, often looking down at water (lakes, canyons, streams) or sitting in places where food is being prepared, or in a position of importance ('Last Supper' dreams) or where people behind the dreamer are waiting for food, payment, services, or information (conducting an orchestra, serving at an altar).

(d) Representation of the anally masturbating fingers – these appear in dreams represented as parts of the body, people, animals, tools or machines, either singly or in groups of four or five, with qualities of faecal contamination variously represented or denied, such as negroes, men in brown helmets, soiled or shiny garden tools, white gloves, people dressed in black, earth-moving tractors, dirty children, worms, rusty nails, etc.

(e) Dreams showing the process of intrusion into the anus of the object (Abraham 1921, 389) – most frequently seen as entering a building or a vehicle, either furtively, by a back entrance, the door has wet paint, the entrance is very narrow, protective clothing must be worn, it is underground, under water, in a foreign country or closed to the public, etc.

(f) Idealization of the rectum as a source of pseudo-analysis – this is frequent and may appear as secondhand bookshops, piles of old newspapers, filing cabinets, public libraries – one patient before an examination dreamed that he fished in the Fleet Street sewer and caught an encyclopaedia.

Clinical material

I have chosen the following material to show the complexity of the connexions to orality and genitality which infuse the anal masturbatory situation and its attendant projective identification with such defensive power.

Three years of analytic work with a late adolescent young man had begun to press toward the dependent relationship to the breast which his history suggested would be extremely disturbed, for he had been a poor feeder, a complaining baby, and a tyrannical child in his dependence on his mother. We knew something of his capacity for scathing mockery and of a terrible way of laughing contemptuously, but this had seldom been unleashed in the consulting room, where his behaviour tended to be superficially co-operative, 'churning out fantasies', as he called it, all with an air of insincerity which made

107

even the simplest account of a daily happening sound like confabulation. This we had already understood as 'pretending to be insincere' but indistinguishable to himself from 'pretending to pretend to be insincere', all of which related to a deeply fixed paranoid feeling of being overheard by a hidden persecutor.

He dreamed that he was among friends and seemed once again, as in school days, to be the head boy. As they came over the *brow* of a hill, he saw a man, whom he knew to be a murderer, among some gravestones, just wandering about. Reassuring his friends that he knew how to handle the man, he approached him with an aide and, pretending to be friendly, led him down to the *bottom*, hoping to extract a confession.

ASSOCIATIONS – his tongue seems to be exploring the back of his teeth which feel old and cracked. That makes him think of putting on some slippers like the ones his father used to have. INTERPRETATION – that his teeth are represented by the gravestones and his tongue as the murderer among his victims. His device in the dream is to rid his mouth of these dangerous qualities and transform them into slippery fingers which can be led down to his bottom, where the victims can be identified in his faeces. But by this device his finger-in-his-bottom becomes confused with father's penis-in-mother's-vagina, an important source of the Nazi-daddy-who-kills-mummy's-Jewish-babies whom we know so well from earlier work. ASSOCIATIONS – he feels as if a circular saw were cutting his thigh (reference to surgery for hernia in puberty). He imagines himself with his back to double doors and the analyst outside trying to pull them open (projection of the buttock-spreading on to the analyst-surgeon-daddy). ASSOCIATION – an ornately carved gilt picture frame (the analyst's interpretation is an ornate picture intended to frame him by revealing his guilt), the Mafia – the black hand. A boat going through a canal which is shaped to fit its keelless hull (the Mafia-fascist daddy getting the big black penis-finger into his anal canal, reassuring him in an Italian accent: 'No keel!')

These associations are typical of the punning which characterizes the compulsive anal masturbatory fantasies.

Four weeks later, approaching the Christmas holiday, in a state of mounting resentment and increasing difficulty at work due to acting out, he came fifteen minutes late and tracked mud from an unpaved road (a shortcut from the underground station to the consulting room) into my room. Only once before had he done this.

ASSOCIATIONS – he had rubbishy dreams over the weekend and feels reluctant to impose them on the analyst. INTERPRETATION – this conscious wish to spare is contrasted by an unconscious wish to dirty the analyst inside and out with his faeces, a bit of which has been acted out by tracking the dirt into the room. Patient looked with surprise at the floor, and apologised. ASSOCIATIONS – On Saturday night he dreamed he was tossing and turning in pain due to a dislocated finger (shows uninjured left index finger). INTERPRETATION – link with the gravestone dream. The weekend distress felt as due to the removal of his murderer-finger (Mafia) from its accustomed location. ASSOCIATIONS – but then he seemed at school, idle and bored. He wandered into the men's lavatory, where there seemed to be a nice big clean bathtub. He decided to have a bath, but then it changed to a small, filthy station toilet with pornographic writing and pictures on the wall, just opposite the basement of a big department store. He couldn't decide what to do, because the staff of the store kept watching him suspiciously. He kept going in and out of the lavatory, until finally he entered the store to steal something.

This dream shows with unusual clarity the way in which the current separation situation (the dislocated finger at the boring weekend) leads to a sequence of infantile events, first wetting himself (the bath) with warm urine, and then exploring his anus (the filthy toilet), becoming more and more sexually aroused (the pornography) and preoccupied with projective identification fantasies about the bottom of mother's body (the toilet-rectum across from the department-store-vagina with the watchful staff-penis) and his wish to rob her.

Sunday night's dream, approaching with some anxiety the Monday session, reveals the continuation of the infantile state, now a baby with soiled nappy, bottom, and cot. In the dream he wanted to change his clothes for a party he and friends were giving at his flat, but already every room was filled with guests, laughing, drinking and smoking (his soiled cot and nappy). But then he was in the park and felt happy among the greenery, even though he had on nothing but an undershirt (the baby has kicked off its nappy and idealizes its soiled bottom and cot). He finds a football to kick and soon others have joined him in the game (playing with his faeces).

This latter state, self-idealization through athletics, had appeared literally in hundreds of dreams in the first two years of his analysis. Here we see in detail its derivation. It is worth mentioning that this patient had suffered from a chronic, but non-ulcerative diarrhoea since early childhood which had only abated some eight months earlier in the analysis.

The cryptic anal masturbation

Reconstruction from the transference indicates that anal masturbation becomes cryptic very early in childhood and tends to remain both unnoticed and unrecognized in its significance thereafter, except when frank perversions declare themselves in adolescence or later. I have referred to it as 'cryptic' to emphasise here the unconscious skill with which it is hidden from scrutiny.

The most common form (see Freud, and Abraham) utilizes the faecal mass itself as the masturbatory stimulant. Either its retention, slow expulsion, rhythmic partial expulsion and retraction, or the rapid, forced, and painful expulsion are accompanied by the unconscious fantasies which alter the ego state. This change in mental state can be noted in child patients when they return from defaecating during sessions. The habit of reading on the toilet, special methods of cleansing the anus, special concern about leaving a bad smell, anxiety about faecal stain on underclothing, habitually dirty finger nails, surreptitious smelling of fingers, etc. all are tentative indicators of cryptic anal masturbation. But it can skilfully be hidden far afield from the act of defaecation: in bathing habits, the wearing of constrictive undergarments, in cycling, horseback riding or other activities which stimulate the buttocks. Most difficult perhaps of all to locate is the sequestration of anal masturbation in the genital sexual relation, which is invariably the case to some extent while anus and vagina are still confused with one another. On the other hand, like Poe's 'Purloined Letter', it may be flamboyantly in view, as in constipation with enemata, suppositories for recurrent fissure *in ano*, etc. but its significance denied.

While it is not part of my technique to comment on a patient's behaviour on the couch nor to ask for associations to it, scrutiny of the patterns of posture and movement and linking them with dream material does sometimes permit a fruitful interpretation of the behaviour. By this means the series of modifications of the anal masturbation can be revealed and a more successful search for the actual anal stimulation instituted. For instance, a patient who often kept both hands in his pockets recognized through a dream that this was accompanied at times by pulling at a loose thread. This led to the realization that he had a habit of manually teasing apart peri-anal hairs prior to defaecation lest they spoil the shape of his emerging faecal mass.

The analytic process

The early years of analysis in such cases involve primarily the resolution of the self-idealization and spurious independence, through the establishment of the capacity in the transference to utilize the analytic breast for projective relief (the toilet-breast). The relief of confusional states (Klein 1957) takes the forefront, especially those confusions of identity and therefore about time and the adult-child differential which characterize massive projective identification. It is only after several years, when the attachment to the feeding breast is developing and the intolerance to separations is rhythmically being invoked at weekends and holidays, that these processes can be accurately and fruitfully investigated. It seems certain that, unless the cryptic anal masturbation can be discovered and its insidious production of aberrant ego states scotched at source, further progress is seriously impeded.

This brings us to a most important point in our exposition, for I would suggest from my experience that the dynamic here described is often of such a subtle structure, the pressure on the analyst to join in the idealization of the pseudo-maturity so great, and the underlying threats of psychosis and suicide so covertly communicated that many of the 'successful' analyses which break down months or years after termination may fall into this category. It is necessary therefore also to stress that the countertransference position is extremely difficult and in every way repeats the dilemma of the parents, who found themselves with a 'model' child, so long as they abstained from being distinctly parental, either in the form of authority, teaching, or opposition to the relatively modest claims for privileges beyond those to which the child's age and accomplishments could reasonably entitle it.

This seductiveness must not be thought of as mere hypocrisy nor its loving quality a sham. Far from it, a Cordelia-like tenderness can be quite genuine, but the preconditions for loving are incompatible with growth since they are both intensely possessive and subtly denigrating of their objects. Termination of analysis is quietly pursued as a fiat for a non-analytic and interminable relation to the analyst and to psychoanalysis. Needless to say, therefore, the configuration described in this paper is of special interest and concern for the analyst with patients who have a professional or social link with psychoanalysis.

In my experience, where the seduction of the analyst to idealize the achievement of pseudo-maturity, in its newly modified and 'analysed' edition, is firmly resisted, interruption of the analysis may be forced by the patient for ostensibly 'realistic' reasons. This may be done through engineering a geographical shift, a change in marital status, by promoting opposition from parent or marital partner, by contracting financial obligations which render payment for the analysis infeasible, etc., while still clinging to the idealized positive transference. If the analytic penetration is to succeed, a prolonged period of violently negative transference and manifest unco-operativeness must be expected and may prove intractable. This takes the form of injured innocence, self-pity, and the constant complaint that the analyst's implication that anal masturbation exists and continues in fact is either doctinaire, a projection, or a manifestation of outside interference (e.g., from a supervisor).

Thanks to the constant clarification brought by dreams it is usually possible for the analyst to persevere. Gradually, by urging improved co-operation about consciously withheld associations and closer attention to body habits, the analyst can bring the hidden anal masturbation to light. With this the feeding-breast transference breaks through the restrictions imposed upon it by the idealization-of-the-faeces. Full-blown, painful and analytically fruitful experiences of separation anxiety become possible for the first time.

It is at this point in the analytic process that the relation to obsessional characterology becomes evident. The oscillation of the two states, pseudo-maturity and obsessional states, can be seen to take place, as the Oedipus complex in its genital and pregenital aspects takes the forefront of the transference. It can be understood that, for all the oedipal implications of earlier material which had required interpretation, a full experience of oedipal conflict only becomes possible when the differentiation of adult and infantile parts of the self has been thus arduously established.

Further clinical material

The clinical material which follows is intended to demonstrate the way in which strengthening of the alliance to good objects internally and to the analyst in the transference make possible a new stand against old anal habits. The patient in question came to analysis because of lack of direction in his work but analysis soon revealed also the pseudo-mature structure outlined in the paper. It also brought to light a little noticed continuation of anal habits and preoccupations which could be traced back in the anamnesis to nocturnal games with an older brother, probably never overtly sexual. But the unconscious splitting-off and projecting of a bad part of the self into the brother had played a large part in the self-idealization which underlay the patient's 'goodness' as a child. In fact the brother was by no means a bad child nor a bad sibling.

Approaching a Christmas holiday, the patient's recurrent fissure *in ano* became active again as the material swung toward patterns of anal intrusion into internal objects already well known by this fourth year of the analysis.

On a Tuesday, he reported having felt ill and cold since the unsatisfactory session of the day before. He dreamed that he was in a house with a man his younger brother's age and yet it was also the patient himself as a younger man. This fellow seemed friendly and pleasant at first and was telling the patient that the bodies of police inspectors, often in a state of advanced decomposition, were being found all over Britain. Only when he indicated that there was one such in the next room under a sheet did the patient become alarmed. When the young man invited him to see it and the patient demurred, a tense situation arose. The patient backed toward the door and finally dashed out as the young man lunged for his throat. To his surprise there were policemen outside who reassured him that road blocks were already established and the young murderer would be dealt with.

In the second dream of the same night he found himself walking on the pavement, naked but for a tiny bath-towel, acutely embarrassed that his penis was visible. Thinking to get home more quickly and cut short the distress, he headed for a station, but was intercepted by a tramp who invited him to his nearby lodgings. He gladly accepted, but once in the tramp's bed he could not get to sleep, for the tramp stood upright by the bed all night and frightened him.

Note the contrast in these two dreams. In the first he is able to resist involvement in anal sadistic oedipal attacks on police-inspector daddies and finds himself comforted by the external relation to the analyst and analytic road-block process. But in the second dream oedipal humiliation in the bath-analysis drives him back to the anal preoccupation with a bad tramp-brother's faecal-penis in his rectum (the constipation which is a regular prelude to activity of his anal fissure).

On the Friday he complained of his constipation and noted that he had begun to diet in an obsessional way. An amusing incident had occurred the previous evening in which a 'fat' fly was buzzing about the house, finally landing on a vase. As he announced his intention to 'show the old gentleman to the door', picking up the vase with the sluggish fly on it, his young son wittily took the patient's arm and led *him* toward the door. He dreamed that he was waiting for a haircut in a queue, but it took so long, despite the fact that both man and wife were barbering on two chairs, that he despaired. Then he found himself lying comfortably in a little flat-bottomed boat going through a little tunnel (like one he'd been on as a child on a visit to Father Christmas at a big department store). When the boat was meant to make a right-angled turn to the left, it became stuck, so the patient put his right hand into the water, making a scooping motion (as he had done the night before when the kitchen sink drain was blocked, to clear it). But he realized with a shock that his fingers were in the mouth of a tramp, lying in the water beneath the boat, who was about to bite him (anxiety about the constipation leading to the tearing open of his fissure, in contrast to the gentle 'showing-the-fat-old-gentleman-(fly)-to-the-door').

In this dream confirmation of the intolerance of separation (the couch-boat turning to the left; in fact when the patient leaves the couch it is *he* who makes a right-angled turn to the right) and turning to the tramp-faeces brother inside the mother's Father-Christmas-tunnel, is impressive. Note how the wish to rid himself gently of his oedipal rival (as his son's joke makes clear) leads him again to the alliance with the tramp brother, the constipated faecal penis and the tearing-open-the-fissure type of anal masturbatory defaecation. The infantile wish to make daddy old and expel him anally is still over-poweringly active, even though the patient's struggle against an abandonment to anal sadism has well commenced.

Three weeks later, on a Monday, he reported himself in a peculiar mood, full of intense and mixed feelings toward the analysis, aware that a recent insight helped him to curb a frequent type of provocative behaviour toward his wife but very worried and resentful about the coming holiday break. He dreamed that he was at a pond near my consulting room, waiting to go to his session. A man was fishing, though there are no fish in that pond, and had one of his two hooks stuck in the bottom. The patient had to free it, but was afraid the man would cruelly keep the line tight and cause the patient to be hooked. In fact this is exactly what happened. Determined to be free, he tore the hook out of his finger with pliers, tearing a piece of the flesh with it. To have it dressed he needed to go to a town outside London to see the American ambassador. He was being feted in a horsedrawn carriage before returning to the States; but, nonetheless, left the carriage and dressed the patient's finger and took him to his home. There the patient, feeling very happy, watched the ambassador and his family have their lunch, separated from him by a perforated partition.

Here, before a holiday, the struggle to accept the oedipal distress (wound on his finger, linked to circumcision), and to free himself from the addiction to the anal masturbation (the man with his hook caught in the bottom of the pond, linked to the tramp–brother faecal penis) has proceeded with remarkable rapidity and clarity of insight. It is interesting that subsequently on two occasions he developed a paronychia of an index finger at weekends.

Summary

For the purpose of illustrating a current trend of our researches into the intimate connexion between projective identification and anal masturbation, I have chosen to describe the transference manifestations of a type of character disorder seen with relative frequency among the many intelligent, gifted and outwardly successful people who seek analysis, namely of 'pseudomaturity'. The concept of projective identification, first described by Melanie Klein, has opened the way to a new fruitful investigation of hitherto unexplored aspects of anality. By demonstrating how projective identification with internal objects is induced by anal masturbation, a richer conception of the derivation and significance of the narcissistic evaluation of faeces is unfolded, thus linking the anal phase more surely to symptom and character pathology.

References

Abraham, K. (1920) 'The narcissistic evaluation of excretory processes in dreams and neurosis' in *Selected Papers*, London: Hogarth Press, (1927).
——(1921) 'Contributions to the theory of the anal character' *ibid*.
Deutsch, H. (1942) 'Some forms of emotional disturbance and their relationship to schizophrenia', *Psychoanalytical Quarterly*, 11.
Freud, S. (1905) *Three Essays on the Theory of Sexuality*, *SE, 7*.
——(1908) 'Character and anal erotism' *SE, 9*.
——(1917) 'On transformations of instinct as exemplified in anal erotism' *SE*, 17.
——(1918) 'From the history of an infantile neurosis', *SE*, 17.
Heimann, P. (1962) 'Notes on the anal stage', *International Journal of Psycho-Analysis*, 43.
Jones, E. (1913) 'Hate and anal erotism in the obsessional neurosis', in

Papers on Psycho-Analysis, 2nd and subsq. editions, London: Baillière (1918).

——(1918) 'Anal–erotic character traits.' *ibid*.

Klein, M. (1946) 'Notes on some schizoid mechanisms' in M. Klein, P. Heimann, S. Isaacs, and J. Riviere *Developments in Psycho-Analysis*, London: Hogarth Press (1952) 292–320 (also in *The Writings of Melanie Klein* vol. 3, 1–24).

——(1957) *Envy and Gratitude* London: Tavistock (also in *The Writings of Melanie Klein* vol. 3, 176–235).

Meltzer, D. (1963) 'A contribution to the metapsychology of cyclothymic states.' *International Journal of Psycho-Analysis*, 44.

Spitz, R. (1949) 'Autoerotism', *Psychoanalytic Study of the Child*, 3–4.

Winnicott, D. W. (1965) *The Maturational Processes and the Facilitating Environment*, London: Hogarth Press.

3

Contribution to the psychopathology of psychotic states: the importance of projective identification in the ego structure and the object relations of the psychotic patient

HERBERT ROSENFELD

This article was first published in 1971 in P. Doucet and C. Laurin (eds) *Problems of Psychosis*, The Hague: Excerpta Medica, 115–28.

Following the suggestion of the organizers of the Symposium that I should discuss the importance of projective identification and ego splitting in the psychopathology of the psychotic patient, I shall attempt to give you a survey of the processes described under the term: 'projective identification'.

I shall first define the meaning of the term 'projective identification' and quote from the work of Melanie Klein, as it was she who developed the concept. Then I shall go on to discuss very briefly the work of two other writers whose use appeared to be related to, but not identical with, Melanie Klein's use of the term.

'Projective identification' relates first of all to a splitting process of the early ego, where either good or bad parts of the self are split off from the ego and are as a further step projected in love or hatred into external objects which leads to fusion and identification of the projected parts of the self with the external objects. There are important paranoid anxieties related to these processes as the objects filled with aggressive parts of the self become persecuting and are experienced by the patient as threatening to retaliate by forcing themselves and the bad parts of the self which they contain back again into the ego.

In her paper on schizoid mechanisms Melanie Klein (1946) considers first of all the importance of the processes of splitting and

denial and omnipotence which during the early phase of development play a role similar to that of repression at a later stage of ego
development. She then discusses the early infantile instinctual impulses
and suggests that while the 'oral libido still has the lead, libidinal and
aggressive impulses and phantasies from other sources come to the
fore and lead to a confluence of oral, urethral and anal desires, both
libidinal and aggressive'. After discussing the oral libidinal and
aggressive impulses directed against the breast and the mother's
body, she suggests that:

> 'the other line of attack derives from the anal and urethral impulses
> and implies expelling dangerous substances (excrements) out of
> the self and into the mother. Together with these harmful
> excrements, expelled in hatred, split off parts of the ego are also
> projected into the mother. These excrements and bad parts of the
> self are meant not only to injure but also to control and to take
> possession of the object. In so far as the mother comes to contain
> the bad parts of the self, she is not felt to be a separate individual
> but is felt to be the bad self. Much of the hatred against parts of the
> self is now directed towards the mother. This leads to a particular
> form of identification which establishes the prototype of an
> aggressive object relation. I suggest for these processes the term
> *projective identification*.'

Later on in the same paper Melanie Klein describes that not only
bad, but also good parts of the ego are expelled and projected into
external objects who become identified with the projected good parts
of the self. She regards this identification as vital because it is essential
for the infant's ability to develop good object relations. If this process
is, however, excessive, good parts of the personality are felt to be
lost to the self which results in weakening and impoverishment of
the ego. Melanie Klein also emphasizes the aspect of the projective
processes which relates to the forceful entry into the object and the
persecutory anxieties related to this process which I mentioned
before. She also describes how paranoid anxieties related to
projective identification disturb introjective processes. 'Introjection
is interfered with, as it may be felt as a forceful entry from the
outside into the inside in retribution for violent projections'. It will
be clear that Melanie Klein gives the name 'projective identification'
both to the processes of ego splitting and the 'narcissistic' object
relations created by the projection of parts of the self into
objects.

I shall now discuss some aspects of the work of Dr Edith Jacobson
who describes psychotic identifications in schizophrenic patients

identical with the ones I observed and described as 'projective identification'. She also frequently uses the term 'projective identification' in her book *Psychotic Conflict and Reality* (Jacobson 1967).

In 1954 Edith Jacobson discussed the identifications of the delusional schizophrenic patient who may eventually consciously believe himself to be another person. She relates this to early infantile identification mechanisms of a magic nature which lead to 'partial or total blending of the magic self and object images, founded on phantasies or even the temporary belief of being one with or of becoming the object, regardless of reality'. In 1967 she describes these processes in more detail. She discusses 'the psychotic's regression to a narcissistic level, where the weakness of the boundaries between self and object images gives rise to phantasies, or experiences of fusion between these images. These primitive introjective or projective identifications are based on infantile phantasies of incorporation, devouring, invading (forcing oneself into), or being devoured by the object'. She also says 'We can assume that such phantasies, which pre-suppose at least the beginning distinction between self and object, are characteristic of early narcissistic stages of development and that the child's relation to the mother normally begins with the introjective and projective processes'; and that the 'introjective and projective identifications (of the adult patient) depend on the patient's fixation to early narcissistic stages and upon the depth of the narcissistic regression'. In discussing clinical material of the Patient A she described this fear that any affectionate physical contact might bring about experiences of merging, which in turn might lead to a manifest psychotic state. Her views that the introjective and projective identifications observed in the adult patient depend on the fixation to early narcissistic phases where these identifications originate, seem identical with my own views and there is nothing in her clinical and theoretical observations which I have quoted above with which I would disagree. She stresses, however, that she differs from Melanie Klein and my own opinion in so far as she does not believe that the projective identifications of the adult patient observable in the transference or acted out by the patient with objects in his environment are in fact a repetition of the early infantile projective and introjective processes, but are to be understood as a later defensive process, as in her view early processes cannot be observed in the transference. She also disagrees with my analytic technique of verbally interpreting the processes of projective identification when they appear in the transference, which I regard as of central importance in working through psychotic processes in the transference situation.[1]

Margaret Mahler in 1952 described symbiotic infantile psychoses and suggested that the mechanisms employed are introjective and projective ones and their psychotic elaboration. Her ideas seem to be closely related, but nevertheless quite distinct from what I have described as projective identification. She describes the early mother/infant relationship as a phase of object relationship in which the infant behaves and functions as though he and his mother were an omnipotent system (a dual unity with one common boundary, a symbiotic membrane as it were). In 1967 she says, 'the essential feature of symbiosis is hallucinatory or delusional, somatopsychic, omnipotent fusion with the representation of the mother and, in particular, delusion of common boundary of the two actually and physically separate individuals'. She suggests that 'this is the mechanism to which the ego regresses in cases of psychotic disorganization'. In describing the symbiotic infantile psychosis she says that the early mother–infant symbiotic relationship is intense. The mental representation of the mother remains or is regressively fused with that of the self. She describes the panic reactions caused by separations 'which are followed by restitutive productions which serve to maintain or restore the symbiotic parasitic delusion of oneness with the mother or father'. It is clear that Mahler has introjective or projective processes in mind as the mechanisms which produce the symbiotic psychosis. I have, however, found no clear description of these mechanisms in her papers. She seems to see the symbiotic psychosis as a defence against separation anxiety which links up closely with my description of the narcissistic object relation serving a defensive function. The symbiotic processes described by Mahler have some resemblance to the parasitical object relations I shall describe later. Projective identification which includes ego splitting and projecting of good and bad parts of the self into external objects is not identitical with symbiosis. For projective identification to take place some temporary differentiation of 'me' and 'not me' is essential. Symbiosis, however, is used by Mahler to describe this state of undifferentiation, of fusion with the mother, in which the 'I' is not yet differentiated from the 'not I'.

In my own work with psychotic patients I have encountered a variety of types of object relations and mental mechanisms which are associated with Melanie Klein's description of projective identification. First of all, it is important to distinguish between two types of projective identification, namely, projective identification used for communication with other objects and projective identification used for ridding the self of unwanted parts.

I shall first discuss projective identification used as a method of communication. Many psychotic patients use projective processes for communication with other people. These projective mechanisms of the psychotic seem to be a distortion or intensification of the normal infantile relationship, which is based on non-verbal communication between infant and mother, in which impulses, parts of the self and anxieties too difficult for the infant to bear are projected into the mother and where the mother is able instinctively to respond by containing the infant's anxiety and alleviating it by her behaviour. This relationship has been stressed particularly by Bion. The psychotic patient who uses this process in the transference may do so consciously but more often unconsciously. He then projects impulses and parts of himself into the analyst in order that the analyst will feel and understand his experiences and will be able to contain them so that they lose their frightening or unbearable quality and become meaningful by the analyst being able to put them into words through interpretations. This situation seems to be of fundamental importance for the development of introjective processes and the development of the ego: it makes it possible for the patient to learn to tolerate his own impulses and the analyst's interpretations make his infantile responses and feelings accessible to the more sane self, which can begin to think about the experiences which were previously meaningless and frightening to him. The psychotic patient who projects predominantly for communication is obviously receptive to the analyst's understanding of him, so it is essential that this type of communication should be recognized and interpreted accordingly.

As a second point I want to discuss projective identification used for denial of psychic reality. In this situation the patient splits off parts of his self in addition to impulses and anxieties and projects them into the analyst for the purpose of evacuating and emptying out the disturbing mental content which leads to a denial of psychic reality. As this type of patient primarily wants the analyst to condone the evacuation processes and the denial of his problems, he often reacts to interpretations with violent resentment, as they are experienced as critical and frightening since the patient believes that unwanted unbearable and meaningless mental content is pushed back into him by the analyst.

Both the processes of communication and evacuation may exist simultaneously or alternatively in our psychotic patients and it is essential to differentiate them clearly in order to keep contact with the patient and make analysis possible.

As a third point I want to discuss a very common transference relationship of the psychotic patient which is aimed at controlling the analyst's body and mind, which seems to be based on a very early infantile type of object relationship.

In analysis, one observes that the patient believes that he has forced himself omnipotently into the analyst, which leads to fusion or confusion with the analyst and anxieties relating to the loss of the self. In this form of projective identification the projection of the mad parts of the self into the analyst often predominates. The analyst is then perceived as having become mad, which arouses extreme anxiety as the patient is afraid that the analyst will retaliate and force the madness back into the patient, depriving him entirely of his sanity. At such times the patient is in danger of disintegration, but detailed interpretations of the relationship between patient and analyst may break through this omnipotent delusional situation and prevent a breakdown.

There is, however, a danger that the verbal communication between patient and analyst may break down at such times as the analyst's interpretations are misunderstood and misinterpreted by the patient and the patient's communications increasingly assume a concrete quality, suggesting that abstract thinking has almost completely broken down. In investigating such situations, I found that omnipotent projective identification interferes with the capacity of verbal and abstract thinking and produces a concreteness of the mental processes which leads to confusion between reality and phantasy. It is also clinically essential for the analyst to realize that the patient who uses excessive projective identification is dominated by concrete thought processes which cause misunderstanding of verbal interpretations, since words and their content are experienced by the patient as concrete, non-symbolic objects. Segal in her paper 'Some aspects of the analysis of a schizophrenic' (1950) points out that the schizophrenic patient loses the capacity to use symbols when the symbol becomes again the equivalent of the original object, which means it is hardly different from it. In her paper 'Notes on symbol formation' (1957) she suggests the term 'symbolic equation' for this process: she writes:

> 'The symbolic equation between the original object and the symbol in the internal and external world is, I think, the basis of the schizophrenic's concrete thinking. This non-differentiation between the thing symbolized and the symbol is part of a disturbance in the relation between the ego and the object. Parts of the ego and internal objects are projected onto an object and identified with it. The differentiation between the self and the object is obscured then; since a part of the ego is confused with the

object, the symbol which is a creation and a function of the ego becomes in turn confused with the object which is symbolized.'

I believe that the differentiation of the self and object representation is necessary to maintain normal symbol formation which is based on the introjection of objects experienced as separate from the self.[2] It is the excessive projective identification in the psychotic process which obliterates differentiation of self and objects, which causes confusion between reality and phantasy and a regression to concrete thinking due to the loss of the capacity for symbolisation and symbolic thinking.[3]

It is, of course, extremely difficult to use verbal interpretations with the psychotic patient when interpretations are misunderstood and misinterpreted. The patient may become extremely frightened, may cover his ears and try to rush out of the consulting room and the analysis is in danger of breaking down. At such times it is necessary to uncover the projective processes used for the purpose of communication between patient and analyst, which will establish some possibility of simple verbal interpretations to explain to the patient and help him to understand the terrifying situation due to the concrete experience. It is essential for the analyst to remember that all three types of projective identification which I have described so far exist simultaneously in the psychotic patient, and one-sided concentration on one process may block the analysis and meaningful communication between patient and analyst.

There is one further aspect of the psychopathology of psychotic patients that is linked with projective identification – that is the importance of primitive aggression, particularly envy, and the use of projective identification to deal with it.

When the psychotic patient living in a state of fusion (projective identification) with the analyst begins to experience himself as a separate person, violent destructive impulses make their appearance. His aggressive impulses are sometimes an expression of anger related to separation anxiety, but generally they have a distinctly envious character. As long as the patient regards the analyst's mind and body and his help and understanding as part of his own self he is able to attribute everything that is experienced as valuable in the analysis as being part of his own self, in other words he lives in a state of omnipotent narcissism. As soon as a patient begins to feel separate from the analyst the aggressive reaction appears and particularly clearly so after a valuable interpretation, which shows the analyst's understanding. The patient reacts with feelings of humiliation, complains that he is made to feel small; why should the analyst be able to remind him of something which he needs but which he cannot provide for himself. In his envious anger the patient tries to destroy and spoil the analyst's interpretations by ridiculing or making them meaningless. The analyst may have the distinct experience in his counter transference that he is meant to feel that he is no good and has nothing of value to give to the patient. There are often physical symptoms connected with this state because the patient may feel sick and may actually vomit. This concrete rejection of the analyst's help can often be clearly understood as a rejection of. the mother's food[4] and her care for the infant repeated in the analytic transference situation. When the patient had previously made good progress in the treatment this 'negative therapeutic reaction' is often quite violent, as if he wants to spoil and devalue everything he had previously received, disregarding the often suicidal danger of such a reaction. Many patients experience this violent envy directed against the good qualities of the analyst as quite insane and illogical and as the inner saner part of the patient experiences these envious reactions as unbearable and unacceptable, many defences against this primitive envy are created.

One of these defences relates to the splitting off and projection of the envious part of the self into an external object, which then becomes the envious part of the patient. This kind of defensive projective identification follows the model of Melanie Klein's description of the splitting off and projection of bad parts of the self, which I quoted in the beginning of this paper.

Another defence against envy relates to omnipotent phantasies of the patient of entering the admired and envied object and in this way insisting that he is the object by taking over its role. When total projective identification has taken place with an envied object envy is entirely denied, but immediately reappears when the self and object become separate again. In my paper on 'The psychopathology of narcissism' (1964) I stressed that:

'projective identification was part of an early narcissistic relationship to the mother, where recognition of separateness between self and object is denied. Awareness of separation would lead to feelings of dependence on an object and therefore to anxiety (see Mahler 1967). In addition, dependence stimulates envy when the goodness of the object is recognized. The omnipotent narcissistic object relations, particularly omnipotent projective identification, obviate both the aggressive feelings caused by frustration and any awareness of envy.'

I believe that in the psychotic patient projective identification is more often a defence against excessive envy, which is closely bound up with the patient's narcissism, rather than a defence against separation anxiety. In my paper 'Object relations of an acute schizophrenic patient in the transference situation' (1964) I tried to trace the origin of the envious projective identification in schizophrenia. I suggested:

'If too much resentment and envy dominates the infant's relation to the mother, normal projective identification becomes more and more controlling and can take on omnipotent delusional tones. For example, the infant who in phantasy enters the mother's body driven by envy and omnipotence, takes over the role of the mother, or breast, and deludes himself that he is the mother of breast. This mechanism plays an important role in mania and hypomania, but in schizophrenia it occurs in a very exaggerated form.'

Finally, I want to draw attention to two similar types of object relations: a parasitical and a delusional one. In the parasitical object relation the psychotic patient in analysis maintains a belief that he is living entirely inside an object – the analyst – and behaves like a parasite living on the capacities of the analyst, who is expected to function as his ego. Severe parasitism may be regarded as a state of total projective identification. It is, however, not just a defensive state to deny envy or separation but is also an expression of aggression, particularly envy. It is the combination of defence and acting out of the aggression which makes the parasitic state a particularly difficult therapeutic problem.

The parasitic patient relies entirely on the analyst, often making him responsible for his entire life. He generally behaves in an extremely passive, silent and sluggish manner, demanding everything and giving nothing in return. This state can be extremely chronic and the analytic work with such patients is often minimal. One of my depressed patients described himself as a baby, which was like a stone heavily pressing into my couch and into me. He felt he was making it impossible for me either to carry him or to look after him and he feared that the only thing that I could possibly do was to expel him, if I could not stand him any longer. However, he was terrified that he could not survive being left. He not only felt that he had a very paralysing effect on the analysis but that he was paralysed and inert himself. Only very occasionally was it possible to get in touch with the intense feelings either of hostility or overwhelming pain and depression bound up with this process. There was no joy when the analyst was felt to be helpful and alive, as it only increased the patient's awareness of the contrast between himself and the analyst and at times produced a desire to frustrate him, and with this he returned to the *status quo* of inertia, which was felt to be unpleasant but preferred to any of the intense feelings of pain, anger, envy or jealousy which might fleetingly be experienced. As I suggested before, extreme parasitism is partly a defence against separation anxiety, envy or jealousy, but it often seems to be a defence against any emotion which might be experienced as painful. I often have the impression that patients, like the one I described, who experience themselves as dead and are often experienced by the analyst as so inactive that they might as well be dead, use their analyst's aliveness as a means of survival. However, the latent hostility prevents the patient from getting more than minimal help or satisfaction from the analysis. In the more active forms of parasitism the insidious hostility dominates the picture and is much more apparent.

Dr Bion in his book *Transformations* (1965) describes a more active case of parasitism. He emphasizes that such patients are particularly unrewarding. The essential feature is simultaneous stimulation and frustration of hope and work that is fruitless, except for discrediting analyst and patient. The destructive activity is balanced by enough success to deny the patient fulfilment of his destructiveness. 'The helpful summary of such a case is described as "chronic murder of patient and analyst" or "an instance of parasitism": the patient draws on the love, or benevolence of the host to extract knowledge and power which enables him to poison the association and destroy the indulgence on which he depends for his existence.'

It is important to differentiate the very chronic forms of parasitism from the massive intrusion and projective identification into the analyst which resembles parasitism but is of shorter duration and responds more easily to interpretations. It occurs at times when separation threatens or when jealousy or envy is violently stimulated in the transference or in outside life. Meltzer (1967) describes a primitive form of possessive jealousy which plays an important role in perpetuating massive projective identification of a peculiar withdrawn, sleepy sort.

The other form of living entirely inside an object occurs in severely deluded schizophrenic patients who seem to experience themselves as living in an unreal world, which is highly delusional but nevertheless has qualities of a structure which suggests that this hallucinatory world represents the inside of an object, probably the mother. The patient may be withdrawn, preoccupied with halluci-nations, in the analysis occasionally projecting the hallucinatory experience on to the analyst, which leads to mis-identifying him and others with his delusional experience. Sometimes the patient may describe himself as living in a world, or object, which separates him entirely from the outside world and the analyst is experienced as a contraption, an actor or a machine and the world becomes extremely unreal. The living inside the delusional object seems to be definitely in opposition to relating to the outside world, which would imply depending on a real object. This delusional world or object seems to be dominated by an omnipotent and sometimes omniscient part of the self, which creates the notion that within the delusional object there is complete painlessness and freedom to indulge in any whim. It also appears that the self within the delusional object exerts a powerful suggestive and seductive influence on saner parts of the personality in order to persuade or force them to withdraw from reality and to join the delusional omnipotent world. Clinically, the patient may hear a voice making propaganda for living inside the mad world by idealizing it and praising its virtue by offering a complete satisfaction and instant cure to the patient. This persuasion or propaganda to get inside the delusional world implies clinically the constant stimulus to all parts of the self to use omnipotent projective identification (forcing the self inside the object) as the only possible method to solve all problems. This situation leads to constant acting out with external objects which are used for projective identification. When, however, projective identification becomes directed towards the delusional object, the saner parts of the self may become trapped or imprisoned within this object and physical and mental paralysis amounting to catatonia may result.

The psychoanalytic treatment of the processes related to projective identification in the psychotic patient

As this paper deals primarily with the psychopathology of psychotic states, I can only briefly discuss my psychoanalytic technique in dealing with psychotic patients to emphasize my contention that the investigation of the psychopathology of the psychotic and the therapeutic approach are closely interlinked.

In treating psychotic states it is absolutely essential to differentiate those parts of the self which exist almost exclusively in a state of projective identification with external objects, or internal ones such as the delusional object I described above and the saner parts of the patient which are less dominated by projective identification and have formed some separate existence from objects. These saner parts may be remnants of the adult personality, but often they represent more normal non-omnipotent infantile parts of the self, which during analysis are attempting to form a dependent relationship to the analyst representing the feeding mother. As the saner parts of the self are in danger of submitting to the persuasion of the delusional self to withdraw into the more psychotic parts of the personality, and to get entangled in it, the former need very careful attention in analysis to help them to differentiate the analyst as an external object from the seductive voice of the omnipotent parts of the self related to the internal delusional object, which can assume any identity for the purpose of keeping up the domination of the whole self. As there is always a conflict, amounting sometimes to a violent struggle, between the psychotic and saner parts of the personality, the nature of this conflict has also to be clearly understood in order to make it possible to work through the psychotic state by means of analysis. For example, the structure and the intentions of the psychotic parts of the patient, which are highly narcissistically organized, have to be brought fully into the open by means of interpretations, as they are opposed to any part of the self which wants to form a relationship to reality and to the analyst who attempts to help the ego to move towards growth and development. The interpretations have also to expose the extent and the method used by the psychotic narcissistic parts of the personality in attempting to dominate, entangle and to paralyse the saner parts of the self. It is important to remember that it is only the sane dependent parts of the self separate from the analyst that can use introjective processes uncontaminated by the concreteness caused by the omnipotent projective identifications; the capacity for memory and growth of the ego depends on these normal introjective processes. When the dependent non-psychotic parts of the personality become stronger, as the result of analysis, violent negative therapeutic reactions usually occur as the psychotic narcisstic parts of the patient oppose any progress and change of the *status quo*, a problem which I recently discussed in detail in a paper on 'The Negative Therapeutic Reaction' (Rosenfeld 1969).

Case presentation

I shall now bring some case material of a schizophrenic patient in order to illustrate some aspects of projective identification and ego splitting.

PATIENT A

Had been diagnosed several years ago as schizophrenic, when he had an acute psychotic breakdown which was characterized by over-whelming panic, confusion and fears of complete disintegration. He did not hallucinate during the acute phase, nor are the delusional aspects of the psychosis dominant at the present time, but he is unable to work or to maintain a close relationship with men or women in the outside world. He had been treated by another analyst for several years before starting analysis with me more than a year ago. The previous analyst in his report to me emphasized the patient's tendency to slip into a state of projective identification with the analyst at the beginning of each session leading to the patient's becoming confused and unable to speak in an audible and under-standable way. The analyst interpreted to the patient that he expected him, the analyst, to understand him even if he could not talk or think, since he believed himself to be inside the analyst; as a result of such interpretations he generally started to speak more distinctly. During the analysis with me there were further improvements and he felt at times more separate, so that the saner parts of his self were able to form to some extent a dependent relationship to me. However, from time to time, particularly after he had made some progress, or when there were long separations, he fell back to a parasitical relationship of living inside me (projective identification), which led to states of confusion, inability to think and talk, claustrophobia and paranoid anxieties of being trapped by me. When envy was aroused through experiences in the real world, for example when he met a man who was successful in his relationship with women or in his work, after a short conscious experience of envy A would frequently become identified with him. This was followed by severe anxieties of losing his identity and feelings of being trapped, rather than leading to the delusion that he was the envied man or that he was able to function in the outside world similarly to the man with whom projective identification and confusion had taken place.

Last year, in the autumn, I had to interrupt the patient's analysis for a fortnight which disturbed him considerably. Consciously, he seemed unconcerned about my going away which I had of course discussed with him several months before. However, two weeks before the interruption he became acutely anxious and confused and for a day he feared that he would have another breakdown and have to go into hospital. The disturbance started with the patient's complaint that he could not drag himself away from the television screen where he was watching the Olympic games. He felt forced, almost against his will to look at it until late at night. He complained that he was drawn into the hot climate of Mexico which made him feel that being there would make him well. He was also compelled to look at the athletes, or wrestlers and weightlifters and felt he was, or ought to be, one of them. He asked me questions: Why have I to be an athlete? Why can't I be myself? He felt that this looking at television was like an addiction which he could not stop and which exhausted and drained him. At times he felt so strongly 'pulled inside the television' that he felt claustrophobic and had difficulty in breathing. Afterwards during the night he felt compelled to get up and see whether the taps of the washbasin in his flat were closed and whether the stoppers in the basin were blocking up the drainage. He was terrified that both his bath and the basin might overflow and eventually he confessed that he was afraid of being drowned and suffocated. I interpreted to him that after he felt that he was making progress and feeling separate from me he was suddenly overcome with impatience and envy of me and other men who were able to move about and were active. I suggested that it was the envious part which drove him into the identification with other men and myself in order to take over their strength and potency, and in this way the omnipotent part of himself could make him believe that he could be mature and healthy instantly. He agreed with the interpretation without any difficulty and started to speak very fast: he said he knew all this and was quite aware of it, but he also knew that this belief was quite false and that it was a delusion and he was angry at having to listen to a voice in him which was very persuasive and stimulated him to take over the mind and body of other people. I also interpreted to him that I thought that the threatening separation was stimulating his wish to be suddenly grown up and independent in order not to have to cope with the anxieties of being separate from me. He then told me that he was falling every night into a very deep sleep from which he could not easily awake in the morning and so he had arrived late for his session. He compared the feeling of being pulled into the television screen, which seemed to have become identified with the delusional object, to being pulled into this deep sleep. He now spoke fairly fluently and more distinctly and conveyed that he felt now more separate from me. He said he felt disgusted with himself for being a parasite and he also complained that the television experience and his bed were draining his life out of him, so that he had a strong impulse to smash both; he was glad that he had been able to control this in reality. I acknowledged his own observation that his looking at television and being pulled into a deep sleep were experienced by him as parasitical experiences where he felt he was getting into other objects. I pointed out that he felt angry with that part of himself which stimulated him to get inside external objects, the athletes representing me as a successful man who was travelling abroad during the break, and also into internal objects which were represented by his bed. I stressed that at first he felt he probably could control and possess these objects entirely when he got inside them, but very soon he felt enclosed and trapped and persecuted, which roused his wish to destroy the bed and the television screen which had turned into persecuting objects. I thought that his fear of being trapped and his anger related also to the analysis and the analyst. The patient's obsessions about the stoppers of the basin were also related to his fear of being trapped and drowned. It seemed that he had constantly to find out whether after his intrusion into objects he was trapped and was in danger of drowning and suffocating inside, or whether there was a hole through which he could escape.

Simultaneously with the projective identification related to the delusional television experience, the patient was violently pulled into relations to prostitutes. He explained to me that there was a part of him which persuaded him whenever he felt lonely or anxious that he needed to have a lovely big prostitute for nourishment and this would make him well. During the session he assured me that he realized the falsity of the voice, but in fact he very rarely could resist. He felt he wanted to get inside the prostitutes in an excited way in order to devour them, but after intercourse he felt sick and disgusted and convinced that he had now acquired syphilis of the stomach. The patient, during this session, many times asserted that he knew quite well the difference between reality and the delusional persuasion and he also knew what was wrong. But it was clear to me that in spite of this knowledge he was again and again put temporarily into a deluded state by a psychotic omnipotent and omniscient part of him which succeeded in seducing and overpowering the saner part of his personality and induced him to deal with all his difficulties and problems, including his envy, by projective identification. During the session, the saner part of the patient seemed to receive help and support from the analyst's interpretations, but he felt humiliated and angry that he could not resist the domination and persuasion of the psychotic part when he was left on his own. In attempting to examine the reason for listening so readily to the internal voice, I found that he was promised cure, freedom from anxiety and from dependence on myself. I was then able to interpret that the separation made him more aware of feeling small and dependent on me, which was humiliating and painful and increased his envy of me. By omnipotently intruding into me, he could delude himself that from one moment to the next he became grown up and completely all right and could manage without me.

I shall now briefly describe the relationship between ego splitting, projective identification and the persecutory anxieties related to these processes in this patient. On the following session he reported that he felt much better, but in the middle of the session he became very silent and then admitted with shame that he had been intensely anti-semitic some time ago for a period of over six months. He had regarded the Jews as degraded people who were only out to exploit others in order to extract money from them in a ruthless way. He hated exploiters and wanted to attack and smash them for it. I interpreted that while he was aware that this happened in the past, he now felt awful towards me because after yesterday's session he had got rid of the greedy parasitical exploiting part of his self but had pushed it into me. He felt now that I had become his greedy expoiting self and this made him feel intensely suspicious about me. He replied that he feared that I must now hate and despise him, and that the only thing which he could do was to destroy himself or this hated part of himself. I interpreted his fear of my retaliation because when he saw me as a greedy, exploiting Jew he attacked and despised me, and feared that I would hate him because he believed I could not bear that he had pushed his own greedy self into me, not only as an attack but because he could not bear it himself and wanted to get rid of it. I suggested that it was when he felt that I could not accept his bad and hated self that he attacked himself so violently. In fact, the greatest anxiety during this session was related to violent attacks that were directed against his bad self which built up to a crescendo, so that he feared he would tear himself to pieces. He calmed down considerably after the interpretations.

The next session showed progress in relation to the splitting processes, followed in subsequent sessions by some experience of depression. In the beginning of the session the patient reported that he had some difficulty in getting up, but he was glad that he remembered a dream. In this dream he was observing a group of Olympic runners in a race on the television screen. Suddenly he saw a number of people crowding in on to the track and interfering with the race. He got violently angry with them and wanted to kill them for interfering and deliberately getting in the way of the runners. He reported that he had been looking at the television screen for only a short time the night before and had been thinking about the last session in which he had been afraid of damaging himself when he tried to cut off and destroy bad parts of himself. He now was determined to face up to whatever was going on in him. He had no associations to the dream, apart from the fact that the interfering people looked quite ordinary. I pointed out that in this dream he showed in a very concrete way what he felt he was doing when he was looking at television. The interfering people seemed to be the parts of himself which he experienced as worming their way into the track in Mexico when he was greedily and enviously looking at television. In this dream it was quite clear that people representing him were not competing by running, but were simply trying to interfere with the progress of the race. I was then able to show him another aspect of the extremely concrete form of projection which did not only relate to the Olympic runners but to the analyst. I interpreted that he felt when the analysis was making good progress he experienced my interpretations and thoughts as something which he was watching with admiration and envy, like the athletes on television. He felt that the envious parts of himself actually could worm their way into my brain and interfere with the quickness of my thinking. In the dream he was attempting to face up to the recognition that these parts of himself actually existed and he wanted to control and stop them. I also related this process to the patient's complaints that his own thought processes were often interfered with and I related this to an identification with the analyst's mind which he often enviously attacked. Actually, the patient's co-operation during the last week had been very positive, which had led to considerable unblocking of his mind, so that a great number of his projective identifications and splitting processes had shown them-selves clearly in the analysis and could be related to the transference situation. In the dream he had actually succeeded in what he announced he tried to do, namely, to face up to the processes by bringing them into the transference rather than attempting to destroy and get rid of them by splitting and projection. This also enabled him to face up to his acute fear of damaging both his objects and his self through his projective identifications. My interpretations seemed to diminish his anxiety about having completely destroyed me and my brain so that I could be experienced as helpful and undamaged, and for certain periods I was introjected as good and undamaged, a process leading gradually to a strengthening of the ego. One of the difficulties of working through such situations in the analysis is the tendency to endless repetition, in spite of the patient's understanding that very useful analytic work is being done. It is important in dealing with patients and processes of this kind to accept that much of the repetition is inevitable. The acceptance by the analyst of the patient's processes being re-enacted in the transference helps the patient to feel that the self, which is constantly split off and projected into the analyst, is acceptable and not so damaging as feared.

I want now to describe briefly a short depressive spell in the patient's illness which throws some light on his internal anxieties related to damage to objects and his self. A few days after the session I reported before the patient became increasingly concerned about injuries he believed he had done to other people, but most of all he was horrified about what was going on inside himself. For half an hour he experienced intense anxiety and reported that he was too frightened to look inside himself. Suddenly he saw his brain in a terrible state as if many worms had eaten their way into it. He feared that the damage was irreparable and his brain might fall to pieces. Despairingly he said how could he allow his brain to get into such an awful state! After a pause he suggested that his constant relations to prostitutes had something to do with the state of affairs. I interpreted that he felt that he had forced himself during the last weeks into people such as the prostitutes and the athletes and that he was afraid to see that damage outside. The damage to his brain seemed identical to the damage he feared he had done to external objects. He then began to talk about his brain as a particularly valuable and delicate part of his body which he had neglected and left unprotected. His voice sounded now much warmer and more concerned than ever previously, so I felt it necessary to interpret that his brain was also identified with a particularly valuable important object relationship, namely, the analysis and the analyst which represented the feeding situation to him. This he had usually displaced on to the prostitutes to whom he always went for nourishment. I gave him now detailed interpretations of the intensity of his hunger for me, his inability to wait and I described his impulses and the self which he had experienced as boring himself omnipotently into my brain, which contained for him all the valuable knowledge which he longed to possess. Throughout the hour the patient felt great anxiety and almost unbearable pain because he feared he could not repair the damage. However, he was clearly relieved through the transference interpretations which helped him to differentiate and disentangle the confusion between inside and outside, phantasy and reality. I think it was particularly the interpretations about my brain, which showed him that I could still think and function, which both helped him to understand this very concrete phantasy in relation to his own thought processes and to relieve his anxiety about the damage he feared he had done to me.

In this case material I have tried to illustrate some of the processes of projective identification and ego splitting and the part they play in the psychopathology of psychotic patients.

Summary

'Projective identification' relates first of all to a splitting process of the early ego, where either good or bad parts of the self are split off from the ego and are as a further step projected in love or hatred into external objects, which leads to fusion and identification of the projected parts of the self with the external objects. There are important paranoid anxieties related to these processes as the objects filled with aggressive parts of the self become persecuting and are experienced by the patient as threatening to retaliate by forcing themselves and the bad parts of the self which they contain back again into the ego.

In this paper I have discussed a number of processes related to projective identification which play an important part in psychotic patients. First of all, I am distinguishing between two types of projective identification: the projective identification used by psychotic patients for communication with other objects, which seems to be a distortion or intensification of the normal infantile relationship which is based on non-verbal communication between infant and mother; and secondly, the projective identification used for ridding the self of unwanted parts, which leads to a denial of psychic reality. As a third point I am discussing projective identification representing a very common transference relationship of the psychotic patient which is aimed at controlling the analyst's body and mind, which seems to be based on a very early infantile type of object relationship. My fourth point is projective identification used by the psychotic patient predominantly for defensive purposes to deal with aggressive impulses, particularly envy. The fifth point I am drawing attention to are those object relations of the psychotic patient in analysis where he maintains the belief that he is living entirely inside an object – the analyst – and behaves like a parasite using the capacities of the analyst, who is expected to function as his ego. Severe parasitism may be regarded as a state of total projective identification. I am also discussing the parasitical state which is related to living entirely in a delusional world. Sixthly, I am discussing the *psychoanalytic treatment* of the processes related to projective identification in the psychotic patient. Finally, I shall present case material of a schizophrenic patient in order to illustrate some aspects of projective identification and ego splitting.

Notes

1 When Edith Jacobson describes the defensive nature of the projective identification in her adult psychotic patients she stresses the projection of bad parts of the self into external objects in order to avoid psychotic confusions, in other words she sees the projective identification of the adult psychotic as the attempt to split off and project into a suitable external object those parts of the self which are unacceptable to the adult ego: the external object would then represent the patient's 'bad self'.

2 Dr Segal (1957) also stresses greater awareness and differentiation of the separateness between the ego and object in normal symbol formation. She thinks that symbolization is closely related to the development of the ego and the objects which occur in the depressive position. She emphasizes 'that symbols are in addition to other factors created in the internal world as a means of restoring, recreating, recapturing and owning again the original object. But in keeping with the increased reality sense, they are now felt as created by the ego and therefore never completely equated with the original object.'

3 The loss of the capacity for abstract and symbolic thinking of the schizophrenic patient, which leads on to very concrete modes of thinking, has been described by many writers such as Vigotsky, Goldstein and others. Harold Searles (1962) in his paper 'The differentiation between concrete and metaphorical thinking in the recovering schizophrenic patient' suggests that the concrete thought disorders depend on the fluidity of the ego boundaries when self and object are not clearly differentiated.

In one of his cases he describes 'abundant evidence of massive projection, not only on to human beings around him but also on to trees, animals, buildings and all sorts of inanimate objects'. Only when ego boundaries gradually become firmly established through treatment can figurative or symbolic thinking develop. Searles' observations have a close relationship to my own observation that excessive projective identification, leading to fusion between self and object, always causes loss of the capacity for symbolic and verbal thinking.

4 It is of course important to differentiate between a patient's rejection of the analyst's bad handling or misunderstanding, which would repeat a

bad feeding situation from the envious aggression of the child which occurs in a good setting. The latter is not only difficult for the primitive ego of the child to tolerate but creates a particularly difficult problem for any loving and caring mother.

References

Bion, W. (1962) *Learning from Experience*, London: Heinemann; paperback Maresfield Reprints, London: H. Karnac Books (1984).

——(1965) *Transformations*, London: Heinemann; paperback Maresfield Reprints, London: H. Karnac Books (1984).

Klein, M. (1946) 'Notes on some schizoid mechanisms' in M. Klein, P. Heimann, S. Isaacs, and J. Riviere *Developments in Psycho-Analysis*, London: Hogarth Press (1952) 292–320 (also in *The Writings of Melanie Klein* vol. 3, 1–24).

Jacobson, E. (1954) 'Contribution to the metapsychology of psychotic identifications', *Journal of the American Psychoanalytical Association*, 2.

——(1967) *Psychotic Conflict and Reality*, New York: International Universities Press.

Mahler, M. (1952) 'On child psychosis and schizophrenia. Autistic and symbiotic infantile psychoses', *Psychoanalytic Study of the Child*, 7.

——(1967) 'On human symbiosis and the vicissitudes of individuation', *Journal of the American Psychoanalytical Association*, 15, 4.

Meltzer, D. (1967) *The Psychoanalytic Process*, London: Heinemann.

Rosenfeld, H. (1964) 'Object relations of an acute schizophrenic patient in the transference situation' in *Recent Research on Schizophrenia*, Psychiatric Research Reports of the American Psychiatric Association.

——(1965) *Psychotic States: A Psychoanalytic Approach*, London: Hogarth Press.

——(1969) 'The Negative Therapeutic Reaction' in P. Giovacchini (ed.) *Tactics and Techniques in Psychoanalytic Theory* Vol. 2, New York: Jason Aronson (1975).

Searles, H. F. (1962) 'The differentiation between concrete and metaphorical thinking in the recovery of a schizophrenic patient', *Journal of the American Psychoanalytical Association*, 10.

Segal, H. (1950) 'Some aspects of the analysis of a schizophrenic', *International Journal of Psycho-Analysis*, 31, 268–78; also in *The Work of Hanna Segal*, New York: Jason Aronson (1981) 101–20.

Segal, H. (1957) 'Notes on symbol formation', *International Journal of Psycho-Analysis*, 38, 391–7; also in *The Work of Hanna Segal* and reprinted here, pp. 160–77.

4

Projective identification –
some clinical aspects

BETTY JOSEPH

This article is published in J. Sandler (ed.) *Projection, Identification, Projective Identification*, New York: International Universities Press, 1987.

The concept of projective identification was introduced into analytic thinking by Melanie Klein in 1946. Since then it has been welcomed, argued about, the name disputed, the links with projection pointed out, and so on; but one aspect seems to stand out above the firing line, and that is its considerable clinical value. It is this aspect that I shall mainly concentrate on today, and mainly in relation to the more neurotic patient.

Melanie Klein became aware of projective identification when exploring what she called the paranoid-schizoid position, that is, a constellation of a particular type of object relations, anxieties, and defences against them, typical for the earliest period of the individual's life and, in certain disturbed people, continuing throughout life. This particular position she saw as dominated by the infant's need to ward off anxieties and impulses by splitting both the object, originally the mother, and the self and projecting these split-off parts into an object, which will then be felt to be like, or identified with, these split-off parts, so colouring the infant's perception of the object and its subsequent introjection.

She discussed the manifold aims of different types of projective identification, for example, splitting off and getting rid of unwanted parts of the self that cause anxiety or pain; projecting the self or parts of the self into an object to dominate and control it and thus avoid any feelings of being separate; getting into an object to take over its capacities and make them its own; invading in order to damage or destroy the object. Thus the infant, or adult who goes on using such mechanisms powerfully, can avoid any awareness of separateness, dependence, admiration, or its concomitant sense of loss, anger, envy, etc. But it sets up anxieties of a persecutory type, claustrophobic, panics and the like.

We could say that, from the point of view of the individual who uses such mechanisms strongly, projective identification is a phantasy and yet it can have a powerful effect on the recipient. It does not always do so and when it does we cannot always tell how the effect is brought about, but we cannot doubt its importance. We can see, however, that the concept of projective identification, used in this way, is more object-related, more concrete and covers more aspects than the term projection would ordinarily imply, and it has opened up a whole area of analytic understanding. These various aspects I am going to discuss later, as we see them operating in our clinical work; here I want only to stress two points: first, the omnipotent power of these mechanisms and phantasies; second, how, in so far as they originate in a particular constellation, deeply interlocked, we cannot in our thinking isolate projective identification from the omnipotence, the splitting and the resultant anxieties that go along with it. Indeed, we shall see that they are all part of a balance, rigidly or precariously maintained by the individual, in his own individual way.

As the individual develops, either in normal development or through analytic treatment, these projections lessen, he becomes more able to tolerate his ambivalence, his love and hate and dependence on objects, in other words, he moves towards what Melanie Klein described as the depressive position. This process can be helped in infancy if the child has a supportive environment, if the mother is able to tolerate and contain the child's projections, intuitively to understand and stand its feelings. Bion elaborated and extended this aspect of Melanie Klein's work, suggesting the importance of the mother being able to be used as a container by the infant, and linking this with the process of communication in childhood and with the positive use of the counter-transference in analysis. Once the child is better integrated and able to recognize its impulses and feelings as its own, there will be a lessening in the pressure to project, accompanied by an increased concern for the object. In its earliest forms projective identification has no concern for the object, indeed it is often anti-concern, aimed at dominating, irrespective of the cost to the object. As the child moves towards the depressive position, this necessarily alters and, although projective identification is probably never entirely given up, it will no longer involve the complete splitting off and disowning of parts of the self, but will be less absolute, more temporary and more able to be drawn back into the individual's personality – and thus be the basis of empathy.

In this paper I want, first, to consider some further implications of the use of projective identification, and then to discuss and illustrate different aspects of projective identification, first in two patients more or less stuck in the paranoid-schizoid position, and then in a patient beginning to move towards the depressive position.

To begin with: some of the implications, clinical and technical, of the massive use of projective identification as we see it in our work. Sometimes it is used so massively that we get the impression that the patient is, in phantasy, projecting his whole self into his object and may feel trapped or claustrophobic. It is, in any case, a very powerful and effective way of ridding the individual of contact with his own mind; at times the mind can be so weakened or so fragmented by splitting processes or so evacuated by projective identification that the individual appears empty or quasi-psychotic. This I shall show with C, the case of a child. It also has important technical implications; for example, bearing in mind that projective identification is only one aspect of an omnipotent balance established by each individual in his own way, an interpretative attempt on the part of the analyst to locate and give back to the patient missing parts of the self must of necessity be resisted by the total personality, since it is felt to threaten the whole balance and lead to more disturbance. I shall discuss this in case T. Projective identification cannot be seen in isolation.

A further clinical implication that I should like to touch on is about communication. Bion demonstrated how projective identification can be used as a method of communication by the individual putting, as it were, undigested parts of his experience and inner world into the object, originally the mother, now the analyst, as a way of getting them understood and returned in a more manageable form. But we might add to this that projective identification is, by its very nature, a kind of communication, even in cases where this is not its aim or its intention. By definition projective identification means the putting of parts of the self into an object. If the analyst on the receiving end is really open to what is going on and able to be aware of what he is experiencing, this can be a powerful method of gaining under-standing. Indeed, much of our current appreciation of the richness of the notion of counter-transference stems from it. I shall later try to indicate some of the problems this raises, in terms of acting-in, in my discussion of the third case, N.

140

I want now to give a brief example of a case to illustrate the concreteness of projective identification in the analytic situation, its effectiveness as a method of ridding the child of a whole area of experience and thus keeping some kind of balance, and the effect of such massive projective mechanisms on her state of mind. This is a little girl aged 4, in analytic treatment with Mrs Elizabeth Da Rocha Barros, who was discussing the case with me. The child had only very recently begun treatment, a deeply disturbed and neglected child, whom I shall call C.

A few minutes before the end of a Friday session C said that she was going to make a candle; the analyst explained her wish to take a warm Mrs Barros with her that day at the end of the session and her fear that there would not be enough time, as there were only three minutes left. C started to scream, saying that she would have some spare candles; she then started to stare through the window with a vacant, lost expression. The analyst interpreted that the child needed to make the analyst realize how awful it was to end the session, as well as expressing a wish to take home some warmth from the analyst's words for the weekend. The child screamed: 'Bastard! Take off your clothes and jump outside.' Again the analyst tried to interpret C's feelings about being dropped and sent into the cold. C replied: 'Stop your talking, take off your clothes. You are cold. I'm not cold.' The feeling in the session was extremely moving. Here the words carry the concrete meaning, to the child, of the separation of the weekend – the awful coldness. This she tries to force into the analyst and it is felt to have been concretely achieved. 'You are cold, I am not cold.'

The moments when C looked completely lost and vacant, as in this fragment, were very frequent and were, I think, indicative not only of her serious loss of contact with reality, but of the emptiness, vacantness of her mind and personality when projective identification was operating so powerfully. I think that much of her screaming is also in the nature of her emptying out. The effectiveness of such emptying is striking, ·as the whole experience of loss and its concomitant emotions is cut out. One can again see here how the term 'projective identification' describes more vividly and fully the processes involved than the more general and frequently used terms, such as 'reversal' or, as I said, 'projection'.

In this example, then, the child's balance is primarily maintained by the projecting out of parts of the self. I want now to give an example of a familiar kind of case to discuss various kinds of projective identification working together to hold a particular narcissistic omnipotent balance. This kind of balance is very firmly structured, extremely difficult to influence analytically and leads to striking persecutory anxieties. It also raises some points about different identificatory processes and problems about the term 'projective identification' itself.

A young teacher, whom I shall call T, came into analysis with difficulties in relationships, but actually with the hope of changing careers and becoming an analyst. His daily material consisted very largely of descriptions of work he had done in helping his pupils, how his colleagues had praised his work, asked him to discuss their work with him, and so on. Little else came into the sessions. He frequently described how one or other of his colleagues felt threatened by him, threatened in the sense of feeling minimized or put in an inferior position by his greater insight and understanding. He was, therefore, uneasy that they felt unfriendly to him at any given moment. (Any idea that his personality might actually put people off did not enter his mind.) It was not difficult to show him certain ideas about myself – for example, that when I did not seem to be encouraging him to give up his career and apply for training as an analyst, he felt that I, being old, felt threatened by this intelligent young person coming forward, and, therefore, would not want him in my professional area.

Clearly, simply to suggest, or interpret, that T was projecting his envy into his objects and then feeling them as identified with this part of himself might be theoretically accurate, but clinically inept and useless; indeed it would just be absorbed into his psychoanalytic armoury. We can see that the projective identification of the envious parts of the self was, as it were, only the end result of one aspect of a highly complex balance which he was keeping. To clarify something of the nature of this balance, it is important to see how T was relating to me in the transference. Usually he spoke of me as a very fine analyst and I was flattered in such ways. Actually he could not take in interpretations meaningfully, he appeared not to listen properly; he would, for example, hear the words partially and then re-interpret them unconsciously, according to some previous theoretical and psychoanalytical knowledge, then give them to himself with this slightly altered and generalized meaning. Frequently, when I interpreted more firmly, he would respond very quickly and argumentatively, as if there were a minor explosion which seemed destined, not only to expel from his mind what I might be going to say, but enter my mind and break up my thinking at that moment.

In this example we have projective identification operating with various different motives and leading to different identificatory processes – but all aimed at maintaining his narcissistic omnipotent balance. First we see the splitting of his objects – I am flattered and kept in his mind as idealized; at such moments the bad or unhelpful aspect of myself is quite split off, even though I don't seem to be achieving much with him; but this latter has to be denied. He projects part of himself into my mind and takes over; he 'knows' what I am going to say and says it himself. At this point, a part of the self is identified with an idealized aspect of myself, which is talking to, interpreting to, an idealized patient part of himself; idealized because it listens to the analyst part of him. We can see what this movement achieves in terms of his balance. It cuts out any real relationship between the patient and myself, between analyst and patient, as mother and child, as a feeding couple. It obviates any separate existence, any relating to me as myself; any relationship in which he takes in directly from me. T was, in fact, earlier in his life slightly anorexic. If I manage for a moment to get through this T explodes, so that his mental digestive system is fragmented, and by this verbal explosion, as I said, T unconsciously tries to enter my mind and break up my thinking, my capacity to feed him. It is important here, as always with projective identification, to distinguish this kind of unconscious entering, invading and breaking up from a conscious aggressive attack. What I am discussing here is how these patients, using projective identification so omnipotently, actually avoid any such feelings as dependence, envy, jealousy, etc.

Once T has in phantasy entered my mind and taken over my interpretations, and my role at that moment, I notice that he has 'added to', 'improved on', 'enriched' my interpretations, and I become the onlooker, who should realize that my interpretations of a few moments ago were not as rich as his are now – and surely I should feel threatened by this young man in my room! Thus the two types of projective identification are working in harmony, the invading of my mind and taking over its contents and the projecting of the potentially dependent, threatened and envious part of the self into me. This is, of course, mirrored in what we hear is going on in his outside world – the fellow students who ask for help and feel threatened by his brilliance – but then he feels persecuted by their potential unfriendliness. So long as the balance holds so effectively, we cannot see what more subtle, sensitive, and important aspects of the personality are being kept split off, or why – we can see that any relationship to a truly separate object is obviated – with all that this may imply.

A great difficulty is, of course, that all insight tends to get drawn into this process; to give a minute example: one Monday, T really seemed to become aware of exactly how he was subtly taking the meaning out of what I was saying and not letting real understanding develop. For a moment he felt relief and then a brief, deep feeling of hatred to me emerged into consciousness. A second later he added quietly that he was thinking how the way that he had been feeling just then towards me, that is, the hatred, must have been how his fellow students had felt towards him on the previous day when he had been talking and explaining things to them! So, immediately that T has a real experience of hating me because I have said something useful, he uses the momentary awareness to speak about the students, and distances himself from the emerging envy and hostility, and the direct receptive contact between the two of us is again lost. What looks like insight is no longer insight but has become a complex projective manoeuvre.

At a period when these problems were very much in the forefront of the analysis, T brought a dream, right at the end of a session. The dream was simply this: T was with the analyst or with a woman, J, or it might have been both, he was excitedly pushing his hand up her knickers into her vagina, thinking that if he could get right in there would be no stopping him. Here, I think under the pressure of the analytic work going on, T's great need and great excitement were to get totally inside the object, with all its implications, including, of course, the annihilation of the analytic situation.

To return to the concept of projective identification; with this patient I have indicated three or four different aspects: attacking the analyst's mind; a kind of total invading, as in the dream fragment I have just quoted; a more partial invading and taking over aspects or capacities of the analyst; and finally putting parts of the self, particularly inferior parts, into the analyst. The latter two are mutually dependent, but lead to different types of identification. In the one, the patient, in taking over, becomes identified with the analyst's idealized capacities; in the other, it is the analyst who becomes identified with the lost, projected, here inferior or envious parts of the patient. I think it is partly because the term is broad and covers many aspects that there has been some unease about the name itself.

I have so far discussed projective identification in two cases caught up in the paranoid-schizoid position, a borderline child and a man in a rigid omnipotent narcissistic state. Now I want to discuss aspects of projective identification as one sees it in a patient moving towards the depressive position. I shall illustrate some points from the case of a man as he was becoming less rigid, more integrated, better able to tolerate what was previously projected, but constantly also pulling back, returning to the use of the earlier projective mechanisms; then I want to show the effect of this on subsequent identifications and the light that it throws on previous identifications. I also want to attempt to forge a link between the nature of the patient's residual use of projective identification and its early infantile counterpart and the relation of this to phobia formation. I bring this material also to discuss briefly the communicative nature of projective identification.

To start with this latter point, as I said earlier, since projective identification, by its very nature means the putting of parts of the self into the object, in the transference we are of necessity on the receiving end of the projections and, therefore, providing we can tune into them, we have an opportunity par excellence to understand them and what is going on. In this sense, it acts as a communication, whatever its motivation, and is the basis for the positive use of counter-transference. As I want to describe with this patient, N, it is frequently difficult to clarify whether, at any given moment, projective identification is primarily aimed at communicating a state of mind that cannot be verbalized by the patient or whether it is aimed more at entering and controlling or attacking the analyst, or whether all these elements are active and need consideration.

A patient, N, who had been in analysis many years, had recently married and, after a few weeks, was becoming anxious about his sexual interest and his potency, particularly in view of the fact that his wife was considerably younger. He came on a Monday, saying that he felt that 'the thing' was never really going to get right, 'the sexual thing', yes, they did have sex on Sunday, but somehow he had to force himself and he knew it wasn't quite all right, and his wife noticed this and commented. It was an all-right kind of weekend, just about. He spoke about this a bit more and explained that they went to a place outside London, to a party; they had meant to stay the night in an hotel nearby, but couldn't find anywhere nice enough and came home and so were late. What was being conveyed to me was a quiet, sad discomfort, leading to despair, and I pointed out to N how he was conveying an awful long-term hopelessness and despair, with no hope for the future. He replied to the effect that he supposed that he was feeling left out, and linked this with what had been a rather helpful and vivid session on the Friday, but now, as he made the remark, it was quite dead and flat. When I tried to look at this with him, he agreed, commenting that he supposed he was starting to attack the analysis, etc.

The feeling in the session now was awful; N was making a kind of sense and saying analytic things himself, which could have been right, for example about the Friday, and which one could have picked up, but, since they seemed flat and quite unhelpful to him, what he seemed to me to be doing was putting despair into me, not only about the reality of his marriage and potency, but also about his analysis, as was indicated, for example, by the useless, and by now somewhat irrelevant, comment about being left out. N denied my interpretation about his despair about the progress of the analysis, but in such a way, it seemed to me, as to be encouraging me to make false interpretations and to pick up his pseudo-interpretations as if I believed in them, while knowing that they and we were getting nowhere. He vaguely talked about this, went quiet and said: 'I was listening to your voice, the timbre changes in different voices. W (his wife), being younger, makes more sounds per second, older voices are deeper because they make less sounds per second, etc.' I showed N his great fear that I showed with my voice, rather than through my actual words, that I could not stand the extent of his hopelessness and his doubts about myself, about what we could achieve in the analysis and, therefore, in his life, and that I would cheat and in some way try to encourage. I queried whether he had perhaps felt that, in that session, my voice had changed in order to sound more encouraging and encouraged, rather than contain the despair he was expressing. By this part of the session my patient had got into contact and said with some relief that, if I did do this kind of encouraging, the whole bottom would fall out of the analysis.

First, the nature of the communication, which I could understand primarily through my counter-transference, through the way in which I was being pushed and pulled to feel and to react. We see here the concrete quality of projective identification structuring the counter-transference. It seems that the way N was speaking was not asking me to try to understand the sexual difficulties or unhappiness, but to invade me with despair, while at the same time unconsciously trying to force me to reassure myself that it was all right, that interpretations, now empty of meaning and hollow, were meaningful, and that the analysis at that moment was going ahead satisfactorily. Thus it was not only the despair that N was projecting into me, but his defences against it, a false reassurance and denial, which it was intended I should act out with him. I think that this also suggests a projective identification of an internal figure, probably primarily mother, who was felt to be weak, kind, but unable to stand up to emotion. In the transference (to over-simplify the picture) this figure is projected into me, and I find myself pushed to live it out.

We have here the important issue of teasing out the motivation for this projective identification: was it aimed primarily at communicating something to me; was there a depth of despair that we had not previously sufficiently understood; or was the forcing of despair into me motivated by something different? At this stage, at the end of the session, I did not know and left it open.

I have so much condensed the material here that I cannot convey adequately the atmosphere and to and fro of the session. But towards the end, as I have tried to show, my patient experienced and expressed relief and appreciation of what had been going on. There was a shift in mood and behaviour as my patient started to accept understanding and face the nature of his forcing into me, and he could then experience me as an object that could stand up to his acting in, not get caught into it, but contain it. He could then identify temporarily with a stronger object, and he himself became firmer. I also sensed some feeling of concern about what he had been doing to me and my work – it was not openly acknowledged and expressed – but there is some movement towards the depressive position with its real concern and guilt.

To clarify the motivation as well as the effect of this kind of projective identification on subsequent introjective identification, we need to go briefly into the beginning of the next session, when N brought a dream, in which he was on a boat like a ferry boat, on a grey-green sea surrounded by mist; he did not know where they were going. Then nearby there was another boat which was clearly going down under the water and drowning. He stepped on to this boat as it went down. He did not feel wet or afraid, which was puzzling. Amongst his associations we heard of his wife being very gentle and affectionate, but he added that he himself was concerned; was she behind this really making more demands on him? She, knowing his fondness for steak and kidney pudding, had made him one the night before. It was excellent, but the taste was too strong, which he told her!

Now the interesting thing, I think, was that, on the previous day I had felt rather at sea, as I said, not knowing exactly where we were going, but I was clear that the understanding about the hopelessness and the defences against it was right, and, though I had not thought it out in this way, my belief would have been that the mists would clear as we went on. But what does my patient do with this? He gratuitously steps off this boat (this understanding) on to one that is going down, and he is not afraid! In other words, he prefers to drown in despair rather than clarify it, prefers to see affection as demands, and my decent, well-cooked steak and kidney inter-pretations as too tasty. At this point, as we worked on it, N could see that the notion of drowning here was actually exciting to him.

Now we can see more about the motivation. It becomes clear that N was not just trying to communicate and get understood something about his despair, important as this element is, but that he was also attacking me and our work, by trying to drag me down by the despair, when there was actually progress. After a session in which he expressed appreciation about my work and capacity to stand up to him, he dreamt of willingly stepping on to a sinking boat, so that either, internally, I collude and go down with him or am forced to watch him go under and my hope is destroyed and I am kept impotent to help. This activity also leads to an introjective identification with an analyst-parent who is felt to be down, joyless and impotent, and this identification contributes considerably to his lack of sexual confidence and potency. Following this period of the analysis, there was real improvement in the symptom.

Naturally these considerations lead one to think about the nature of the patient's internal objects, for example, the weak mother, that I described as being projected into me in the transference. How much is this figure based on N's real experience with his mother, how much did he exploit her weaknesses and thus contribute to building in his inner world a mother, weak, inadequate and on the defensive, as we saw in the transference? In other words, when we talk of an object projected on to the analyst in the transference, we are discussing an internal object that has been structured in part from the child's earlier projective identifications, and the whole process can be seen being revived in the transference.

I want now to digress and look at this material from a slightly different angle, related to the patient's very early history and anxieties. I have shown how N pulls back and goes into an object, in the dream, into the sinking boat, as in the first session he goes into despair, which is then projected into me, rather than his thinking about it. This going into an object, acted out in the session, is, I believe, linked with a more total type of projective identification that I indicated in the sexual dream of T, and referred to briefly at the beginning of this paper, as being connected with phobia formation. At the very primitive end of projective identification is the attempt to get back into an object, to become, as it were, undifferentiated and mindless and thus avoid all pain. Most human beings develop beyond this in early infancy; some of our patients attempt to use projective identification in this way over many years. N, when he came into analysis, came because he had a fetish, a tremendous pull towards getting inside a rubber object which would totally cover, absorb, and excite him. In his early childhood he had nightmares of falling out of a globe into endless space. In the early period of analysis he would have severe panic states when alone in the house, and would be seriously disturbed or lose contact if he had to be away from London on business. At the same time there are minor indications of anxieties about being trapped in a claustrophobic way, for example, at night he would have to keep blankets on the bed loose or throw them off altogether; in intercourse phantasies emerged of his penis being cut off and lost inside the woman's body. As the analysis went on, the fetishistic activities disappeared and real relationships improved, and the projecting of the self into the object could clearly be seen in the transference. He would get absorbed in his own words or ideas or in the sound of my words and my speaking, and the meaning would be unimportant compared with the concrete nature of the experience. This type of absorption into words and sounds, with the analyst, as a person, quite disregarded, is not unlike the kind of process that one sometimes sees in child patients, who come into the playroom, on to the couch, and fall so deeply asleep that they are unable to be woken by interpretations. It is, therefore, interesting to see in N how he has always concretely attempted to get into an object, apparently largely in order to escape from being outside, to become absorbed and free from relating and from thought and mental pain. And yet we know that this is only half the story, since the object he mainly got into was a fetish and highly sexualized. And still in the modern dream of getting into the drowning boat there was masochistic excitement that he tried to pull me into and in this sense it needs to be compared with T. I described how, as his constant invading and taking over was being analysed, we could see in T's sexual dream an attempt totally to get inside me with great excitement. I suspect there is much yet to be teased out about the relation between certain types of massive projective identification of the self and erotization.

Now I want to return to the material that I quoted and to the question of projective identification in patients who are becoming more integrated and nearer to the depressive position. We can see in the case of N, unlike T who is still imprisoned in his own omnipotent, narcissistic structure, that there is now a movement, in the transference, towards more genuine whole object relations. At times he can really appreciate the strong containing qualities of his object; true he will then try to draw me in and drag me down again, but there is now potential conflict about this. The object can be valued and loved, at times he can consciously experience hostility about this, and ambivalence is present. As his loving is freed, he is able to introject and identify with a whole valued and potent object, and the effect on his character and potency is striking. This is a very different quality of identification from that based on forcing despairing parts of the self into an object, which then in his phantasy

149

becomes like a despairing part of himself. It is very different from the type of identification we saw in T, where the patient invaded my mind and took over the split and idealized aspects, leaving the object, myself, denuded and inferior. With N, in the example I have just given, he could experience and value me as a whole, different and properly separate person with my own qualities, and these he could introject and thereby feel strengthened. But we still have a task ahead, to enable N to be truly outside and able to give up the analysis, aware of its meaning to him and yet secure.

Summary

I have tried in this paper to discuss projective identification as we see it operating in our clinical work. I have described various types of projective identification, from the more primitive and massive type to the more empathic and mature. I have discussed how we see alterations in its manifestation as progress is made in treatment and the patient moves towards the depressive position, is better integrated and able to use his objects less omnipotently, relate to them as separate objects and introject them and their qualities more fully and realistically, and thus also to separate from them.

PART THREE

On thinking

Introduction

In her earliest work Klein was very much interested in the
epistemophilic instinct and in the way children's anxieties interfered
with their intellectual curiosity (Klein 1921, 1928). Her investigation
of these anxieties, which she thought were basically caused by
phantasies of exploring the inside of the mother's body and
destroying its contents, led her on to the work she reported in *The
Psycho-Analysis of Children* (1932). After that she gave no further
attention to the idea of an epistemophilic instinct and, with the
exception of one paper on symbolism, she did not make thinking and
disorders of thought a central theme of her later work, at least not
explicitly. But two of her ideas were important starting points of
later work on thinking. One was her theory about symbols (1930),
the second the idea of projective identification (1946). Her idea about
symbols is that interest in the original object, the mother's body, is
repressed and displaced to objects in the external world. If anxiety
about the mother's body is too acute because of phantasied attacks
upon it, no displacement takes place and symbol formation comes to
a standstill.

In an outstanding paper on symbol formation developed from
Klein's work on symbolism, Hanna Segal distinguished between
symbol formation in the paranoid-schizoid position, which she
called symbolic equation, and symbol formation in the depressive
position, which she called symbol proper (Segal 1957, reprinted
here, pp. 160–77). In symbolic equations, the symbol is confused
with the object to the point of *being* the object; her example is a
psychotic man who could not play the violin because it meant
masturbating in public. In such a state of mind the ego is confused

with the object through projective identification; it is the ego which creates the symbol; therefore the symbol is also confused with the object. In the depressive position, where there is greater awareness of differentiation and separateness between ego and object and recognition of ambivalence towards the object, the symbol, a creation of the ego, is recognized as separate from the object. It *represents* the object instead of being equated with it, and it becomes available for use to displace aggression and libido away from the original objects to others, as Klein described in her symbolism paper.

True symbols, as distinct from symbolic equations (also often referred to as 'concrete symbols'), are thus the precipitate of the mourning intrinsic to the depressive position, of the recognition of the independent existence of the object. In her paper on phantasy (1964b) Segal describes the process by which unconscious phantasies are used as hypotheses (preconceptions in Bion's phrasing) to be tested against reality, so leading to discrimination between internal and external reality and laying the foundation for thinking and the use of symbols proper.

In a remarkable series of papers and books Bion uses the idea of projective identification as a central concept in developing a theory of thinking that has had a profound effect on the conceptual and technical repertoire of all Kleinian analysts (1962a (reprinted here) 1962b, 1963, 1965, 1967 (reprinted in volume 2 of the present work), 1970). In this body of work Bion suggests three models for understanding the process of thinking.

The first model is similar to Segal's idea of an unconscious phantasy being used as a hypothesis for testing against reality. In Bion's formulation of it, a pre-conception, of, for example, a breast, is mated with a realization, that is, an actual breast, which gives rise to a conception, which is a form of thought.

In the second model, a pre-conception encounters a negative realization, a frustration, that is, no breast available for satisfaction. What happens next depends on the infant's capacity to stand frustration. Klein had pointed out that in earliest experience an absent, frustrating object is felt to be a bad object. Bion took this idea further. If the infant's capacity for enduring frustration is great, the 'no-breast' perception/experience is transformed into a thought, which helps to endure the frustration and makes it possible to use the 'no-breast' thought for thinking, that is, to make contact with, and stand, his persecution and then split it off when the external breast arrives again. Gradually this capacity evolves into an ability to imagine that the bad feeling of being frustrated is actually occurring because there is a good object which is absent but which may return.

If, however, capacity for frustration is low, the 'no-breast' experience does not develop into the thought of a 'good breast absent'; it exists as a 'bad breast present'; it is felt to be a bad concrete object which must be got rid of by evacuation, that is, by omnipotent projection. If this process becomes entrenched, true symbols and thinking cannot develop.

The third model came to be called the formulation of the container and the contained (Bion 1962b). (An elegantly concise description of this model is given in Edna O'Shaughnessy's paper 'W. R. Bion's theory of thinking and new techniques in child analysis' (1981b), reprinted in volume 2 of the present work.) In this model the infant has some sort of sensory perception, need, or feeling which to him feels bad and which he wants to get rid of. He behaves in a way 'reasonably calculated to arouse in the mother feelings of which the infant wishes to be rid' (Bion 1962a). This type of projective identification is thus 'realistic'; it is not only an omnipotent phantasy, but leads to behaviour that arouses the same sort of feeling in the mother. If the mother is reasonably well-balanced and capable of what Bion calls 'reverie', she can accept and transform the feelings into a tolerable form which the infant can reintroject. This process of transformation Bion calls 'alpha function'. If all goes reasonably well, the infant reintrojects not only the particular bad thing transformed into something tolerable, but eventually he introjects the function itself, and thus has the embryonic means within his own mind for tolerating frustration and for thinking. Symbolization, a 'contact barrier' between conscious and unconscious, dream thoughts, concepts of space and time can develop.

The process can, of course, go wrong, either because of the mother's incapacity for reverie or the infant's envy and intolerance of the mother being able to do what he cannot. If the object cannot or will not contain projections, the individual resorts to increasingly forceful projective identification. Reintrojection is effected with similar force. Through such forceful reintrojection the individual develops within himself an internal object that will not accept projections, that is felt to strip the individual greedily of all the goodness he takes in, that is omniscient, moralizing, uninterested in truth and reality testing. With this wilfully misunderstanding internal object the individual identifies and the stage may be set for psychosis.

Of all Bion's ideas, the notions of container and contained and alpha function have been the most widely accepted and more or less well understood. Their adoption has led to a less pejorative attitude towards patients' use of projective identification and to a better ˙

conceptualization of the distinction between normal and pathological projective identification. The container/contained model of the development of thinking has lessened the divide between emotion and cognition, for it is as much concerned with describing how emotions become meaningful as with describing a model of how the capacity to think develops (cf. Thorner 1981a and b). Further, to Bion the external object is an integral part of the system. Klein has often been accused, wrongly I think, of paying no attention to the environment. Bion's formulation shows not just *that* the environment is important, but *how* it is important.

In 'A theory of thinking', and indeed in his later work, Bion did not do as much as he might have to link his three models. It is surely repeated experiences of alternations between positive and negative realizations that encourage the development of thoughts and thinking. And the return of an absent mother gives rise to a particularly important instance, repeated many times in childhood (and in an analysis), of a mother taking in and transforming, or failing to transform, the bad-breast-present experience.

In subsequent work (1962b) Bion further elaborates the model of container/contained and thinking as an emotional experience of getting to know oneself or another person, which he designates as 'K', in distinction from the more usual psychoanalytic preoccupations with love (L) and hate (H). He also describes the evasion of knowing and truth, which he calls 'minus K'. He says that K is as essential for psychic health as food is for physical well-being. In other words, K is synonymous with Klein's epistemophilic instinct, though in a more elaborated form.

In subsequent work (1963) Bion develops the idea of the 'Grid', an instrument for use not in sessions, where any conscious theoretical preoccupation intrudes on the analyst's receptiveness, but afterwards where deliberate conscious thinking can be constructive. The horizontal axis of the grid represents the uses to which thoughts may be put; the vertical axis of the grid represents genetic growth in sophistication and abstractness. Few analysts I know have systematically used the grid to examine their clinical material after sessions in the fashion Bion recommends. Most have used it as a method of understanding Bion's own ideas. But that is not to say it has not influenced the way Kleinian analysts work and think. It is typical to find that one person has been much influenced by the idea of the 'definitory hypothesis', another by lying and its relation to 'Column 2' (use of false thoughts to deny the dangerous unknown); another puzzles over the relation of 'myth' to 'pre-conceptions', and so forth. In other words, few analysts use the grid as a whole but nearly everyone finds aspects of it useful in his or her thinking.

Bion also develops the idea of fluctuation between the paranoid-schizoid and depressive positions, which he represents by the sign Ps<---->D, as a factor in the development of thinking (1963). This movement back and forth from the paranoid-schizoid to the depressive position was originally pointed out by Klein herself, but Bion focuses on the dimension of dispersal/disintegration (Ps) on the one hand and integration (D) on the other, ignoring for the time being the other elements of the paranoid-schizoid and depressive constellations as described by Klein. This emphasis has helped many analysts to look for moment-to-moment shifts in a session from integration and depression towards fragmentation and persecution and back again rather than looking for major shifts of character and orientation. Further, Bion's formulation draws attention to the positive aspects of the paranoid-schizoid chaos, to the need to be able to face the possibility of a catastrophic feeling of disintegration and meaninglessness. If one cannot tolerate the dispersal and threatened meaninglessness of the paranoid-schizoid position, one is likely to push towards integration prematurely or to hold on to a particular state of integration and meaning past its time (cf. Eigen 1985).

In later work (1965 and 1970) Bion discusses in some detail the idea of there being an essential unknowable truth, which he calls 'O', in every session which both analyst and patient dread because they feel the experience of it to be catastrophic. He emphasizes that one cannot know or master this reality, one can only 'be' it – a statement based on an earlier distinction between using thinking to learn from experience and using thinking to increase the learner's store of acquired knowledge without producing any change in himself. In the face of the unknowable and frightening 'O', Bion advocates 'faith' (F), by which he means a willingness by the analyst to abandon his usual props in order to approach the 'O' of the session as closely as possible. He suggests that the analyst should eschew 'memory', that is, attempts to hold on to what he knows about his patient or about psychoanalytic theories, and, equally, that he should give up 'desire', meaning future aspirations for his patient or himself, in order to concentrate fully on the immediate unknowable reality. (See 'Notes on memory and desire', 1967, reprinted in volume 2 of the present work and see also *Attention and Interpretation*, 1970.)

Reaction to these injunctions has been mixed. A few analysts are entranced by the idea of eradicating memory and desire. Some angrily repudiate the notions of 'O' and 'F' as mystical nonsense. Others agree with the idea of catastrophe inhering in apprehension of reality and truth and with the idea of abstaining from memory and desire, though most of the analysts I have talked to feel that a really conscientious attempt to eradicate memory and desire would lead the analyst into a psychotic state. These cautious abrogators of memory and desire are doubtful about the enthusiastic exponents, thinking that too uncritical an adoption of the ideas of 'O' and 'F' and doing away with memory and desire can turn into an idealization of ignorance and indolence.

This notion of a dreaded state of catastrophe as a basic and continuous aspect of human experience is one that was also fundamental in the work of Esther Bick, She did not think of her work on it as being a contribution to the theory of thinking, but at the same time she presents this sense of catastrophe as the ultimate and basic experience which is both the focus of existence and the thing that everyone uses thought and thinking to evade. She thought of the central catastrophe as a primary infantile experience of unintegration; but she emphasizes its continuation into adult life, and her descriptions of it are consistent with Bion's conception of 'O', of unintegration, in the encounter with truth, but where Bick emphasizes catastrophe as a primary infantile experience, Bion emphasizes catastrophe as inhering in the encounter with truth. Bick's idea is that catastrophe is experienced as falling apart, falling endlessly into space, or as one's insides liquefying and pouring out uncontrollably. She thinks the response to this anxiety is a desperate use of all the senses to hold the self together – focusing on bright objects, on sounds, on being held, on the feeling of the nipple in the mouth; later on some form of activity and movement and thinking itself may serve this function of holding the self together. Her descriptions give extraordinarily vivid meaningfulness to the facts of infant observation as well as to patients' material. She used the term 'adhesive identification' to describe a form of holding oneself together by an attachment to the object in which there is no projection, no introjection, only 'sticking' followed by psychic damage and tearing apart when individual and object are separated. In this very primitive level of thinking and experiencing there is no concept of depth; it is a two-dimensional world. She put some of these ideas into her very brief paper 'The experience of the skin in early object relations' (1968, reprinted here, pp. 187–91). Meltzer has found her version of the idea of adhesive identification useful in studying autistic children (Meltzer 1975). But Bick herself did not write about her ideas further and, in my view, did not really make an effective conceptual link between adhesive identification, projection, and introjection.

Thus Segal has developed Klein's idea of symbolism, showing

how crucially true symbolism is linked to the depressive position, and Bion has developed Klein's idea of projective identification, showing how normal projective identification is essential to the development of realistic thinking and how thought disorders are pervaded by pathological projective identification. Both have immeasurably enriched the Kleinian reservoir of clinical understanding and theoretical formulations.

1

Notes on symbol formation

HANNA SEGAL

This article was originally a paper read at the meeting of the Medical Section of the British Psychological Society in May 1955, based on an earlier paper presented at a Symposium on Symbolism at St Anne's House, London, in November 1954, and was first published in the *International Journal of Psycho-Analysis*, 38, 391–7. The postscript, 1979, was first published in *The Work of Hanna Segal*, New York: Jason Aronson (1981) 60–5.

The understanding and interpretation of unconscious symbolism is one of the main tools of the psychologist. Often he is faced with the task of understanding and recognizing the meaning not only of a particular symbol but also of the whole process of symbol formation. This applies particularly to work with patients who show a disturbance or inhibition in the formation or free use of symbols, as for instance, psychotic or schizoid patients.

To give a very elementary example from two patients. One – whom I will call A – was a schizophrenic in a mental hospital. He was once asked by his doctor why it was that since his illness he had stopped playing the violin. He replied with some violence: 'Why? do you expect me to masturbate in public?'

Another patient, B, dreamt one night that he and a young girl were playing a violin duet. He had associations to fiddling, masturbating, etc., from which it emerged clearly that the violin represented his genital and playing the violin represented a masturbation phantasy of a relation with the girl.

Here then are two patients who apparently use the same symbols in the same situation – a violin representing the male genital, and playing the violin representing masturbation. The way in which the symbols function, however, is very different. For A, the violin had become so completely equated with his genital that to touch it in public became impossible. For B, playing the violin in his waking life was an important sublimation. We might say that the main difference between them is that for A the symbolic meaning of the violin was conscious, for B unconscious. I do not think, however, that this was the most important difference between the two patients. In the case of B, the fact that the meaning of the dream became completely conscious had in no way prevented him from using his violin. In A, on the other hand, there were many symbols operating in his unconscious in the same way in which the violin was used on the conscious level.

Taking another example – this time from a schizophrenic patient in an analytical situation: One session, in the first weeks of his analysis, he came in blushing and giggling, and throughout the session would not talk to me. Subsequently we found out that previous to this hour he had been attending an occupational therapy class in which he was doing carpentry, making a stool. The reason for his silence, blushing, and giggling was that he could not bring himself to talk to me about the work he was doing. For him, the wooden stool on which he was working, the word 'stool' which he would have to use in connexion with it, and the stool he passed in the lavatory were so completely felt as one and the same thing that he was unable to talk to me about it. His subsequent analysis revealed that this equation of the three 'stools', the word, the chair, and the faeces, was at the time completely unconscious. All he was consciously aware of was that he was embarrassed and could not talk to me.

The main difference between the first and second patient quoted in their use of the violin as the symbol for the male genital was not that in the one case the symbol was conscious and in the other unconscious, but that in the first case it was felt to *be* the genital, and in the second to *represent* it.

According to Ernest Jones's (1916) definition, the violin of A, the schizophrenic, would be considered a symbol. Similarly in the dream of B. But it would not be a symbol in B's waking life when it was used in sublimation.

In his paper written in 1916 (Jones 1916), Jones differentiated unconscious symbolism from other forms of 'indirect representation', and made the following statements about true unconscious symbolism:

(i) A symbol represents what has been repressed from consciousness, and the whole process of symbolization is carried on unconsciously.

161

(ii) All symbols represent ideas of 'the self and of immediate blood relations and of the phenomena of birth, life and death'.

(iii) A symbol has a constant meaning. Many symbols can be used to represent the same repressed idea, but a given symbol has a constant meaning which is universal.

(iv) Symbolism arises as the result of intra-psychic conflict between the 'repressing tendencies and the repressed'. Further: 'Only what is repressed is symbolized; only what is repressed needs to be symbolized'.

He further distinguishes between sublimation and symbolization. 'Symbols', he says, 'arise when the affect investing the symbolized idea has not, as far as the symbol is concerned, proved capable of that modification in quality which is denoted by the term sublimation.'

Summarizing Jones's points, one might say that when a desire has to be given up because of conflict and repressed, it may express itself in a symbolical way, and the object of the desire which had to be given up can be replaced by a symbol.

Further analytical work, and particularly play analysis with young children, has fully confirmed some main points of Jones's formulation. The child's first interests and impulses are directed to his parents' bodies and his own, and it is those objects and impulses existing in the unconscious which give rise to all further interests by way of symbolization. Jones's statement, however, that symbols are formed where there is no sublimation soon gave rise to disagreement. In fact, Jones himself as well as Freud wrote many interesting papers analysing the content of works of art. In 1923, in her paper 'The role of the school in libidinal development' (Klein 1923), Melanie Klein did not agree with this view on the relation between symbolization and sublimation. She tried to show that children's play – a sublimated activity – is a symbolic expression of anxieties and wishes.

We might consider it as a question of terminology, and accept Jones's view that we should call symbols only those substitutes which replace the object without any change of affect. On the other hand, there are very great advantages in extending the definition to cover symbols used in sublimation. In the first place the wider definition corresponds better to common linguistic usage. Jones's concept excludes most of that which is called 'symbol' in other sciences and in everyday language. Secondly, and I shall elaborate this point later, there seems to be a continuous development from the primitive symbols as described by Jones to the symbols used in self-expression, communication, discovery, creation, etc. Thirdly, it is difficult to establish a connexion between the early primitive desires and processes in the mind and the later development of the individual, unless the wider concept of symbolism is admitted. In the analytical view, the child's interest in the external world is determined by a series of displacements of affect and interests from the earliest to ever new objects. And, indeed, how could such a displacement be achieved otherwise than by way of symbolization?

In 1930, Melanie Klein (Klein 1930) raised the problem of inhibition in symbol formation. She described an autistic little boy of four, Dick, who could not talk or play; he showed no affection or anxiety, and took no interest in his surroundings apart from door-handles, stations, and trains, which seemed to fascinate him. His analysis revealed that the child was terrified of his aggression towards his mother's body, and of her body which he felt had turned bad because of his attacks on it; because of the strength of his anxieties he had erected powerful defences against his phantasies about her. There resulted a paralysis of his phantasy life and of symbol formation. He had not endowed the world around him with any symbolic meaning and therefore took no interest in it. Melanie Klein came to the conclusion that if symbolization does not occur, the whole development of the ego is arrested.

If we accept this view it follows that the processes of symbolization require a new and more careful study. To begin with, I find it helpful, following C. Morris (1938), to consider symbolizing as a *three*-term relation, i.e. a relation between the thing symbolized, the thing functioning as a symbol and a *person* for whom the one represents the other. In psychological terms, symbolism would be a relation between the ego, the object, and the symbol.

Symbol formation is an activity of the ego attempting to deal with the anxieties stirred by its relation to the object. That is primarily the fear of bad objects and the fear of the loss or inaccessibility of good objects. Disturbances in the ego's relation to objects are reflected in disturbances of symbol formation. In particular, disturbances in differentiation between ego and object lead to disturbances in differentiation between the symbol and the object symbolized and therefore to concrete thinking characteristic of psychoses.

Symbol formation starts very early, probably as early as object relations, but changes its character and functions with the changes in the character of the ego and object relations. Not only the actual content of the symbol, but the very way in which symbols are formed and used seem to me to reflect very precisely the ego's state of development and its way of dealing with its objects. If symbolism is seen as a three-term relation, problems of symbol formation must always be examined in the context of the ego's relation with its objects.

I shall try to describe briefly some basic attitudes of the ego to the objects, and the way in which I think they influence the processes of symbol formation and the functioning of symbolism. My description is based here on Melanie Klein's (1946) concept of the paranoid-schizoid position and of the depressive position. According to her, the oral stage of development falls into two phases, the earlier being the point of fixation of the schizophrenic group of illnesses, the later that of the manic-depressive. In my description, which will of necessity be very schematic, I shall select only those points which are directly relevant to the problem of symbol formation.

The chief characteristics of the infant's first object relations are the following. The object is seen as split into an ideally good and a wholly bad one. The aim of the ego is total union with the ideal object and total annihilation of the bad one, as well as of the bad parts of the self. Omnipotent thinking is paramount and reality sense intermittent and precarious. The concept of absence hardly exists. Whenever the state of union with the ideal object is not fulfilled, what is experienced is not absence; the ego feels assailed by the counterpart of the good object – the bad object, or objects. It is the time of the hallucinatory wish-fulfilment, described by Freud, when the thought creates objects which are then felt to be available. According to Melanie Klein, it is also the time of the bad hallucinosis when, if the ideal conditions are not fulfilled, the bad object is equally hallucinated and felt as real.

A leading defence mechanism in this phase is projective identification. In projective identification, the subject in phantasy projects large parts of himself into the object, and the object becomes identified with the parts of the self that it is felt to contain. Similarly, internal objects are projected outside and identified with parts of the external world which come to represent them. These first projections and identifications are the beginning of the process of symbol formation.

The early symbols, however, are not felt by the ego to be symbols or substitutes, but to be the original object itself. They are so different from symbols formed later that I think they deserve a name of their own. In my paper of 1950 I suggested the term 'equation'. This word, however, differentiates them too much from the word 'symbol' and I would like to alter it here to 'symbolic equation'.

The symbolic equation between the original object and the symbol in the internal and the external world is, I think, the basis of the schizophrenic's concrete thinking where substitutes for the original objects, or parts of the self, can be used quite freely, but, as in the two examples of schizophrenic patients which I quoted, they are hardly different from the original object: they are felt and treated as though they were *identical* with it. This non-differentiation between the thing symbolized and the symbol is part of a disturbance in the relation between the ego and the object. Parts of the ego and internal objects are projected into an object and identified with it. The differentiation between the self and the object is obscured. Then, since a part of the ego is confused with the object, the symbol – which is a creation and a function of the ego – becomes, in turn, confused with the object which is symbolized.

Where such symbolic equations are formed in relation to bad objects, an attempt is made to deal with them as with the original object, that is by total annihilation and scotomization. in Melanie Klein's paper quoted above (1930), it seemed as though Dick had formed no symbolic relations to the external world. The paper was written very early on in Dick's analysis, and I wonder, on the basis of my own experience with schizophrenics, whether it did not, perhaps, subsequently transpire that Dick had formed numerous symbolic equations in the external world. If so, then these would have carried the full anxiety experienced in relation to the original persecutory or guilt-producing object: his mother's body, so that he had had to deal with them by annihilation, that is by total withdrawal of interest. Some of the symbols which he had formed as his analysis progressed, and he started to show an interest in certain objects in the consulting room, seemed to have had the characteristics of such symbolic equations. For instance, when he saw some pencil shavings he said: 'Poor Mrs Klein'. To him the shavings were Mrs Klein cut into bits.

This was the case in the analysis of my patient Edward (Segal 1950). At one stage in the analysis a certain degree of symbol formation on a symbolic equation basis had occurred, so that some anxiety was displaced from the person of his analyst, felt as a bad internal object, on to substitutes in the external world. Thereupon the numerous persecutors in the external world were dealt with by scotomization. That phase of his analysis, which lasted several months, was characterized by an extreme narrowing of his interests in the external world. At that point also his vocabulary became very poor. He forbade himself and me the use of many words which he felt had the power to produce hallucinations and therefore had to be abolished. This is strikingly similar to the behaviour of a Paraguayan tribe, the Abipones, who cannot tolerate anything that reminds them of the dead. When a member of the tribe dies, all words having any affinity with the names of the deceased are immediately dropped from the vocabulary. In consequence, their language is most difficult to learn, as it is full of blocks and neologisms replacing forbidden words.

The development of the ego and the changes in the ego's relation to its objects are gradual, and so is the change from the early symbols, which I called symbolic equations, to the fully formed symbols in the depressive position. It is therefore only for the sake of clarity that I shall make here a very sharp differentiation between the ego's relations in the paranoid-schizoid position and in the depressive position respectively, and an equally sharp differentiation between the symbolic equations and the symbols which are formed during and after the depressive position.

When the depressive position has been reached, the main characteristic of object relation is that the object is felt as a whole object. In connexion with this there is a greater degree of awareness and differentiation of the separateness between the ego and the object. At the same time, since the object is recognized as a whole, ambivalence is more fully experienced. The ego in this phase is struggling with its ambivalence and its relation to the object is characterized by guilt, fear of loss or actual experience of loss and mourning, and a striving to re-create the object. At the same time, processes of introjection become more pronounced than those of projection, in keeping with the striving to retain the object inside as well as to repair, restore and re-create it.

In favourable circumstances of normal development, after repeated experiences of loss, recovery, and re-creation, a good object is securely established in the ego. Three changes in relation to the object, as the ego develops and integrates, affect fundamentally the ego's reality sense. With an increased awareness of ambivalence, the lessening of the intensity of projection, and the growing differentiation between the self and the object, there is a growing sense of reality both internal and external. The internal world becomes differentiated from the external world. Omnipotent thinking, characteristic of the earlier phase, gradually gives way to more realistic thinking. Simultaneously, and as part of the same process, there is a certain modification of the primary instinctual aims. Earlier on, the aim was to possess the object totally if felt as good, or to annihilate it totally if felt as bad. With the recognition that the good and the bad objects are one, both these instinctual aims are gradually modified. The ego is increasingly concerned with saving the object from its aggression and possessiveness. And this implies a certain degree of inhibition of the direct instinctual aims, both aggressive and libidinal.

This situation is a powerful stimulus for the creation of symbols, and symbols acquire new functions which change their character. The symbol is needed to displace aggression from the original object, and in that way to lessen the guilt and the fear of loss. The symbol is here not an equivalent of the original object, since the aim of the displacement is to save the object, and the guilt experienced in relation to it is far less than that due to an attack on the original object. The symbols are also created in the *internal* world as a means of restoring, re-creating, recapturing and owning again the original object. But in keeping with the increased reality sense, they are now felt as created by the ego and therefore never completely equated with the original object.

Freud (1923) postulates that a modification of instinctual aims is the basic pre-condition of sublimation. In my view the formation of symbols in the depressive position necessitates some inhibition of direct instinctual aims in relation to the original object and therefore the symbols become available for sublimation. The symbols, created internally, can then be re-projected into the external world, endowing it with symbolic meaning.

The capacity to experience loss and the wish to re-create the object within oneself gives the individual the unconscious freedom in the use of the symbols. And as the symbol is acknowledged as a creation of the subject, unlike the symbolic equation, it can be freely used by the subject.

When a substitute in the external world is used as a symbol it may be used more freely than the original object, since it is not fully identified with it. In so far, however, as it is distinguished from the original object it is also recognized as an object in itself. Its own properties are recognized, respected, and used, because no confusion with the original object blurs the characteristics of the new object used as a symbol.

In an analysis we can sometimes follow very clearly the changes in the symbolic relations in the patient's attitude to his faeces. On the schizoid level the patient expects his faeces to be the ideal breast; if he cannot maintain this idealization his faeces become persecutory, they are ejected as a bitten-up, destroyed and persecuting breast. If the patient tries to symbolize his faeces in the external world the symbols in the external world are felt to be faeces – persecutors. No sublimation of anal activities can occur under these conditions.

On the depressive level, the feeling is that the introjected breast has been destroyed by the ego and can be re-created by the ego. The faeces may then be felt as something created by the ego out of the object and can be valued as a symbol of the breast and at the same time as a good product of the ego's own creativity.

When this symbolic relation to faeces and other body products has been established a projection can occur on to substances in the external world such as paint, plasticine, clay, etc., which can then be used for sublimation.

When this stage of development has been achieved, it is of course not irreversible. If the anxieties are too strong, a regression to a paranoid-schizoid position can occur at any stage of the individual's development and projective identification may be resorted to as a defence against anxiety. Then symbols which have been developed and have been functioning as symbols in sublimation, revert to concrete symbolic equations. This is mainly due to the fact that in massive projective identification the ego becomes again confused with the object, the symbol becomes confused with the thing symbolized and therefore turns into an equation.

In the example of the schizophrenic patient A quoted at the beginning of this paper, there was a breakdown of an already established sublimation. Prior to his schizophrenic breakdown, the violin had been functioning as a symbol and used for purposes of sublimation. It had only become concretely equated to the penis at the time of his illness. Words which had certainly developed at the time when the ego is relatively mature, become equated with the objects that they should represent, and become experienced as concrete objects when projective identification occurs with the resulting confusion between the symbols created by the ego: the word, or even the thought, and the object that they were to symbolize.

I should like at this point to summarize what I mean by the terms 'symbolic equation' and 'symbol' respectively, and the conditions under which they arise. In the symbolic equation, the symbol-substitute is felt to *be* the original object. The substitute's own properties are not recognized or admitted. The symbolic equation is used to deny the absence of the ideal object, or to control a persecuting one. It belongs to the earliest stages of development.

The symbol proper, available for sublimation and furthering the development of the ego, is felt to *represent* the object; its own characteristics are recognized, respected, and used. It arises when depressive feelings predominate over the paranoid-schizoid ones, when separation from the object, ambivalence, guilt, and loss can be experienced and tolerated. The symbol is used not to deny but to overcome loss. When the mechanism of projective identification is used as a defence against depressive anxieties, symbols already formed and functioning as symbols may revert to symbolic equations.

Symbol formation governs the capacity to communicate, since all communication is made by means of symbols. When schizoid disturbances in object relations occur, the capacity to communicate is similarly disturbed: first because the differentiation between the subject and the object is blurred, secondly because the *means* of communication are lacking since symbols are felt in a concrete fashion and are therefore unavailable for purposes of communication. One of the ever-recurring difficulties in the analysis of psychotic patients is this difficulty of communication. Words, for instance, whether the analyst's or the patient's, are felt to be objects or actions, and cannot be easily used for purposes of communication.

Symbols are needed not only in communication with the external world, but also in internal communication. Indeed, it could be asked what is meant when we speak of people being well in touch with their unconscious. It is not that they have consciously primitive phantasies, like those which become evident in their analyses, but merely that they have some awareness of their own impulses and feelings. However, I think that we mean more than this; we mean that they have actual *communication* with their unconscious phantasies. And this, like any other form of communication, can only be done with the help of symbols. So that in people who are 'well in touch with themselves' there is a constant free symbol-formation, whereby they can be consciously aware and in control of *symbolic expressions* of the underlying primitive phantasies. The difficulty of dealing with schizophrenic and schizoid patients lies not only in that they cannot communicate with us, but even more in that they cannot communicate with themselves. Any part of their ego may be split off from any other part with no communication available between them.

The capacity to communicate with oneself by using symbols is, I think, the basis of verbal thinking – which is the capacity to communicate with oneself by means of words. Not all internal communication is verbal thinking, but all verbal thinking is an internal communication by means of symbols – words.

An important aspect of internal communication is the integration of earlier desires, anxieties, and phantasies into the later stages of development by symbolization. For instance, in the fully developed genital function, all the earlier aims – anal, urethral, oral – may be symbolically expressed and fulfilled, a point beautifully described in Ferenczi's *Thalassa* (1923).

169

And this takes me to the last point of my paper. I think that one of the important tasks performed by the ego in the depressive position is that of dealing not with depressive anxieties alone, but also with unresolved earlier conflicts. A new achievement belonging to the depressive position; the capacity to symbolize and in that way to lessen anxiety and resolve conflict, is used in order to deal with the *earlier* unresolved conflicts by symbolizing them. Anxieties, which could not be dealt with earlier on, because of the extreme concreteness of the experience with the object and the object-substitutes in symbolic equations, can gradually be dealt with by the more integrated ego by symbolization, and in that way they can be integrated. In the depressive position and later, symbols are formed not only of the whole destroyed and re-created object characteristic of the depressive position, but also of the split object – extremely good and extremely bad – and not only of the whole object but also of part-objects. Some of the paranoid and ideal object relations and anxieties may be symbolized as part of the integrative process in the depressive position.

The fairy tale is an example in point. It deals basically with the witch and the fairy godmother, Prince Charming, the ogre, etc., and has in it a great deal of schizophrenic content. It is, however, a highly integrated product, an artistic creation which very fully symbolizes the child's early anxieties and wishes. I should like to illustrate the function of the fairy tale by some material from the analysis of an adolescent schizophrenic. This girl had been hallucinated and openly schizophrenic since the age of four. She had, however, a great many depressive features and there were in her life phases of relatively greater integration. In these phases, when she felt less persecuted, and, as she told me, could experience some longing for her parents, she used to write fairy tales. In the bad phases, the bad figures of her fairy tales came to life and persecuted her. One day, after many weeks of silence, when she was obviously hallucinated in a very persecutory way she suddenly turned round to me and asked with great fear 'What are the Lancashire witches?' I had never heard of the Lancashire witches, she had never mentioned them before, but I knew that she herself came from Lancashire. After some interpretations she told me that when she was about 11 (she had at that time actually a whole year free of hallucinations), she had written a fairy tale about Lancashire witches. The phase of her analysis following this session has been very revealing. It turned out that the Lancashire witches represented both herself and her mother. The anxiety situation went right back to early childhood, when she saw herself and her mother as devouring one another or devouring

170

father. When a greater degree of integration was achieved and she established a more realistic relation to her parents, the earlier situation was dealt with by symbol formation: by writing the fairy tale about the Lancashire witches. In the subsequent deterioration of her health, the early persecutory situation recurred with concrete intensity but in a new form. The fairy tale come to life: the Lancashire witches – the fairy-tale figures which she had created – had become a concrete external reality. In the consulting room it was quite clear how this concretization of the fairy tale depended on projective identification. She turned to me and asked me about the Lancashire witches. She expected me to know who they were. In fact, ·she thought that I was a Lancashire witch. She had unconsciously phantasied that she had put into me the part of herself which had invented the Lancashire witches, and she had lost contact with this part. She lost all sense of reality in this projection and all memory that she had created this symbol, the 'Lancashire witches'. Her symbol became confused with me, an actual external object, and so became for her a concrete external reality – I had turned into a Lancashire witch.

The way in which the maturing ego, in the process of working through the depressive position, deals with the early object relations, is of paramount importance. Some integration and whole object relations can be achieved in the depressive position, accompanied by the splitting off of earlier ego experiences. In this situation, something like a pocket of schizophrenia exists isolated in the ego and is a constant threat to stability. At worst, a mental breakdown occurs and earlier anxieties and split-off symbolic equations invade the ego. At best, a relatively mature but restricted ego can develop and function.

However, if the ego in the depressive position is strong enough and capable of dealing with anxieties, much more of the earlier situations can be integrated into the ego and dealt with by way of symbolization, enriching the ego with the whole wealth of the earlier experiences.

The word 'symbol' comes from the Greek term for throwing together, bringing together, integrating. The process of symbol formation is, I think, a continuous process of bringing together and integrating the internal with the external, the subject with the object, and the earlier experiences with the later ones.

Postscript 1979: Notes on symbol formation

Since writing this paper, and largely under the influence of Bion's work on the relationship between the container and the contained, I have come to think that it is not projective identification *per se* that leads to concretization. One has to take into account the particular relationship between the projected part and the object projected into: the container and the contained. For a more detailed explanation, I refer the reader to chapter 7 of *The Work of Hanna Segal*, New York: Jason Aronson (1981). In relation to symbol formation, this relationship is of great importance. I want to give two examples.

In the first one, the environmental factor plays an important role. A neurotic young man was able much of the time to function on a depressive level. He could communicate in a symbolic way and had numerous sublimations. These achievements were, however, insecure and at moments of stress, he tended to use massive projective identification accompanied by regression to concrete levels of functioning. Sometimes, for instance, he had near-hallucinatory states of mind.

He came to one session very perturbed because on waking up he had a hallucinatory experience. It differed from hallucination only in so far as he clung desperately to the belief that it must be the product of his own mind. When he woke up, he felt that his head was solid and he saw a motorcycle riding into his head. The rider had a kind of mask on, which made his head look like a finger. He felt terrified and thought his head would explode. Then he looked at his own index finger, and got frightened because his finger looked like a gorilla. He emerged from a state of acute anxiety only when he made himself remember the previous session, in which he was disturbed by a very intrusive noise of motorcycles outside the consulting room windows. He thought the motorcycles were connected with my son. He associated the gorilla to a psychotic boy who was described in a paper as looking like a gorilla. The finger he associated to anal masturbation, about which he had spoken a few days earlier. His anal masturbation was always associated with violent projective identification into the anus of the analyst/mother, as described by Meltzer (1966). We could analyse that the motorcycles outside the window represented his own intrusive self identified with his finger and penis, projected into an external object – the motorcycle – and intruding into him. It is important in this connection that there was in the external world an actual intrusive object into which this projection fitted. It repeated a childhood situation in which there was, in fact, a very intrusive older sibling interfering with his relation to the mother even when he was a tiny baby. Thus, his projections were concretized for him in the external world.

My second example was a much more disturbed young woman. In her case, the disturbance seemed to spring from excessive envy and narcissism projected into an overly narcissistic mother. This patient was not psychotic but she may well have been the most difficult patient I have ever had to understand. Her verbal communications were very difficult to follow. I often had difficulty in grasping the conscious meaning. She tended to misuse words, mix languages. There were non sequiturs and contradictions in what she said. Often there was little connection between what she said, what she meant to say and what she actually thought. The unconscious meaning was even more confused. In other patients, when verbal communications are so difficult, one may get important non-verbal clues. With her, the non-verbal clues were often lacking or misleading. The tone of her voice or her facial expression often bore no relation to her state of mind. Typically, she would greet me with a friendly, relaxed smile, giving no indication that she was in fact in a turmoil of anxiety, confusion and hostility. Her symbolism was at times very concrete. She had states of bodily excitement, bizarre bodily sensations, psychosomatic, hypochondriacal, hysterical symptoms and often complained that she had no feelings, only physical sensations. She often responded to interpretations by physical sensation. Words were experienced as concrete things, felt as a lump inside her. This was often accompanied by fears of cancer. In those situations, one could often see that she felt she had invaded my speech and made it into a physical possession of hers. But there was an opposite phenomenon. Her speech could be called completely abstract. She spoke most of the time in metaphors, clichés, technical terms. She often generalized in a way which left no meaning. Sometimes she spoke for a long time, and I realized she had said nothing concrete or real that I could get hold of. At the same time, I could observe how she emptied my words of all meaning as if she listened to an interpretation and immediately translated it into some philosophical or psychoanalytic abstract term, often distorting its meaning completely. The underlying phantasy was that she entered me and emptied me of all contents and she felt equally emptied by me. Stealing was an ever-recurring theme. At other times, she might communicate dissociated fragments of bits of her experience that seemed to function as Bion's 'bizarre objects' (Bion 1957).

173

In those modes of functioning, one can see a disturbance between the container and the contained. When she was overly concrete, the projected part was totally identified with the container, when her communication was empty of meaning, the container and the contained had a relation of mutually emptying one another. When she was fragmented and produced 'bizarre objects' type of associations, her projections had split the container into fragments.

In her case, this mutually destructive relation between the part she projected and the container seems to be related to envy and to narcissism. Nothing was allowed to exist outside herself which could give rise to envy. I would like to give some material to illustrate this.

She had several dreams characteristic of her, depicting her narcissism. For instance, she dreamed she was in bed with a young man, glued and fused to him, but the young man was herself. Following several such dreams, she brought a different one: 'She was in a house, the roof of which was disintegrating. She did not want to take any notice because she lived in the middle floor between the ground and the top floor.' She had a number of useful, and surprisingly comprehensible, associations to the dream. She owned one of three apartments in a house. The owner of the house wanted her to participate in the costs of repairing the attic. She was furious about it because she felt it wasn't fair. It was true she signed a contract that she would, but she had been foolish to agree to it. Her own apartment was not in danger from the leaking roof, being in the middle, but she felt bad about it because of her friends who lived in the top apartment. Then she said that the middle must be her tummy and started complaining of her physical symptoms and the state of her mind. The attic must be her head, which she thought was in a terribly disintegrated state. She couldn't think; she couldn't work. She thought her head should be entirely my concern. I had interpreted to this patient her repudiation of the analytic contract that we should both be concerned with her head and related the friends who live in the top flat to internal objects, thoughts and feelings that she did not want to concern herself with. But somewhat later in the session I noticed that, despite her lamentations about her head, there was something very superior in her attitude. I particularly noted that, though she complained later in the session of how empty she felt and unable to communicate, she seemed to take quite some pride in her metaphors, which were getting more and more flowery as her session progressed. When I drew her attention to this, she rather reluctantly said that while she was speaking of the middle floor, she was in fact thinking of the 'first floor', which in her native language is a colloquial expression for belonging to superior, upper classes.

Thus, it was her narcissism which prevented her from relating to and taking care of internal objects. That, in turn, seemed to prevent her symbolizing and communicating. The pain in her tummy – her middle floor – is where she kept me, totally controlled by and identified with her gut. If she integrated me into her head, she would be aware of her own feeling of dependence, felt by her as great inferiority. Also, the middle floor, which is also the first floor, represented both her superiority and her illness.

Verbalization can be looked at from the angle of the relation between the container and the contained. Unlike the unconscious forms of symbolism, speech has to be learned. Though the baby begins by producing sounds, those sounds have to be taken up by the environment to be converted into speech, and words or phrases have to be learned from the environment. The infant has had an experience and the mother provides the word or phrase which binds this experience. It contains, encompasses and expresses the meaning. It provides a container for it. The infant can then internalize this word or phrase containing the meaning. My patient had the greatest difficulty in experiencing any interpretation, any phrase of mine as containing and giving expression to *her* meaning. Strange things happened to my interpretations. They could become a pain in her belly or sexual excitement. They could be learned by heart and applied to others. They were frequently fed back to me as her own product but usually a bit distorted, often deprived of emotional meaning, sometimes completely reversed. She had a dream, associations to which illustrated this difficulty. To understand them, I refer you to a beautiful passage in Helen Keller's autobiography (1954) where she described how she first rediscovered speech. For a long time her teacher had tried to communicate with her by writing on her hand. Helen did not respond. After a long period of breaking and smashing things without concern, she broke a doll and for the first time cried about it. That afternoon when the teacher tried again to communicate with her and wrote a word on her palm, Helen Keller understood and responded. Thus, a capacity to understand symbolic communication followed immediately and directly from her first experience of depressive feelings, an experience very familiar to those who analyse autistic children. This sequence was first described by Emilio Rodrigue (1955) in 'The analysis of a three-year-old mute schizophrenic'. To return to my patient's dream. She dreamed of a little girl with long nails and ferocious teeth greedily attacking a table, scratching and biting. Her first associations were to my having given her my vacation date; this probably stirred up her greed. She produced a kind of lament, without any genuine feeling, of how primitive she was, how the little girl in the dream represented her, etc. But then she added another association. She recently read a book by, or about, a little girl who lost her sight and hearing and was like a little wild animal until the day she *invented* a sign language and taught it to her teacher. (The book was obviously Helen Keller's, read by my patient.) I think Helen Keller's description and my patient's version of it exemplify different kinds of symbol formation. With all her handicaps, Helen Keller had achieved a complete communication with her audience; but my poor patient was not yet able to speak in a way easily understandable to others. She still had not accepted that she learned to speak from her mother.

References

Bion, W. R. (1957) 'Differentiation of the psychotic from the non-psychotic personalities', *International Journal of Psycho-Analysis* 38, 266–75; also in W. R. Bion, *Second Thoughts*, London: Heinemann (1967) 43–64; reprinted in paperback, Maresfield Reprints, London: H. Karnac Books (1984).

Ferenczi, S. (1923) *Thalassa: A Theory of Genitality*, New York: W. W. Norton (1968).

Freud, S. (1923) *The Ego and the Id*, SE 19, 1–66.

Jones, E. (1916) 'The theory of symbolism', in E. Jones, *Papers on Psycho-Analysis*, 2nd edn, London: Baillière, Tindall & Cox (1918).

Keller, H. (1954) *Story of My Life*, New York: Doubleday.

Klein, M. (1923) 'The role of the school in the libidinal development of the child', in *The Writings of Melanie Klein*, vol. 1, London: Hogarth Press (1975), 59–76; paperback New York: Dell Publishing Co., (1977)).

——(1930) 'On the importance of symbol formation in the development of the ego', in *The Writings of Melanie Klein*, vol. 1, 219–32.

——(1946) 'Notes on some schizoid mechanisms', in M. Klein, P. Heimann, S. Isaacs, and J. Riviere, *Developments in Psycho-Analysis*, London: Hogarth Press (1952) 292–320; also in *The Writings of Melanie Klein* vol. 3, 1–24.

Meltzer, D. (1966) 'The relation of anal masturbation to projective identification', *International Journal of Psycho-Analysis*, 47, 335–42 and reprinted here on pp. 102–16.

Morris, C. (1938) 'Foundations of the theory of signs', *International Encyclopaedia of Unified Science*, Chicago: University of Chicago Press.

Rodrigue, E. (1955) 'The analysis of a three-year-old mute schizophrenic', in M. Klein, P. Heimann, and R. Money-Kyrle (eds) *New Directions in Psycho-Analysis*, London: Tavistock Publications, 140–79; in paperback, Tavistock Publications (1971).

*——(1956) 'Notes on symbolism', *International Journal of Psycho-Analysis*, 37, 147–58.

*Rycroft, C. (1956) 'Symbolism and its relation to primary and secondary processes', *International Journal of Psycho-Analysis*, 37, 137–46.

Segal, H. (1950) 'Some aspects of the analysis of a schizophrenic', *International Journal of Psycho-Analysis*, 31, 268–78; also in *The Work of Hanna Segal*, New York: Jason Aronson, 101–20; reprinted in paperback, London: Free Association Books (1986).

——(1952) 'A psycho-analytical approach to aesthetics', *International Journal of Psycho-Analysis*, 33, 196–207; also in *The Work of Hanna Segal*, 185–206.

——(1955) 'Depression in the schizophrenic', *International Journal of Psycho-Analysis*, 37, 339–43; also in *The Work of Hanna Segal*, 121–29.

* No reference is made in the 1957 text to these two contributions, as the three papers were written and read almost concurrently.

2

A theory of thinking

W. R. BION

This article was originally a paper read at the 22nd International Psycho-Analytical Congress, Edinburgh, July–August 1961, and was first published in the *International Journal of Psycho-Analysis*, 43, 306–10.

(i) In this paper I am primarily concerned to present a theoretical system. Its resemblance to a philosophical theory depends on the fact that philosophers have concerned themselves with the same subject-matter; it differs from philosophical theory in that it is in intended, like all psychoanalytical theories, for use. It is devised with the intention that practising psychoanalysts should restate the hypotheses of which it is composed in terms of empirically verifiable data. In this respect it bears the same relationship to similar statements of philosophy as the statements of applied mathematics bear to pure mathematics.

The derived hypotheses that are intended to admit of empirical test, and to a lesser extent the theoretical system itself, bear the same relationship to the observed facts in a psychoanalysis as statements of applied mathematics, say about a mathematical circle, bear to a statement about a circle drawn upon paper.

(ii) This theoretical system is intended to be applicable in a significant number of cases; psychoanalysts should therefore experience realizations that approximate to the theory.

I attach no diagnostic importance to the theory, though I think it may be applicable whenever a disorder of thought is believed to exist. Its diagnostic significance will depend upon the pattern formed by the constant conjunction of a number of theories of which this theory would be one.

It may help to explain the theory if I discuss the background of emotional experience from which it has been abstracted. I shall do this in general terms without attempting scientific rigour.

(iii) It is convenient to regard thinking as dependent on the successful outcome of two main mental developments. The first is the development of thoughts. They require an apparatus to cope with them. The second development, therefore, is of this apparatus that I shall provisionally call thinking. I repeat – thinking has to be called into existence to cope with thoughts.

It will be noted that this differs from any theory of thought as a product of thinking, in that thinking is a development forced on the psyche by the pressure of thoughts and not the other way round. Psychopathological developments may be associated with either phase or both, that is, they may be related to a breakdown in the development of thoughts, or a breakdown in the development of the apparatus for 'thinking' or dealing with thoughts, or both.

(iv) 'Thoughts' may be classified, according to the nature of their developmental history, as preconceptions, conceptions or thoughts, and finally concepts; concepts are named and therefore fixed conceptions or thoughts. The conception is initiated by the conjunction of a preconception with a realization. The preconception may be regarded as the analogue in psychoanalysis of Kant's concept of 'empty thoughts'. Psychoanalytically the theory that the infant has an inborn disposition corresponding to an expectation of a breast may be used to supply a model. When the preconception is brought into contact with a realization that approximates to it, the mental outcome is a conception. Put in another way, the preconception (the inborn expectation of a breast, the *a priori* knowledge of a breast, the 'empty thought') when the infant is brought in contact with the breast itself, mates with awareness of the realization and is synchronous with the development of a conception. This model will serve for the theory that every junction of a preconception with its realization produces a conception. Conceptions therefore will be expected to be constantly conjoined with an emotional experience of satisfaction.

(v) I shall limit the term 'thought' to the mating of a preconception with a frustration. The model I propose is that of an infant whose expectation of a breast is mated with a realization of no breast available for satisfaction. This mating is experienced as a no-breast, or 'absent' breast inside. The next step depends on the infant's capacity for frustration: in particular it depends on whether the decision is to evade frustration or to modify it.

(vi) If the capacity for toleration of frustration is sufficient the 'no-breast' inside becomes a thought, and an apparatus for 'thinking' it

179

develops. This initiates the state, described by Freud in his 'Two principles of mental functioning', in which dominance by the reality principle is synchronous with the development of an ability to think and so to bridge the gulf of frustration between the moment when a want is felt and the moment when action appropriate to satisfying the want culminates in its satisfaction. A capacity for tolerating frustration thus enables the psyche to develop thought as a means by which the frustration that is tolerated is itself made more tolerable.

(vii) If the capacity for toleration of frustration is inadequate, the bad internal 'no-breast', that a personality capable of maturity ultimately recognizes as a thought, confronts the psyche with the need to decide between evasion of frustration and its modification.

(viii) Incapacity for tolerating frustration tips the scale in the direction of evasion of frustration. The result is a significant departure from the events that Freud describes as characteristic of thought in the phase of dominance of the reality principle. What should be a thought, a product of the juxtaposition of preconception and negative realization, becomes a bad object, indistinguishable from a thing-in-itself, fit only for evacuation. Consequently the development of an apparatus for thinking is disturbed, and instead there takes place a hypertrophic development of the apparatus of projective identification. The model I propose for this development is a psyche that operates on the principle that evacuation of a bad breast is synonymous with obtaining sustenance from a good breast. The end result is that all thoughts are treated as if they were indistinguishable from bad internal objects; the appropriate machinery is felt to be, not an apparatus for thinking the thoughts, but an apparatus for ridding the psyche of accumulations of bad internal objects. The crux lies in the decision between modification and evasion of frustration.

(ix) Mathematical elements, namely straight lines, points, circles, and something corresponding to what later become known by the name of numbers, derive from realizations of two-ness as in breast and infant, two eyes, two feet, and so on.

(x) If intolerance of frustration is not too great, modification becomes the governing aim. Development of mathematical elements, or mathematical objects as Aristotle calls them, is analogous to the development of conceptions.

(xi) If intolerance of frustration is dominant, steps are taken to evade perception of the realization by destructive attacks. In so far as preconception and realization are mated, mathematical conceptions are formed, but they are treated as if indistinguishable from things-in-themselves and are evacuated at high speed as missiles to annihilate space. In so far as space and time are perceived as identical with a bad object that is destroyed, that is to say a no-breast, the realization that should be mated with the preconception is not available to complete the conditions necessary for the formation of a conception. The dominance of projective identification confuses the distinction between the self and the external object. This contributes to the absence of any perception of two-ness, since such an awareness depends on the recognition of a distinction between subject and object.

(xii) The relationship with time was graphically brought home to me by a patient who said over and over again that he was wasting time – and continued to waste it. The patient's aim is to destroy time by wasting it. The consequences are illustrated in the description in *Alice in Wonderland* of the Mad Hatter's tea-party – it is always four o'clock.

(xiii) Inability to tolerate frustration can obstruct the development of thoughts and a capacity to think, though a capacity to think would diminish the sense of frustration intrinsic to appreciation of the gap between a wish and its fulfilment. Conceptions, that is to say the outcome of a mating between a preconception and its realization, repeat in a more complex form the history of preconception. A conception does not necessarily meet a realization that approximates sufficiently closely to satisfy. If frustration can be tolerated, the mating of conception and realizations whether negative or positive initiates procedures necessary to learning by experience. If intolerance of frustration is not so great as to activate the mechanisms of evasion and yet is too great to bear dominance of the reality principle, the personality develops omnipotence as a substitute for the mating of the preconception, or conception, with the negative realization. This involves the assumption of omniscience as a substitute for learning from experience by aid of thoughts and thinking. There is therefore no psychic activity to discriminate between true and false. Omniscience substitutes for the discrimination between true and false a dictatorial affirmation that one thing is morally right and the other wrong. The assumption of omniscience that denies reality ensures that the morality thus engendered is a function of psychosis. Discrimination between true and false is a function of the non-psychotic part of the personality and its factors. There is thus potentially a conflict between assertion of truth and assertion of moral ascendancy. The extremism of the one infects the other.

(xiv) Some preconceptions relate to expectations of the self. The preconceptual apparatus is adequate to realizations that fall in the narrow range of circumstances suitable for the survival of the infant.

One circumstance that affects survival is the personality of the infant himself. Ordinarily the personality of the infant, like other elements in the environment, is managed by the mother. If the mother and child are adjusted to each other, projective identification plays a major role in the management; the infant is able through the operation of a rudimentary reality sense to behave in such a way that projective identification, usually an omnipotent phantasy, is a realistic phenomenon. This, I am inclined to believe, is its normal condition. When Klein speaks of 'excessive' projective identification I think the term 'excessive' should be understood to apply not to the frequency only with which projective identification is employed but to excess of belief in omnipotence. As a *realistic* activity it shows itself as behaviour reasonably calculated to arouse in the mother feelings of which the infant wishes to be rid. If the infant feels it is dying it can arouse fears that it is dying in the mother. A well-balanced mother can accept these and respond therapeutically: that is to say in a manner that makes the infant feel it is receiving its frightened personality back again, but in a form that it can tolerate – the fears are manageable by the infant personality. If the mother cannot tolerate these projections the infant is reduced to continue projective identification carried out with increasing force and frequency. The increased force seems to denude the projection of its penumbra of meaning. Reintrojection is affected with similar force and frequency. Deducing the patient's feelings from his behaviour in the consulting room and using the deductions to form a model, the infant of my model does not behave in a way that I ordinarily expect of an adult who is thinking. It behaves as if it felt that an internal object has been built up that has the characteristics of a greedy vagina-like 'breast' that strips of its goodness all that the infant receives or gives, leaving only degenerate objects. This internal object starves its host of all understanding that is made available. In analysis such a patient seems unable to gain from his environment and therefore from his analyst. The consequences for the development of a capacity for thinking are serious ; I shall describe only one, namely, precocious development of consciousness.

(xv) By consciousness I mean in this context what Freud described as a 'sense-organ for the perception of psychic qualities'.

I have described previously (at a Scientific Meeting of the British Psycho-Analytical Society) the use of a concept of 'alpha-function' as a working tool in the analysis of disturbances of thought. It seemed convenient to suppose an alpha-function to convert sense data into alpha-elements and thus provide the psyche with the material for dream thoughts, and hence the capacity to wake up or go to sleep, to be conscious or unconscious. According to this theory consciousness depends on alpha-function, and it is a logical necessity to suppose that such a function exists if we are to assume that the self is able to be conscious of itself in the sense of knowing itself from experience of itself. Yet the failure to establish, between infant and mother, a relationship in which normal projective identification is possible precludes the development of an alpha-function and therefore of a differentiation of elements into conscious and unconscious.

(xvi) The difficulty is avoided by restricting the term 'consciousness' to the meaning conferred on it by Freud's definition. Using the term 'consciousness' in this restricted sense it is possible to suppose that this consciousness produces 'sense-data' of the self, but that there is no alpha-function to convert them into alpha-elements and therefore permit of a capacity for being conscious or unconscious of the self. The infant personality by itself is unable to make use of the sense data, but has to evacuate these elements into the mother, relying on her to do whatever has to be done to convert them into a form suitable for employment as alpha-elements by the infant.

(xvii) The limited consciousness defined by Freud, that I am using to define a rudimentary infant consciousness, is not associated with an unconscious. All impressions of the self are of equal value; all are conscious. The mother's capacity for reverie is the receptor organ for the infant's harvest of self-sensation gained by its conscious.

(xviii) A rudimentary conscious could not perform the tasks that we ordinarily regard as the province of consciousness, and it would be misleading to attempt to withdraw the term 'conscious' from the sphere of ordinary usage where it is applied to mental functions of great importance in rational thinking. For the present I make the distinction only to show what happens if there is a breakdown of interplay through projective identification between the rudimentary consciousness and maternal reverie.

Normal development follows if the relationship between infant and breast permits the infant to project a feeling, say, that it is dying, into the mother and to reintroject it after its sojourn in the breast has made it tolerable to the infant psyche. If the projection is not accepted by the mother the infant feels that its feeling that it is dying is stripped of such meaning as it has. It therefore reintrojects, not a fear of dying made tolerable, but a nameless dread.

(xix) The tasks that the breakdown in the mother's capacity for reverie have left unfinished are imposed on the rudimentary consciousness; they are all in different degrees related to the function of correlation.

(xx) The rudimentary consciousness cannot carry the burden placed on it. The establishment internally of a projective-identification-rejecting-object means that instead of an understanding object the infant has a wilfully misunderstanding object – with which it is identified. Further its psychic qualities are perceived by a precocious and fragile consciousness.

(xxi) The apparatus available to the psyche may be regarded as fourfold:

(a) Thinking, associated with modification and evasion.
(b) Projective identification, associated with evasion by evacuation and not to be confused with normal projective identification (para. xiv on 'realistic' projective identification.)
(c) Omniscience (on the principle of *tout savoir tout condamner*).
(d) Communication

(xxii) Examination of the apparatus I have listed under these four heads shows that it is designed to deal with thoughts, in the broad sense of the term, that is including all objects I have described as conceptions, thoughts, dream thoughts, alpha-elements and beta-elements, as if they were objects that had to be dealt with (a) because they in some form contained or expressed a problem, and (b) because they were themselves felt to be undesirable excrescences of the psyche and required attention, elimination by some means or other, for that reason.

(xxiii) As expressions of a problem it is evident they require an apparatus designed to play the same part in bridging the gap between cognizance and appreciation of lack and action designed to modify the lack, as is played by alpha-function in bridging the gap between sense-data and appreciation of sense-data. (In this context I include the perception of psychic qualities as requiring the same treatment as sense-data.) In other words just as sense-data have to be modified and worked on by alpha-function to make them available for dream thoughts, etc., so the thoughts have to be worked on to make them available for translation into action.

(xxiv) Translation into action involves publication, communication, and commonsense. So far I have avoided discussion of these aspects of thinking, although they are implied in the discussion and one at least was openly adumbrated; I refer to correlation.

(xxv) Publication in its origin may be regarded as little more than one function of thoughts, namely making sense-data available to consciousness. I wish to reserve the term for operations that are necessary to make private awareness, that is awareness that is private to the individual, public. The problems involved may be regarded as technical and emotional. The emotional problems are associated with the fact that the human individual is a political animal and cannot find fulfilment outside a group, and cannot satisfy any emotional drive without expression of its social component. His impulses, and I mean all impulses and not merely his sexual ones, are at the same time narcissistic. The problem is the resolution of the conflict between narcissism and social-ism. The technical problem is that concerned with expression of thought or conception in language, or its counterpart in signs.

(xxvi) This brings me to communication. In its origin communication is effected by realistic projective identification. The primitive infant procedure undergoes various vicissitudes, including, as we have seen, debasement through hypertrophy of omnipotent phantasy. It may develop, if the relationship with the breast is good, into a capacity for toleration by the self of its own psychic qualities and so pave the way for alpha-function and normal thought. But it does also develop as a part of the social capacity of the individual. This development, of great importance in group dynamics, has received virtually no attention; its absence would make even scientific communication impossible. Yet its presence may arouse feelings of persecution in the recipients of the communication. The need to diminish feelings of persecution contributes to the drive to abstraction in the formulation of scientific communications. The function of the elements of communication, words and signs, is to convey either by single substantives, or in verbal groupings, that certain phenomena are constantly conjoined in the pattern of their relatedness.

(xxvii) An important function of communications is to achieve correlation. While communication is still a private function, conceptions, thoughts, and their verbalization are necessary to facilitate the conjunction of one set of sense-data with another. If the conjoined data harmonize, a sense of truth is experienced, and it is desirable that this sense should be given expression in a statement analogous to a truth-functional statement. The failure to bring about this conjunction of sense-data, and therefore of a commonplace view, induces a mental state of debility in the patient as if starvation of truth was somehow analogous to alimentary starvation. The truth of a statement does not imply that there is a realization approximating to the true statement.

(xxviii) We may now consider further the relationship of rudimentary consciousness to psychic quality. The emotions fulfil for the psyche a function similar to that of the senses in relation to objects in space and time: that is to say, the counterpart of the commonsense view in private knowledge is the common emotional view; a sense of truth is experienced if the view of an object which is hated can be conjoined to a view of the same object when it is loved, and the conjunction confirms that the object experienced by different emotions is the same object. A correlation is established.

(xxix) A similar correlation, made possible by bringing conscious and unconscious to bear on the phenomena of the consulting room, gives to psychoanalytic objects a reality that is quite unmistakable even though their very existence has been disputed.

The experience of the skin
in early object-relations

ESTHER BICK

This article was originally a paper read at the 25th International Psycho-Analytical Congress, Copenhagen, July 1967, and was first published in the *International Journal of Psycho-Analysis*, 49, 484–6.

The central theme of this brief communication is concerned with the primal function of the skin of the baby and of its primal objects in relation to the most primitive binding together of parts of the personality not as yet differentiated from parts of the body. It can be most readily studied in psychoanalysis in relation to problems of dependence and separation in the transference.

The thesis is that in its most primitive form the parts of the personality are felt to have no binding force amongst themselves and must therefore be held together in a way that is experienced by them passively, by the skin functioning as a boundary. But this internal function of containing the parts of the self is dependent initially on the introjection of an external object, experienced as capable of fulfilling this function. Later, identification with this function of the object supersedes the unintegrated state and gives rise to the phantasy of internal and external spaces. Only then the stage is set for the operation of primal splitting and idealization of self and object as described by Melanie Klein. Until the containing functions have been introjected, the concept of a space within the self cannot arise. Introjection, i.e. construction of an object in an internal space is therefore impaired. In its absence, the function of projective identification will necessarily continue unabated and all the confusions of identity attending it will be manifest.

The stage of primal splitting and idealization of self and object can now be seen to rest on this earlier process of containment of self and object by their respective 'skins'.

The fluctuations in this primal state will be illustrated in case material, from infant observation, in order to show the difference between unintegration as a passive experience of total helplessness, and disintegration through splitting processes as an active defensive operation in the service of development. We are, therefore, from the economic point of view, dealing with situations conducive to catastrophic anxieties in the unintegrated state as compared with the more limited and specific persecutory and depressive ones.

The need for a containing object would seem, in the infantile unintegrated state, to produce a frantic search for an object – a light, a voice, a smell, or other sensual object – which can hold the attention and thereby be experienced, momentarily at least, as holding the parts of the personality together. The optimal object is the nipple in the mouth, together with the holding and talking and familiar smelling mother.

Material will show how this containing object is experienced concretely as a skin. Faulty development of this primal skin function can be seen to result either from defects in the adequacy of the actual object or from phantasy attacks on it, which impair introjection. Disturbance in the primal skin function can lead to a development of a 'second skin' formation through which dependence on the object is replaced by a pseudo-independence, by the inappropriate use of certain mental functions, or perhaps innate talents, for the purpose of creating a substitute for this skin container function. The material to follow will give some examples of 'second-skin' formation.

Here I can only indicate the types of clinical material upon which these findings are based. My present aim is to open up this topic for a detailed discussion in a later paper.

Infant observation: Baby Alice

One year of observation of an immature young mother and her first baby showed a gradual improvement in the 'skin–container' function up to twelve weeks. As the mother's tolerance to closeness to the baby increased, so did her need to excite the baby to manifestations of vitality lessen. A consequent diminution of unintegrated states in the baby could be observed. These had been characterized by trembling, sneezing, and disorganized movements. There followed a move to a new house in a still unfinished condition. This disturbed severely the mother's holding capacity and led her to a withdrawal from the baby. She began feeding whilst watching television, or at night in the dark without holding the baby. This brought a flood of somatic disturbance and an increase of unintegrated states in the baby. Father's illness at that time made matters worse and the mother had to plan to return to work. She began to press the baby into a pseudo-independence, forcing her on to a training-cup, introducing a bouncer during the day, whilst harshly refusing to respond to the crying at night. The mother now returned to an earlier tendency to stimulate the child to aggressive displays which she provoked and admired. The result by six-and-a-half months was a hyperactive and aggressive little girl, whom mother called 'a boxer' from her habit of pummelling people's faces. We see here the formation of a muscular type of self-containment – 'second-skin' in place of a proper skin container.

Analysis of a schizophrenic girl: Mary

Some years of analysis, since age 3½, have enabled us to reconstruct the mental states reflected in the history of her infantile disturbance. The facts are as follows: a difficult birth, early clenching of the nipples but lazy feeding, bottle supplement in the third week but on breast until 11 months, infantile eczema at 4 months and scratching until bleeding, extreme clinging to mother, severe intolerance to waiting for feeds, delayed and atypical development in all areas.

In the analysis, severe intolerance to separation was reflected from the start as in the jaw-clenched systematic tearing and breaking of all materials after the first holiday-break. Utter dependence on the immediate contact could be seen and studied in the unintegrated states of posture and motility on the one hand, and thought and communication on the other, which existed at the beginning of each session, improving during the course, to reappear on leaving. She came in hunched, stiff-jointed, grotesque like a 'sack of potatoes' as she later called herself, and emitting an explosive 'SSBICK' for 'Good morning, Mrs Bick'. This 'sack of potatoes' seemed in constant danger of spilling out its contents partly due to the continual picking of holes in her skin representing the 'sack' skin of the object in which parts of herself, the 'potatoes', were contained (projective identification). Improvement from the hunched posture to an erect one was achieved, along with a lessening of her general total dependence, more through a formation of a second skin based on her own muscularity than on identification with a containing object.

189

Analysis of an adult neurotic patient

The alternation of two types of experience of self – the 'sack of apples' and 'the hippopotamus' – could be studied in regard to quality of contact in the transference and experience of separation, both being related to a disturbed feeding period. In the 'sack of apples' state, the patient was touchy, vain, in need of constant attention and praise, easily bruised and constantly expecting catastrophe, such as a collapse when getting up from the couch. In the 'hippopotamus' state, the patient was aggressive, tyrannical, scathing, and relentless in following his own way. Both states were related to the 'second-skin' type of organization, dominated by projective identification. The 'hippopotamus' skin, like the 'sack' were a reflection of the object's skin inside which he existed, whilst the thin-skinned, easily bruised, apples inside the sack, represented the state of parts of the self which were inside this insensitive object.

Analysis of a child: Jill

Early in the analysis of a 5-year-old child, whose feeding period had been characterized by anorexia, skin-container problems presented themselves, as in her constant demand from mother during the first analytic holiday, that her clothes should be firmly fastened, her shoes tightly laced. Later material showed her intense anxiety and need to distinguish herself from toys and dolls, about which she said: 'Toys are not like me, they break to pieces and don't get well. They don't have a skin. We have a skin!'

Summary

In all patients with disturbed first-skin formation, severe disturbance of the feeding period is indicated by analytic reconstruction, though not always observed by the parents. This faulty skin-formation produces a general fragility in later integration and organizations. It manifests itself in states of unintegration as distinct from regression involving the most basic types of partial or total, unintegration of body, posture, motility, and corresponding functions of mind, particularly communication. The 'second skin' phenomenon which replaces first skin integration, manifests itself as either partial or total type of muscular shell or a corresponding verbal muscularity.

Analytic investigation of the second skin phenomenon tends to produce transitory states of unintegration. Only an analysis which perseveres to thorough working-through of the primal dependence on the maternal object can strengthen this underlying fragility. It must be stressed that the containing aspect of the analytic situation resides especially in the setting and is therefore an area where firmness of technique is crucial.

PART FOUR

Pathological organizations

Introduction

This is an area of much development. Klein's followers have made very little change in her basic conceptions of the paranoid-schizoid and depressive positions, but, as they have continued to explore psychosis, narcissism, borderline states, addiction, sexual perversion, and perverse character structure, they have developed richer and more complex ideas about the defensive arrangements in these various pathologies. The idea of 'pathological organizations' has been gradually evolved as a central concept to order the clinical phenomena encountered. Many authors have contributed to the development of the concept, and the word 'organization' has been in use for some time, first as 'narcissistic organization' (Rosenfeld and Sohn), then as 'defensive organization' (O'Shaughnessy). More recently John Steiner has used the term 'pathological organization' which is now being generally adopted.

There are two main strands of thought in the idea of the pathological organization. The first is the dominance of a bad self over the rest of the personality; many authors point out a perverse, addictive element in this bondage, indicating that it involves sado-masochism, not just aggressiveness. The second strand is the idea of development of a structured pattern of impulses, anxieties, and defences which root the personality somewhere between the paranoid-schizoid and depressive positions. This pattern allows the individual to maintain a balance, precarious but strongly defended, in which he is protected from the chaos of the paranoid-schizoid position, that is, he does not become frankly psychotic, and yet he does not progress to a point where he can confront and try to work through the problems of the depressive position with their intrinsic

195

pain. There may be shifting about and even at times the appearance of growth but an organization of this sort is really profoundly resistant to change. The defences appear to work together to make a rigid system which does not develop the flexibility characteristic of the defences of the depressive position, and efforts by the individual to make reparation, so characteristic of the depressive position, are usually too narcissistic to bring lasting resolution. There is considerable variation in the psychopathology of pathological organizations but the analyses of these patients tend to get stuck, either to be very long, only partially successful, or sometimes interminable. The various authors are concerned with the question of whether the destructiveness of these organizations is primary or defensive. Often it is both, and indeed it is implicit in the work of many of the authors that the organizations they discuss are compromise formations, that is, that they are simultaneously expressions of death instinct and systems of defence against it.

The clinical phenomena of pathological organizations have been reported for many years; by Freud in his discussions of the negative therapeutic reaction (1916, 1923, 1924, 1937); by Abraham on the narcissistic defence (1919); and, among Kleinians, by Joan Riviere (1936) in her discussion of the negative therapeutic reaction as a defence against the task, felt to be impossible, of repairing damaged internal objects.

Bion is one of the first of the more recent group of authors to tackle the problem of how an organization of this sort arises. His model of what he calls 'minus K' paints a chilling picture of the inner world when reverie and alpha function fail (Bion 1962b, especially chapter 28). One wonders, he says, why such a thing as minus K should exist and says he will explore one factor only: envy. In his model the hypothetical infant projects his fear of dying into the breast together with envy and hate of the breast. Because of the projected envy, the breast is felt enviously to remove the good elements from the fear of dying and to force the worthless residue back into the infant. Worse still, the envious breast takes away the infant's will to live. When the object is reintrojected, it becomes an extremely destructive internal object, bent on stripping the infant, or what is left of the infant, of any qualities he still possesses, enviously asserting moral superiority, arousing guilt but only to show superiority, not to put anything right. The ego becomes partially identified with this envious stripping internal object to form what other authors variously call the bad self, the destructive self, or the narcissistic self, which attempts in diverse ways to rule the internal world.

In his paper 'Schizoid phenomena in the borderline' (1979, reprinted here, pp. 203–29), Henri Rey explores the role of schizoid phenomena as a relatively persistent personality organization which is neither neurotic nor psychotic but forms a frontier state. He emphasizes the concrete thinking typical of the schizoid mode of being together with its concomitant splitting, projective identification, denial, and inability to assimilate introjected objects. He emphasizes that the schizoid personality finds itself caught in a fluctuation between claustrophobia and agoraphobia. Because of his projections the space containing the schizoid person is felt to be hostile and dangerous, but to come out of his dangerous enclosing space leaves him lost in a state of fragmentation with no container. Rey gives many vivid examples of schizoid behaviour and thought, including difficulties in negotiating the depressive position which are likely to be dealt with by manic reparation in which the magical curative power of the penis is aggressively flaunted. He relates Klein's and Bion's concepts of psychic development and thinking to Piaget's conceptualization of the development of concepts of space and time. He gives little idea, however, of the possible constellation of factors, environmental and intrapsychic, that lead to people getting stuck in a schizoid mode of being rather than being able to move on to the integration of the depressive position.

Narcissism is a topic that has led many Kleinian analysts to further exploration of the first main strand of thinking about pathological organizations, namely to the dominance of the 'bad self' over the rest of the personality. As Segal points out (1983), Klein gave us all the conceptual and technical tools to understand narcissism but says very little about it herself. Klein clearly states, however, that she does not agree with Freud's idea that the infant goes through a stage of primary narcissism in which libido is attached to the ego. She states as her hypothesis that 'auto-eroticism and narcissism include the love for and relation with the internalized good object which in phantasy forms part of the loved body and self' (M. Klein 1952b). She makes a distinction between temporary narcissistic states, which involve withdrawal to an idealized internal object, and what she calls 'narcissistic structure' which, in contrast, is a more long-lasting organization involving projective identification to control objects and reintrojection of them in a way that affects the structure of the ego and the superego (M. Klein 1946). Klein did not spell out this brief reference, nor did she make an explicit connection between envy and narcissism, though it is implicit in *Envy and Gratitude* (1957) that she thought of narcissism as a defence against envy.

Herbert Rosenfeld has made some notable contributions to our understanding of the workings of the death instinct and defences against it in narcissism (1964 and 1971b, reprinted here). In his 1964 paper, 'On the psychopathology of narcissism: a clinical approach', Rosenfeld describes the way the self is identified with the good and enviable qualities of an object in such a way that the boundary between self and object is blurred, and, indeed, the self claims the object's qualities as its own without any recognition of their origin. The aim of this omnipotent identification, which he says takes place simultaneously by introjection and by projection, is to deny the separateness of the object and hence dependence on it; this denial makes it possible to evade painful feelings of envy, helplessness, and depressive anxiety. Indeed, the object, external or internal, is barely recognized to exist. This 1964 paper is often referred to as the paper concerned with 'libidinal narcissism', which is perhaps not a happy choice of term for it sounds benign, whereas I think Rosenfeld, like other Kleinian analysts, regards all but the most temporary states of narcissism as basically destructive, suffused with death instinct, and not to be confused with self-respect and caring for oneself.

During the 1960s and 1970s several Kleinian analysts began to work further on the idea of narcissistic and perverse relationships between parts of the self. Following on Klein's idea of a distinction between good and bad parts of the personality, Meltzer (1968, reprinted here) states that the aim of the destructive part of the personality is to create confusion and chaos so that the good infantile self will abandon psychic and external reality and willingly submit to the voluptuous despair offered by the bad self. The claim of the bad self, he suggests, is that it offers protection from terror of dead babies killed in phantasied attacks on the good parental intercourse and its products. None of the other authors traces the grip of the bad self to so specific a cause. (See also Meltzer, 1973.)

In 'On the fear of insanity' (1969), Money-Kyrle suggests that the infant mind is born into chaos and madness – 'We are born mad and become sane' – is his way of putting it. As the individual develops, the mad part of the self feels that its independence and omnipotence are threatened by sanity and that sanity will expose it to envy as well as dependence. So the mad self tries to dominate the sane self, leading to the situation described by Meltzer in 'Terror, persecution, dread' (1968).

But perhaps the paper which brings these issues to the fore most cogently is 'A clinical approach to the psychoanalytic theory of the life and death instincts: an investigation into the aggressive aspects of narcissism' (1971b, reprinted here), in which Rosenfeld describes what he calls destructive narcissism, an organization based on idealization of the bad self. He describes the perverse quality of the bad self and its triumph in seducing the good self and defeating the analyst. At times the bad self appears to whip up a delusional world into which the libidinal, dependent self disappears and a situation close to mania develops. The clinical aim of the analyst, he says, is to rescue the libidinal self and help the patient to become aware of the destructive omnipotence of the bad part of himself; once exposed, there is some hope that the bad self will be deflated and reveal itself, as one of my patients put it, as a 'poor devil' instead of '*the* Devil'.

In 'Cruelty and narrowmindedness' (1985a, though written years earlier, reprinted here), Brenman stresses again the theme of domination of one part of the self over another. He describes the omnipotent idealization of a cruel superego and the identification of the self with it in a fashion that blurs the boundaries between self and object and denies helplessness, the needs of the self, and dependence on good objects. In order to evade conscious guilt, mental perceptions are narrowed to justify cruelty and to ignore goodness in objects.

Leslie Sohn's concept of the *identificate*, described in 'Narcissistic organization, projective identification, and the formation of the identificate' (1985a, but written much earlier, reprinted here), is another way of describing the formation and maintenance of the bad self. His idea is developed from Rosenfeld's 1964 narcissism paper with its stress on omnipotent identification which takes over, virtually steals, the good qualities of the object in order to evade dependence and envy. This part of the self, which Sohn calls the 'identificate', not only triumphs over the object and the rest of the self but wipes the rest of the self out; it claims to be the whole of the self. Unlike Rosenfeld, Sohn thinks that it is only omnipotent projective identification that effects this result, not omnipotent introjective identification. Rosenfeld thinks both defences occur simultaneously.

With Segal's paper 'A delusional system as a defence against the re-emergence of a catastrophic situation' (1972) we begin to move towards the second strand of thinking about pathological organizations, that is, to the idea of a constellation of defences that leads to the personality getting stuck in uneasy equilibrium between the paranoid-schizoid and depressive positions. Segal discusses a man who suffered in infancy a catastrophic situation of being flooded by destructive and self-destructive impulses, threatening annihilation. He developed a delusional system in which dependence on objects was supposedly excluded in order to prevent the dreaded flooding from happening again. The delusional system contained elements of restitution, though the major aim was sadistic control of external reality and aggressive attack on his objects. The delusion was frankly psychotic, though the various obsessional rituals he had developed, in combination with a great deal of unacknowledged support from his relatives, had prevented an overt psychosis. This paper thus moves towards the idea of a defensive equilibrium between the paranoid-schizoid and depressive positions, though Segal's patient was much nearer the paranoid-schizoid pole than is characteristic of most pathological organizations described by other authors.

In 'A clinical study of a defensive organization' (1981a, reprinted here) Edna O'Shaughnessy discusses a somewhat similar situation in a much less ill man. She suggests that a 'defensive organization' is likely to develop when a typically anxious, persecuted individual with a weak ego arrives at the depressive position, finds its pains and responsibilities impossible to negotiate, and develops a defensive organization instead. She distinguishes defences from defensive organization on the grounds that a defensive organization is much more fixed and pathological than individual defences which allow greater scope for working through anxieties and moving forward to more integrated states. She describes her patient's initial collapse in which his mental state was extremely precarious, close to the chaos and madness of the paranoid-schizoid position; this was followed by reinstatement of his defensive organization; in the third phase of his analysis he misused this organization for perverse and omnipotent purposes; in the fourth phase he made very gradual progress to a more integrated state.

In her paper 'Expiation as a defence' (1981a) Ruth Riesenberg-Malcolm describes a patient's perverse use of guilt to appear responsible and depressed, while in fact avoiding the real responsibilities of the depressive position – again the emphasis on perversion of internal reality that so many of these papers describe.

Betty Joseph tackles the problem too, especially in 'Addiction to near-death' (1982, reprinted here) in which she describes the addictive quality and sexual pleasure in the relationship between the destructive and dependent parts of the self. The patient stirs up despair, depression, and fear of persecution, all of them real at some level, but in a way that creates a masochistic situation in which the patient gets caught up and tries to get his analyst caught up too. She describes a possible defensive basis for this sort of masochistic addiction. Such patients cannot stand waiting, she says, or even the simplest sort of guilt. She suggests that in infancy depressive pain must have been a torment and thinks they tried to get away from the torment by taking over the infliction of pain on themselves, building it into a world of perverse excitement and preventing consistent progress towards the depressive position. In this, as in several other of her papers, Joseph is dealing with what she and other colleagues have come to call 'perversions of character', even though no overt sexual perversion may be present. The paper is also especially important because it links the two strands of thinking about pathological organizations, the perverse relation between parts of the self and the maintenance by the individual of an uneasy equilibrium between the paranoid-schizoid and depressive positions.

John Steiner (1982) gives a formulation that states more explicitly an observation made by several other analysts, that there is a continuum in degree of malignancy of the narcissistic/destructive organization. In Steiner's description, everyone has a primitive destructive aspect of the self and a healthy self. In psychosis the destructive self dominates and destroys the healthy parts; in normal individuals the destructive self is less split off so that it can be contained and neutralized by the healthy part of the personality; in borderline and narcissistic states there is some sort of unhealthy liaison between the two. Steiner thinks that each part of the personality contains both good and bad aspects. This not only disguises the destructive nature of the more destructive part, but also allows perverse elements to be associated with the libidinal self, so that in the perverse relationship between the two parts of the self, the libidinal, dependent self is much too willing a victim.

In 'The interplay between pathological organizations and the paranoid-schizoid and depressive positions' (1987, reprinted here) Steiner clearly states the idea of the pathological organization as a set of defences not only against the fragmentation and confusion of the paranoid-schizoid position, but also against the mental pain of the depressive position. Although in the pathological organization primitive phantasies and mental mechanisms characteristic of the paranoid-schizoid position are used, Steiner suggests that, when they take the form of a stable organization of defences, they have a sort of pseudo-integration which can masquerade as the integration of the depressive position and give the illusion of providing relative stability and avoidance of depressive pain. Like O'Shaughnessy and Joseph, he stresses that there are both defensive aspects in such an organization and elements more directly expressive of death instinct. Whether intrinsically destructive or defensive, there are very frequently addictive, perverse elements which strongly resist change and are indeed opposed to any true grasp of psychic reality.

Thus it is clear that this set of Kleinian analysts have been moving towards the same sort of conceptualization, obviously influencing one another but without being particularly aware at the time of a common theme. Many questions remain, particularly, perhaps, how it is that a bad object is sometimes and in some patients felt to be a separate entity inside the personality, whereas at other times and in other patients it takes over the ego in a destructive amalgam that avoids madness but never allows anything like a full encounter with depressive anxiety. Bion's hypothesis is that envy is a crucial factor, with which all the authors I have described agree. A low threshold for tolerance of frustration and pain, Joseph adds. Deprivation by the external object both in the past and in the present is a factor that Rosenfeld finds important (Rosenfeld 1978a and 1986). It is likely that this is a topic on which many Kleinians will continue to work.

1

Schizoid phenomena in the borderline

J. H. REY

This article was first published in J. Le Boit and A. Capponi (eds) *Advances in the Psychotherapy of the Borderline Patient*, New York: Jason Aronson (1979) 449–84.

The schizoid mode of being

The period that followed the Second World War revealed a remarkable change in the kind of patients seen by, or referred to, the psychotherapist and the psychoanalyst. The bulk of patients seemed to consist of a certain kind of personality disorder which defied classification into the two great divisions of neurosis and psychosis. We now know them as borderline, narcissistic, or schizoid personality organization. This simplification is the result of a long process of attempts at classification of all kinds.

An attempt has been made in this essay to extract aspects of human behaviour and mental processes that seem to constitute the core of what we now know as schizoid or borderline personality organization. It can be found not only in those people with such a personality as will be described but also in people who may break down into schizophrenia, depression or mania, or as the underlying core of personality in people with hysterical or obsessional personality. By studying the 'schizoid' traits in these various states I hope to be able to define the schizoid personality and the schizoid mode of being in its more or less pure form and distinguish it from the other states of which it may form part. It seems that those people represent a group of persons who have achieved a kind of stability of personality organization in which they live a most limited and abnormal emotional life which is neither neurotic nor psychotic but a sort of frontier state.

Schizoid and/or borderline patients when seen by the psychiatrist are usually in their early twenties. They complain of an inability to make contact with others and find it impossible to maintain any warm and steady relationship. If they actually manage to enter into a relationship it rapidly becomes intensely dependent and results in disorders of identity. They rapidly and transiently form identification with their objects, experience a loss of their sense of identity with accompanying intense anxiety, fear of fragmentation or dissolution of the self. They seldom establish a firm sexual identity and vacillate in their experience of maleness and femaleness. They are not homo-sexuals but have fears that they may be and their choice of love object, or attempts at choice of love object, is just as vacillating. They are demanding controlling, manipulating, threatening, and devaluing towards others. They accuse society and others for their ills and are easily persecuted. This may be associated with grandiose ideas about themselves. In fact, their feelings are dominated by phantasies of relative smallness and bigness. When threatened by feeling small and unprotected and in danger they may defend themselves by uncontrollable rages and various forms of impulsive behaviour. Other aspects of their abnormal affectivity are reflected in the sense of futility they complain of and which is characteristic of them. This is reflected as well in the special kind of depression from which they suffer, a form of depersonalized depression, that is, boredom, uselessness, lack of interest, etc., but with a marked deadening of the pain aspect of true depression. Together with this deadness there is a search for stimulants and production of sensory experience by means of alcohol, drugs, hashish, cutting themselves, perversions, promiscuity, etc. They often complain of various abnormal sensations, body image disturbance of various kinds as well as depersonalization and derealization experiences. Their body ego is no more structured and stable than their personality, ego or self. Their underlying state of perplexity and confusion is frequently apparent.

Their work performance varies a great deal. Often when they come to treatment they have given up their studies or their work or they are doing some form of manual or low-level occupation although they may have achieved university standards. However, their working capacity may be preserved if they work in a structured situation.

There is one difference in my personal experience in the way the two sexes present themselves, with many more men responding to the description I have given than women. In the case of women, hysterical manifestations, that is, hysterical mechanisms of defence mark the underlying personality structures and they show more often than men histrionic behaviour, acting out, hysterical fits, and overtly the claustro-agoraphobic syndrome.

The claustro-agoraphobic syndrome, however, is basic to both sexes; only certain manifestations of it are different. As Guntrip (1968) has so clearly described, the schizoid person is a prisoner. He craves love but is prevented from loving because he is afraid of the destructive force of his love so far as his object is concerned. He dares not love for fear that he will destroy. He finds himself enclosed in a dilemma, enclosed in a limited space and with limited objects and limited relationships.

It is the mechanisms at work in this 'limitation state' that I intend to describe. Kindness and support in the transference situation is not enough to treat these patients. A thorough knowledge of their mental processes, phantasies, and underlying structures subtending their behaviour is essential in combination with affective understanding.

I will begin with internal part-objects and their language, projective identification, because we must begin somewhere in this Tower of Babel which makes up the schizoid structure. I mean this expression literally because these part-objects whose structure we need to understand, speak to each other and speak to us in a confusion of languages which demand special interpretation.

In normal interpersonal relationships one or another aspect of the whole ego corresponds with one or another aspect of the ego of the other person. It is a relationship at the level of the integrated ego. Moreover, in normal conduct, apart from certain aspects of love and hate, when we tend to be concrete, the ego makes use of conventional signs which are conscious and of symbols which may be conscious or unconscious, both however existing at a representational level. Schizoid communication by contrast often takes place at a level of 'merchandise', a sort of barter agreement in which the subject feels himself to be given 'things', made to accept 'things', where 'things' are done to him, etc.

Thus, after weeks or even months of refusing to speak of her intimate feelings a patient said: 'You don't understand. If I speak to you I hit you, I poison you with the rotting and mouldy things which I am full of.' She had previously simulated a suicide attempt in order to get her stomach washed out, to clean out some of these contents. Another patient said: 'When you speak to me and ask me questions you bite me and tear out a piece of my flesh. I won't speak any more, I won't listen.' It is a well accepted fact by psycholinguists that at first the utterances of the mother are considered to be experienced by the child as perceptual parts of mother like any other parts.

Moreover, more or less normal people think in terms of persons, not objects placed somewhere in a container. But in contrast, this is just how schizoid thought functions. Thoughts are material objects contained somewhere and expelled into something or other; even the containing object is itself contained somewhere. It is thus that the schizophrenic is the patient who most concretely shows the true problem of claustrophobia and agoraphobia. In the consulting room he sits near the door or the window even if this can't be opened sufficiently for him to escape. He feels himself to be engulfed, immured in one object or another, and feels that he does the same thing with the objects which are inside him.

A schizophrenic patient illustrated this by explaining why he was frightened to lie on the couch. He was afraid of becoming engulfed in it and, being so tall that his feet overlapped the couch, he feared that his father would see his legs poking out and cut them off. He could not distinguish between the couch and his mother in his unconscious phantasy and felt himself caught inside his mother with only his feet showing. This is concrete thinking where the idea is equivalent to the object and where these idea-objects are always contained or containing.

We must now consider the characteristics of these objects and their fate when they are displaced. This will lead us to examine the notion of partial objects and of splitting and denial. It is remarkable that these ideas which took on an increasing importance in Freud's thought remained unused, or almost so, by the adherents of classical psychoanalysis. To quote Laplanche and Pontalis (1967): 'It is of some interest to note that it was in the field of psychosis – the very area where Bleuler too, from a different theoretical standpoint speaks of *Spaltung* – that Freud felt the need to develop a certain conception of the splitting of the ego. It seemed to us worth outlining this conception here even though few psychoanalysts have adopted it; it has the merit of emphasizing a typical phenomenon despite the fact that it does not provide an entirely satisfactory explanation of it' (p. 429). Similar comments could be applied to the concept of partial objects and of denial since these concepts are interdependent. I think it is necessary to make an important distinction between a pathological part-object and a normal part-object which is only partial in the sense that it forms one of the parts of an object which is capable of being assembled into a whole. Thus the maternal breast is a part-object only by comparison with the whole mother formed by the integration of her various parts, and functions in an infant's phantasy like an object endowed with capacity for action, love, and hate.

Splitting plays a part in normal development also, for example, splitting of good and bad aspects of the object as well as of the subject and also the splitting of one object from others. But the schizophrenic behaves differently. Under the sway of persecutory anxiety and the fear of catastrophic dissolution of the ego, primitive and elemental anxieties which arise from the beginning of life, he proceeds to use splitting repetitively and intensively to get rid of bad parts of himself which leads to a fragmentation of the object and of the ego. The fragmented parts of the ego as well as fragmented parts of internal objects with the impulses and anxieties belonging to these fragments are projected into his objects which acquire by projective identification these split-off aspects of the self, now projected and denied. These objects become persecutors, and are introjected, but cannot be assimilated and are in turn projected into an external object (or even into an internal object in an intrapsychic relation) and the vicious circle continues. These objects, some of which Bion has called bizarre objects, are important as elements in the thinking not only of the schizophrenic but also of the schizoid patient. These processes do not only apply to bad aspects of the object or of the self. From fear of destruction, the good parts of the object or the ego are also split off and projected in the same manner into objects which are expected to look after them while they contain them, preserving and protecting them.

In the course of psychotherapy the schizoid, having projected his good parts into the therapist in order to preserve them, as if depositing them in a bank, becomes frantic if he cannot find his therapist because the loss of the therapist means also the loss of elements of the self and of his objects. Moreover, since the reparative activity of the schizoid is based on concrete reparation, as if he were rebuilding a house with its bricks, the loss of the bricks contained in the therapist makes reconstruction impossible. This, in my opinion, is one of the fundamental reasons for the schizoid's refusal to form an ordinary transference relationship with the therapist. Unless one can interpret this mistrust, which is fundamentally justified and which the therapist needs to understand, it is extremely difficult to ever obtain the confidence of the schizoid patient. Concurrently with these internal splits, the therapist, too, is split into good and bad objects and the transference relationship changes constantly and remains unstable and fragmented for a long time, changing not only from day to day but from minute to minute during the session.

Thus, a young schizophrenic whom I treated in hospital perceived me either as an object whom she could not do without, from whom she could not separate, and to whom she wanted perpetually to adhere, or within an instant as an object which she attacked so vigorously that I had to defend myself from her by force. One day she illustrated the change from a neurotic transference to a psychotic transference in a remarkable way: she spoke to me about her life at home in a reasonable manner and in contact with reality, and then all of a sudden, with astonishing rapidity, she went to the door and with piercing eyes and voice trembling with emotion she said: 'Get down here in front of me, obey. You know how for years you have mistreated my mother and me, the cruelties and torture that you have done. When you came to my room at three a.m. in the morning, etc., etc.'

External reality had disappeared and only psychic reality remained. The image of the father and of me had become one. By projective identification I had become her father with his characteristics partly real and partly attributed to him by the patient by that same process of projective identification. At the end of five minutes, which seemed as long as five centuries, when I wondered what was going to happen, she became calm and resumed a more or less normal conversation. But she remained mistrustful, close to the door as if she might await the return of the 'feared ones' which she called 'they' and which would come to take her away to a hellish fate. She could not be friends with me because 'they' became angry and punished her. It was best to be on good terms with 'they'. She asked if she could kill me to convince 'they' that she did not love me. On the other hand, the idea of losing me was intolerable; after she let down the tyres of my car so that I would be killed in an accident, she hid herself to watch me and ran after me to warn me that if I went in the car I was in great danger, without telling me why.

The fear of separation from the object and the desire to penetrate into it and fuse with it into a primal unity can be so intense that it surpasses human understanding.

Thus, a paranoid and persecuted patient complained ceaselessly with years of virulent reproaches full of rage and despair because I did not love her, after having seduced her by my interpretations and having led her to believe that she was loved. She found proof of my wish to torture her in the fact that I did not let her penetrate into me physically and fuse with me. On this subject she lost all contact with reality and insisted that such a fusion was possible. One proof of my refusal which made the analysis almost impossible consisted in reproaching me as often as she could that I was not in agreement with what she was saying. This produced two people, not one person, and I became a monster which, at least at that moment, she hated.

It is clear from what I have just said that the question of his identity is a major problem for the schizoid. The enormous difficulty of acquiring a stable ego is the result of faulty introjective identification, made very difficult by persecutory feelings and a fear of the object created by the projection of destructive, envious, and insatiable impulses which can become incredibly violent. They are neither heterosexual nor homosexual, not even bisexual. This arises from the fact that their identifications depend both on an internal object which is not assimilated and on a containing external object in which they live, and hence this identity depends on the state of the object and varies with it, with its identity and its actions. They have an external shell or carapace but no vertebral column. They live as parasites in the shell which they seem to have borrowed or stolen and this creates a feeling of insecurity.

Thus, an extremely schizoid young man, who during his treatment went through a breakdown diagnosed by all the psychiatrists except me as totally schizophrenic, would dress himself at night in clothes typical of a London businessman. He would enter his parents' bedroom at three o'clock in the morning, wake them and say to his father: 'Am I now the person you wanted me to be?' Previously he had dressed himself in his mother's clothes for a number of years. Under the pressure of the psychotherapeutic group where he received treatment, which attempted to confront him with his lack of initiative and his failure to leave home and go to work, he decided to become a man.

One day some workmen happened to be working on road works in front of his house; he urinated in a bottle which he put at the front door as a gesture of contempt; he looked at himself in a mirror, brushed his hair in the style of Wellington and in a military manner marched around the courtyard, took some of his neighbor's washing which was drying on the hedge between their houses and threw it into her garden. He invited the workers to tell him who gave them permission to be there and then returned to his house. Since it was the first of May, a special day for workers, he sang a patriotic anticommunist song. Then he convinced himself that he was in danger because the workers were Communists and would attack him. Moreover, the BBC would begin to talk about him and the Irish rebels would come to get him. He had become important, but persecuted, and his homosexual passivity and his feminine identification entered into the conflict as a passive defence. Finally, to separate himself, to undo the identification with his parents, he became irritable, oppositional, and aggressive. They could no longer look after him and he was admitted to the hospital as an inpatient.

During individual sessions with me he sat on the floor to look up at me from a lower position as a sign of respect, like a baby. Then he said that if he lay down, or sat down, etc., he would, like a baby, fail to orient himself in relation to the things around him. Later he became preoccupied with multiple aspects of his personality: he no longer knew which parts of his parents he was made of, and each piece had a nationality: his father was English, his mother German/Polish, who now lives in England. Each 'piece' had a special and separate characteristic. His father is a professor, but in addition was a military man through family tradition, but at the same time a pacifist; he is upper and lower class, conservative and socialist, etc. He began to believe that his mother · was Jewish. He gave a nationality to each of these 'pieces': one 'piece' of him was Prussian, and very rigid, one 'piece' English, one 'piece' Polish, etc. Then he wanted to become a Jew and soon after he no longer wanted to. First he admired them, then he criticized them. Finally he explained to me why he wanted to become Jewish: it was because the Jews were fragmented, dispersed, persecuted, and dispossessed, living in a Tower of Babel of languages and of different nationalities and yet found their unity and their own identity by the fact that they were Jewish and this fact could transcend and unite all these fragments into an integrated whole.

What a marvellous unconscious description of the integrative functions of the object! He had to have this schizoid regression, this dissociation of parts which had been assembled in a faulty way in order to separate out the elements and to reconstruct the edifice. This example illustrates clearly the problem which integration of the ego poses for the schizophrenic or schizoid person.

Schizophrenic breakdown

I have had the occasion to treat a young schizophrenic who had an attitude resembling catatonia and very interesting rituals in which a gesture of her limbs or her face was always annulled by an opposing gesture controlling and undoing the preceding gesture. I eventually understood that these gestures were either sexual or aggressive and needed to be controlled. After the death of her father she adopted typically catatonic postures and said that she could not move because she would come into collision with her father who was enclosed inside her.

Later, with other patients, I came to understand that the opposite of immobility could be seen in paroxysmal movements such as those of an epileptic fit, which by contrast results in the projection of internal contents outside where they can be attacked and destroyed. Then I came to understand the extreme mental rigidity of the schizoid who has to control all his objects, both internal and external. The anxiety of his sexual persecutory and destructive impulses is so great that no autonomy can be allowed to his objects. The fear of fragmentation is catastrophic.

Thus a schizoid man could alter nothing of his life or his attitudes and he said that he could never live anywhere else than at his home because if he moved he would have to take with him his room with all his furniture and things as they were without changing anything.

Transformation, representation, and symbolization

The second fact to consider with the schizoid is the mental apparatus necessary for the transformation of sensory or sensorimotor experience into representations, into images, into symbols and signs, and into memories, such transformations being essential both for the maintenance of ordinary human relationships and for the construction of a normal mental apparatus for thinking.

We have seen that the elements of thought in the schizoid have a concrete character which Freud himself described as one of the essential qualities of the system unconscious, namely, the representation of things instead of the representation of words. This defect in the function of transformation seems to be a basic defect in the schizoid. But at the same time we know that the schizoid is in many cases capable of great intelligence even though he treats people as things, and in this way removes the affectivity which for him is dangerous and persecuting. The coexistence of a schizoid type of personal relationship and of a highly developed intelligence can only be explained by a split in the ego which results in a partial ego, which is intellectual and highly developed such as Piaget or Hartmann would describe, and another part of the ego in which the development has been arrested at the schizoid stage and where the depressive position has not been worked through.

During psychotherapy with the schizoid, progress in treatment depends on the possibility of undoing this schizoid structure and of allowing normal symbolization of bizarre objects and of sensory experiences to occur, that is to say, make other modes of communication possible. It is sometimes possible to achieve this end

211

without a catastrophic reaction, that is to say, without the coherent parts of the ego disintegrating. In other cases this is impossible and the patient needs to go through a frankly schizophrenic episode. For some this is a good thing, because it is the only way of returning to the point of bifurcation between normal and abnormal development where the growth of a paralyzed affectivity, previously enslaved and rigidly controlled, may be resumed. No one, I believe, can predict if this happens whether the patient will become a chronic schizophrenic or will progress towards new horizons.

The same situation applies to the schizophrenic in a clinically obvious schizophrenic state: does he have the potential to resume his development or not? This chiefly depends on the capacity of his mental apparatus for symbolic transformation and on the stage he has reached in relation to the depressive position. Indeed, there is a group of patients for whom the schizoid state is a regression and constitutes a defence against the suffering and pain of the depressive state; these patients have a better outlook than those who are true schizophrenics, that is to say, who have never reached the depressive state. A 'schizoaffective' state where clinically the patient oscillates between a state of schizophrenia and depression is also well known and these cases again have a more favourable outcome with psychotherapy. We also know of cases who, without treatment, change from schizophrenia to depression or vice versa in the course of time.

Among those who have studied the function of transformation and representation in the mental apparatus, the work of Bion (1965) stands out as especially significant. I would like to give an example of defective transformation. Bion says, 'In psychoanalytic theories statements by patients or by analysts are representations of an emotional experience. If we can understand the process of representation this will help us to understand the representation and that which is represented.'

A patient told me the following dream:

'I am dining with friends and get up from the table. I am thirsty and I start to drink. I realize that the bottle in my mouth has a neck shaped like a feeding bottle; there is no teat, but I think I can feel the flange which normally holds the teat in place. While I think of this I begin to see the bottle more clearly. I hold it in front of my face and see that it has the shape of a feeding bottle. In the bottle I see water. The level of the water falls and bubbles of air mount through the liquid, and because of this I am aware that some of the water has become part of me; but I cannot feel this thing that becomes part of me. I am anxious because I can neither understand nor feel the water passing from a state separate from me to become an intimate part of me. While I am thinking thus, the bottle becomes bigger. I see at that moment that on the inside of the bottle facing me, words are engraved on the surface in raised letters which give instructions on how to wean an infant.'

In this dream the subject failed to transform the experience of the movement of water from the exterior to the interior of his body into a good experience in the form of a representation and a memory. He did not participate in the experience. He did not understand what happened; he tells us that he lacks the experience of the change. This can only be the experience in the mouth where the presence of water produces a sensation, a sensation which is needed to make the work of transformation possible. One part of the experience is lacking; it is as if he had been fed through a tube. But he tells us what was lacking, it was the teat and it was the experience of weaning, and of suckling from a mother. He took the bottle himself and gave himself a drink. The teat no doubt represents a maternal breast and a mother whose presence and whose bodily contact is absolutely necessary for the awareness and recording of the experience. It seems that in the absence of the good object, part of the work of assimilation did not take place.

Reparation

In addition to structural mechanisms of the schizoid phase and its mechanisms of defence I would like to consider a fundamental aspect of schizoid mentality. This is the law of the talion and the absence of the capacity for reparation which governs the whole behaviour of the schizoid. It is this law of vengeance which is responsible through its incredible power in the schizoid not only for the stunted mental structure, but also for its lack of humanity. By the law of the talion I mean: 'An eye for an eye and a tooth for a tooth'; 'Let the punishment fit the crime'; 'If I have stolen my hand will be cut off, if I have transgressed I will be punished, you have stolen and I will cut off your hands', etc. There is no forgiveness, no compassion, no reparation. There is only the terrible vengeance and anger of Jehovah preached by the prophets of the Old Testament.

Reparation in the schizoid state also obeys the law of the inverse talion. Like everything I have already described, it has to be concrete. I call this *repair* to distinguish it from reparation. We could perhaps call it reconstruction in contrast to reparation. This reconstruction has some things in common with the restitution with which Freud was concerned. Reparation, on the other hand, is a notion unknown to Freud, and plays a fundamental role in the work of Melanie Klein. Even Freud's ideas on restitution remained sketchy and far from complete, as were his ideas on splitting and denial. Almost all analysts have rejected the fundamentally new theme which appears in his work after 1920 in which the life instinct as a constructive force was contrasted with the death instinct as an instinct of disintegration. People have quarrelled about words and have forgotten that analysis is rooted on observation. The study of the schizoid personality structure has led us back to the observations of a master on splitting, projection, and denial which his ultraconservative disciples had well buried. In reconstruction or repair, infantile omnipotence is retained and an attempt is made to reconstruct the damaged one. Reparation, by contrast, is not and cannot be an omnipotent act.

The manic defence

We will now consider the role of the manic state. On the one hand its role is a defence against the anxiety of disintegration and of schizoid persecution, and on the other hand a defence against the pain of the depressive state. One can observe this from the point of view of psychiatry in the clinical syndrome of hypomania, but also as a potential psychodynamic state during psychotherapy. We must not forget that the manic state can represent an exaggeration of a normal phase of maturation and of reparation. In manic states or in the manic defence we are no longer concerned with the maternal breast but with the penis. I believe that in all depressive states the object with which the subject has a relationship is, contains, or symbolically represents the maternal breast which as a partial object represents the mother who is destroyed, emptied, poisoned and thus in a depressed state; the subject feels this is his fault and becomes identified with this depressed object and, consequently, depressed himself.

The object of the manic state is the penis which is needed by the subject for the task of reparation: through it he can regain the destroyed object either as a direct substitute by identification or by recreating the contents of the mother, that is to say, by making her pregnant by filling her empty breasts, etc. The more the maternal object is destroyed by the subject's attacks, the more must the penis become omnipotent and the subject by identification becomes omnipotent also. In this manner the destroyed state of the object is denied. There is no reparation proper and after the manic phase the patient returns to his depression or his schizoaffective state at the level of maturation which he had previously reached.

A very schizoid patient dreamed that on his nose he was balancing a long pole which reached right to the sky with a baby balanced on the end. As he awakened he said to himself: 'This fucking penis is good for nothing, it is so big that it is useless.' On the couch, the patient of whom I have already spoken had identified his whole body with a phallus and he felt himself enlarge physically and be invaded by delusions of grandeur.

In the manic state we have a pseudo penis which repairs nothing; it serves to deny the reality of destroyed objects and presents itself as the universal substitute, which leads to the formation of a false self. Meanwhile, the aggressive impulses continue to destroy the object.

Manic reactions can actually represent a pathological deviation of a normal phase of development. I believe that when the separated fragments of the ego reunite, whether in a mosaic or in a fusion, it is done with the help of the phantasied action of the phallus. This is achieved on the one hand by an identification with the penis, adopting its characteristics and functions and, on the other hand, because, although a partial object it usually functions, as we have explained, as a representation of the whole object, the father, and enters into the relationship with the maternal breast, the partial object representing the mother. We have here the prototypes of the sexual identity of the two sexes and the prototype of the relationship between them. The role of the penis as a creator integrating and repairing through reproduction becomes clear in this model.

On the other hand, in the manic state there is a partial identification with the immeasurably grandiose aspect of the erect penis. The manifestations of this aspect are omnipotent, contemptuous, and persecutory as well. It is always present in a latent form in the schizoid and, when seen clinically as delusions of grandeur in paranoid states or as a feature of the depression of the manic depressive, illustrates the role of the phallus in the grandiosity seen in these conditions.

The patient referred to earlier, who felt himself to vary in size both physically and mentally, explained that he felt he had a permanent personality for the first time when he experienced the presence inside him of a hard column extending from his anus to his mouth which could resist all attacks. Later in his grandiose state he identified with Jesus Christ, grew a beard and became a carpenter, designed religious motifs and wanted to preach in church.

The depressive position

It will not be possible to go into the mechanism by which a depressive state develops even though this forms an essential phase in treatment. This is work about which much has been written and I want to concentrate on schizoid states. Suffice that we remember that in this process destructive impulses lose their intensity and loving impulses play a fundamental role. The good and the bad parts of the ego and also of the object unite gradually into a whole and the law of the talion loses its virulence. Primitive compassion begins to take over from the total egocentricity characteristic of the beginnings of life. The object achieves a life of its own and the subject becomes an object related to like any other object.

The change from schizoid states to schizophrenia

These phases of development belong to the preverbal period. Instead of the biphasic development. Freud proposed we have here to understand a triphasic evolution: first an archaic preverbal phase and an archaic verbal phase where the distinction can be thought of as an example of ontogeny repeating phylogeny, and, then, after the age of six, seven, or eight, a phase in which external reality dominates. I take the view that nonverbal schemata give a structure to verbal thought which in turn influences the pre-existing nonverbal schemata. This reciprocal relationship sheds light on the disorders of verbal thought which are seen when a schizoid individual becomes schizophrenic. The task of defining what happens when this change from a schizoid to a schizophrenic state occurs is not easy. The more I understand the language and structure of the schizoid the more I find the distinction difficult.

From the point of view of classical psychiatry it is quite simple: are there delusions or hallucinations? If there are, it is schizophrenia, if not, it isn't. But in fact, when one works not only longitudinally but simultaneously in depth as the psychoanalyst does, the situation is quite different. We can see this if we compare material from schizoid patients with the delusional ideas of someone floridly schizophrenic.

Let us take an extreme case, a patient who had four schizophrenic breakdowns, each presenting a different clinical picture. In his hebephrenic–catatonic state, which began with an intense interest in the universe and the stars, he felt himelf to be communicating with an extraterrestrial universe. As proof he took out of his briefcase

216

some little oval and circular shaped pieces of ivory colored paper and assured me that their extraterrestrial origin was obvious. Much later he admitted that although at first he had firmly believed this, he later came to realize that he himself had simply collected these pieces of paper from somewhere.

We see here the interplay of a number of schizoid mechanisms. First of all the wish to be omnipotent to participate in the universe, which he held very strongly. To achieve this wish without becoming mad he had to avoid destroying external reality and instead tried to transform it. With the external physical proof he could thus reinforce the internal psychic reality of his wish. For this he had through the phantasy of projective identification transformed the pieces of paper and obtained in this way a formal proof of his experience. He had thus decided not to completely abandon external reality, but to grossly transform it by a process of splitting, by omnipotent wishing and by projective creation.

Some schizoid patients are past masters at the art of choosing objects which are precisely appropriate for their projections, that is, which have characteristics so similar to their projection that it becomes very difficult to make a distinction between the object and the projected phantasy.

It seems to me then that the schizophrenic goes further and does not concern himself with the existence of external reality but declares and delusionally believes whatever he wishes, having made a regression to a very primitive, infantile, stage where the distinction between psychic reality and external reality is almost nonexistent and hardly concerns him. There is only one reality, the reality of the internal phantasy world. In the schizoid world we find various gradations of abnormality in the type of morbid processes I have just described.

The space–time continuum and displacement in the borderline

An attempt will be made now to examine the clinical observations previously described, in terms of the organization of space and time as in any other branch of knowledge. Piagetian observations, ideas and constructs have been extensively used both explicitly and implicitly but by no means exclusively. The main source for this work is clinical observation during treatment and psychoanalytical psychotherapy supervisions and interpretations of data. I have made use of Piaget only for the reason that psychoanalysis has never

217

studied the structure of external reality, of space, displacement and time as have he and his pupils.

During the treatment of patients, especially of claustrophobic and agoraphobic patients, it appeared more and more evident to me that a fundamental organization of objects in space (including the patient himself) was underlying the mode of behaviour observed. All sorts of physical and mental situations which claustrophobic and agoraphobic patients experience are very likely to refer to a primary situation which all the other secondary situations are substitutes for and symbolic of.

Claustrophobic persons are afraid to be in an enclosed situation, they develop extreme anxiety or panic and want to get out. The 'situation' may be a room, a traffic jam, a marriage. When they are not contained they become agoraphobic and develop anxiety or panic. Thus they may be housebound, or may only travel so far alone from the place of safety and no further, or have to be accompanied. The manifestations of those conditions are well known. However, it was when I made the observation that this condition is really a basic one in schizoid states and schizophrenia that I realized it had a very important meaning. By a basic condition I mean that whenever schizoid and schizophrenic patients are seen in the context of dynamic treatment they reveal claustro-agoraphobic basic fears not in the least evident when their behaviour is assessed from a purely phenomenological psychiatric approach. The mental and emotional disturbances of the schizoid state are disturbances in the early, primitive, and basic organization of the human being, ontogenetically speaking. It is the importance that Piaget gives to the early structuralization of space that led me to attempt the explanation of the way of life of the schizoid in terms of the early organization of space, movement, and time.

Spatial development of the infant and his world

The foetus is at first contained within the uterus which is itself contained inside the mother. It is relatively deprived of freedom of movement and displacement, although a certain degree of movement is possible. On the other hand it moves with the mother in the mother's external space. After birth one could say that the mother through her care, feeding, warmth support, etc., recreates partially this uterine state for the baby. Although restricted still, the baby's personal space allows him more freedom than in the womb. It could be called the marsupial space. The baby now moves in the mother's space but only in that portion of her space which is his personal space. As he grows up his personal space increases until it has coincided with the maternal space and, if the mother is normal, for instance, not claustro-agoraphobic, that space will coincide with general space where the subject will be an object amongst objects. Simultaneously with this process a space internal to the subject is formed where psychic internal objects live in intrapsychic relationships. They are experienced very concretely at first, for example, as sensations or elaborated perceptions and even more elaborated later as representations of a very complex nature.

It would seem that everybody has an external personal space of some kind which persists, somewhat like the notion of territory in ethology and in which our object relations are somewhat different from those in the universal space. However, as Piaget has pointed out and described so clearly space is not a Newtonian absolute space, neither is time absolute time; they are both constructs. The infant and the child have to construct their objects and their space, space being the relative positioning of objects as in the Einsteinian model.

The idea then would be to look at some aspects and stages of those early constructions and how they appear either unevolved or distorted as structures underlying the schizoid mode of being. The pure Piagetian approach is unsatisfactory, for although emotions, affects, and drives are accepted as intrinsic parts of the cognitive structures, they are not referred to as such. I will therefore present my own psychoanalytical and Piagetian-inspired elaborations.

Objects that are familiarly looked upon and treated as individual wholes by adults are certainly not experienced as such for the infant, and the child has to 'construct' them, linking parts by action schemas as described by Piaget, that is, by interiorized actions of the subject on the object. Piaget says the child co-ordinates 'the actions among themselves in the form of practical schemas, a sort of sensorimotor preconcept, characterized by the possibility of repeating the same action in the presence of the same objects or generalizing it in the presence of analogous others.'

For Piaget more complex schemas are not just the association or synthesis of previously isolated elements. Thus, he writes of the sensorimotor schema that 'it is a definite and closed system of movements and perceptions. The schema presents, in effect, the double characteristics of being structured (thus structuring itself the field of perception or of understanding) and of constituting itself beforehand as totality without resulting from an association or from a synthesis between the previously isolated elements' (Battro 1973). For Piaget the 'sensorimotor schemas are not simply what we

219

sometimes call patterns, that is to say they have further power to generalize and further power to assimilate' (Battro 1973).

As to schemas relative to persons, he says that 'they are cognitive and affective simultaneously. The affective element is perhaps more important in the domain of persons and the cognitive element in the domain of things, but it is only a question of degree.' Thus, he says that 'an affective schema' means simply the affective aspect of schemas which are otherwise also intellectual.

So to summarize, for Piaget action is at the very beginning the source of all manifestations of life. It precedes thought, it controls perception and sensation, and it is by a process of combinations of actions of the subject on his object, followed by the internalization of these action schemas, that the precursors of thought are generated. Thus the infant puts his thumb in his mouth, then he extends this action to other objects than his thumb, then elaborates the action by using a rod or some such object to extend the reach of his arm to get to objects that he will take to his mouth or elsewhere.

I do not know if a study has been made of such a way of thinking in Freud's writings apart from the structural theory itself. But it is interesting to note that in the Rat Man, for instance. Freud makes constant references to psychical structures. In fact, Part II is entitled, 'Some general characteristics of obsessional structures' (Freud 1909). He says that 'obsessional structures can correspond to every sort of psychical act' (p. 221). He says:

'In this disorder (obsessional neurosis) repression is affected not by means of amnesia but by a severance of causal connections brought about by a withdrawal of affect. These repressed connections appear to persist in some kind of shadow form (which I have elsewhere compared to an endopsychic perception) and they are thus transferred, by a process of projection, into the external world, where they bear witness to what has been effaced from consciousness.'

This is as good a definition of mental structure as any structuralist could wish.

For the object-relations psychoanalyst, therefore, there exists in the behaviour of adults primitive object relationships or schemas, normal or pathological, which govern aspects of behaviour. Some of these primitive internalized object relations may have remained unintegrated and function autonomously. Part-object psychology or the psychology of part-object, part-subject, part-states, etc., relates to the study of the aspect of the genetic development of object relationships.

Starting with the need of the infant expressed as desire for gratification, there is little doubt that the infant wishes to make part of his endogenous space, that is, the precursor of the self, the gratifying objects he needs for survival and growth. His early discovery of the appearance and disappearance of the object in his space (i.e., early ego or self) will prompt him to desire the good objects as part of himself or of his good space in the only way he is capable, the concrete. The frustration of not being able to always keep the object in his spaces (i.e., internal space and personal space) will increase the desire for the object to be his possession. The growth of this desire and the need for securing such objects, if it reaches great intensity, will become greed. The frustration, anger, anxiety resulting from the nonpossession of the desired gratifying objects will lead to the desire to deprive of it the other space containing the desired objects, for the other space containing the objects is now in a state of no-pain or pleasure, a state previously experienced by the infant. The wish is not only to possess the object but to deprive the other space as he is deprived himself. This is envy.

Further, the infant left in his self-space whilst waiting for the gratifying object will have to substitute objects of his own self-space, for example, parts of his own body, or toys, etc. Thus in the place of the breast mother he will have thumb, excrements, or genitals as part of his space. They may prove helpful to wait for the appearance of the external breast-mother and thus temporarily relieve anxiety or frustration following nongratification. Nongratification may lead to punishing the nonself space by putting frustrating objects, say faeces, into it, thus substituting for the good breast or transforming it into a bad object. However, those parts of the self-space put into the nonself-space are still considered to be somehow part of the self-space and a particular kind of bond is formed between self-space and nonself-space by displacement in or out of them, that is, by introjection and projection. This bond gives to early object relationship a quality of possessiveness and identification between objects which are at the roots of introjective and projective identification processes. This process is by no means abnormal when it is concerned with displacement of objects for need gratification and communication purposes.

Its persistence and distortions are, however, responsible for a large number of typical features of the schizoid way of experiencing. It creates the feeling of living in the object because part of oneself is in the object; it creates the need for never leaving the object out of control; it creates a sense of impending doom through the possible loss of part of the self if the object is lost. And it results in persecutory feelings if the projected or displaced part of the self is believed to have envious, greedy, and destructive impulses and accounts for innumerable other schizoid manifestations.

We must now proceed with the systematic examination of schizoid manifestations in terms of our space-time model and also illustrate with examples. First of all, I will try to show how one must extend the claustro-agoraphobic syndrome from a specific syndrome to a basic universal organization of the personality. A claustrophobic woman is seen for assessment for psychotherapy. She says she is afraid that something terrible will happen to her if she goes out. She insists she does not know what it is. I point out that there are only two possibilities, either it is something she will do to others or something others will do to her. She says after a lot of hesitation, 'I'm afraid I'll do something mad.' After more hesitation, she says, 'I'll shout and people will think I'm mad.' I say, 'Shouting is something coming out of you, what else could come out of you?' She becomes extremely tense and nervous and after a while asks to be allowed to leave. I say that, of course, she can leave if she so desires, but on the other hand if she can have the courage to say what thought is making her so uncomfortable that she wants to leave, it might save her months of treatment and misery. She plucks up the courage and says 'urine and faeces'. I will leave out the rest of the interview. This is a routine happening in various forms. What years of study of my own patients and patients treated by others has revealed I will put in schematic form.

It will be noticed that the patient wanted to remove herself from the space where she was in contact with what she felt as a threatening object. She wanted to leave the room. However, we also know that phobics avoid certain situations, for instance, eating in public; they will not go to a restaurant, or to the cinema, or to shops. They restrict their outside space until they are housebound. It is important to understand what the ultimate space into which they retire corresponds to in the unconscious.

The outside world or outside space is in such an instance transformed by projective identification into the body or internal space of the subject himself, identified with the internal space of the mother, and thus entering and coming out of a room is coming out of that which the room stands for – ultimately, the mother's body. A primitive imprinted state of birth experiences persists in the hierarchies of transformation and representation of that early experience. What is fixed in the mind is not necessarily the original experience of birth but one or another experience of a primitive similar state belonging to the hierarchy of space constructions, such as the marsupial space described previously. When something comes out of the body such as a shout, urine, faeces, semen, saliva, vomit, it fires the system 'coming out of' and produces the attached affect. The mechanism involved is the identification by projective identification of the subject with the contents of his own body and of his body identified with that of the mother. He thus experiences himself coming out of mother.

As I have said, the primitive emotional experience, the affect, has been dominant in the structurization of the self- and nonself-spaces. Displacement, then, of any kind of objects including the subject himself from self-space to nonself-space or vice versa is experienced in a primitive manner. Space in certain circumstances is experienced as it was once experienced in a part of the personality, split off from the rest and this way of experiencing space persists. The panic associated with that state and the bodily anguish and sensations are but persistence of the experience when the ego was mostly body ego. The coming into activity of that split-off archaic part of the adult self takes over and paralyses the more adult ego, and thus, adult methods of coping with danger are not any longer available.

However, I realized the fundamental structure underlying it all when I came across the same experiences as a basic state with schizophrenics, for example, their difficulty lying on the couch from fear of merging and disappearing into it, and, out of the blue, expressing the same fear about mother; or their difficulty staying in the room with me unless they could be near the door or the window, even with bars; or the case of a person who has to be by the door of a plane at 10,000 feet in the air to avoid panic. And, of course, as I have said, it is not only the mother but the early spatial structures constructed to replace the mother's internal space that are suffused with primitive emotional experiences.

As those spaces are structured by objects and their displacement, the objects in these spaces are gratifying or nongratifying, persecuting or protecting, good or bad. Here are two dreams from two very schizoid patients. One dreamt that he was quite happy inside mother. He then felt he wanted to find out about outside. He got out and started enjoying himself sexually and also doing aggressive things. Then he became anxious as he felt some people might be angry with him, and that he was outside in the open and unprotected. So he got back inside mother. Unfortunately, he realized that it was not much safer because he could do things to his mother from inside that would put him in danger just the same.

Another schizoid young man dreamt that he was living in a sort of tunnel-like building and he was moving about in the tunnel in a sort of trolley. At intervals there were openings from which he could see the outside world. Sometimes the trolley would stop and he would get out to mix in with this outside world, especially for sexual purposes. Then he would get back and resume the inside life. However, one day he was seized with a panic at the thought that the tunnel might close and he would be enclosed forever and he desperately wanted to get out. There is nowhere for the claustro-agoraphobic.

An example of coming out of a containing space and something coming out of the body and their linking together by a common experience is given by the following patient. He was the most severe claustro-agoraphobic I have come across. He dreamt that he had passed a stool several hundred feet long and it was still attached to his anus. It was unseparated from him. We proceeded with the session and when the end of the session approached he sat on the couch in a state of extreme terror saying, 'Help me, help me, if I come out of the room outside I will only be a mass of liquefied shit.'

Here we can see that coming out of the room was associated with faeces coming out of him and the identification with the faeces was complete as he felt he would be nothing else than the faeces. Further, he could not in the dream let the faeces be separate from him. As he was himself identified with the faeces he was afraid to be in an open space, unprotected after he left me. This patient could only go to the lavatory to defaecate if somebody knew he was in the toilet. He thus also demonstrates the fear of fragmentation if a part of him separates from the rest, and a fear of dissolution of self by identification with another object, e.g., the faeces.

It is obvious that problems of identity, for example, being small or adult, being male or female, and so on, are understandable on the above basis of transient identification with objects. Demandingness, controlling impulses, possessiveness are all clearly connected with the fact that the parts of the self-space put into the nonself-space and vice versa cannot be allowed separateness and dictate such behaviour to prevent catastrophic loss of parts of the self. To prevent loss of self, objects must be kept at a distance and vice versa. Thus a young schizoid man in an attempt to solve this problem would remain in his room and communicate with others by watching children play from his window and communicating with others at a distance by telephone. A woman attempted to live in my personal space by constantly walking near my residence or using the telephone to penetrate into my flat. When there was nobody there she would let the telephone ring and fall asleep being in my personal space. So the schizoid person, to prevent pain, anxiety, depression, etc., splits parts of himself, projects them and denies their existence. Immediately he experiences the opposite feelings: fear of loss, of fragmentation, attempts to remake contact, etc., and the vicious circles goes on.

Internal and personal spaces are not the same. Personal-space objects are transitional between universal space and internal space. There is a story about Voltaire, that he built himself a tomb half in the church and half outside to confound those who argued whether he was an atheist. The relative positioning of objects in space is astonishing at times. We know of the preoccupation of obsessionals not to let objects touch each other and the need for symmetry. But sometimes positioning is even more explicit. A very schizoid girl wondered if, when objects were on top of each other, for example, a bird flying over her head, it meant sexual intercourse. After the death of her father, she could not move because any movement would either hurt her father inside her or would have a sexual connotation. The relative positioning of objects was extremely meaningful to her. She would put her right foot on top of the left and do a short, quick tapping movement. This was sexual and was undone by putting the right foot from forward to backwards and instead of tapping she then did a larger and wider movement in the opposite direction.

I will now consider how immature 'concepts' of time are involved in this way of being in the same way as those of space. A little autistic boy who wanted his sessions to be at the same time every day (and which I could not do) would take my watch and set it at the time he wanted. The time was the time indicated by the watch face, watches being very special spatial devices. We had to play a game of going from London to Brighton, and returning by train. We had to go from station to station and then return through each station in reverse order. Any fault on my part and everything had to be started all over again. He had seriated space as Piaget has demonstrated but could not decentre from it. He could pass from A to B to C to D, etc., but not from D to A to return to A. He had to move from each position to the next like Achilles and the tortoise, or like Zeno's arrow. These examples lead us to examine more closely the elements of displacement and movement and of time.

Piaget describes a simple experiment carried on with children of various ages. There are two tunnels, one visibly longer than the other. Two dolls, each on a separate track and moving at a fixed speed, are made to enter their respective tunnels at exactly the same time and to emerge at the distal end, also at exactly the same time. Children of a certain age repeatedly say the two dolls moved at the same speed although they agree that one tunnel is longer. The tunnels are removed and the experiment repeated. This time, the same children will say that the doll overtaking the other one goes faster. However, if the tunnels are put back again, they say that the dolls were going at the same speed. They are clearly basing their judgement on the relative positioning of the dolls irrespective of length and time. In that way and by combining a large number of delightfully simple experiments it is possible to reconstruct the stages through which the growing child passes as he constructs his adult ideas of space, speed, and time. At least these notions are involved in the notion of time: seriation or the ordering of events in time, e.g., *B* comes after *A*, *C* after *B*, etc., then class inclusion, e.g., if *B* comes after *A* and *C* after *B*, then *A–C* is greater than *A–B* or a whole class is greater than the subclass; finally, there is the measurement of time.

Similarly the notion of causality is developed in stages and depends on the emergence of other notions such as those of the permanent object, of space and of time leading to an objective view of causality instead of a magico-phenomenal one.

A woman, a very intelligent woman patient at that, said to me very seriously that she knows she will be married to me and live with me in my country of origin; that she will be married and live with her husband in England; and it will be the same with many other men – all simultaneously and without seeing any contradiction. In fact, she was angry by my suggesting there could be some difficulty in realizing this project.

Time past is time future which is time present, says T. S. Eliot. But this is obviously time inconsistent. Time as a seriation process makes it impossible to go back in time. To be in the same place years later is not the same as previously. But displacement and movement to the schizoid can be disastrous, as it may tear part of him away and leave him fragmented or empty or lost and it can do the same to his objects. Therefore, movements may be very slow or immobility may set in, as in the case of the girl with her father in her internal space. Movement brings about separation and loss, and if it comes fast, catastrophe. Rigidity, fixity, frigidity, impotence – are all defences against that possibility.

A very severely ill woman one day revealed to her therapist that she could not leave the hospital immediately after her session. This would be incompatible with her not collapsing. To take the bus and disappear quickly was dreadful. She wandered on the hospital ground first and then very slowly moved away, very gradually. The speed at which she moved from one place to another mattered very much. In depression, movements of the body and limbs become slower and slower until a state of depressive stupor is reached, and

226

ultimate nonmovement is found in suicide. In mania, the contrary takes place, the speed of every movement including speed is increased and the patient cannot keep in one place. The sense of the passage of time is greatly altered in both states.

Piaget says, 'Psychological time is the connection between work accomplished and activity (force and rapidity of action) or time is plastic; it expands according to the deceleration or contracts according to the acceleration of action . . . or time is conferred at its point of departure with the impression of psychological duration inherent in the attitudes of expectations, effort, and of satisfaction in brief in the activity of the subject.' The schizoid patient, paralysed in his activities, empty of actions with objects, can only experience duration in relationships in a completely abnormal way.

It is necessary at this point to return to the relationship between localization of object and the most important notion of permanence of subject. Piaget describes frequently a little experiment how in the first half year of mental life an infant who is about to grasp an object will stop his hands if the object is covered with a handkerchief. At a later stage, the baby will try to lift the handkerchief, to look for the object at the place *A* where it has just been covered. But Piaget then observes if the object placed at *A* is displaced to *B* in front of the child watching the displacement that he will often look for the object at *A*, where he had been successful in finding it in previous occasions. It is only towards the end of the first year that he looks unhesitatingly for the object at the place to which it has been displaced. Before this, he ignores series of displacements but is fixated on his own action on the object. Thus, object permanence, says Piaget, is closely linked with its localization in space.

It is absolutely vital here to differentiate between the concept of object in Piaget and the libidinal object of psychoanalysis. Piaget describes an object as a permanent object at the end of the sensorimotor stage, at about eighteen months. Where the subject himself is an object amongst objects this concept applies to all objects and in no way considers the question of libidinal investment which renders an object meaningful and unique to the infant. The libidinal object is meaningful long before the completion of the sensorimotor object. Of vital interest for understanding distortions of self and object of the schizoid person are the stages of object formation described by Piaget, especially because of the specific use of objects of the physical world for identification purposes in schizoid mechanisms of defence.

Since the individual has also to construct his own body image as that of other bodies in space and to gradually reach a sense of permanence of his identity, similar considerations apply here. As Marcel Proust has Swann say in *Swann's Way*, if one wakes up in the night in the dark, not knowing the time or where one is, then one does not know who one is. It is extremely interesting that Piaget has demonstrated by lovely, simple little experiments that the concept of identity of matter takes place in definite stages and that the concept of identity occurs, for instance, before the concept of conservation of quantity. Thus, by showing changing shapes of the same object, for instance, water, in differently shaped containers, it will take time before the child can say it is the same water. It will take more time before he is decentred from spatial ties such as believing there is more water in the tall thin tube than in the other. Only when able to co-ordinate two independent variables simultaneously, as width and height, will he achieve the right answer.

We now begin to understand the kind of level of organization of mental operations used by the schizoid patient when he feels instability, confusion of identity, disorder of body image, fears of impermanence, etc., since he is bound to experience himself differently in various localities, in various situations, with various objects.

The difficulty existing outside the space with which existence and permanence are so closely linked is enormous for the schizoid. Thus a young man only had a sense of existence when he drove his motor bike so long as there was a car in front of him or if his engine was going. If he passed the car or the engine stopped, he became depersonalized. A young woman, although she had changed greatly in analysis, could only be the person she was in her mother's head. A young man who, often having lived alone for a considerable time in a room in a boarding house, made progress, started studying, but had to move out of his room to study, in order to have people about him, as he could not bear to be alone. So he sat in various public places like bars and cafes. Then he went through a phase when the place had to move with him and so he sat on buses and wandered everywhere whilst studying. Was he being carried by mother everywhere? In fact, after months of this behaviour he had a dream that he was standing in a bus holding a baby, his baby, somewhat monstrous. Then the baby grew up and appeared normal but he lost him. In his association he said the baby was also himself. Some phobics, and perhaps most, will go nowhere unless accompanied, and this can reach amazing extremes with some patients.

For this paper I have attempted to introduce concepts of space, movement and time as the basic elements, the weft and warp of primitive human behaviour. Primitive thought is centred on the first moves taken by the infant to structure space. This is done by the action of the subject on his objects and vice versa. Primitive notions of time then follow. Patterns of behaviour belonging to any stage may persist and become active at any time later.

References

Battro, M. (1973) *Piaget Dictionary of Terms*, E. Ritschverimann and S. F. Campbell (eds). Oxford: Pergamon.

Bion, W. (1965) *Transformations*, London: Heinemann; paperback Maresfield Reprints, London: H. Karnac Books (1984); and in *Seven Servants: Four Works by Wilfred Bion*, New York: Jason Aronson (1977).

Freud, S. (1909) 'Notes upon a case of obsessional neurosis', *SE* 10, 153–310.

Guntrip, H. (1968) *Schizoid Phenomena: Object Relations and the Self*, London: Hogarth Press.

Laplanche, J. and Pontalis, J. B. (1967) *The Language of Psycho-analysis*, tr. Donald Nicholson-Smith, New York: W. W. Norton (1973).

2

Terror, persecution, dread – a dissection of paranoid anxieties

DONALD MELTZER

This article was originally a paper read at the 25th International Psycho-Analytical Congress, Copenhagen, in July 1967 and was first published in the *International Journal of Psycho-Analysis*, 49, 396–400.

This brief paper is intended as a contribution to the exploration of the paranoid-schizoid position in object relations, as defined by Melanie Klein. It is the result of analytic work employing the deeper understanding of personality made possible by her discoveries of the role of splitting processes in the formation of psychic structure and the mechanism of projective identification in the dynamics of object relations.

A spectrum of psychic pains is subsumed under the category of paranoid anxieties, the study of which has been begun in detail by other authors, for instance, confusion by Rosenfeld, catastrophic anxiety by Segal and Bion, nameless dread by Bion. Less well-defined terms such as hopelessness, despair, helplessness must also be dealt with, but this paper is limited to three: terror, persecution, and dread. I attempt to define these metapsychologically and to show their place and interaction in the analytical process, employing a case presentation to show them at work and their interrelation.

Case material

Although this cultured and intelligent man in his late thirties entered analysis because of somatic symptoms, extensive character pathology was soon revealed. Early in analysis the narcissistic structure expressed itself clearly as in the following dream. He was walking uphill on a lonely woodland track and saw another man about his age, a former business client of very paranoid disposition, ahead of him. When the track divided, instead of going to the right as he had intended, he followed the other man, going down on to a beach which he recognized as belonging to the village where he had been born (and from which he had departed at the age of 6 months when his parents emigrated). On the beach he listened with admiration as the other man declaimed at length about his income and importance, how even on holiday he had to keep in constant touch with his office, as they could do nothing without his advice.

As this part of his infantile structure showed up several times in dreams as a fox, having a reference to a childhood picture story book, it came to be known as his 'foxy' part and could be seen to be the source of several types of mental content and phenomena. It produced a constant punning and caricaturing of other people's words (including analytic interpretations); elaborated an endless stream of cleverly screened pornographic limericks; supplied a relentless line of cynical and snobbish argument; and carried on a visual and auditory scrutiny of his environment just outside consciousness. This latter produced a series of dreams in the transference which indicated a most intimidating monitoring of the analyst's technique and way of life. For instance, he knew that I had a colleague who lived in a road that he regularly drove along on his way to analysis. On the night after I had borrowed this colleague's car, and despite my having taken the precaution of parking it around the corner, the patient dreamed that my colleague had a hole, about the size of a car, in the road before his house. The patient had not consciously, however, either seen the borrowed car, noted the absence of my usual one, nor noted the vacancy in front of the colleague's house.

The know-it-all quality of this 'foxy' part and its hold over other infantile structures did not however, yield in the slightest to the analytic investigation. Rather it seemed paradoxically to strengthen its hold as a result of two revelations, both of which were reconstructed from the dreams before they were admitted to by the patient. The first of these was a secret sadomasochistic masturbatory perversion and the second was a terror of fire. This paradoxical strengthening of the symptoms had a peculiarly defiant quality. He asserted that his perversion was the only pleasure in his life and sustained him from suicide; while the terror of fire was claimed as absolutely rational on the one hand and sanctified by trauma during the war, on the other. He did not in the least acknowledge that these two arguments were mutually exclusive.

A further area of psychopathology which resisted investigation was his relationship to his ageing mother, whose development of a chronic ailment had been shortly followed by the somatic symptoms which led the patient to analysis. While his relation to her had been cool and even contemptuous from late adolescence, her illness was extremely persecuting to him. He appropriated from his siblings, in a slavish custodial manner, the supervision of the mother's health, financial problems and household affairs, consciously motivated by devotion to his long-deceased father, as if charged by him exclusively with the mother's care. The persecutory element was linked with the perversion, whose secret pleasures were felt as the oasis in a desert of deprivation spitefully imposed by the ailing mother out of her own incapacity for pleasure. The constellation had arisen slowly when it had become clear with the passage of years that his mother would not remarry. It had replaced the tyrannical and jealously possessive demeanour toward her which characterized the years immediately following his father's death. The turning point had occurred at the event of his mother's home being considerably damaged, though not beyond repair, by incendiary bombs. At the time he had been able to fight the fire with courage, but shortly thereafter developed his terror of fire and would rush from the house at the hint of a raid to sleep in a nearby ditch, leaving his mother alone in the undamaged part of the house.

In the following years the perversion crystallized a fixed pattern – dressed in a chauffeur's uniform, sitting on the inner tube of a car tyre, holding a glass of whisky, he would masturbate genitally and anally. The expulsive significance of the orgasm was indicated in analysis in a dream in which, sitting on the tube over a well, he defaecated and then threw his clothes down the well. The prehistory of the perversion was of interest and could be accurately dated to an incident in which his father had needed to remove, repair, blow up, and replace a punctured tyre of the family car during an outing, the spare being missing. The little boy was overwhelmed with sexual excitement watching his father and thereafter developed several symptoms and secret activities. One of these was the habit of sucking on the dirty tyres of his bicycle. The other was an exciting game of letting the air out of a bicycle tyre, waiting then until a policeman would come along, attempting to blow it up with his mouth as the policeman watched. But he also developed a fear of riding in the family car which was sternly dealt with.

In order to comprehend the anxieties which the analysis found to underlie the perversion and the character pathology, another factor must be noted, again a mixture of trauma and fate. The patient was the youngest child and only boy. A particular traumatic incident of early childhood had assumed a screen memory function. When he was 5, probably (after being reunited with his mother following her protracted illness which had entirely altered the family plans for the future) he was on a country stroll with his nanny when they came upon a dead infant, left under a hedge. This incident became fixedly bound in his mind to his own naughty habit; when given lunch in the garden he would always secretly throw away into the hedge the detested cold fatty meat. It formed the core of the 'dead baby' material, as will be seen later on.

For the first three years of his analysis, which was occupied largely with his tendencies to massive projective identification and 'pseudo-maturity'[1], this constellation of perversion, character pathology and symptoms were kept from analysis by acting out in which his 'foxy' part was split off into a close business associate by whom he felt dominated. But as this lessened and his own 'foxiness' became more conscious and clearly manifest in the transference, two things happened. First of all there took shape a new hopefulness about the possibility of being released through analysis from his constricted life. Consequently, with the acceptance of some measure of dependence on the analytic process, his conscious cooperation became divested of its lacunae of secretiveness. Secondly his attitude toward mental pain altered, so that his cowardice, earlier paraded as a cynical self-interest and snobbery, was allowed a central place in the analytic investigation.

In the following years, the fourth and fifth year of analysis, the material made possible a dissection of his persecutory anxieties. Progress toward a deeper infantile dependence (on the analytic breast as an introjective object) could commence – the threshold of the depressive position was reached in the analytic process.[1]

As the work of the two months prior to the fifth Christmas break and the one month after seem so crucial and clear, I will try to describe them in some detail.

The struggle to abandon the perversion could be seen clearly as a struggle to put his faith in the analysis and analytic parents. He dreamed he was at school taking a Latin exam. He thought it might be a trick question, but decided to decline the noun in the straightforward manner of 'Mensa' (a pun on Meltzer). Or he dreamed he was visiting his old school and had to decide whether to drive with the chauffeur and boys or to accompany the pleasant mistress (to choose between 'foxy' and analysis).

The uncertainty seemed to relate to doubts about the strength, not the goodness or sincerity, of the analytic parents. The night after I had had a tiny cut over one eye, which the patient hadn't consciously noticed, he dreamed that he was complaining to the analyst about a cut over one eye he himself had received in a plane crash and that he might have been killed due to the pilot's carelessness. The intensity of the dependence was apparent.

But as his confidence grew, so did his identification with a capable and courageous 'daddy'. This was manifest in dreams and behaviour in which he confronted situations he had always cowered from, as well as persons who represented the 'foxy' and 'vixen' aspects of his own infantile structure. In one dream he protected his son's guinea-pig from a weasel; in another he chased away hoodlums assaulting an old man. But when confronted in a dream with a former friend who had developed a paranoid breakdown, the best he could do was to hide in the nursery. In reality when this man had paid him an unexpected visit, he could not help placating him when he demanded that my patient join in a bizarre prayer to 'the Spirit'. This, we knew, touched terribly closely on his terror of fire and, as he now revealed, of ghosts, or spirits. We had already seen many dreams in which spirit lamps caught fire. It became clear also that his dislike of swimming was in fact a terror of deep water, not from fear of drowning but a terror of monsters seizing him from below. Material also indicated that this constellation played a part in his impotence and aversion to the female genital.

It was very close to Christmas; his mother seemed to be losing ground and his inner trust in the vitality of good objects seemed to collapse as the theme of the 'dead baby' once more took hold. He was dreaming again of a dead octopus on the front step, of squashed worms in the lawn, or a dead crab under a rock. He had an experience of terror one morning when some flour fell from a bread roll as he drew it from the oven, flaring in the gas fire. He lay in paralysed terror one night when a sound from his daughter's bedroom was construed as an explosion of the TV machine. Some nights later he was seized by a paralysing terror at sounds downstairs felt to be an insane intruder. His dreams reflected the renewed hopelessness. The Nazis were counter-attacking in England or Brighton was being bombed.

However in fact he felt better during the holiday and noted gains in his vigour and courage. He was terribly grief-stricken in a dream in which his mother had died and her belongings were being stored. But the couch which was being carried away was the analytic couch. He understood by himself how closely linked now were the analysis, his mother and his internal good objects. In a later dream he was scolded by a woman for starting a fire in the stove with his methylated spirit lamp. She ordered him to stay back saying that she'd called the fire brigade and in the meantime the automatic spray-pipe would keep things under control. In a word, his internal mother forbade his manic reparativeness, telling him that her internal penis would suffice until the 'daddy' arrived.

By this time the three different qualities of anxiety, persecution, dread, and terror, were very distinct in his conscious experience. This was of course to some extent due to alteration in the economics of anxiety in that he was more depressed than persecuted by damaged objects, less cowardly toward bad parts of himself and dreaded persons containing them, and more aware that the terror situations had a basis in psychic reality which could be both comprehended and corrected. Attention in the work could now be turned to the problem of the recurrent destruction and restoration of the internal mother's babies and its transference manifestations in regard to the analyst's children, publication and interpretation – brain children. This work involved the prevention of the destructive attacks (his masturbation attacks, as in the perversion) by greater responsibility for psychic reality. But also true reparation was made possible by the relinquishment of the acting out of his manic reparativeness, so epitomized in his snobbish contempt for manual work and idealization of intellectual pursuits. One such episode was the following. After dreaming that he chased a wasp from the family car, he developed an episode of abdominal pain, which lasted several days. It resolved after a dream in which his father was repairing the inner tube of a tyre, though the patient half-hoped that the butt of the nail had been left in the tyre. After the following sessions in which his critical and competitive attitude toward the analytic-daddy was scrutinized, he dreamed that a terrible noise coming from a gap in the hedge terrified him, until a little terrier dog appeared. But when it ran ahead of him to his mother's house, it seemed to turn into his father's boxer dog.

In the working through of this problem during the following year, many episodes occurred, clustering about the separations, of attacks on the mother's internal babies in masturbatory or acted-out forms. His various forms of manic reparation were reduced and the resolution of his oedipal conflict instituted. The attacks of terror disappeared and the residual clinging to the perversion was finally abandoned.

Discussion of clinical material

The material demonstrates how the systematic analysis of the transference made it possible for us to see the different qualities of his anxieties and the organization of his narcissism as a defensive structure. He was *terrified* of the 'dead babies', the 'fire-bomb' babies, the ghostly 'burning-flour-off-the-bap' babies. He was *persecuted* by his damaged objects – his dead father, his impaired mother, his defective analyst – by whom he was deprived of pleasure, of leisure, of money, of comfort; for whom he had to work, to be respectable, to earn a living, to know about a world of economics, health, morality and politics in which he felt no interest. He *dreaded* and was submitted to the tyranny of his 'foxy' part, which demanded his participation in his perversion long after it had ceased to be his oasis of secret pleasure. This destructive part prevented him from admiring or respecting anyone by its slander, its omniscient propaganda. It kept him in a state of impotence by its denigration of the female genital, while it threatened him with homosexual desires by presenting penises as delicious suckable nipples. But, above all, 'foxy' offered him protection from the terror of the dead babies – or so it claimed. Only in the transference, as in the dream of the little-dog-in-the-hedge, did he come to realize that this 'foxy' part had never protected him, that in fact he had been protected all along by an external good object, fundamentally his mother; in the transference by the analyst, psychoanalysis, the analytic breast, with its power to project, despite his enfeebled introjective power, a reparative vitality into his inner world – just as his mother had nourished the recalcitrant little boy who secretly threw the cold meat into the hedge. The series of dreams of live and dead babies (the dead crab, the dead octopus, the terrifying gap-in-the-hedge, etc.) gradually showed him the real nature of his dependence and enabled him to rebel against his tyrant, 'foxy', as seen in the dreams such as that of the weasel, or the assault on the old man. Submission to 'foxy' and the perversion had yielded to the acknowledgement of absolute dependence at infantile levels on his primal good objects in psychic reality.

Only with this step forward did an amelioration of his persecution by damaged objects begin to give way to depressive concern for them, in dreams, in the transference, in his relations to his mother. Where despair had yielded to hopelessness, hope now arose.

Theoretical discussion and summary

Terror is a paranoid anxiety whose essential quality, paralysis, leaves no avenue of action. The object of terror, being in unconscious fantasy dead objects, cannot even be fled from with success. But in psychic reality the vitality of an object, of which it may be robbed, can also be returned to it, as the soul to the body in theological terms. This can only be accomplished by the reparative capacity of the internal parents and their creative coitus.

When dependence on the reparative capacity of the internal objects is prevented by oedipal jealousy and/or destructive envy, this restoration cannot occur during the course of sleep and dreaming. Only an object in external reality, which bears the transference significance of the mother's breast at infantile levels, can accomplish the task. This may be undertaken innumerable times without being acknowledged, if the infantile dependence is blocked by the denigrating activity of envy or the obstinacy born of intolerance to separation.

Where dependence on internal good objects is rendered infeasible by damaging masturbatory attacks and where dependence on a good external object is unavailable or not acknowledged, the addictive relationship to a bad part of the self, the submission to tyranny, takes place. An illusion of safety is promulgated by the omniscience of the destructive part and perpetuated by the sense of omnipotence generated by the perversion or addictive activity involved. The tyrannical, addictive bad part is dreaded. It is important to note that, while the tyrant may behave in a way that has a resemblance to a persecutor, especially if any sign of rebellion is at hand, the essential hold over the submissive part of the self is by way of the dread of loss of protection against the terror. I have come to the conclusion that intolerance of depressive anxieties alone will not produce the addictive constellation of submission to the tyrant – nor in combination with persecution by the damaged object. Where a dread of loss of an addictive relation to a tyrant is found in psychic structure, the problem of terror will be found at its core, as the force behind the dread and the submission.

Until such a narcissistic organization is dismantled and a rebellion against the tyranny of the bad part is mounted, progress into the threshold of the depressive position is impossible. Furthermore, until this occurs, factors in psychopathology such as intolerance of separation, or of depressive pain, or cowardice in the face of persecution cannot be accurately estimated. The dread felt in relation to the tyrant is fundamentally a dread of loss of the illusory protection against the terror and may be seen to appear especially at times when rebellion has been undertaken in alliance with good objects which are then felt to be inadequate or unavailable, as during analytic holiday breaks.

Note

1 See my paper 'The relation of anal masturbation to projective identification' *International Journal of Psycho-Analysis*, 1966, 47, 335–42 (reprinted here, pp. 102–16) and my book *The Psychoanalytical Process* (London: Heinemann, 1967).

3

A clinical approach to the psychoanalytic theory of the life and death instincts: an investigation into the aggressive aspects of narcissism

HERBERT ROSENFELD

This article was originally an invited contribution to the 27th International Psycho-Analytical Congress, Vienna, 1971, and was first published in the *International Journal of Psycho-Analysis*, 52, 169–78.

When Freud introduced his dualistic theory of the life and death instincts in 1920 a new era in the development of psychoanalysis began which gradually opened up a deeper understanding of aggressive phenomena in mental life. Many analysts objected to the theory of the death instinct and were tempted to discard it as purely speculative and theoretical; however, others soon recognized its fundamental clinical importance.

Freud emphasized that the death instinct was silently driving the individual towards death and that only through the activity of the life instinct was this death-like force projected outwards and appeared as destructive impulses directed against objects in the outside world. Generally the life and death instincts are mixed or fused in varying degrees, and Freud maintained that the instincts, meaning the life and death instincts, 'hardly ever appear in "a pure form" '. While states of severe defusion of the instincts do resemble Freud's description of the unfused death instinct – for example, a wish to die or to withdraw into a state of nothingness – on detailed clinical examination we find that the death instinct cannot be observed in its original form, since it always becomes manifest as a destructive process directed against objects and the self. These processes seem to operate in their most virulent form in severe narcissistic conditions.

I shall therefore attempt in this paper to clarify particularly the destructive aspects of narcissism and relate this to Freud's theory of the fusion and defusion of the life and death instincts.

In Freud's writings following his more speculative approach in 'Beyond the pleasure principle', it became clear that he used the theory of the life and death instincts to explain many clinical phenomena. For example, in 'The economic problem of masochism' (1924) he said:

'Moral masochism thus becomes a classical piece of evidence for the existence of 'instinctual fusion': its dangerousness lies in its origin in the death instinct and represents that part of the latter which escaped deflection on to the outer world in the form of an instinct of destruction.'

In the 'New introductory lectures' (1933) he discussed the fusion of Eros and aggressiveness and attempted to encourage analysts to use this theory clinically. He said:

'This hypothesis opens a line of investigation which may some day be of great importance for our understanding of pathological processes. For fusions may be undone and such defusions of instincts may be expected to bring about the most serious consequences to adequate functioning. But this point of view is still too new. No one has so far attempted to make practical use of it.'

Only four years later, in 'Analysis terminable and interminable' (1937), Freud returned to the clinical application of this theory of the death instinct for the understanding of deep-seated resistances against analytic treatment, saying:

'Here we are dealing with the ultimate things which psychological research can learn about: the behaviour of the two primal instincts, their distribution, mingling and defusion. No stronger impression arises from the resistances during the work of analysis than of there being a force which is defending itself by every possible means against recovery and which is absolutely resolved to hold on to illness and suffering.'

He linked this with his previous theory of the negative therapeutic reaction, which he had related to an unconscious sense of guilt and the need for punishment, now adding:

'These phenomena are unmistakable impressions of the power in mental life which we call the instinct of aggression or of destruction according to its aims and which we trace back to the original death instinct of living matter. . . . Only by the concurrent or mutually opposing action of the two primal instincts – Eros and death instinct – never by one or the other alone, can we explain the rich multiplicity of the phenomena of life.'

Later on in the same paper he suggested that we may have to examine all instances of mental conflict from the point of view of a struggle between libidinal and destructive impulses.

In discussing his psychoanalytical approach to narcissistic neurosis in 1916 Freud emphasized the impenetrable stone wall which he encountered. However, when in 1937 he described the deepseated resistances to analytic treatment he did not explicitly relate the resistances in narcissistic conditions to the resistances in states of inertia and in the negative therapeutic reactions, which he did attribute to the death instinct. One of the main reasons for this omission may be that Freud's whole theory of primary narcissism had originally been based on the idea of the individual's directing his libido towards the self and of secondary narcissism being due to a withdrawal of libido from the object back onto the self – and only after he had clarified his ideas on the pleasure principle and the reality principle in 1911, and brought these ideas in relation to love and hate in 'Instincts and their vicissitudes' (1915) did he begin to feel that there was some important connection between a pleasurable narcissistic stage and hatred or destructiveness towards the external object when the object begins to impinge on the individual. For example, in 1915 he states: 'When during the stage of primary narcissism the object makes its appearance, the second opposite to loving, namely hating, also attains its development.'

In the same paper he emphasizes the primary importance of aggression:

'Hate, as a relation to objects, is older than love. It derives from the narcissistic ego's primordial repudiation of the external world with its outpouring stimuli.'

Something of the same line of thought can be seen in Freud's view of the Nirvana principle, which he sees as a withdrawal or regression to primary narcissism under the dominance of the death instinct – where peace, an inanimate state and giving in to death are equated.

Hartmann *et al.* (1949) seemed to have a similar impression of Freud's ideas on the relation of aggression to narcissism when they wrote:

'Freud was used to comparing the relation between narcissism and object love to that between self-destruction and destruction of the object. This analogy might have contributed to his assumption of self-destruction as of the primary form of aggression to be compared with primary narcissism.'

From all this it is clear that Freud must have realized the obvious relation between narcissism, narcissistic withdrawal and the death instinct; but he did not work it out in any detail either theoretically or clinically. As I shall go on to show later in this paper, I feel these connections are of considerable clinical significance.

Returning now to the question of the hidden transference in the sense of clinical resistances which Freud (1937) related to the silent opposition of the death instinct, it is important to realize that he thought that these resistances could not be successfully treated by analysis: he apparently believed that the hidden silent aggression of the death instinct could not be analysed unless it emerged as an open negative transference and that interpretations could do nothing to 'activate' it.

Abraham went much further than Freud in studying the hidden negative transference and in clarifying the nature of the destructive impulses which he encountered in his clinical work with narcissistic patients. In psychotic narcissistic patients he stressed the haughty superiority and aloofness of the narcissist and interpreted the negative aggressive attitude in the transference. As early as 1919 he had contributed to the analysis of the hidden negative transference by describing a particular form of neurotic resistance against the analytic method. He found in these patients a most pronounced narcissism, and he emphasized the hostility and defiance hidden behind an apparent eagerness to co-operate. He described how the narcissistic attitude attached itself to the transference and how these patients depreciate and devalue the analyst and grudge him the analytic role representing the father. They reverse the position of patient and analyst to show their superiority over him. He emphasized that the element of envy was unmistakable in these patients' behaviour and in this way clinically and theoretically he connected narcissism and aggression. It is, however, interesting to note that Abraham never attempted to link his findings with Freud's theory of the life and death instincts.

Reich was opposed to Freud's theory of the death instinct. He did, however, make fundamental contributions to the analysis of narcissism and the latent negative transference. He also emphasized, contrary to Freud, that the patient's narcissistic attitudes and latent conflicts, which include negative feelings, could be activated and brought to the surface in analysis and then worked through. He thought 'that every case without exception begins analysis with a more or less explicit attitude of distrust and criticism which, as a rule, remains hidden' (Reich 1933).

He considered that the analyst has constantly to point to what is hidden and he should not be misled by an apparent positive transference towards the analyst. Reich studied in detail the character armour where the narcissistic defence finds its concrete chronic expression. In describing the narcissistic patient he stressed their superior, derisive and envious attitude, as well as their contemptuous behaviour. One patient who was constantly preoccupied with thoughts of death complained in every session that the analysis did not touch him and was completely useless. The patient also admitted his boundless envy, not of the analyst, but of other men towards whom he felt inferior. Gradually Reich realized and was able to show the patient his triumph over the analyst, and his attempts to make him feel useless, inferior and impotent so that he could achieve nothing. The patient was then able to admit that he could not tolerate the superiority of anyone and always tried to tear people down. Reich states: 'There then was the patient's suppressed aggression, the most extreme manifestation of which had thus far been his death wishes.'

Reich's findings in connection with latent aggression, envy and narcissism have many similarities to Abraham's description of the narcissistic resistance in 1919.

Of the many analysts who have accepted Freud's theory of the interaction between the life and death instincts Melanie Klein's contribution deserves particular consideration as her work is essentially based on this assumption both theoretically and clinically. She also made important contributions to the analysis of the negative transference. She found that envy, particularly in its split-off form, was an important factor in producing chronic negative attitudes in analysis, including 'negative therapeutic reactions'. She described the early infantile mechanisms of splitting the objects and the ego, which enable the infantile ego to keep love and hate apart. In her contributions to narcissism she stressed more the libidinal aspects and suggested that narcissism is in fact a secondary phenomenon which is based on a relationship with an internal good or ideal object, which in fantasy forms part of the loved body and self. She thought that in narcissistic states withdrawal from external relationships to an identification with an idealized internal object takes place.

Melanie Klein wrote in 1958 that she observed in her analytical work with young children a constant struggle between an irrepressible urge to destroy their objects and a desire to preserve them. She felt that Freud's discovery of the life and death instincts was a tremendous advance in understanding this struggle. She believed that anxiety arises from the 'operation of the death instinct within the organism, which is expressed as a fear of annihilation.'

In order to defend itself against this anxiety the primitive ego uses two processes: 'Part of the death instinct is projected into the external object which hereby becomes a persecutor, while that part of the death instinct, which is retained in the ego, turns its aggression against the persecutory object.'

The life instinct is also projected into external objects, which are then felt to be loving or idealized. She emphasizes that it is characteristic for early development that the idealized and the bad persecuting objects are split and kept wide apart, which would imply that the life and death instincts are kept in a state of defusion. Simultaneously with the splitting of the objects the splitting of the self into good and bad parts takes place. These processes of ego splitting also keep the instincts in a state of defusion. Almost simultaneously with the projective processes another primary process, introjection, starts, 'largely in the service of the life instinct: it combats the death instinct because it leads to the ego taking in something life-giving (first of all food) and thus binding the death instinct working within.'

This process is essential in initiating the fusion of the life and death instincts.

As the process of splitting of the object and the self and therefore the states of defusion of the instincts originate in early infancy at a phase which Melanie Klein described as the 'paranoid schizoid position', one may expect the most complete states of defusion of instincts in those clinical conditions where paranoid schizoid mechanisms predominate. We may encounter these states in patients who have never completely outgrown this early phase of development or have regressed to it. Melanie Klein emphasized that early infantile mechanisms and object relations attach themselves to the transference and in this way the processes of splitting the self and objects, which promote the defusion of the instincts, can be investigated and modified in analysis. She also stressed that through investigating these early processes in the transference she became convinced that the analysis of the negative transference was a precondition for analysing the deeper layers of the mind. It was particularly through investigating the negative aspects of the early infantile transference that Melanie Klein came up against primitive envy which she regarded as a direct derivative of the death instinct. She thought that envy appears as a hostile, life-destroying force in the relation of the infant to its mother and is particularly directed against the good feeding mother because she is not only needed by the infant but envied for containing everything which the infant wants to possess himself. In the transference this manifests itself in the patient's need to devalue analytic work which he has found helpful. It appears that envy representing almost completely defused destructive energy is particularly unbearable to the infantile ego and early on in life becomes split off from the rest of the ego. Melanie Klein stressed that split-off, unconscious envy often remained unexpressed in analysis, but nevertheless exerted a troublesome and powerful influence in preventing progress in the analysis, which ultimately can only be effective if it achieves integration and deals with the whole of the personality. In other words the defusion of the instincts has gradually to change to fusion in any successful analysis.

Freud's theory of the fusion and defusion of the life and death instincts seems vital for the understanding of defused destructive processes.

Hartmann *et al.* stressed in 1949 that 'little is known about the fusion and defusion of aggression and libido'. Hartmann himself concentrated on studying the function of neutralized libidinal and aggressive energy, which is probably one of the aspects of the normal fusion of the basic instincts. He also stressed the importance of deneutralization of libido and aggression in psychotic states such as schizophrenia and stated that defusion and deneutralization may be interrelated (1953).

Freud suggested that defusion of the instincts becomes manifest clinically when regression to earlier phases of development takes place.

I have attempted to clarify the origin of the processes of defusion and fusion of the instincts by relating them to Melanie Klein's theory of the process of splitting of objects and the ego. This splitting is a normal defence mechanism in early life aimed at protecting the self and object from the danger of annihilation by the destructive impulses deriving from the death instinct. This may explain why defusion of the instincts plays an important role in the psychopathology of narcissistic patients and why defused destructive impulses can be observed distinctly in patients emerging from narcissistic states.

For this reason I shall concentrate on the examination of the libidinal and destructive aspects of narcissism and shall attempt to clarify in my clinical material how some of the severe defusions of the instincts arise and indicate the factors contributing to normal and pathological fusions.

I introduced the concept of pathological fusion for those processes where in the mixing of libidinal and destructive impulses the power of the destructive impulses is greatly strengthened, while in normal fusion the destructive energy is mitigated or neutralized.

Finally I shall present case material to illustrate the clinical importance of defused and split-off aggression in creating obstacles to analysis, such as chronic resistances and negative therapeutic reactions.

In my previous work on narcissism (1964) I stressed the projective and introjective identification of self and object (fusion of self and object) in narcissistic states, which act as a defence against any recognition of separateness between the self and objects. Awareness of separation immediately leads to feelings of dependence on an object and therefore to inevitable frustrations. However, dependence also stimulates envy, when the goodness of the object is recognized. Aggressiveness towards objects therefore seems inevitable in giving up the narcissistic position and it appears that the strength and persistence of omnipotent narcissistic object relations is closely related to the strength of the envious destructive impulses.

In studying narcissism in greater detail it seems to me essential to differentiate between the libidinal and the destructive aspects of narcissism. In considering narcissism from the libidinal aspect one can see that the over-valuation of the self plays a central role, based mainly on the idealization of the self. Self-idealization is maintained by omnipotent introjective and projective identifications with good objects and their qualities. In this way the narcissist feels that everything that is valuable relating to external objects and the outside world is part of him or is omnipotently controlled by him.

Similarly, when considering narcissism from the destructive aspect, we find that again self-idealization plays a central role, but now it is the idealization of the omnipotent destructive parts of the self. They are directed both against any positive libidinal object relationship and any libidinal part of the self which experiences need for an object and the desire to depend on it. The destructive omnipotent parts of the self often remain disguised or they may be silent and split off, which obscures their existence and gives the impression that they have no relationship to the external world. In fact they have a very powerful effect in preventing dependent object relations and in keeping external objects permanently devalued, which accounts for the apparent indifference of the narcissistic individual towards external objects and the world.

In the narcissism of most patients libidinal and destructive aspects exist side by side but the violence of the destructive impulses varies.

In the narcissistic states where the libidinal aspects predominate destructiveness becomes apparent as soon as the omnipotent self-idealization is threatened by contact with an object which is perceived as separate from the self. The patient feels humiliated and defeated by the revelation that it is the external object which, in reality, contains the valuable qualities which he had attributed to his own creative powers. In analysis one observes that when the patient's feelings of resentment and revenge at being robbed of his omnipotent narcissism diminishes, envy is consciously experienced, since it is then that he becomes aware of the analyst as a valuable external person.

When the destructive aspects predominate the envy is more violent and appears as a wish to destroy the analyst as the object who is the real source of life and goodness. At the same time violent self-destructive impulses appear, and these I want to consider in more detail. In terms of the infantile situation the narcissistic patient wants to believe that he has given life to himself and is able to feed and look after himself. When he is faced with the reality of being dependent on the analyst, standing for the parents, particularly the mother, he would prefer to die, to be non-existent, to deny the fact of his birth, and also to destroy his analytic progress and insight representing the child in himself, which he feels the analyst, representing the parents, has created. Frequently at this point the patient wants to give up the analysis but more often he acts out in a self-destructive way by spoiling his professional success and his personal relations. Some of these patients become suicidal and the desire to die, to disappear into oblivion, is expressed quite openly and death is idealized as a solution to all problems.

As the individual seems determined to satisfy a desire to die and to disappear into nothing which resembles Freud's description of the 'pure' death instinct, one might consider that we are dealing in these states with the death instinct in complete defusion. However, analytically one can observe that the state is caused by the activity of destructive envious parts of the self which become severely split off and defused from the libidinal caring self which seems to have disappeared. The whole self becomes temporarily identified with the destructive self, which aims to triumph over life and creativity represented by the parents and the analyst by destroying the dependent libidinal self experienced as the child.

The patient often believes that he has destroyed his caring self, his love, for ever and there is nothing anybody can do to change the situation. When this problem is worked through in the transference and some libidinal part of the patient is experienced as coming alive, concern for the analyst, standing for the mother, appears which mitigates the destructive impulses and lessens the dangerous defusion.

There are some narcissistic patients where defused destructive impulses seem to be constantly active and dominate the whole of their personality and object relations. They express their feelings in an only slightly disguised way by devaluing the analyst's work with their persistent indifference, tricky repetitive behaviour and some-times open belittlement. In this way they assert their superiority over the analyst representing life and creativity by wasting or destroying his work, understanding and satisfaction. They feel superior in being able to control and withhold those parts of themselves which want to depend on the analyst as a helpful person. They behave as if the loss of any love object including the analyst would leave them cold and even stimulate a feeling of triumph. Such patients occasionally experience shame and some persecutory anxiety but only minimal guilt, because very little of their libidinal self is kept alive. It appears that these patients have dealt with the struggle between their destructive and libidinal impulses by trying to get rid of their concern and love for their objects by killing their loving dependent self and identifying themselves almost entirely with the destructive narcissistic part of the self which provides them with a sense of superiority and self-admiration.

One narcissistic patient, who kept relations to external objects and the analyst dead and empty by constantly deadening any part of his self that attempted object relations, dreamt of a small boy who was in a comatose condition, dying from some kind of poisoning. He was lying on a bed in the courtyard and was endangered by the hot midday sun which was beginning to shine on him. The patient was standing near to the boy but did nothing to move or protect him. He only felt critical and superior to the doctor treating the child, since it was he who should have seen that the child was moved into the shade. The patient's previous behaviour and associations made it clear that the dying boy stood for his dependent libidinal self which he kept in a dying condition by preventing it from getting help and nourishment from the analyst. I showed him that even when he came close to realizing the seriousness of his mental state, experienced as a dying condition, he did not lift a finger to help himself or to help the analyst to make a move towards saving him, because he was using the killing of his infantile dependent self to triumph over the analyst and to show him up as a failure. The dream illustrates clearly that the destructive narcissistic state is maintained in power by keeping the libidinal infantile self in a constant dead or dying condition.

Occasionally the analytic interpretations penetrated the narcissistic shell and the patient felt more alive. He then admitted that he would like to improve but soon he felt his mind drifting away from the consulting room and became so detached and sleepy that he could scarcely keep awake. There was an enormous resistance, almost like a stone wall, which prevented any examination of the situation, but gradually it became clear that the patient felt pulled away from any closer contact with the analyst, because as soon as he felt helped there was not only the danger that he might experience a greater need for the analyst but he feared that he would attack him with sneering and belittling thoughts. Contact with the analyst meant a weakening of the narcissistic omnipotent superiority of the patient and the experience of a conscious feeling of overwhelming envy which was strictly avoided by the detachment.

The destructive narcissism of these patients appears often highly organized, as if one were dealing with a powerful gang dominated by a leader, who controls all the members of the gang to see that they support one another in making the criminal destructive work more effective and powerful. However, the narcissistic organization not only increases the strength of the destructive narcissism, but it has a defensive purpose to keep itself in power and so maintain the *status quo*. The main aim seems to be to prevent the weakening of the organization and to control the members of the gang so that they will not desert the destructive organization and join the positive parts of the self or betray the secrets of the gang to the police, the protecting superego, standing for the helpful analyst, who might be able to save the patient. Frequently when a patient of this kind makes progress in the analysis and wants to change he dreams of being attacked by members of the Mafia or adolescent delinquents and a negative therapeutic reaction sets in. This narcissistic organization is in my experience not primarily directed against guilt and anxiety, but seems to have .the purpose of maintaining the idealization and superior power of the destructive narcissism. To change, to receive help, implies weakness and is experienced as wrong or as failure by the destructive narcissistic organization which provides the patient with his sense of superiority. In cases of this kind there is a most determined chronic resistance to analysis and only the very detailed exposure of the system enables analysis to make some progress.

In many of these patients the destructive impulses are linked with perversions. In this situation the apparent fusion of the instincts does not lead to a lessening of the power of the destructive instincts; on the contrary the power and violence is greatly increased through the erotization of the aggressive instinct. I feel it is confusing to follow Freud in discussing perversions as fusions between the life and death instincts because in these instances the destructive part of the self has taken control over the whole of the libidinal aspects of the patient's personality and is therefore able to misuse them. These cases are in reality instances of pathological fusion similar to the confusional states where the destructive impulses overpower the libidinal ones.

In some narcissistic patients the destructive narcissistic parts of the self are linked to a psychotic structure or organization which is split off from the rest of the personality. This psychotic structure is like a delusional world or object, into which parts of the self tend to withdraw. It appears to be dominated by an omnipotent or omniscient extremely ruthless part of the self, which creates the notion that within the delusional object there is complete painlessness but also freedom to indulge in any sadistic activity. The whole structure is committed to narcissistic self-sufficiency and is strictly directed against any object relatedness. The destructive impulses within this delusional world sometimes appear openly as overpoweringly cruel, threatening the rest of the self with death to assert their power, but more frequently they appear disguised as omnipotently benevolent or life-saving, promising to provide the patient with quick, ideal solutions to all his problems. These false promises are designed to make the normal self of the patient dependent on or addicted to his omnipotent self, and to lure the normal sane parts into this delusional structure in order to imprison them. When narcissistic patients of this type begin to make some progress and to form some dependent relationship to the analysis, severe negative therapeutic reactions occur as the narcissistic psychotic part of the self exerts its power and superiority over life and the analyst, standing for reality, by trying to lure the dependent self into a psychotic omnipotent dream state which results in the patient losing his sense of reality and his capacity for thinking. In fact there is a danger of an acute psychotic state if the dependent part of the patient, which is the sanest part of his personality, is persuaded to turn away from the external world and give itself up entirely to the domination of the psychotic delusional structure. This process has similarities to Freud's description of the giving up of object cathexis and the withdrawal of the libido into the ego. The state I am describing implies the withdrawal of the self away from libidinal object cathexis into a narcissistic state which resembles primary narcissism. The patient appears to be withdrawn from the world, is unable to think and often feels drugged. He may lose his interest in the outside world and want to stay in bed and forget what had been discussed in previous sessions. If he manages to come to the session, he may complain that something incomprehensible has happened to him and that he feels trapped, claustrophobic and unable to get out of this state. He is often aware that he has lost something important but is not sure what it is. The loss may be felt in concrete terms as a loss of his keys or his wallet, but sometimes he realizes that his anxiety and feeling of loss refers to having lost an important part of himself, namely the sane dependent self which is related to the capacity for thinking. Sometimes the patient develops an acute hypochondriacal fear of death which is quite overwhelming. One has here the impression of being able to observe the death instinct in its purest form, as a power which manages to pull the whole of the self away from life into a deathlike condition by false promises of a Nirvana-like state, which would imply a complete defusion of the basic instincts. However, detailed investigation of the process suggests that we are not dealing with a state of defusion but a pathological fusion similar to the process I described in the perversions. In this narcissistic withdrawal state the sane dependent part of the patient enters the delusional object and a projective identification takes place in which the sane self loses its identity and becomes completely dominated by the omnipotent destructive process; it has no power to oppose or mitigate the latter while this pathological fusion lasts; on the contrary, the power of the destructive process is greatly increased in this situation.

Clinically it is essential to help the patient to find and rescue the dependent sane part of the self from its trapped position inside the psychotic narcissistic structure as it is this part which is the essential link with the positive object relationship to the analyst and the world. Secondly, it is important gradually to assist the patient to become fully conscious of the split-off destructive omnipotent parts of the self which control the psychotic organization, because this can only remain all-powerful in isolation. When this process is fully revealed it becomes clear that it contains the destructive envious impulses of the self which have become isolated and then the omnipotence which has such a hypnotic effect on the whole of the self gets deflated and the infantile nature of the omnipotence can be exposed. In other words, the patient becomes gradually aware that he is dominated by an omnipotent infantile part of himself which not only pulls him away towards death but infantilizes him and prevents him from growing up, by keeping him away from objects who could help him to achieve growth and development.

I shall now briefly report some case material from a narcissistic neurotic patient to illustrate the existence of a split-off, omnipotent, destructive part of himself which became more conscious during analysis and lost some of its violence. The patient is an unmarried business man of 37, who has been in treatment for several years. He came to analysis because of character problems and was consciously very determined to have analysis and to co-operate in it. However, there was a chronic resistance to the analysis, which was very elusive and repetitive. The patient had to leave London occasionally for short business trips and he often returned too late on Mondays and so missed either part or the whole of his session. He frequently met women during these trips and brought to analysis many of the problems which arose with them. It was, of course, clear from the beginning that some acting out was taking place but only when he regularly reported murderous activities in his dreams after such weekends did it become apparent that violently destructive attacks against the analysis and the analyst were hidden in the acting out behaviour. The patient was at first reluctant to accept that the acting out of the weekend was killing, and therefore blocking the progress of, the analysis, but gradually he changed his behaviour and the analysis became more effective and he reported considerable improvement in some of his personal relationships and his business activities. At the same time he began to complain that his sleep was frequently disturbed and that he woke up during the night with violent palpitations which kept him awake for several hours. During these anxiety attacks he felt that his hands did not belong to him; they seemed violently destructive as if they wanted to destroy something by tearing it up, and were too powerful for him to control so that he had to give in to them. He then dreamt of a very powerful arrogant man who was nine feet tall and who insisted that he had to be absolutely obeyed. His associations made it clear that this man stood for a part of himself and related to the destructive over-powering feelings in his hands which he could not resist. I interpreted that he regarded the omnipotent destructive part of himself as a superman who was nine feet tall and much too powerful for him to disobey. He had disowned this omnipotent self, which explained the estrangement of his hands during the nightly attacks. I further explained this split-off self as an infantile omnipotent part which claimed that it was not an infant but stronger and more powerful than all the adults, particularly his mother and father and now the analyst. His adult self was so completely taken in and therefore weakened by this omnipotent assertion that he felt powerless to fight the destructive impulses at night. The patient reacted to the interpretation with surprise and relief and reported after some days that he felt more able to control his hands at night. He became gradually more aware that the destructive impulses at night had some connection with analysis because they increased after any success which could be attributed to it. Thus he saw that the wish to tear at himself was related to a wish to tear out and destroy a part of himself which depended on the analyst and valued him. Simultaneously the aggressive narcissistic impulses which had been split off became more conscious during analytic sessions and he sneered saying: 'Here you have to sit all day wasting your time'. He felt that he was the important person and he should be free to do anything he wanted to do, however cruel and hurting this might be to others and himself. He was particularly enraged by the insight and understanding which the analysis gave him. He hinted that his rage was related to wanting to reproach me for helping him, because this interfered with his omnipotent acting-out behaviour. He then reported a dream, that he was running a long-distance race and he was working very hard at it. However, there was a young woman who did not believe in anything that he was doing. She was unprincipled, nasty and did everything to interfere and mislead him. There was a reference to the woman's brother, who was called 'Mundy'. He was much more aggressive than his sister and he appeared in the dream snarling like a wild beast, even at her. It was reported in the dream that this brother had had the task of misleading everybody, during the previous year. The patient thought that the name 'Mundy' referred to his frequent missing of the Monday sessions a year ago. He realized that the violent uncontrolled aggressiveness related to himself but he felt the young woman was also himself. During the last year he had often insisted in his analytic sessions that he felt he was a woman, and was very contemptuous of and superior to the analyst. Lately, however, he occasionally dreamt of a little girl who was receptive and appreciative of her teachers, which I had interpreted as a part of him which wanted to show more appreciation of the analyst, but was prevented from coming into the open by his omnipotence. In the dream the patient admits that the aggressive omnipotent part of himself, represented as male, which had dominated the acting out until a year ago, had now become quite conscious. His identification with the analyst is expressed in the dream as a determination to work hard at his analysis. The dream, however, is also a warning that he would continue his aggressive acting out in analysis by asserting in a misleading way that he could present himself omnipotently as a grown-up woman instead of allowing himself to respond to the work of the analysis with receptive feelings relating to a more positive infantile part of himself. In fact the patient was moving in the analysis towards a strengthening of his positive dependence, which enabled him to expose openly the opposition of the aggressive narcissistic omnipotent parts of his personality; in other words, the patient's severe instinctual defusion is gradually developing into normal fusion.

Summary

I have attempted in this paper to investigate clinical conditions where aggressive impulses predominate and examine their relation to Freud's theory of the defusion and fusion of the life and death instincts. I have found that even in the most severe states of defusion of the instincts clinical states which resemble Freud's description of the death instinct in its original form reveal on detailed analysis that it is the destructive aspect of the death instinct which is active in paralysing, or psychically killing, the libidinal parts of the self derived from the life instinct. I therefore think that it is not possible to observe an unfused death instinct in the clinical situation.

Some of these destructive states cannot be described as defusions because they are really pathological fusions, in which the psychic structure dominated by a destructive part of the self succeeds in imprisoning and overpowering the libidinal self, which is completely unable to oppose the destructive process.

It seems that certain omnipotent, narcissistic states are dominated by the most violent destructive processes, so that the libidinal self is almost completely absent or lost. Clinically it is therefore essential to find access to the libidinal dependent self, which can mitigate the destructive impulses. In analysing the omnipotent structure of the narcissistic state the infantile nature of the process has to be exposed in order to release these dependent parts which can form good object relations leading to the introjection of libidinal objects which are the basis of normal fusion.

References

Abraham, K. (1919) 'A particular form of neurotic resistance against the psychoanalytic method' in *Selected Papers*, London: Hogarth Press (1942).

—— (1924) 'A short study of the development of the libido viewed in the light of mental disorders' in *Selected Papers*, London: Hogarth Press (1942).

Freud, S. (1911) 'Formulations on the two principles of mental functioning', *SE* 12.

—— (1914) 'On narcissism: an introduction', *SE* 14.

—— (1915) 'Instincts and their vicissitudes', *SE* 14.

—— (1916–17) 'Introductory lectures on psycho-analysis', *SE* 15–16.

—— (1920) 'Beyond the pleasure principle', *SE* 18.

—— (1923) 'The ego and the id', *SE* 19.

—— (1924) 'The economic problem of masochism', *SE* 19.

—— (1933) 'New introductory lectures on psycho-analysis', *SE* 22.

—— (1937) 'Analysis terminable and interminable', *SE* 23.

Hartmann, H. (1953) 'Contribution to the metapsychology of schizophrenia', in *Essays on Ego Psychology*, London: Hogarth Press (1964).

——, Kris, E. & Loewenstein, R. M. (1949) 'Notes on the theory of aggression', *Psychoanalytic Study of the Child*, 3–4.

Kernberg, O. F. (1970) 'Factors in the psychoanalytic treatment of narcissistic personalities', *Journal of the American Psychoanalytical Association*, 18, 51–85.

Klein, M. (1946) 'Notes on some schizoid mechanisms' in M. Klein, P. Heimann, S. Isaacs, and J. Riviere *Developments in Psycho-Analysis*, London: Hogarth Press (1952) 292–320 (also in *The Writings of Melanie Klein* vol. 3, 1–24).

—— (1952) 'The origins of transference', *International Journal of Psycho-analysis*, 33, 433–8; also in *The Writings of Melanie Klein*, vol. 3, London: Hogarth Press (1975), 48–56; also paperback New York: Dell Publishing Co. (1977).

—— (1957) *Envy and Gratitude* in *The Writings of Melanie Klein*.

—— (1958) 'On the development of mental functioning', *International Journal of Psycho-Analysis*, 39, 84–90.

Reich, W. (1933) *Character-Analysis*, New York: Orgone Institute Press (1949).

Rosenfeld, H. (1964) 'On the psychopathology of narcissism', *International Journal of Psycho-Analysis*, 45, 332–7; also in *Psychotic States*, London: Hogarth Press (1965) 169–79.

—— (1969) 'Notes on the negative therapeutic reaction' in P. Giovacchini (ed.) *Tactics and Techniques in Psychoanalytic Theory* vol. 2, New York: Jason Aronson (1975).

—— (1970) 'On projective identification', paper read to the British Psycho-Analytical Society, first published in 1971 in P. Doucet and C. Laurin (eds) *Problems of Psychosis*, The Hague: Excerpta Medica, 115–28 and reprinted here on pp. 117–37.

4

Cruelty and narrowmindedness

ERIC BRENMAN

This article is a development of the paper on 'Cruelty and narrowmindedness' read at the European Congress in October 1970; for reasons of confidentiality it was not published until 1985 when it appeared in the *International Journal of Psycho-Analysis*, 66, 273–81.

In normal development love modifies cruelty; in order to perpetuate cruelty, steps have to be taken to prevent human love from operating. My contention is that in order to maintain the practice of cruelty, a singular narrowmindedness of purpose is put into operation. This has the function of squeezing out humanity and preventing human understanding from modifying the cruelty. The consequence of this process produces a cruelty which is 'inhuman'.

If we consider the Oedipus myth from the angle of the role played by the Gods, we can follow this process. The God Apollo had ordained that Oedipus would kill his father Laius and marry his mother Jocasta. No mortal, that is, human, intervention could be proof against the God's prediction. Here we see the omnipotent narrowminded persistence: nothing can stand in the way of the omnipotent Gods' determination.

Laius' only hope was that Oedipus should not survive. Here we see counter-cruelty presented as the only solution. Oedipus was delivered to a shepherd with orders to abandon him on a mountain; but human compassion, the antidote to cruelty, intervened, as the shepherd had not the heart to do this and entrusted the child to a Corinthian shepherd. But this humanity was of no avail.

As a result of cruel destiny, Oedipus killed his father on his journey to escape patricide, emphasizing again the impotence of human understanding. After marrying Jocasta, Oedipus had to root out his father's murderer, and pursued this course with persistent vigour, excluding all human counsel. The tragic revelation led to his plucking out his eyes, and his abandonment to cruel exile.

What this myth shows, over and above the accepted interpretation, is that the powerful omnipotent Gods are determined to triumph over human compassion and understanding, and this in itself prompts counter-cruelty. The revelation of guilt likewise leads to the relentless cruel judgement of loveless exile, with the deprivation of human comfort; equivalent to the cruelty of the superego. Some human comfort was, however, derived from his daughter Antigone.

It seems to me that this myth shows another interesting feature; the omnipotent cruel and relentless gods are actually worshipped and revered and given a higher status than human love; I think that it is because they are in fact 'loved' (as well as feared) more than humanity that such catastrophes take place.

When love and hate clash, either we feel guilt and make reparation, or we are persecuted by guilt. To avoid either consequence, we can pervert the truth, draw strength from a good object and feel free to practise cruelty in the name of goodness. It is as though we omnipotently hijack human righteousness and conduct cruelty in the name of justice.

We now take for granted that omnipotent behaviour belongs to the nature of man. History affords us many examples of this: the Hitler regime, idealized omnipotent national conquest, revolutions and their subsequent regimes. This perversion is well illustrated by the Spanish Inquisition, which took the Christian ethic of tolerance, understanding and brotherly love, and tortured ruthlessly in the name of Christianity.

In Greek tragedy the chorus sees the tragedy in a broader spectrum, but only hopelessly observes while the Tragic Hero is locked in the narrow confines of his destiny. The analyst witnesses, as the chorus does, but hopes that intervention of understanding can modify the process. In my clinical examples I refer to patients who are persistently cruel and who persist with their grievances in a cruel way and, by projection, experience the interpretations of the analyst as having the identical qualities of cruelty. I also wish to show the narrowing of perception (narrowmindedness) that facilitates this process, and with it the avoidance of psychotic catastrophe.

Clinical example

The patient, a Jewish woman of 42, born in Eastern Europe, presented with belligerent complaints of suffering. She had had two previous attempts at analysis. She complained of intolerable suffering. She was in agony of spirit, depressed in a tortured way. She had unbearable backache which was unresponsive to medical treatment, agonizing headaches, stabbing pains in her eyes, with an inability to concentrate, inability to see clearly, and difficulty in focusing her eyes for any long period.

I learned in the course of treatment that she had tormented her husband, humiliated and derided him, left him for long periods, having affairs with his knowledge; she neglected her child, and was cruel and spiteful to her acquaintances. She believed, however, that she was the victim of cruel fate, and she felt cruelly treated by almost everyone.

Her previous analysis, which lasted one year, was spent screaming at her analyst, reproaching her, and complaining of inhuman treatment.

By the time she came to me for treatment, her husband had divorced her. She spent the first period of analysis screaming at me and complaining.

In the analysis I felt trapped in a cruel siege, unable to interpret meaningfully as she went on and on with her grievances, which she documented with the relish of a collector of antiques.

She accused me of being a cold, merciless Anglo-Saxon, and complained that I forced her to yield to my analytic theory, with complete disregard for her human plight.

The combination of cruel attacks on me and, by projection, the guilt of cruelty that was alleged to be mine, showed her particular need to have someone who could both tolerate being the victim of cruelty and who could bear the guilty responsibility for these attacks.

For example, she dreamed that she parked a lorry at a parking meter. The lorry, however, was too big and took up too many spaces. She was approached by a traffic-warden who questioned her. She immediately rammed the lorry into a telephone kiosk and smashed it up.

She associated the traffic-warden with the small-mindedness of a petty official, later attributed to me. Apart from many other meanings in her dream, the rage which smashed up all forms of communication (the telephone) was her reaction to what she perceived as my smallminded omnipotent officialdom; her perception of me was as one who could only moralize, only see where she was doing 'wrong' (a harsh superego). She felt I could not see her need to park the lorry; to find a resting place or home. She felt I could have no sympathy with her requirements for more space, more time, more sessions, or with her plight.

Therefore, living in such a cruel and narrowminded reproachful environment, all she could do was to smash up our means of communication: the analysis.

It is of interest to note that she herself had no conscious knowledge of her need to 'park' herself and be given a 'home' by me. She saw me as behaving like a Tin God, but was not aware of her need for me.

She obtained some relief from my interpretation. I was also able to show her some of her own behaviour; that she was acutely 'switched on' to my faults, showing the acumen of a specialist. She was 'switched off' to any goodness and helpfulness which might be in me, to her own dependent needs, and to the fact that she really behaved in this way.

This patient was uprooted from her home by the Nazis at the age of 14, and her parents were taken to a concentration camp where they subsequently perished. This tragedy played a vital part in her development. However, it did not seem to me that the picture of me as a traffic-warden corresponded to the brutality of the Nazis, but rather to the officiousness of the projected child part of herself.

I learned in the course of subsequent sessions that she had uprooted – left her husband and child to go abroad for her artistic pursuits, with little regard for their needs, or indeed, her own.

Gradually I was able to study the dossier she had built up about me. I was depicted as complacent and smug, and she seemed determined to put an end to my peace of mind. She maintained that I practised analysis solely in order to make money and in order to believe I knew everything about life. She tried to make me feel that my whole belief in psychoanalysis was based on a lie motivated by my greedy omniscience. Above all, she wanted to know if I could face this false life I had built up; face the illusion and the guilt and have to give it up with nothing to fall back on. She even begrudged the fact that I could practise as a doctor if I realized psychoanalysis was a delusion; I was to be left with nothing at all.

These attacks on me were her attempt to destroy my goodness and creativity, but above all, I felt at the time that she conveyed to me an ordeal that she felt I would not have the courage to face. I knew what I was supposed to experience, and that she had to face this in herself; she wanted the experience of someone who could share such a predicament and give her the strength to face this in her life. Her cruel fate was to realize that she had built her life on a lie, and that she had nothing left. The lie was for her quite specific. She was a woman of talent who had created works of art depicting deep human qualities, but her personal life was devoid of these qualities.

She felt alone, unloved, and persecuted by a reproachful superego.

The capacity to tolerate these projections, and my sharing her task in facing the way she had built up her life, gave her some security. She gradually was able to see this as an internal problem which tormented her whenever she had to make a decision. For example, when she had to buy kitchen units, she felt that if she bought a large unit she would be tortured with the thought that she had spent too much money. On the other hand, if she bought a small unit, she was tortured with thoughts of being mean and stupid and thereby spoiling the whole character of the kitchen. Both thoughts were cruel and relentless, and she felt exhausted.

In actual fact, whatever decision she made would not be all that bad in reality. However, each 'voice' in the argument had this cruel quality. If she spent extra money she was reproached for producing a state of utter bankruptcy, and she would regret it for the rest of her life; she would be excommunicated and forced to live in guilt. Equally, if she was careful with money her whole mean character would be exposed and disgraced so that she would again be derided and reproached for spoiling the whole house.

The quality in all this cruelty, her behaviour to me, her picture of my behaviour to her, and the elements in the internal conflict, all had the same unbearable consequence – that she would be excommunicated, left alone, unlovable, with the reproach that she had ruined everything irreparably, and there would be no chance of forgiveness or opportunity for reparation. To my mind it was characterized by another quality; there was no 'rest of her life' available to carry on with. The whole of life was narrowed to these elements, and there was nothing else. Every issue was one of life-and-death. It followed closely the pattern of fanatic puritanism, in which any one sin leads to eternal damnation.

Gradually some elements of a good understanding analyst began to develop, relieving the cruelty. But I wish to show what happened to this understanding.

During a session she experienced feeling understood, and she felt that I empathized with her predicament; she obtained great relief from her physical pain. By the next session (after a weekend break), her memory of the good session was lost.

She did, however, produce a dream: she was a student at the University hostel in Kiev, where there was a special area provided for her to rest and find shelter, and she was nursed by a couple who understood her as an individual.

She associated that it was odd of her to find comfort in the capital of the Ukraine, which she considered was the capital of pogroms against the Jews. She felt it perverse and strange to give such qualities to such people, who did not deserve this. She came to realize:

(1) That she had destroyed the good memory of an understanding session; equated with love.
(2) That the good humanity was given to omnipotent racists who practised cruelty, but whose cruelty was denied; instead they were idealized as so comforting.

In this she re-enacted her past history, when she had despised her parents, identified herself with fair-haired, blue-eyed Aryans, and likened herself to them, in spite of their arrogant contempt of her Jewish qualities.

So it could be seen that she identified herself with cruel omnipotent gods, perverting the good aspects of her parents and my analysis. She bestowed the attributes of human understanding and love on to the tormentors with whom the omnipotent part of herself identified.

She did come to realize that in her belief that she was the champion of humanity (that was the way she practised cruelty) she stole the humanity from her parents and me, and she was the perpetrator of cruelty. It was she who practised the Inquisition in her analysis, in the name of righteousness, with fanatic persistence, and even contrived to suffer in its cause.

Later on, she dreamed of going to a station with a time-bomb in her belly. This she associated with an explosive outburst with her ex-husband when he was boarding a train, accusing him of infidelity. This she 'timed' to justify her outrage and squeeze out of her mind that she had left him for three months for an affair. By narrowing her mind to his possible infidelity she occluded her guilt and could produce the explosion for this isolated incident. This coincided with my approaching holidays.

The same night she dreamed of an Amazon woman, who was evil but did not know what she had done. This woman's head was cruelly smashed again and again, and the onlookers thought this was just. Among the onlookers was the figure of Justice, but instead of being blindfolded, this figure of Justice had daggers in her eyes.

She associated that she had wanted to paint a picture of Amazon life. If she created a picture of other people's cruelty she could justifiably attack it in a relentless way. But in order to do this, the vision of Justice was not made impartial by blindfolding; instead the eyes were filled with daggers. Here she could both 'look daggers' and have her perceptions attacked by daggers. (One is reminded of the fate of Oedipus.)

The daggers in the eyes of the figure of Justice she associated to the stabbing pain in her eyes, and her inability to concentrate and have any breadth of vision. The analysis of this relieved the pains in her eyes but confronted her with guilt, and she could now see the injustice of her attacks that had been so righteously upheld.

The analysis of the guilt is of course essential; the experiencing of it is made difficult by the narrowminded unforgiving torture of the superego.

She could defend herself against this by a desire to devote her life to what she believed to be an all-righteous cause, by fighting for Israel.

The rationalization of self-centred omnipotent narrowmindedness, and the defence against guilt, was perpetuated in the name of survival. Consequently all issues were felt as struggles of life-and-death, and so became unbearable. She thus so narrowed her perception that she was constantly in the position of the baby whose only horizon was the nipple, and it was right and natural to focus her life on satisfying her needs, and to demand that I too focus my mind on the satisfaction of her needs.

The great tragedy of her life was that at the age of 14 she had had to leave her country with her brother and sister to escape extermination by the Nazis and so survive. Her parents stayed behind and were murdered. So her survival was felt to be at the expense of her parents' lives, and she felt she should have shared their fate. The guilt over this never left her, and she felt reparation was impossible. It was not only the burden of guilt that prevented the enjoyment of life, but she began to see there was a 'kill-joy' part of herself in operation. (In fact, this was the cause of a good deal of guilt.)

She realized there was a part of herself that behaved in a particularly cruel way. If I did not satisfy her completely and make her feel special and unique, she killed my analysis and my work in a vicious annihilation. When I pointed this out to her she claimed that I condemned her to feeling guilty and tortured as unlovable for the rest of her life.

The fact that I tolerated this, contained it, continued to try to understand and help her, brought her no joy. She could not see that she was killing joy and comfort; only the pain she suffered. She screamed and shouted at the pain that she felt I inflicted on her.

When she saw that it was the good parents in me she destroyed in her self-absorption, she obtained dramatic relief and eventually could appreciate me and feel sorry. She could then experience guilt, together with a more understanding superego, and have more strength and hope to deal with *it*.

This was in contrast to her actual past, where I have reason to believe that her mother submitted to her attacks, with the patient introjecting a hopelessly destroyed and reproachful mother.

Developments in the analysis

In an earlier account of this patient, I described how she was locked in the narrow confines of cruelty and cut off from a 'home'. Gradually some concept of a home was built in the analysis, which enabled humanity to counteract cruelty. Following the dream about 'Kiev' we saw the beginning of her realization of her need for a home for the needy baby part of herself, and her recognition that she stole from her parents and myself and gave our good attributes to the cruel 'ideal Aryans' with whom she identified.

We also discovered that she had her own ways of trying to provide herself with a home. She could establish a comforting home if she was in a blurred state of mind, with no distinction between herself and her object. She got a feeling of 'belonging' in intense physical sexual union. She also had a feeling of security in her manic paranoid episodes when all the goodness was felt to be inside her. But none of these experiences could nourish her and assist in growth. All these processes destroyed the really helpful separate breast-mother-analyst.

The analysis of these issues enabled her to recognise the paramount importance of her search for a home for the needy parts of herself. She came to value the psychological home I gave her and the home given to her by friends; she began to admire people who provided homes and those who could admit their need for homes.

She described vividly to me how she met a Russian Jew who managed to leave the Soviet Union and was in transit to Israel. This man had sacrificed an important prestigious position in his field of work. He assumed, for her, heroic proportions and she yearned to be united with such a man, who could keep a concept of home alive in him, risk prison in his country, and finally achieve his home in Israel.

She spoke with genuine admiration about the fact that this Russian Jew had given up his worldly success for more human aspirations. After meeting this man, however, she had a dream in which she was fishing in the River Thames. She caught something at the end of her line but she could not pull in her catch, however hard she tried. Eventually she followed the line and it was attached to a metal box which was embedded in rock. The box had written on it 'Bank X' and inside 'Cafe Y'. I use 'X' and 'Y' to disguise identity.) Bank 'X' was associated with her ex-husband's bank and the time when money seemed inexhaustible. Cafe 'Y' was associated with a cafe where she used to meet her artistic friends who would 'run the world' in a superior fashion from their coffee tables. The Thames was associated with the publishers of artistic books which she hoped would publish her art.

She soon realized that in spite of the preface to the dream of the sacrifice of worldly success for a 'human home', her yearning for money and success were firmly embedded and rock-like. This dream does contain an element of her search for 'omnipotent gods' (Cafe 'Y'), but it did not seem to me sinister and cruel in nature. The overall picture is her search for money and success, which had some realistic basis. She was not nursed in a 'cruel perverse home' as she was in the dream about Kiev. She was fishing for money and success and there was a struggle between the different parts of herself. She struggled with her ambivalence, instead of reverting to a perverse solution to obviate this.

But what I consider the most striking development was the way she reacted to the realization of what she was doing in the dream. She did not have to 'pluck out her eyes', narrow her perception, justify herself or feel mercilessly reproached. She could look at this part of herself, give it a home, and realize it was her task to struggle with these elements. I believe this was the result of my having a 'home' to these parts of her as well as the needy parts, and the subsequent introjection of my 'psychological home'. This enabled the analysis to proceed in a way in which insight could be used constructively rather than being regarded as the cruel reproach of a moralizing superego.

On her own reflection, she recognized the power of these forces and thought about the way she behaved with her son, being rejecting if he were not highly successful. She felt genuine guilt and seemed determined to give him a proper home whatever he achieved or did not achieve.

A most significant part of her development was the giving of a home to the memory of her mother. She had described her mother, perhaps not inaccurately, as always anxious, always complaining about father and nagging her if she, the patient, was not 'just so', and not at all interested in the patient's work or enjoyment. She stood somewhere between a broken-down mother and a demanding figure. Now she could see her mother as depressed and unhappy but always striving: a woman who gained satisfaction from making a good physical home for the family, who always fed and clothed her well and did what she could in 'her way'. It was a sad picture in many ways, but there was one feature that left its mark – this was her mother's struggling and carrying on in spite of adversity and depression. It was this quality of her mother that the patient felt sustained her (the patient) in her journey across Europe and Turkey when she left her native land at the age of 14.

It was through the realization of what I endured in giving her a 'psychological home' that she gave a home to the memory of her real mother, drew strength from this and felt free to avail herself of new loving experiences without feeling she abandoned her mother. She could now begin to live in a more generous world which reduced her hatred and helped her to deal with her aggression, and mitigated the vicious circle of her previous cruel and narrow world.

Second clinical example

In the first example, I described how the patient narrowed her perception to the picture of a nipple as the means of survival. In the second clinical example the penis took the place of the nipple and was the focal point in the patient's world.

This patient was a homosexual male aged 30. It first seemed that his narrowmindedness was localized in sensuous satisfaction, but it soon became apparent that the penis stood for very much more. His whole life revolved around worshipping penises. He had sexual adventures in public lavatories many times a day, mainly of fellatio or being the passive partner in anal intercourse. He would go into eulogies about these penises – they were straight, upright, noble, etc. The fact that these penises belonged to men who sometimes robbed him of money or assaulted him did not lead to any modification of his views. Any strength he obtained from me was denied and attributed to·these penises.

For example, he would be relieved of some misery in a session, proceed to lose all the understanding I gave him, and turn to these 'magnificent' penises for relief, only to be plunged into depression, once again. This pattern was repeated again and again. In essence the buggery was always cruel and was used to triumph over the good internal object, linked in the analysis with my understanding.

In the countertransference he produced a feeling of helplessness in me and a feeling that there was nothing I could do against the powerful omnipotence of the religion of phallic worship. He tried to force me to believe in his system and to get me to admit my impotent envy of his exciting exploits.

When this picture of a phallic world began to break down, and he experienced depression, he would eulogize depressive writers and try to make me believe that only those who saw the futility of human life were the true giants of the human mind; and the others, like me, were pathetic cowards. Again, there were persistent, narrow, cruel attacks against life itself. What became clear was the omnipotent cruelty, which made creativity and joy as nothing by comparison with his depression.

When he moved to heterosexuality he mercilessly focused his mind on all the defects of his girlfriend and tormented her for her deficiencies with an arrogant belief in his god-like superiority. He was identified with the ideal object and felt entitled to torment the actual girl for her failings.

After laborious analysis he began to come closer to the realization of his cruelty and to approach some feelings of guilt.

His ace card in acting out was to come one day to the session in a distraught state, earlier than his appointment, and go into the waiting room. Soon after arriving, he left my house knowing I could hear him leave, and paraded outside my house, knowing I could see him from my window. He knew I would not call him in, so when he did come to the door, missing about five minutes of his session, he was now armed with righteous reproach. Here was he, the patient, distraught with suffering and I, the analyst, extremely cruel, worshipping my analytic technique and putting it above humanity and suffering. I would never deviate to help him, so he could now establish that the cruelty was mine.

Throughout the whole pattern of this cruelty, the narcissistic preoccupation that he was right, he knew the real truth, he loved the really worthy objects, was persistently maintained. Ultimately he alone walked with 'humanity' and I had none.

I have little doubt about his basic envy of humanity and creativity, but the point I wish to emphasize is the way he narrowed his perception to 'his world' and kept out any fuller understanding. His analysis was not like this all the time, of course, but it is the strength of this feature and its power that I wish to emphasize. This pattern was resurrected at every crisis.

Whatever the perversion and narrow preoccupation may be, I think that it is ultimately goodness, humanity and truth that are so sorely coveted. It also shows in this case the painfulness of guilt in realizing what he had done; he had to frame me for this sin, and was prepared to suffer to vindicate himself.

Theoretical considerations

Freud (1917), in 'Mourning and melancholia' described how the melancholic would both torture his object and cling to it, refusing to establish a new object relationship. Abraham (1924) made the observation that in the cruelty of melancholia these patients treated the object as if they owned it. Both Freud and Abraham emphasized the regression to narcissism, with no differentiation between self and object.

As I understand Melanie Klein's concept of the depressive position (1934), a development takes place in which the infant begins to realize the separateness of himself and the object. As I see it, he is therefore confronted with inferiority and envy of the mother, a realization of the human non–ideal mother, whom he does not own; and therefore has to confront frustration, guilt, and the anxiety of losing this mother.

In order to remain in the narcissistic position, attacks are made on this awareness, which include attacks on the internal object. These attacks destroy the awareness of the human mother and the patient is therefore left in a cruel, loveless world.

To put this another way: perception develops from the nipple to the breast, to the body, face, and ultimately the mother's mind and love, producing a picture of 'Mummy'. This can be introjected and be given a 'home' inside the infant's mind and feed the infant's capacity to love. It is the obliteration of the concept of the whole human mother that narrows the picture of the world to a cruel loveless place.

Furthermore, the attacks on the real mother for not being the 'ideal breast' (which satisfies through narcissistic identification the demand to have the ideal, and be the ideal) leads to the incorporation of a superego which demands that the infant has to satisfy it for the rest of his life. Therefore he lives in a cruel, exacting, narrow world, which feeds his fear and hatred, and he is forced to worship this system, subordinate himself and identify with it, partly out of fear, and partly because it contains his own vengeful omnipotence. This superego–ego ideal dominates his life. That which Freud and Abraham described as the patient clinging to his object and treating his object as if he owns it, now becomes, through introjection, a patient possessed by a cruel superego which will not let him be free.

He is therefore confined to his narrow loveless narcissistic demands, governed by narrow loveless narcissistic gods. Added to this the infant casts out and abandons the real human mother to cruel exile, and introjects a mother that does the same to him, and therefore gives him no home. In addition, the narcissistic part of the personality exiles the needy real baby part of himself. A home is therefore only given to gods and the godlike narcissistic part of the self, leading to a 'false self' and living a lie.

This problem is complicated still further as the infant may have been denied a good home in the first place. He may have had a mother who rejected the baby part of him, could not stand his anxieties, and failed in this sense to provide a home for this baby. His anxious needy self may have been psychologically cast out and abandoned in cruel exile. He may have had a mother who could only tolerate an 'ideal baby' and rejected the real baby, or he may have had a mother who over-indulged him and satisfied his omnipotent cravings. In either case, he lusts for vengeance and the re-creation of the 'ideal world'.

By the time the patient arrives for analysis we are therefore faced with a complex problem. But it seems to me the clinical task is to enable the patient to make use of a fuller, understanding, loving world which is the only experience that can rescue him.

I have attempted to show in this paper how such patients try to confine the analyst's understanding to the justification of their grievances under the guise of moral justice, and squeeze out or prevent any fuller love from modifying this situation. In doing so, they cast themselves into exile, devoid of love, at the mercy of the primitive superego.

The sum total of this narcissistic organization ensures that the patient does not find a good home in which to grow up, enjoy life and have the experience of human sharing.

With a 'good home', problems of cruelty are humanized by interaction with parents. I cannot help speculating: 'Would Oedipus have behaved as he did had he been brought up at home?' His tragedy was that he started life in exile and finished in exile.

The converse of the cruel vicious circle is mutual shared concern; the mother giving a home for the baby inside her mind, and the baby giving a home for the real mother inside his mind.

Conclusion

The normal process that leads to seeing the mother as a separate person who feels pain, joy and gives creatively, is, in cases of cruelty, viciously squeezed out of perception, leading to a narrow mind.

The narrowing of perception restricts the imagery of the whole object to the role of a nipple that the patient owns, and so restricts conscious love and conscious guilt.

Demands are put on this object to be ideal and consider the patient ideal, or be vengefully punished.

Goodness is hijacked and perverted to the side of cruelty to give it strength and avoid catastrophe. This perversion is worshipped as a religion and the analyst is required to convert to this worship, and 'God help you if you don't'. The introjection of this leads to a cruel superego and establishes a hopeless vicious circle of cruelty and slavish devotion to a cruel perverse moralizing god. The real mother is cast out and abandoned and the real needy 'Baby part' is likewise cast into exile.

Unfavourable early and analytic environment may: support the omnipotent delusion; enact counter-cruelty; provide its own omnipotent cruelty as a model for identification; collapse or die. All may have disastrous consequences.

The role of the analyst is to widen the patient's perception against militant attacks designed to keep both his and the patient's minds narrowed, and to supply the right environment by his careful analysis. The fuller understanding of the analyst must be matched against the narrowmindedness, as this fuller understanding is the means of modifying cruelty and allowing goodness, strength to deal with hatred, and forgiveness to intervene.

By this means a 'home' is given to new good experiences; this enables the good aspects of the original 'home' to be rehoused inside the patient's mind. An exiled mother comes home, becomes an ally in the work of goodness and the task of mitigating cruelty is strengthened and shared.

Summary

The contention of this paper is that human understanding modifies cruelty, and that in order that cruelty can remain unmodified various mechanisms are employed. The most important processes include the worship of omnipotence which is felt to be superior to human love and forgiveness, the clinging to omnipotence as a defence against depression, and the sanctification of grievance and revenge. In order to avoid conscious guilt, the perceptions of the mind are narrowed to give ostensible justification to the cruelty, and the obviation of redeeming features in the object.

The paper explores how these processes operate and how by virtue of projection the analyst's interpretations are perceived as cruel, and how the patient arranges to be locked in this vicious circle.

Technical problems of dealing with these forces are explored together with the task of bringing alive the human concern that modifies cruelty.

References

Abraham, K. (1924) 'A short study of the development of the libido, viewed in the light of mental disorders' in *Selected Papers on Psychoanalysis*, London: Hogarth Press (1942), 418–501.

Freud, S. (1917) 'Mourning and melancholia', *SE* 14.

Klein, M. (1934) 'A contribution to the psychogenesis of manic-depressive states', in *The Writings of Melanie Klein*, London: Hogarth Press (1975).

5

Narcissistic organization, projective identification, and the formation of the identificate

LESLIE SOHN

This article was first published in 1985 in the *International Journal of Psycho-Analysis*, 66, 201–13.

In the paper, 'The dissection of the psychical personality', which is presented as Lecture XXXI in 1933, the editors of the *Standard Edition* direct our attention to the fact that the lecture is largely derived from at least four chapters in 'The ego and the id'. Despite this, Freud predicts that the response to the lecture will be a furthering of the reserve and caution of his audience towards his material. Freud says in his preface, written in the summer of 1932, that this is a lecture only by an artifice of the imagination, in which he critically revises previous expositions, but in the lecture, with almost a jaunty musicality, he says,

> 'We wish to make the ego the matter of our enquiry, our very own ego. But is that possible? After all, the ego is in its very essence a subject; how can it be made into an object? Well, there is no doubt that it can be. The ego can take itself as an object, can treat itself like other objects, can observe itself, criticize itself, and do Heaven knows what with itself. In this, one part of the ego is setting itself over against the rest. So the ego can be split; it splits itself during a number of its functions – temporarily at least. Its parts can come together again afterwards. That is not exactly a novelty, though it may perhaps be putting an unusual emphasis on what is generally known. On the other hand, we are familiar with the notion that pathology, by making things larger and coarser, can draw our attention to normal conditions which would otherwise have escaped us. Where it points to a breach or a rent, there may normally be an articulation present. If we throw a crystal to the

floor, it breaks; but not into haphazard pieces. It comes apart along its lines of cleavage into fragments whose boundaries, though they were invisible, were predetermined by the crystal's structure. Mental patients are split and broken structures of this same kind. Even we cannot withhold from them something of the reverential awe which peoples of the past felt for the insane. They have turned away from external reality, but for that very reason they know more about internal, physical reality and can reveal a number of things to us that would otherwise be inaccessible to us (pp. 58–9).'

My paper is an attempt, via clinical presentation, to look at the lines of cleavage in the ego structures of a differing group of patients, to examine the fragmentations, and sometime restoration, and the identifications resultant upon such changes, and therefore attempts to look at a possible furthering of a considerable body of thought and practice of psychoanalytic work with narcissistic patients and their pathology, by an examination of the varying processes of identification that are engaged upon by such patients in their lives and in their psychoanalyses. The paper would therefore have to show clearly the presence of a transference, because Freud himself felt that these patients had either no capacity for transference or at best a marked diminution of such capacity.

The term primary narcissism implies an objectless state, yet in the writings of many analysts on the subject, terms such as confusion of self and objects, projection of aggression into objects, demands upon objects of varying intensity keep occurring.

The question therefore arises, how, in a situation traditionally reserved to imply an objectless state, has a body of work arisen upon apparently clinically observable conditions, which resemble Freud's description of primary narcissism but which are spoken about in Rosenfeld's terms (1964) as primitive object relations.

Looking at two short excerpts from papers which have served as models over the years for the psychoanalyst's views of processes of normal identification, we can contrast the presentation of those working with narcissistic patients and their experiences with such patients. Freud, in his paper 'Identification' from 'Group psychology' (1921), states:

'Identification is known to psycho-analysis as the earliest expression of an emotional tie with another person. It plays a part in the early history of the Oedipus complex. A little boy will exhibit a special interest in his father; he would like to grow like him and be like him, and take his place everywhere. . . . At the same time as this identification with his father, the boy has begun to develop a true object-cathexis towards his mother, according to the attachment [anaclitic] type. He then exhibits, therefore, two psychologically distinct ties: a straightforward sexual object-cathexis towards his mother and an identification with his father which takes him as his model. The two subsist side by side for a time without any mutual influence or interference. In consequence of the irresistible advance towards a unification of mental life, they come together at last; and the normal Oedipus complex originates from their confluence (p. 105).

In her paper, 'On identification' (1955), Melanie Klein states:

'In normal development, in the second quarter of the first year, persecutory anxiety diminishes and depressive anxiety comes to the fore, as a result of the ego's greater capacity to integrate itself and to synthesize its objects. This entails sorrow, and guilt about the harm done (in omnipotent phantasies) to an object which is now felt to be both loved and hated; these anxieties and the defences against them represent the depressive position . . . internalization is of great importance for projective processes, in particular that the good internalized breast acts as a focal point in the ego, from which good feelings can be projected on to external objects. It strengthens the ego, counteracts the processes of splitting and dispersal and enhances the capacity for integration and synthesis. The good internalized object is thus one of the preconditions for an integrated and stable ego and for good object relations (p. 312).'

'Integration', she feels, 'implies being alive, loving, and being loved by the internal and external good object; that is to say, there exists a close link between integration and object relations'. She continues later, in the same context, 'a securely established good object, implying a securely established love for it, gives the ego a feeling of riches and abundance which allows for an outpouring of libido and projection of good parts of the self into the external world without a sense of depletion arising'. In a footnote to this paper, Klein refers to Freud's 'Group psychology and the analysis of the ego', saying that on re-reading this, she felt that Freud was aware of the process of identification by projection, although it was with introjection that he was mainly concerned (p. 313). She, of course, is referring in such cases, to a balance between giving out, and taking in, between introjection and projection.

In his paper 'Psychopathology of narcissism' (1964), Rosenfeld introduces us to a considerable and growing body of opinion which has undertaken a study of the narcissistic patient, and states: 'In narcissistic object relations omnipotence plays a prominent part. The object, usually a part-object, the breast, may be omnipotently incorporated, which implies that it is treated as the infant's possession; or the mother or breast are used as containers into which are omnipotently projected the parts of the self which are felt to be undesirable as they cause pain or anxiety' (pp. 332–3). He continues,

> 'Identification is an important factor in narcissistic object relations. It may take place by introjection, or by projection. When the object is omnipotently incorporated the self becomes so identified with the incorporated object, that all separate identity, or any boundary, between self and object is denied. In projective identification, parts of the self omnipotently enter an object, for example, the mother, to take over certain qualities, which would be experienced as desirable, and therefore claim to be the object or part-object.'

He feels that identification by introjection and by projection usually occur simultaneously (to which we will return later).

Rosenfeld continues, 'In narcissistic object relations defences against any recognition of separateness between self and object play a predominant part. Awareness of separation would lead to feelings of dependence on an object and therefore to anxiety'. He discusses the implication of dependence, its stimulus to envy and its awareness. The omnipotent narcissistic object relations obviate the aggressive feelings caused by frustration and any awareness of envy, so that omnipotent possession of the breast and its functions cannot frustrate him, or arouse his envy.

Such a formulation, however, brings up a problem. If such a balance, as Rosenfeld describes, is to be maintained in the narcissistic organization, the idea expressed earlier of the object, or part-object, as a container, has to be re-thought; because a successful, or even partially successful, narcissism, must 'view' an object peculiarly, by its own defined terms, and if an evacuation into a containing object occurs omnipotently, it must immediately or omnipotently undergo a denial of the evacuation itself or denial of the awareness of the containing potential of the object because that too will promote envy of the object. If there are, or are felt to be, introjective processes occurring, these too would create a similar difficulty. It is because of this that I feel there is a minimum of introjective identificatory processes, and we should be more concerned in this paper with the projective mechanism; because the greater the degree of introjective processes the less would we be concerned with this kind of development and therefore the less with these kinds of illnesses.

One is tempted to consider the severe and usually irreversible psychoses, in very young people, to be related to this gross interference with introjective processes. These patients are reported to us as having been good children, good learners and full of promise. It is as if when the illness manifests, that a facade which has been present is suddenly removed, for whatever reason, and the exposed, possibly totally undernourished ego, which has until then been falsely maintained by projective processes, is called upon to account for itself, and collapses. The rapid deterioration of such people is well known to all of us.

Rosenfeld speaks about the projection into an object without any concern for it, which he feels takes place because the object is de-valued. My feeling is that the projection itself is one of the reasons for such a de-valuation and the maintenance of the experience of de-valuation, particularly if the projection is bound up with maximal envy, and its denial, and its consequence.

We already have two beliefs accounting for the difficulties encountered in undertaking a psychoanalysis of such patients, the extreme difficulties in 'containing' such patients, while having essentially to be such a container, without ever having it acknow-ledged or experienced, and the natural evolution of a psychoanalysis which allows, invites or guarantees such cruel projections, and its corollary, the de-valuation. Melanie Klein stated that these patients need constant analysis so that they can prove to themselves that they don't need it (origin unknown).

Rosenfeld speaks of how object relations appear to the analyst, and are also experienced by the patient, as very ideal and desirable. The relation to the lavatory mother is felt as ideal because the patient feels relieved where everything unpleasant can be discharged into the analyst during a session. The patient claims credit for all satisfactory interpretations in a situation felt to be perfect or ideal because it increases the feeling during the session that he (the patient) is good or important. All these patients seem to have in common the feeling that they contain all the goodness which would otherwise be experienced in relation to an object.

This was rather graphically demonstrated by a young woman patient hospitalized during an acute psychosis. She had been given some magazines to read by the sister on the ward. She found them uninteresting and tore them into small pieces; urinated on them and ate them with relish. Only then did she enjoy them, proving to herself that her excreta (urinary) were so much better than anyone else's productivity, and in the case of the sister, so much better than her care and generosity.

We would expect from what has been said that such patients would invariably present as overtly psychotic. If we have been saying that there is a withdrawal from reality, an avoidance of reality testing in the systems of denial that exist, the varying degree of omnipotence, the denial of envy, and therefore of jealousy, in the development of such patients, we would be led to expect that we would always be hearing about psychotic cases. I hope to describe narcissistic patients with a lesser narcissistic or a more object-directed personality structure. I believe that within the study of the problems of narcissism there is a complete spectrum of the process. In the original concept of narcissism as described by Freud, the patients were totally withdrawn, but the spectrum moves along from the psychotic patients through to patients as discussed by Rosenfeld in his two papers, to those who maintain apparently adequate lives but in whom the pattern described occurs as isolated or sets of phenomena which produce a particular character structure, or those in whom the narcissistic organization appears as a persistent or temporary defence during the analysis or life.

The answer to the question – why the difference? – lies, I think, in the degree of envy that is or is not available, and as a result of which the various defences earlier discussed are mobilized. The presentation of these patients and their character structures will therefore vary considerably.

In the psychotic cases, characteristically, there is a history of apparent early normality, which is never borne out in the analysis and certainly not in the transference. There is a gradual development of educational failures; in other words, when faced with a testing of introjective processes, failure occurs, most frequently in the more severely ill patient of this type. There is a sudden development of psychotic symptoms – withdrawal, distressed emotional responses, and a rapidly deepening deterioration in their state. Shading away from this end of the spectrum, we find vague unattached goal-less people, who are always full of unrealized promise and peculiar easy and meaningless adaptabilities, through to somewhat withdrawn patronizing condescending people with major or minor dissatisfactions, quite unaware usually of their potential for envy or jealousy or their actual involvement in both.

In his later paper (1971) 'An investigation into the aggressive aspects of narcissism', Rosenfeld refers to 'the central role of self idealization, or the idealization of the omnipotent destructive parts of the self. They are directed against any postive libidinal object

276

relationship and any libidinal part of the self which experiences a need for and the desire to depend on it. The destructive omnipotent parts of the self often remain disguised or they may be silent and split off, which obscures their existence and gives the impression that they have no relationship to the external world. In fact they have a very powerful effect in preventing dependent object relations in keeping external objects permanently devalued, which accounts for the apparent indifference of the narcissistic individual towards external objects and the world' (p. 173).

The process described is well recognized in an analysis of such patients; that when a patient of this kind feels helped in an analysis, it must be the dependent, libidinal aspects that feel helped. (I use the word 'helped' to imply an analytic intervention, which makes the dependent aspects of the patient feel strengthened.) It is also clearly recognizable that the moment such a process occurs such a new situation is attacked mercilessly, acting out occurs, and the original situation of dominance and triumph recurs. This can readily lead us to understand Rosenfeld's view of the imprisoning quality of the nature, not however of splitting, but of a split within the ego.

During the development of such a psychoanalysis, the patient feels that these aspects of his personality have been split off and projected, but only when he begins to feel that the analysis is beginning to have a specific meaning for him. It is then that he is convinced that he has been robbed of his previously held special powers, and that the robbery has been perpetrated by the analyst during the analysis. It seems therefore that the problem that concerns us lies in the nature of the split in the ego as well as in the splitting processes which follow.

In narcissistic organization we have postulated an omnipotent identification having taken place, but we have not explained at all why such a process is basic to the development of a narcissistic organization and why, though the process itself is seen to occur so commonly, it does not always lead to such an organizational development of such a personality structure. We therefore have to postulate in certain instances, and particularly in the psychotic cases, a permanence of such a process, which differentiates it from the more usual experience of a projective taking-over process, which is variable, changes, and is modifiable and stimulated by the vicissitudes of the ongoing mental life.

To me it appears that in the narcissistic organization, an identification by projective identification has taken place; the process of identification starts the narcissistic organization: that is to say, by becoming the object, which is then felt to be within the possession of the self.

It is this that produces the feeling which we call omnipotence, or which enhances the intrinsic omnipotence that is present in all of us, and accounts for the strong bland arrogance of these patients, who can then think, do, be, and exert all the influences of the original object. It has all the chameleonic satisfaction of being a new object and wishes to stay that way. It is, however, done destructively and can never be used constructively – the destruction being to the state of the ego, and to the object which is consequently devalued. This accounts for the hollowness of such a process, which so differentiates it from normal identification.

The consideration of the narcissistic organization we have been discussing therefore is so different from the ones discussed by Freud and Melanie Klein, as we have an unbalanced situation with introjection kept at a minimum, and a maintained split in the ego with its consequent disposal; it is because of this considerable difference that I dislike the use of the term identification in this context – I would prefer the term 'identificate'.

Something takes place, dictated by envy, followed by omnipotent denial, in which a part of the ego becomes as if concretely differentiated, yet plastic in its manoeuvrings, in which the new roles and functions of this part of the ego assure omnipotent control, by virtue of the enhancement of the omnipotence over the ego-remnants produced by the split that has taken place within it. By 'concrete', I mean that the identificate believes itself to be the whole ego.

The split in certain cases is, I feel, permanent; the stronger the degree of envy, the greater is the permanence of the split and the more dominant is the part which has projectively assumed the new role. It is this omnipotent dominance which accounts for the imprisoning quality described by Rosenfeld; the imprisonment being directed towards the remaining dependent, libidinal aspects of the ego. It is this, so called concretized, split part, which does all the 'becoming' and 'being' that I wish to apply to the term identificate. It is not simply that the identificate becomes God, Napoleon *et al.* which it can do, but it has the plastic quality which I mentioned earlier. It is deprived of any enrichment and concern, it is hidden and covert, and mimics a variety of apparently positive situations.

The commonest version seen in an analysis is where it suddenly takes up a collusive pseudo-alliance in the analytic work with the analyst, and criticizes the hated dependent aspects of the personality which are felt to be ill, and helps in the enquiry into the illness, as if it were a crime, but with complete callow hypocritical indifference to the fate of the 'ill part'.

In working through various problems with the patient, one is always aware of an undercurrent. Although insightful conclusions appear to be reached there is a covert sabotaging process at work which dislocates and disrupts progress. It is as if a Pied-Piper process is at hand, with the dependent parts of the personality constantly being led away to disappearance, leaving the personality like the crippled boy who survived in the story. Simultaneously the same crippling is directed against the analytic work.

A recent example of this was presented in the analysis of a man with severe problems of excessive shyness accompanied by pathological miserliness, during the course of a session. It seemed clearly demonstrable that this process was operating both within him and in the analytic work, whilst it seemed that he was being seriously co-operative, and which seemed to be mirrored in his work with students. He offered an idea. He had always been so impressed with people who 'were helping the police with their enquiries'. He always felt that they were such nice people to be so helpful, without recognizing the relevance of their position in relation to either the crime or the police, or that these helpful ones were possibly the accused — and this from a university don, albeit on the science side!

The narcissistic organization arises in a particular way. The identificate can be stimulated in any one of a variety of ways, depending upon what object or part-object, or what function of object or part-object is fastened upon. If the identification is with a combined parental couple, or more usually a phantasy version of such a compound, the result is the most dangerous, mentally seductive and destructive version of the process, and is more frequently confined to the psychotic end of the clinical spectrum. The destructive potential of this is that despite the relative lateness of such an event in the development scale, the result produced is as if nothing preceded this event in the patient's mental life. An accompaniment of this process is usually omniscience, and I have found that when such identificates occur in the manifestly non-psychotic cases, which are of a more temporary character, the main clinical pattern is usually one of omniscience. There is a state of being in an unquestioning, unquestionable position – usually directed against any threatened guilt or feelings of enquiry which may produce painful feelings of envy and possible concern.

The clinical cases I will be discussing vary from a young, schizophrenic man to people in full-time employment with relatively minor character disturbances. The very nature of the problem as outlined implies a long drawn-out struggle in the analysis with constant interferences and resulting negative therapeutic reactions in such patients, irrespective of diagnosis.

Looking at the literature one is struck by the considerable emphasis on the part played by the utilization of dream material from these patients. So frequently the problem seems to be illustrated in the dreams in a way which is so totally different from the ordinary presentations of these patients. There is a rare and, I sometimes feel, provocative honesty in their dreams. We are given so little by these patients that we cannot be blamed for exploiting their dreams, in an attempt to achieve a therapeutic response. When speaking to these patients, one is perforce directing one's interpretive remarks to an ever-present usurper or an ubiquitous usurping situation, which replaces any new unity created in the analytic situation.

The identificate believes itself to be, and can actually be, the prevailing ego of the patient; the countertransference in such situations, therefore, is not only the stone-wall Freud described that one is up against, but it has another quality. One is made to feel distrust for one's own interpretive work, which can be viewed in so many ways: as an attack upon one's perceptions and awareness, as a natural consequence of the peculiar plasticity and insincerity I have described, but to me very frequently it has been felt to be a projection of the dependent needy parts of the patient, which are felt by the identificate to be so untrustworthy and weak. I have learned to trust this untrustworthiness and to mistrust or be sceptical about feelings of trust in the work until it can be checked and rechecked in the transference.

Recently I had been accused by a very disturbed and disturbing patient of having been untrustworthy, and that he had lost confidence in me. This came at the climax of a week in which we were working in what I thought to be a satisfactory nature, insightful responses were being maintained, until I felt the need to instruct the nursing staff to be particularly vigilant: he is an impulsive delusional man, who periodically runs away and creates considerable damage.

I had felt somewhat uneasy during the session when he reported that he had noticed a dark colour in his urine in the morning, and was making references to the summer holiday with ideas of being free of his mother's attentions. It seemed to me, during the session, that he was emphasizing an interest in business concerns which had nothing to do with him, and that there was no concern with his own business, with his own mental health and ill-health. There was very little else to go on; the atmosphere was friendly and 'confidential'. My disquiet was of this untrusting character, and I felt that despite the friendly atmosphere I had been asked too many questions to which I should know the answers but did not. Two days later in an explosive yet strangely enlightening way we became aware that the peace of the whole week was based on a false promissory relationship, in which I was going to give wild permissions for a variety of mad acts. In fact it was not promissory, it was promised and arranged – we had had a collusive partnership in which all my natural antagonisms to his madness were diluted to much expendable urine. He had successfully taken over my business and was as if free from any good maternal care again.

The fact that I was untrustworthy now in my own way and did not inspire confidence was a compliment.

Clinical material

The first case I wish to report upon is that of a man of 26, employed in a large organization in a professional capacity. He finds his work difficult, although he is intelligent, and he frequently promises himself a higher qualification, which has been suggested by his immediate senior in his section at work. He makes little move in this direction.

In the summer holiday preceding this particular phase in the analysis he had severe anxiety attacks, with what seemed to me to be periods of considerable self-aggrandisement during which people he was talking to admired him considerably. There were, as well, long periods of abstinence from eating, because 'That would be good for him'. On his return to analysis, there were no overt signs of psychotic break-down, but periodically, we were reminded of the therapeutic importance of his experience; of its enriching, though terrifying quality – this was usually associated with a belief of my being bad-smelling later in the session, as if to confirm the successful evacuation of anything bad. In other words, in this instance, there was for him a recognizable result after any evacuation.

A problem which he had was having to present his point of view at work, which created great difficulty and paralysing anxiety. Just prior to the material I report upon, he had failed to get the salary rise he had expected. The departmental head had patiently explained that this was due to his behaviour in the department, and his failure to maintain his work standard; my patient was furious at this rebuff. He had to arrange a meeting at work, over which he had to preside, because his superior was away – he also would have to introduce a man from an overseas division of the organization, who was to introduce some new and original system of work procedure. He was now quite confident of his ability to arrange all this very well – this he announced a fortnight before the meeting. On the morning, however, of this particular experience, the analytic session was totally preoccupied with the impending failure of the whole procedure, and therefore, inevitably of my failure and the failure of psychoanalysis to help. He was worried about the guest speaker, because he was sure he had never been analysed, and he would inform everyone of the man's original work (this although the work was almost required reading in the Department).

He reported a dream. He was driving an 'X 7' car – which was the largest variety of a particular model, of which he had the smallest version (in truth). It was a new car. (The name of the car in the dream was made up, partly of the name of his superior, and an additional name, which ordinarily connotes aggression and rivalry.) The car was driving beautifully and responded to his 'every dictation'. He saw a girl, with whom he had once considered having an affair, he spoke to her, and made an appointment for later, implicitly a sexual meeting. He draws my attention, for the first time, to the fact that the girl is a Jewess, and reminds me how anti-Semitic his parents were; how they would have loathed her, her Jewishness and her darkness. He also reminds me how they hated his brother's wife even though she was not a Jewess. I remembered at that moment how they used to express their hatred of her, by saying, 'We hate her', over and over again. It is clear that he identified himself in this dream with the combined parents, combined as well in their hating capacity, of me, as of the girl with whom he has a date on the next day.

He hates too his awareness of any need, or any reference to his need, for help throughout the preceding days, where he maintained a fluent omniscience (seen in the dream as the car's wonderful response to his dictation). He takes over his superior's role – as he does with my role in the analysis by the possession of the car. So clearly this new identificate, producing the false fluency, is in response to the hatred of the dependent, needy parts of himself which require help which can hardly be supplied in the time available. The most important thing, however, in the dream seems to be the denuding of possession of capacities, all round, produced by the link with the hating parents, who hate newcomers and strangers. It is a very strange experience too, in the middle of an analysis, to be conceived of as a visitor, or guest.

On the next day he was furious – I was a swine, and bad-smelling. He reported during the session that he had asked 'himself' whether he should change his analyst, and he reported a dream. This time he had been driving an AB – the smaller version in the series of models (his own car). It kept on slowing down, as if it had a defective battery that needed bringing to life. He returned to his complaint about my behaviour; that I failed to understand his problems. Quite suddenly he announced after a silence, 'We hate you'.

It was as if in asking a special part of the 'himself' as to whether they should change his analyst, it didn't only refer to changing to 'another analyst, a better one', but also as to whether I should be changed into something else having discovered the hated limping little self. (The car has a strange name – indicating smallness and mischievousness in reality.) These being the actual ill-dependent parts of himself, which needed to be brought to life, that 'help' then came again from the 'We hate you' combined parents, that restored him to the position of unneeding omniscience, via this same process.

My role in the previous day's session, where I seemed to have produced some change in him by being able to understand some of the difficulties, thereby exposing to him his own needy part, seems to have incited this envious attack which becomes so denied in the mad, successful, 'We hate you' experience – which restores dictating omniscience. The procedure adopted to reachieve this position would appear to be the fusion, arranged by, 'I ask myself', which formation is announced by the 'We hate you'. To maintain and strengthen that, I have to be seen as the dark contemptible sister-in-law, dark girl, Jewish figure by the projection of the limping little car feelings into me, and with me now needing to be brought to life and deodorized. Difficulties similar to this occur frequently, in this slow, laborious, analysis – with its stone-walling triumphs and easily uprooted improvement.

The next illustration is of a man also professionally employed. He, like some of the other patients I have treated, is a very nice person, and they form a group at the far/'normal' end of the problem of narcissism. In these patients a relatively normal amount of introjective processes has taken place, allowing for depressive anxieties and reparative processes to have occurred, which mitigate the severity and the permanence of the narcissistic organization. This patient had a self-deprecatory presentation, but once we began to deal with the depressive elements in this illness, we were faced with a problem. He felt better, he had decided on a course of post-graduate study, but a new element entered the analysis.

He would forget everything I said within moments of my having said it. He was convinced that anybody having to listen to me would find my words, as he did, quite incomprehensible. The difficulty, however, lay in his awareness that such a problem had never existed previously. Gradually it was borne in on him that he had evacuated everything I said immediately I had spoken. This immediate experience alternated with experiences in which the session would be lost, as he left the room, or would be lost on the stairs leading away from my room.

We came to learn how he had studied at his university. He had never, if he could help it, directly attended a lecture or seminar, but would find out the subject to be discussed and read it in his room, from books. Although hard-working by nature, when faced with an actual examination he would feel totally empty. His mother would then be expected to reassure him of his capacities. His presentation of these scenes was interesting. She, although a teacher, knew nothing of his subjects, but although she was clearly being helpful in trying to alleviate his anxieties, would not be experienced as a helpful mother, but as someone who obviously knew the work with which he was concerned and therefore when she said he would pass, he felt reassured. (This process touches on the relationship of the narcissistic organization to the perversions, which cannot be gone into here.) We have enough to go on so far in the description of this man to see many of the elements we have spoken about.

He reported a dream. He was abroad during the holidays – and in a window of a slum house saw a woman beckoning to him. He realized that she was a whore (his word) who was attracted to him; he went to her apartment, she turned to him, and he saw that it was his wife. He was only mildly surprised, in the dream. He turned away from her, and found that he was at an exhibition of his paintings in a big gallery. He knows the gallery, and everything seemed much more alive in the environment. There was a vivacity and vitality that ordinarily is not present in this district. He added that during the holidays he had had a strange experience on returning to his home. He had attended a meeting and heard a man speaking, whose flow and delivery he had admired, and who spoke such sense; to his surprise he realized that the speaker was his father. He had also heard, though he had known of it for some time, that in the early years of marriage his father had been excessively promiscuous. He then hesitated to tell me, because of his fear of my disapproval, that he too, recently, had been having meaningless affairs which he had hidden from me – they had coincided with his wife's being ill, when she had been in hospital. His wife has recently begun to paint, an activity which he feels he would love to be able to do.

It seemed to me, therefore, that there was a link between my work and his wife's painting and behind that of the maternality and real helpfulness of his mother; that he enviously attacks all three functions, by perverting the truth of his mother's intentions, by devaluing and taking over, grandiosely and exhibitionistically, his wife's talent and evacuating my 'incomprehensibilities'. It seems to me that with the withdrawal and self-sufficiency in the analysis, as in his learning, in which he was faced with the envy of the analytic work as breast, the identificate process took place.

The question arises in connexion with this case: why could this not be viewed as an envious attack on a particular function, attached to a particular object or part-object, where the envy takes the meaning out of the function by invading it and making it, as in this case, incomprehensible.

The answer lies in two areas. In the 'ordinary' envious attack, there are always signs in the patient or in the material of a fear of retribution – in this process it is distinctly absent. A total take-over of function occurs, withdrawal ensues in a triumphant way, and the patient not only does not feel envious (which anyway can occur in the other cases) but has a peculiar satisfaction as if protected by the identificate. This has a consequence in the countertransference. Certainly for me, there is a singularly unfrightening character of the process in the analysis. All manner of emotions are produced in the analyst, but fear is not one of them – no matter how explosively these patients behave, they do not produce fear. There is an almost surgical precision in the process. I haven't really clarified for myself why this happens, but it does so differentiate it from the more usual procedure. The other reason for my conviction that we are dealing with a problem of narcissism has been indicated to me in the structure of the dream. Herbert Rosenfeld has pointed out to me, in a personal communication, how in the dreams of these patients there is a peculiar character. The identificate exerts its influence as if from afar, and in this dream, he turns away from the slum house, and its scene, and finds himself miles away, at the exhibition, and it's from there that the vivacity and interest emanate, presumably exciting envious responses in the rejected woman.

A final point about this patient which confirms this view, is the dream which occurred later in the same week. He dreams he is in bed with his wife – his penis is erect and he makes love to his wife, and discovers that her vagina has become changed. It is as if the vagina has become moulded completely into the shape of his penis, which has now taken over the whole configuration of the vagina.

I wish now to turn to these problems in the psychotic patient. In these patients, naturally enough by virtue of the illness itself, the processes are very much more complicated. The delusional transference (which at this stage could be thought to be a synonym for the identificate) is based upon projective identification, where a patient feels himself or a part of himself to be within an object, taking over the role applied to that area of the object where the projection is lodged. This may be confused with the infantile transference based upon an actual experienced relation to an object, or more usually to a part-object, which could also possibly be felt to be within the personality of the analyst, or projected into it, that creates difficulty enough with these patients. These patients loathe any reference to the transference – they loathe the fact that it exists, and so much time is spent by them in neutralizing, particularly for themselves, the effects of it, while there exists clearly in the analyst's mind the constant awareness of the paradox that the narcissistic organization and its omnipotence is dependent on the continued presence of a good object for the maintenance of the narcissism and its beliefs.

We are faced in these patients with a peculiar smugness, endowed with an enhanced omnipotence by virtue of the belief, not only in the successful taking over, but a belief in the rectitude of the narcissistic organization. The belief is that what we feel is so very bad for them, is really, on their own terms, so very good for them. We are exposed to repetitive propaganda, trumpeting this combination of rectitude and success, and at the worst moments we are faced with problems of our own intense hatred for this process, which is bent on totally nullifying our usual therapeutic approach.

A short illustration: Mr XY, a 43-year-old man in the throes of a long drawn-out psychotic illness with marked paranoid delusional features. After several months of analysis, he emerged from the waiting room, and instead of turning to the right on his emerging, to walk to the consulting room, turned to the left as if making for the cloakroom and lavatory. He corrected himself on reaching the door of the cloakroom. We had been concerned for some time in the analytic work with delusional memories, about imprisonment, cruelty and deception of his captors, who may be his employers, or the enemy of his employers, whom he should possibly have worked for in the first place. The material has clearly been seen as the cruel subjugation of his own discriminating and differentiating sanity, by the mad cruel aspects of his personality. At the same time, there is a constant demand that there be implicit belief in the actual truth of all the memories, without our recognizing them as being parts of a mental catastrophe. Instead, there is a wish to project any such catastrophic results into my mind, which would be reflected in total, subjugated, believing.

No reference is made by my patient to the wrong turning he took. I do not know whether turning towards the lavatory is an evacuating act, directed towards his confusion or belief that there exists in my anus, or in the anal areas of my mind, goodnesses which a part of himself may batten upon and take over, or both. There was a silence. I felt irrationally angry at the idea of the patient's mind turning towards the lavatory, and at the same time wished I hadn't noticed it. I don't think the latter related to my anger. It was as if I was responding to an invitation, to not notice what I should think about. This only angered me even more, and I wanted to smoke; an activity which I never undertake whilst working with psychotic patients. This led me to realize how much my thinking was being interfered with, and how much I was playing the role of the subsidiary but sane aspects of the patient.

He then reported a dream. He had been in a Land-Rover, with an open back, in which he was standing. It moved, though nobody was driving it. In the dream, he ignores that part. He is more concerned with the trailer which is being pulled behind, which is full of wild animals, felt to be dead. He keeps on looking at it, because the skins are very valuable. He is horrified on waking, because he is a conservationist, and wishes to have no truck with the killing of wild animals for profit. (At the time of this session some years ago, I had a Land-Rover, which he had to pass on the way to the consulting room.) Although this has all the elements to illustrate the problems, I don't wish to go into the material. I use it to illustrate some of the transference and counter-transference situations described – how cruelty in the transference almost invites counter-cruelty in the analyst, yet how the presentation of the dream leads to clarification and understanding.

The main clinical material concerns J, who is 23 years old. He is the fifth child of seven. His parents have been separated, and then divorced, for fourteen years. The mother remarried eight years ago. His childhood is described as uneventful, but so frequently any childhood enjoyment would be spoiled by persistent fantasies of what he was going to *be*. He would be this or that, something great or famous, owning this or that wonderful thing. Schooling was uneventful, until the last years, when he suddenly changed the course of studies so that he could 'help his father' with his new studies. In his first year at university, there occurred a confusional illness with delusional beliefs.

There have been four or five psychotic episodes since. He wanders about during these phases, excessively preoccupied with arranging imaginary business deals, spending money extravagantly, and feels persecuted by Communists, and the threats of Communist invasion of his house and homeland. His father's house, and business, seem a particular magnet to the 'Communist greed'. He has been hospitalized here in London. There have been phases of confusion, running away to his home and returning, and occasionally creating considerable havoc. Despite his total unwillingness to be analysed, he is persistently importunately phoning for extra sessions and constantly demanding a multiplicity of gratifications, mostly that his planning systems should produce concrete results after being filtered through my mind. These all invariably would imply a total restructing of my mind, changing every view held, to become compliant to his wishes. This patient has an excessive mental unsophistication, in that he can manifest stupidity as a symptom to a wild degree. He found the first interpretation, it being a transference interpretation, a total shock. He expected answers which would solve a geographical dilemma or supply clues to a new profession he could undertake. Gradually over the months he became used to analysis. He could produce sudden sleeps, in which he could withdraw from consciousness in a moment, which we later saw were withdrawals which could maintain him in any desired position while maintaining a particular unchanged point of view. They have stopped, but I am convinced that the withdrawals still remain, without any loss of consciousness.

He had always collected his dreams in a book, but never really consulted them. He was amazed at a dream, with two parts, early on in the analysis, where he was talking to old ladies of the family's acquaintance. They were discussing all sorts of marvellous possibilities of his becoming (a) a pianist, (b) an orchestral conductor – this dialogue of the possibilities of 'becoming' frequently features in his dreams – only in this dream, he suddenly saw my face appearing, expressing disapproval, of this 'silly talk'. The next phase of the dream had him talking to a professor, who advised that he be analysed in City X, and I pulled him back, and told him to go to the consulting room.

A position in the work is established. We have achieved an understanding, or feel we have achieved an understanding of a problem relating to wandering abroad, which would always masquerade as purposeful mercantile activity. It related historically to wild travels in his home country, and would be connected with sudden impulses to leave the analysis, for apparently good business reasons. This would frequently be prefaced by long silences, in which he would be preoccupied with his own private thoughts which he couldn't, or wouldn't share with me, or by wandering away from any theme that might be felt to be existing in the analysis. Clearly his wandering around was an identification with a mobile father engaged in huge business transactions, but behind this (because either in the reality event in the past, or in the fantasies, he always ended up in one of two particular family farmhouses) we could work out what couplings were taking place in the identificate. On occasions it would be ski-ing parents, an idealized version of the pre-separated parents. This was a particular disturbing identification. It had a delusional character, and led to considerable hatred of the mother's remarriage as a representative of the new reality, or it would be different and take the form of sailing in which one or other of the parents would be represented. A sailing father came to represent an attack on truth because of a particular childhood event, when he discovered that his father lied, and so on.

In this phase he recounted a dream. The devils, unseen, or evil spirits, equally unseen, were abroad. They were wild, and they hated Rosa, and her purity. (Rosa was a housemaid, who had cared for him, very well, at the time of the separation of the parents.) They had tied her to the railway tracks, and unless she relinquished her purity, she would be killed by an oncoming train, which he could hear in the distance, coming nearer. He was terribly anxious for Rosa's safety, and he had so much love for her. He persuaded her to allow him to make sexual love to her, which would save her life, because the evil spirits would then depart. She reluctantly agreed. They had sexual intercourse, and he heard the train going away. He felt it was a strange dream. He had never had any sexual wishes towards Rosa; anyway she had been so very good to him, and had looked after him so well. The dream clearly implied that the analysis and the analytic work was endangered by what he felt about its truth and its purity. As long as it stood for, or told the truth, it was endangered by his devilish feelings, directed here towards Rosa, a servant, which also showed that the analyst should be the servant of his envy, not its instigator. The link with his dependence and his devilish hatred of it was clear. In the illustration, the envy successfully attacks truth, and institutes in its place his own mad-hypocritical version of truth, giving him an identity of a peculiar saviour. Characteristic of these kind of dreams, the final cruelty is heard from afar, but the actual nature of the origin of this hypocritical saviour was not worked out at the time. Later work showed it to be a semi-perverse version of certain paternal functions and activities, but was closely related to the rubbishy, sanctimonious talk, in dreams and life – when anything and everything was promised.

The family B was particularly admired. The father was a barrister whom he had always admired, covertly originally, for fear of inciting his father's envy and jealousy. Since the analysis he has admired Mr B more openly, and recently has made tentative attempts to begin law studies. A dream occurred. He remembered a winter holiday, at which they were present. He pictured himself, on a particular slope, which did not have a mechanical ski-lift, but one in which you pulled yourself up the slope by pulling on the chain. He was pulling himself up on the chain towards their house at the top, and was looking forward to getting to their house and being with them. They were such a nice, totally integrated family group. Suddenly he found himself preoccupied with choosing a name for his new (non-existent) newspaper. He felt there was a tremendous need for an independent newspaper in his country. They, the Bs, were associated with peace and helpfulness – and therefore clearly linked with the truth of the previous situation, which link was now clearly being attacked and replaced by his own delusional publishing organ, which would independently tell him the news, in his own way, and it was concretely felt to be there, only awaiting a name, and it took over and replaced my independent analytic interpretive news-system – which had its own way of looking at his news-system.

This attack on a link soon became attached to the concept of hard work, and his abomination of it – particularly the kind of work that he felt an analysis demanded; and later in the same week, any awareness that might have existed from an understanding derived from the work on this dream material was toppled. In the next dream he was married to the daughter of family B. All the girls in his home country admired him, but he told them it was too late. He was now the owner of the newspaper and had named it. (I cannot mention the name, but it signified a clear conjunction of parts of both parents again, which was cemented by one of the father's industrial functions.) The important part of this dream is that this idealized family into which he marries, and which puts him into this new admired position, in reality know about his psychotic illnesses, and really only have a relationship to him through having done legal work for both sides of his family. The barrister in fact is loathed, because he has made it clear to him that any marital ideas are unthinkable, so in the dream he brings together the unthinkable and the separated, omnipotently, and so omnipotently erases any knowledge of his illness as well. He still retains two delusional links with this dream – he feels he will marry the daughter, at any time, but at the same time feels dangerously trapped by his 'promised' attachment to the girl.

Some time later we had a session in which he apparently was very ashamed. I did not know that he was ashamed, but I knew that I had an extremely mad patient in my consulting room. He was insulting, he was contemptuous, and I thought at one stage that he would like to hit me, but he did not. He took no notice of my interpretations. The session ended. That evening there was a knock at the door and the patient arrived and told me that he would like a session – so I took him in. He said that he had come to tell me that he was sorry, because I was right, and he proceeded to give a lot of information about why he felt I was right. It seemed to me that it was quite a meaningful process that was going on, and he related the situation he was describing to various situations that had been going on in the analysis.

Then he said to me 'Ah, I am thinking about X' – she was the girl he had known many years before. He had dropped her, because she was said to be a coquette. He said 'What I should have done on the night that I dropped her, was to face the two problems. Either I should have been courageous, and found out whether she was, or was not a coquette, or I should have taken her into the fields and given her cunnilingus'. So what happened was that when we came to the end of the extra session, the whole situation had suddenly changed. The mad part of him was accusing him of being a coquette for having come here, for having decided that I was right and that the analysis had some meaning, and, having licked me with the tongue of his words, I had become the cunt and we were right back in the situation we were in before he had decided that there was something correct and right about analysis and being analysed.

He clearly found himself in an intolerable position of being dependent on my being right and answerable to. Such a threat produced the considerable about-swing I've described. This analysis continues, in its difficult fashion.

The essence of the material presented is that it should illustrate 'successful' defences for obviating any feelings of, or awareness of envy, possibly subserving successful envious attacks; secondly, it should nullify any awareness of dependence, and therefore, possibly, awareness of need and illness; and thirdly, it should maintain the narcissistic organization, by virtue of producing a successful identificate.

Summary

Clinical examples are given, varying from what would appear to be self-sufficient normal people, to overtly psychotic cases, in order to illustrate the development of a narcissistic organization of varying intensity and permanence.

That is to say, an identification via projective identification has taken place, which heightens intrinsic omnipotence, to allow what has been termed the identificate to believe that it has become the desired object – and thereby that within this spuriously organized ego-structure exist the characteristics and functions of the object or part object that has been taken over. Varying forms of such identificatory process are illustrated. The functions of these 'successful defence' manoeuvres are to obviate any feelings of an awareness of envy, although they may be overtly envious attacks within themselves, secondly they nullify any awareness of dependence, and also nullify awareness of need and illness, and thirdly they maintain the narcissistic organization by producing a successful identificate.

References

Freud, S. (1921) 'Identification', in 'Group psychology and the analysis of the ego', *SE* 18.

—— (1933) 'The dissection of the psychical personality', *SE* 22.

Klein, M. (1955) 'On identification', in *New Directions in Psychoanalysis*, London: Tavistock, 309–45.

Rosenfeld, H. (1964) 'On the psychopathology of narcissism: a clinical approach', *International Journal of Psycho-Analysis*, 45, 332–7.

—— (1971) 'A clinical approach to the psychoanalytical theory of the life and death instincts: an investigation into the aggressive aspects of narcissism', *International Journal of Psycho-Analysis*, 52, 169–78 (also reprinted in this volume, pp. 239–55).

6

A clinical study of a defensive organization

EDNA O'SHAUGHNESSY

This article is a revised version of a paper read to the British Psycho-Analytical Association in November 1979 and first published in 1981 in the *International Journal of Psycho-Analysis*, 62, 359–69.

Some patients seek an analysis at a moment when they hope not to extend their contact with themselves or their objects, but, on the contrary, because they desperately need a refuge from these. Once they are in analysis their first aim is to establish, really to re-establish, a defensive organization against objects internal and external which are causing them nearly overwhelming anxiety.

The current lives of the patients I have in mind are permeated by infantile anxieties that have not been much modified. They are patients with a weak ego who, with more persecution than normal, arrive in infancy at the borders of the depressive position as defined by Klein (1935), but are then unable to negotiate it, and instead form a defensive organization. The defensive organization, however, proves precarious, since the combination of a weak ego and acute assailing anxieties that makes a negotiation of the depressive position impossible also makes it impossible for them to sustain a defensive organization. Their lives oscillate between periods of exposure and periods of restriction; they are exposed to intense anxiety from their objects when the defensive organization fails, and suffer restricted, though tolerable, object relations when it is again established.

This paper aims to show how a defensive organization, established and maintained in the conditions provided by an analysis, can strengthen the ego and diminish the area of anxiety. In this way the oscillation between exposure and restriction is halted, and instead the patient is able – in the particular manner open to him – to proceed with his development. The paper aims also to examine the nature of a defensive organization.

A long, twelve-year analysis of Mr M gave me the opportunity of studying the several successive phases – four in all – in the evolution of his defensive organization. In the first phase I could see the desperate situation to which he was exposed when his defensive organization failed. Then, in the next period, when Mr M was able to re-establish his defensive organization, I could study the restricted object relations on which his defensive organization was based and the nature of the relief and benefit it brought him. Later, in the third stage, I could observe how he exploited his defensive organization for the gratification of his cruelty and his narcissism. Finally, in the last phase of the analysis, when Mr M, now with some trusted objects, was able once more to go forward in his development. I could observe how his ego, while much strengthened, was also split in a characteristic way as a consequence of his protracted use of his defensive organization.

To lessen the mass of clinical material, I report a full session only from the beginning and near the end – from the beginning to present fully Mr M's initial predicament so that his defensive organization against it may be understandable, and near the end to contrast Mr M at the start with Mr M in the final phase of his analysis. In between, for brevity, I resort to descriptions aided by images from Mr M's dreams with only a brief indication of their working through by analyst and patient. The four phases of Mr M's analysis – presenting predicament, establishment of a defensive organization, exploitation of the defensive organization, and progress forward – are described in a way that makes clear their distinctness, which was very marked; I have omitted the forerunners of, and returns to, the other phases which, of course, were present in each.

Presenting predicament

Mr M was an only child born after a long labour by Caesarian section. His mother told him there were no more children because she could not bear again the experience of labour. She also told him she breast-fed him for six months while feeling very depressed. Mr M felt his mother to be burdensome but caring. His father was a well-intentioned but chilly and remote man with a grievance about lack of professional recognition. Mr M felt his father 'psychologized' about him.

Mr M recalled his childhood as unhappy and lonely, and

sometimes terrifying. At night he needed a light in his bedroom and also insisted on a light in the passage leading to his parents' bedroom. He slept fitfully and was enuretic. At the age of 7 he became acutely nervous and suffered nightmares. This must have been a period when his defensive organization was failing him. His parents took him to an analyst who treated him for two years; they were of the opinion that this childhood analysis helped him even if it did not remove his problems. In this view I think Mr M's parents were right; his first analysis seems to have helped him to reconstitute a much needed defensive organization, though it did not alter his underlying predicament. Mr M continued his schooling, hating it, afraid of the other children. Isolated and unhappy, he started university. His father urged him to have another analysis, but Mr M was unwilling. Two years later, his father died suddenly. At first Mr M could not absorb the fact of his father's death. Later, alone at home with his mother, Mr M became depressed and increasingly felt ill and frightened. He was 22 when he sought analysis with me.

In the preliminary interview I saw a weak and acutely anxious young man. Mr M spoke of his fears of dying and mutilation, his plagues of sexual phantasies and his excessive masturbation, all of which, he said, were 'driving him nuts'. He told me, too, that he had tried to approach one or two girls at the university but was sexually impotent.

For his first session he arrived laughing to cover terror. He poured out garbled material about 'oral castration', 'homosexuality', 'impotence', 'lesbians', speaking like a confused psychoanalyst and as if his mind was under intolerable pressure. He could barely listen to the few interpretations I made about the pressure and confusion in his mind and his terror of me. At one point, however, I said that because he was terrified of me he was giving me 'analytic' talk and that perhaps there was something else he might otherwise say. At this interpretation his hectic speaking stopped. 'It's hard to daydream. I try to but I can't. People distract me. But in a daydream I get left by myself with my thoughts – then there is nothing except thoughts.' He spoke with intense yearning. This was his first expression, often repeated subsequently, of his longing of a peaceful undistracted relationship to me, a relationship in which he could have what he here calls a 'daydream'. As the psychologizing father in the transference I had already made him distracted; I terrified him, he projected himself into me to gain control of me, and then got confused with me. His longing is to get away from such distracting people, but not to be alone and left with 'nothing except thoughts'. The defensive organization which Mr M later established in the analysis achieved exactly this. It got him away from 'distracting people' and gave him the undisturbed relationship to me for which he yearned.

But in this first phase of his analysis Mr M was very disturbed. The impact of his father's death, held off for some months, had broken down his precarious defensive organization and exposed him to confusion and nearly overwhelming anxieties. I should like to portray Mr M's predicament in more detail as it emerged very early in the analysis in a Friday session. At the start of the session, Mr M had seemed afraid to enter the room. When he did, on his way to the couch, he stopped, bent down and stared into the seat of my chair (I had not yet sat down). He was very anxious and breathing irregularly. On the couch he began: 'You've changed your suit again. It's got stripes. I had been feeling anxious when I was coming here'. His anxiety, already acute, was increasing. I spoke to him, saying he wanted me to realize he was very afraid. Mr M replied: 'It's my breathing, it's abnormal. In an abnormal rhythm. I can't get back to normal breathing. I had a dream last night actually'. In sudden tones of self-admiration he said: 'Some dream!'

He relapsed immediately into anxiety, speaking as if he were watching the dream he was telling. 'I was watching an old film or a film on T.V. The woman who was supposed to be the star disgusted me. She was too old. I felt it disgusting her acting this role. She should be younger. There were two men with her all the time. I saw her in bed with her breasts bared and these two men were on either side of her. They were going to make love or something. But suddenly the man said something in a peevish flippant tone. I was surprised at this. Then the man drew out a big knife and started cutting at the woman between her two breasts. It was horrible. Then I wasn't watching any more, but I had got mixed up with the man in the dream and was stabbing the woman. I was sort of drawn into him and he was writing his name on her flesh with the knife. She was screaming'. He stopped.

Before I could say anything he shouted out angrily: 'You haven't said anything. It wasn't worth it. I wasted it on you'. I said he was angry I wasn't quicker. He felt it showed I didn't value his dream – the star production for me (Mr M gave a giggle) but also, and more important, was his fear that his dream had become real, and that an intercourse was really happening here in the session, pulling him to the seat of my chair to see it, getting into his mind in pictures and also getting into his breathing. Mr M was attentive. I went on to suggest that he had been afraid at the beginning that I had actually changed into the screaming mother of his dream – perhaps my stripes had seemed to him to be screams. Mr M gave a little laugh of relief, and his breathing quietened.

Then the next moment he was saying, thinly boastful but also desperate: 'That dream was very vivid. Usually I can't remember my dreams. They are incoherent. I tried hard to remember that one. It was very vivid', he repeated, desperate to get me talking further about his Sex dream, as I shall call it. I remained quiet. Suddenly Mr M said in a totally tired and dead voice: 'I had another dream actually. I was trying to hitch a lift. There were lots of cars coming along. Then I saw two old people. They also needed a lift. But as soon as I was wanting a lift for them the flow of cars dried up. Then I was with a big Alsatian dog. I thought "I will never get a lift with that dog with me".'

Later I knew that Mr M's dream about Old People was a recurring dream. On this day it had been occasioned by the end of the week, when the flow of cars, that is, the flow of sessions, was ceasing. I interpreted that Mr M felt there was a baby him who was making a hitching gesture, moving his thumb, and needing to be picked up. But his dream, and his sudden tired mood with me, indicated that he felt abandoned with old people who couldn't help him, who instead made him feel tired and dead and that he had to lift or liven them. I reminded him how just before in the session he had been wanting us to talk about his Sex dream in order to enliven both him and me.

It was almost the end of the session. Mr M poured out a disordered sequence: 'haphazard . . . it's your desk. My testicles could get crushed. I'm having a picture. Too far . . .' etc. He was agitated. He was fragmenting his thoughts, talking to rid himself of 'hazards', and to keep me away from him, terrified I was 'Old People', who couldn't either care for him or manage on their own, any more than could his widowed mother, with whom he would spend the weekend.

In this session Mr M is almost overwhelmed by anxieties and confusions. At the start, the room, the analytic chair and the analyst all frightened him: they appeared changed. They had almost become for him actually the world of his Sex dream. Inside his body, his abnormal breathing similarly alarms him: it is the concrete and physical expression of internal copulating analyst-parents. Though he is confused and tending to function in a disordered and concrete way, he has not altogether lost his hold on reality or his capacity to think, but he is terrified that he could. Noticeable, too, is how he has almost no respite. No sooner has he gained a little relief, as he did when his terror of the room and his breathing is understood and interpreted, than another anxiety supervenes. When his objects stop copulating they are inert, depressed 'Old People', who need life from him – an impossible demand when he himself feels he is abandoned and dying on the weekend. The mixture of persecutory and depressive anxieties stirred by his depressed dying objects rouses an enormous and uncontainable agitation in Mr M from which at the end of the session he tries to defend himself by fragmenting and evacuating it.

This defence, like the others his ego attempts during the session, e.g. his thin bravado ('Some dream!'), or his distancing of his frighteningly concrete and invasive Sex dream by seeing it as a film, or his use of the Sex dream for erotization, fails almost instantly, leaving Mr M exposed again to multiple anxieties. His weak ego is throughout unable to sustain its defences.

Mr M's ego is also too weak to resist the pull of his objects. In his Sex dream, for example, he is drawn into the murderous copulation, as in the session he is pulled helplessly over to the seat of my chair. It is his ego's lack of cohesion that vitiates another important defence used by Mr M – projective identification. This was evident already in the first session when he arrived in a state of projective identification with a psychologizing father-analyst, but confused and over-excited, and still terrified. The father transference was very important. Mr M often feared me as a cold, ridiculing, peevish father, a father depicted in many dreams as a monster.

Also in the session above is an interesting anticipation of an aspect of Mr M which emerged only much later in the analysis. This is the Alsatian dog which appears at the end of his Old People dream. It represents a treacherous, destructive, possessive side of him. When it appears it makes him despair – 'I will never get a lift with that dog with me', he says in the dream, and later when it emerged fully it gave him, and me, cause for despair.

But in the present first phase it is not his impulses which trouble Mr M. It is the weak and confused state of his ego and his alarming objects which are causing him almost overwhelming anxiety, to the degree that he felt threatened by a psychotic condition. Mr M did not believe that his objects had the capacity to contain either their feelings or his, and he himself could not hold any one state of mind for more than a moment or two. Above all, Mr M felt a need for stillness and unchangingness, a need really to regain his defensive organization against his borderline condition. He continued to voice his longing for his lost refuge in such terms as: 'I want to cry. I want to put myself away so as not to be troubled'. 'I must regain my former calm', 'If I don't get calm I feel I shall never work again'. During one session he asked: 'Give me peace'.

Though Mr M was suspicious of interpretations, afraid they were trying to excite or mock him or were my outpouring of suffering or deadness or anxiety, he wanted me to interpret to him. This was the transference manifestation of his belief that his objects, for all their terrifying burdensomeness, were trying to care for him, just as he, for all his deadness, would have liked to be able to enliven them. It was particularly interpretations that recognized the extremity of his anxieties and feelings of disorder and confusion – if they could be formulated before Mr M shifted to yet a further anxiety, a task by no means easy – which gave him relief. Then he felt reached by an analyst strong enough to hold him, and in identification his ego strengthened, and gradually the level of Mr M's anxiety, though it remained high, began to drop. At the end of this first period, which lasted for eighteen months, a change occurred in the whole nature of Mr M's relationship to me.

Establishment of a defensive organization

Unlike before, Mr M now came on time to the second, pressing the doorbell hard. Also, unlike before, when he poured out constantly shifting anxieties about himself or the analyst, he was now oblivious of these. Nor did he bother about enlivening me; there was no more erotized 'stimulating' material. Instead, he spoke distantly, thickly, as though his head was muffled with sleep, dropping his words out in a deadened and deadening way which controlled and transfixed me. Mr M had split off his anxiety-laden parts and, in phantasy, projected himself into father's cold penis, which he used for making cold deadening speech that annihilated disturbance in the room, the couch and myself, all of which represented mother's body. In this way he made an emptied, unchanging place for himself in me as a mother-analyst. With a stronger ego he was able now to sustain his control of me and to stay in his state of projective identification without becoming confused, and to prevent the return and re-invasion of himself by unwanted split-off parts.

Mr M had said: 'I want to put myself away so as not to be troubled'. He had now done so – almost. Mr M felt he formed me, in the sessions, into an object in which he could store himself and be free from 'trouble'. In place of the earlier lurching, agitated transference situation there was now a restricted, controlled relationship between Mr M and myself. He was in a sort of daydream state in which only the feel of the couch and the sound of my voice impinged on him. He had nearly no anxiety; and in this minimal way he had a sense of having what he needed. Mr M felt calm. His calm was an enormous relief; he felt he had been saved from an impending psychotic condition.

At the same time that Mr M was forming me into the undisturbing place he could tolerate, he was also splitting off and projecting into me his unwanted states of mind. His unchanging, cold, repetitive behaviour projected into me feelings of being dealt with by a relentless object, of being helpless, of being deadened, of being tortured to the point of madness, of having to endure what I did not like again and again. Mr M was projecting into me the suffering infant he had been, and also expressing, through what he felt he made me endure, his hatred and resentment. Any interpretation that he experienced as my forcing feelings back into him, or that seemed to him evidence of my anxiety or my curiosity (he aroused both in me by his mental state and the lack of almost all information about his existence) he could not take. It was a return of disturbance. Immediately, he flattened and deadened the interpretation to safeguard his new calm state.

Looked at broadly, Mr M had now formed a defensive organization by the interlocking use of several defences, omnipotent control and denial, and the several forms of splitting and projective identification described by Melanie Klein (1955) to organize relations within himself and between himself and his objects. Clinically, he formed the controlling and static transference, characteristic of the operation of a defensive organization in an analysis. He exerted intense pressure on me to form me into, and keep me restricted to, the object he required in order to remain calm. And for five years, analytic work was received by him within the broad framework imposed by this defensive organization.

There is a matter of terminology. I should like to propose, though it is a departure from analytic usage, that the term 'defensive organization', which was introduced by Willi Hoffer (1954), be reserved for the kind of defensive system Mr M established.[1] Unlike defences – piecemeal, transient to a greater or lesser extent, recurrent – which are a normal part of development, a defensive organization is a fixation, a pathological formation when development arouses irresoluble and almost overwhelming anxiety. Expressed in Kleinian terms, defences are a normal part of negotiating the paranoid-schizoid and depressive positions; a defensive organization, on the other hand, is a pathological fixed formation in one or other position, or on the borderline between them. Segal (1972) describes another such defensive organization in a patient more disturbed than Mr M.

To return to Mr M's defensive organization. In his material, oral and genital ideas were infiltrated by anal notions, and anal terms and processes themselves were very prominent. Mr M delivered his words making noises of being at stool; most thoughts and feelings had for him the meaning of unwanted faeces that he wished to evacuate; his highly controlled objects were felt to have been changed into stool. Mr M's functioning, and his relations to his objects, now often had for him a predominantly anal significance, and in this sense, his defensive organization was also an anal organization.

Mr M pictured the kind of object he needed in order to obtain his calm in the following dream. He dreamt that he met a friend who led a hand-to-mouth existence, sleeping in a flat in a broken-down warehouse, which was disused – but his friend said it was safe. The dream is of Mr M leading his 'hand-to-mouth' existence – he often put his hand to his mouth – sleeping in his flat sessions in a broken-down analyst-mother, who was barely able to move, and since Mr M had control of father's penis there could be no copulation and no babies, so that the analyst-mother was also 'disused'. I was both the warehouse-mother in which Mr M stored himself and also his 'aware' house, the container of his own unwanted awarenesses.

But though he had a calm based on the absence of disturbance, he had not the peace of freely relating to an object that freely accepts him. Storing himself in a broken-down warehouse-mother, while it had an affinity – which Mr M felt – with being in the womb, or peacefully lying in a mother's arms, was only the best alternative available to him for this. And though enormously relieved, Mr M still felt unsafe, ill and also 'bad'. He had always to be on the alert for anything that signalled disturbance; as he put it once, he was like a dog that must keep its ears pricked up. His splitting off of awareness made him sleepy, and the intrusion into his head of his intruded-upon objects made his head feel strange and thick. To get his calm, Mr M had to organize his object to give it to him: he had to break his way into it, annihilate its disturbing properties, and control it to make it fit his needs, to the degree that he almost converted it into faeces or destroyed it, and he was troubled by anxiety that he was 'bad'.

After some months he began to ruminate about a monster featured in the newspapers, the 'Abominable Snowman', a monster who had smashed into a house. This expressed Mr M's feelings of breaking into me each day exactly on time with his hard pressing of the doorbell. Mr M asked repeatedly: 'Is the "Abominable Snowman" a real monster?' He knew he was being abominable and coldly controlling but was he so monstrous out of fear that otherwise the object would, as before, cause him feelings he could not endure? Or was he himself really a monster? He could not decide and there were signs of a small monster, signs of what in the future evolution of his defensive organization was to escalate: Mr M found he got a sadistic pleasure from my controlled transfixed condition and from making me endure the projections of his hatred. Sometimes, I caught a smirk hidden in Mr M's flat tones, but usually if I pointed it out a long silence annihilated both smirk and interpretation. Very occasionally he was able to let his awareness that he was not only defending, but also gratifying, himself get near. Once he brought a dream about a strange, damaged animal that was half a mammal, but which had evolved on its jaw a long snout. In the dream Mr M felt responsible for the animal and was very upset. He associated the animals with piglets who like putting their snouts in the dirt. The dream was Mr M's picture of himself as a damaged infant who needed to protect himself by evolving a long snout, but an infant who was also getting a cruel pleasure from using his snout to control me and reduce me to dirt. The analysis of the dream made, unusually during this period, a lot of anxiety break through in the session. The next day, as Mr M needed to split off his upset about his piglet-self, I was almost suffused by the extent of the anxiety and depression he projected into me. But in the main Mr M succeeded in organizing himself and his objects so that he kept the session almost flat and deadened, and himself, though on the alert, almost untroubled and calm.

It was important to Mr M that I understood, in its daily and detailed manifestation, his need to remain calm and destroy potential disturbance emanating from himself or from me, and sometimes interpretations about his holding us together in a controlled and deadened way because he was frightened of freer contact enabled him briefly to bring material that was more alive. He could take in only those interpretations which he did not experience as forcing unwanted feelings into him or as criticisms of him for being a monster. Those interpretations he could accept gave him a different experience from his calm state. He reported that they 'cleared his head', made him 'feel different'. They were an experience of a much more alive relationship occurring between us.

By the fifth year of the analysis, Mr M's life had improved in several ways. He completed his university courses and obtained a job. After one failed attempt he succeeded in moving away from living at home with his mother (this, of course, he was doing instead with me in the analysis) and established himself in a flat. He found one or two friends. It was also evident to me – the overall unchanging character of the sessions notwithstanding – that his ego was definitely strengthening and I was much less frightening to him. But he did not, as I think I was expecting, use this improvement to begin to tolerate more integration of himself or his object. On the contrary, he used his improvement in a quite opposite direction.

Exploitation of the defensive organization

One result so far of Mr M's analysis was the lessening of his fear of being flooded with disturbance from his object. He used me in the fixed form he needed, and he projected unwanted feelings into me, and he trusted me not to move overwhelmingly or to project back into him. Objects so used, can also be abused – and Mr M began to exploit this relationship. It became a venue in which he felt his narcissism and his cruelty could emerge and operate more omnipotently, unrestrained by complaints from the object or interference from himself.

At the beginning the paramount function of Mr M's defensive organization had been defensive. This was now not so. His defensive organization was now equally, at moments predominantly, a vehicle for the omnipotent gratification of his narcissism and his cruelty. His object relations now constituted a narcissistic organization of the type studied by Rosenfeld (1971). In this new form his defensive organization still served a defensive function. It defended Mr M from feeling small and slow, from the fear that he might never be able really to change or be well, and from all the fresh anxiety and guilt, that the use, and now also the abuse, of his defensive organization aroused by his controlling, his separating, and his deadening of his objects, and now further by his triumphant and cruel robbery of them.

In the sessions he was often now openly cruel, refusing me material and producing any jumble that occurred to him, at times when I knew, if he cared to, he was able to communicate much better. Mr M got excited by his cruelty and my flounderings with his disordered material. He did not now ruminate about being an 'Abominable Snowman'. Instead, he omnipotently split off his superego. His triumph over me, felt to be dismayed and disappointed by his perverse use of his improvement, escalated.

Mr M felt increasingly attractive. He used splitting mechanisms to split off not only his superego, as described above, but also to split off realities that interfered with his narcissism. In his burgeoning phantasies he felt he was inside and had inside him not only his father's omnipotent penis, but all his mother's attributes – her breasts, her stimulating beauty, etc. He felt, almost believed, he was the penis, or the breasts, I desired, and that he could consummate his positive and negative Oedipus complex, and that he could stay in analysis for ever. The analysis was to be the fulfilment of what a recent writer has termed 'the golden phantasy', (Smith 1977). In his current life, after one or two failures, Mr M was sexually potent and found at this time several girls ready to chase him and confirm his feeling of power and attractiveness. Now he felt no need of my work. He had contempt for interpretations which he dismissed as 'pedestrian' and a similar contempt for the aware and more realistic part of himself which he felt was also 'pedestrian' – a favourite word of his at this time.

His excited state is well depicted in a dream. In the dream Mr M saw a fellow with combs sticking out all over him and thought: 'That fellow ought to be defused'. There were traffic lights going in the wrong order – red, yellow, red – and the fellow was also looking the wrong way. After telling the dream Mr M paid it no more attention. He moved off quickly to new topics in a jumbled order that I could do nothing with. I tried to show him he was being the fellow of his dream, who, I suggested, was a coxcomb – the combs sticking out all over being his showy bursting excitement. I suggested he was living his dream in the session, feeling excited about giving me his material in the wrong order, like the traffic lights, and looking the wrong way – that is away from his dream that told him about this coxcomb self, that he knew ought to be defused. Mr M did not want to look at these interpretations. I persisted, he got very irritated, and the session ended with his saying contemptuously, 'You annoy me' as he strode out. The smirky piglet had grown into an openly contemptuous and omnipotent coxcomb.

Increasingly at this stage Mr M did not want the part of himself that was aware of what he was doing and knew he was getting dangerously excited and should be defused. He wanted to be free of it. Mr M wanted to be 'free' from all 'trouble' of reality, sanity, anxiety and guilt. He made an increasing split between his cruel narcissistic part which he idealized, and the part of himself capable of awareness, feeling, thought and judgment, which he disowned. The split in Mr M's ego was of the kind described by Freud (1940) in his paper on 'Splitting of the ego in the process of defence'. In Freud's view such a split is 'a rift in the ego which never heals'. The split in Mr M's ego stayed, although the nature of the rift between the two parts changed.

At this stage his omnipotent part was dominant and constantly tried to increase its dissociation from his sane aware part, a process which culminated in an acting out at the end of the sixth year when Mr M became temporarily almost deluded. He quit his job and informed me he was quitting the analysis and not returning after the holidays. He made unrealistic plans for extended travel. In the last weeks of the term he was so insulated by feelings of excitement and omnipotence that I could make little contact with him. I continued to analyse his plans as an enactment of his omnipotent phantasies rather than as the expression of an intention to leave the analysis. At this moment he had deposited all his sense and sanity in me. After the holidays Mr M returned. He said his travels had been a disaster, his firm would not take him back and he had yet to find another job. His experiences during his holidays had defused and collapsed his omnipotence and excitement, leaving him very frightened. His more aware part had forced itself back into his mind again, and he now felt he had been 'crazy'.

He could not, however, bear to know this for very long. He split off his knowledge that his omnipotent feelings were crazy and gave himself a changed and twisted version of his return to analysis: it was his fulfilment of my desires. Soon, he was relating to me in the same overall defensive and highly pathological mode as before.

I worked on this repetitive and, broadly speaking, unchanging transference situation. There were times when Mr M brought me close to despair. My despair arose from my concern about the lack of movement in the analysis: I wondered if we should go on. But it was also Mr M's despair projected into me, which I analysed, that he would hold on to and possess the analysis – there was no more talk of leaving – that he would use it treacherously to inflate his omnipotence and narcissism, but never let it move and come alive, and therefore that he himself would never feel alive. This period saw the full emergence and analysis of what had been foreshadowed long before in an early dream, the Old People dream reported on page 297. At the end of that dream, you will remember, an Alsatian dog appeared and in the dream Mr M says: 'I will never get a lift with that dog with me'. That I did not give him up and persevered in my work with him was, I think, proof to Mr M that his object could withstand the Alsatian dog in him, his relentless and treacherous possessiveness, without being destroyed by it.

Progress forward

Gradually, during the eighth year of the analysis, there were distinct signs of a more alive, less restricted contact between us, as Mr M's defensive organization began to slacken. Instead of a total and perpetual organization of his relationships internal and external to exclude all disturbance, Mr M began to use his defences more transiently and to allow perturbing perceptions and emotions to reach him. Other related changes occurred. His speech altered. He now wanted to talk. There was a broader area in the purview of the analysis: his current life now figured in his thoughts during his sessions. He began to see the beginnings of his return to grappling with those problems that lie on the edge of the depressive position from which his defensive organization had been a much needed retreat. Mr M was not now almost overwhelmed by these returning anxieties: he was better equipped. His ego was stronger, more cohesive, and more able to tolerate anxiety, and the area of anxiety itself had lessened – along with his old, dying, cold and over-impinging objects, he had new relations to warmer, stronger, more contained, alive objects.

With a characteristic configuration, Mr M began to confront his developmental problems. The configuration was a sequel to his protracted use of a defensive organization in the sense given it in this paper, namely a pathological, static formation needed when development is arousing almost overwhelming and irresoluble anxiety. Mr M had a split in his ego: one part was capable of awareness and feeling and tried to progress even though anxiety loomed; his other omnipotent part preferred to stay in a state of projective identification with its objects, and was obstructive and contemptuous of 'pedestrian' efforts to develop. But unlike before, Mr M's aware part was often now the dominant one, and it had started to scrutinize his omnipotent part, which like the defensive organization of which it was the precipitate, still served Mr M as a defence. The existence of a split and deep opposition within the ego, and the continued use for defence of the omnipotent part, are, I think, the characteristic *sequelae* of a defensive organization.

Before concluding I shall report a session from the ninth year which shows this characteristic configuration in operation. The session, when placed alongside the session reported at the start of the paper, also shows the change in Mr M, and, as well, returns us to, and throws new light on, his longing for peace.

It was a Friday session. Mr M began in a sneering, hostile tone saying he was bored. Then in a different voice he said he was tired (he had looked tired) and he now sounded it. He changed back to being sneering and hostile, saying he had to make obeisance, he had to sort of nod his head to the side as he passed the exit door (he had, in fact, nodded to the street door on the way to the consulting room). I commented on his opposite feelings: that he was hating me, feeling I forced him to acknowledge it was exit day, Friday, and also that he was feeling tired.

Straightaway Mr M talked about his weekend sexual plans, talking about having sex again with X – a married woman with whom he was having an affair, and then talking about Y – a girl whose magazine advertisement he had answered, and whom he would also see and have sex with at the weekend, and his tangle with the pair of them; and then he talked about Z, a young Jewish girl who was interested and friendly, and whom he had invited out on Saturday night. He was worried that he was going to lose interest in her. He sounded worried. Acknowledging first his worry that his activities with X and Y might destroy his interest in the young Jewish girl who was friendly and interesting, I linked her with an aspect of myself, who was interested in him and noticed how he felt. I pointed out that he had already, with all the sex talk to me, lost interest in his tiredness and depression that had crept over him on exit day, Friday. The interpretation seemed to reach Mr M and there was a silence.

When he spoke next it was with a lighter, more alive voice. He said he felt better now than when he arrived; then he hadn't felt well, but now he felt relieved as though some weight had been lifted off him. There was another long silence. Then Mr M said he was thinking how it was cold in his flat. He had got some draught excluders and put them round the entrance door, but the gap was too big, and the thing got twisted, it got bent. I suggested to him that he was explaining to me about his draught excluders, his sexual arrangements for the weekend, his talk to me about them in the session. These were his methods of excluding the flatness and tiredness that came into him at the weekend and he was telling me that these methods didn't really close the gap and also that they made him get twisted and bent. Mr M said thoughtfully: 'Well, yes. A perversion. I know'.

After a while he said: 'It's funny to think I have two homes – one here and one in A . . . I like A . . .' (recently he had inherited a property in A . . .). He continued: 'A picture occurs to me of the Jewish cemetery in A . . . which I often go past. Sometimes there are swastikas painted on it. There is a wide pedestrian' – at the word 'pedestrian' he said with a friendly laugh: 'I know what you'll think' – path alongside it along which I sometimes walk'. I interpreted his thoughts about having two homes as expressing the two ways he felt with me. When he first arrived he felt hostile, hating me for the way I force him out at the weekends and he painted me as a Nazi, and preferred his exciting weekend girls to boring Old People analysis.

Now, in the middle of the session he felt at home with me, liked me and felt communicative. I also said that the 'pedestrian path' was important. Today he was not going past the 'Jewish cemetery'; he was on what he often thought of as the pedestrian path of noticing how things are. I suggested that by taking the life and sex out of me, as he had done at the beginning of the session, he felt he reduced me to a cemetery, which then got into his inner world, making him tired and depressed.

It was near the end. Frightened of depression and his exit, Mr M split off his aware part. Abruptly he was like a different patient on the couch. He spoke of his women, X and Y, and described excitedly a film about homosexuals. He sniggered and ended the session saying it had got good reviews and he would take one of them to see it at the weekend.

In this session Mr M was beginning to face, or at least to give a nod in the direction of, a number of disturbing problems: exit day, the persecution of being forced out, his perverse and destructive defences and the tiredness and depression, really deadness, that stem from what he fears is a cemetery he makes in his inner world. We can also see the interaction of the two parts of Mr M. Both arrive and in the beginning they alternate. As the session proceeds his aware part becomes dominant, communicative and thoughtful about his twisted defences, acknowledging that he has a home he likes, and recognizing the existence in himself of Nazis, dead objects, and depression. But when the end comes, Mr M is at this stage still too anxious. He needs to split off his aware part and his omnipotent part, defensive and twisted, completely takes him over, as it will partly do at the weekend.

The atmosphere of the session was characteristic of many in the concluding fourth stage of the analysis. Mr M was able to feel and show his hostility. He was also able to feel affection. His words and thoughts function very differently from early in the analysis, when they tended to become concrete and disordered. Mr M can now take his time. He was not frantic as he used to be at the start, nor dead calm as he was when he first formed his defensive organization, nor dangerously excited as he often was when he later exploited it. I think Mr M himself expressed the change when he said: 'It's funny to think I have two homes'. It was his feeling of having a *home*, i.e. an object he could trust to accept him – in fact he felt he had two homes, one for each part of him, that was beginning to give Mr M a real sense of peace. This peace is different from the calm got by organizing and restricting himself and his objects in order to remain undisturbed. As the session shows, this kind of peace is compatible with disturbance: indeed, it is based on having a home for disturbance.

The last years of Mr M's analysis saw an intricate conflict, and sometimes alliance, between his aware self and his omnipotent self. Gradually he faced some of what had previously been, in a phrase he often used, 'inadmissible evidence' about his object relations, including his terror and refusal of separateness that lay hidden under his omnipotence, and he was able, after his own fashion, to work through some of the feelings and anxieties of the depressive position. The broken-down, disused warehouse, Mr M's image of the mother who housed him, emerged in an important dream as a beautiful historic mansion that should not have been ruined and which the National Trust should restore. This, Mr M's increasing trust partially did.

By the end of his long twelve-year analysis, though his omnipotent part was liable to intrude suddenly into and spoil his relationships, and when he felt persecuted or over-guilty he was liable abruptly to lose interest in his object and become omnipotent and perverse, such states of mind were temporary. They were not seriously disturbing to his stable relationships, foremost among which was a marriage that brought him considerable satisfaction.

Summary

This paper is concerned with those patients whose lives oscillate between periods of overrestricted object relations based on a defensive organization, and periods of exposure to almost overwhelming anxiety from their objects when their defensive organization fails. The paper reports a twelve-year analysis of one such patient, a young man whose defensive organization had broken down. The clinical material shows how, in the conditions an analysis tries to provide – interpretive understanding, emotional containment, and analytic perseverance – he first re-established and then maintained his defensive organization long enough to halt the oscillation between exposure and restriction, and to resume instead his forward development.

In the course of this clinical study, the nature of a defensive organization is itself examined. I suggest that a distinction be drawn between defences and defensive organization. Defences allow for the working through of anxiety and are a normal part of forward development. A defensive organization is an overall pathological formation, a fixation of object relations when progress is impossible;

its benefits come from the elimination of anxiety from object relations, and inherently, as the clinical material shows, such object relations offer the possibility of exploitation.

As regards technique, the paper shows the necessity of recognizing the patient's need to be analysed for a long time within the framework of his defensive organization. This allows his ego to strengthen and the area of his anxieties to diminish – changes which will enable him, often only after many years, to resume his forward development.

Note

1 In fact, another and different proposal to rescue Hoffer's term from obscurity was made in 1971 by Lichtenberg and Slap.

References

Freud, S. (1940) 'Splitting of the ego in the process of defence', *SE* 23.

Hoffer, W. (1954) 'Defensive process and defensive organization: their place in psycho-analytic technique', *International Journal of Psycho-Analysis*, 35, 194–8.

Klein, M. (1935) 'A contribution to the psychogenesis of manic–depressive states', in *The Writings of Melanie Klein*, vol. 1, London: Hogarth Press (1975), 262–89.

——(1946) 'Notes on some schizoid mechanisms', in M. Klein, P. Heimann, S. Isaacs, and J. Riviere *Developments in Psycho-Analysis* London: Hogarth Press (1975) 292–320 (also in *The Writings of Melanie Klein*, vol. 3, 1–24).

——(1955) 'On identification', in *The Writings of Melanie Klein*, vol. 3, 141–75.

Lichtenberg, J. D. & Slap, J. W. (1971) 'On the defensive organization', *International Journal of Psycho-Analysis*, 52, 451–7.

Rosenfeld, H. (1971) 'A clinical approach to the psychoanalytic theory of the life and death instincts: an investigation into the aggressive aspects of narcissism', *International Journal of Psycho-Analysis*, 52, 169–78 and reprinted here, pp. 239–55.

Segal, H. (1972) 'A delusional system as a defence against the re-emergence of a catastrophic situation', *International Journal of Psycho-Analysis*, 53, 393–401.

Smith, S. (1972) 'The golden phantasy. A regressive reaction to separation anxiety', *International Journal of Psycho-Analysis*, 58, 311–24.

7

Addiction to near-death

BETTY JOSEPH

This article was originally a paper presented to a scientific meeting of the British Psycho-Analytic Society, 20 May 1981, and was first published in 1982 in the *International Journal of Psycho-Analysis*, 63, 449–56.

There is a very malignant type of self-destructiveness, which we see in a small group of our patients, and which is, I think, in the nature of an addiction – an addiction to near-death. It dominates these patients' lives; for long periods it dominates the way they bring material to the analysis and the type of relationship they establish with the analyst; it dominates their internal relationships, their so-called thinking, and the way they communicate with themselves. It is not a drive towards a Nirvana type of peace or relief from problems, and it has to be sharply differentiated from this.

The picture that these patients present is, I am sure, a familiar one – in their external lives these patients get more and more absorbed into hopelessness and involved in activities that seem destined to destroy them physically as well as mentally, for example, considerable over-working, almost no sleep, avoiding eating properly or secretly over-eating if the need is to lose weight, drinking more and more and perhaps cutting off from relationships. In other patients this type of addiction is probably less striking in their actual living but equally important in their relationship with the analyst and the analysis. Indeed, in all these patients the place where the pull towards near-death is most obvious is in the transference. As I want to illustrate in this paper, these patients bring material to analysis in a very particular way, for example, they may speak in a way which seems calculated to communicate or create despair and a sense of hopelessness in themselves and in the analyst, although apparently wanting understanding. It is not just that they make progress, forget it, lose it or take no responsibility for it. They do show a strong though frequently silent negative therapeutic reaction, but this negative therapeutic reaction is only one part of a much broader and more insidious picture. The pull towards despair and death in such patients is not, as I have said, a longing for peace and freedom from effort; indeed, as I sorted out with one such patient, just to die, although attractive, would be no good. There is a felt need to know and to have the satisfaction of seeing oneself being destroyed.

So I am stressing here that a powerful masochism is at work and these patients will try to create despair in the analyst and then get him to collude with the despair or become actively involved by being harsh, critical or in some way or another verbally sadistic to the patient. If they succeed in getting themselves hurt or in creating despair, they triumph, since the analyst has lost his analytic balance or his capacity to understand and help and then both patient and analyst go down into failure. At the same time the analyst will sense that there is a real misery and anxiety around and this will have to be sorted out and differentiated from the masochistic use and exploitation of misery.

The other area that I am going to discuss as part of this whole constellation is that of the patient's internal relationships and a particular type of communication with himself – because I believe that in all such patients one will find a type of mental activity consisting of a going over and over again about happenings or anticipations of an accusatory or self-accusatory type in which the patient becomes completely absorbed.

I have described in this introduction the pull of the death instincts, the pull towards near-death, a kind of mental or physical brinkmanship in which the seeing of the self in this dilemma, unable to be helped, is an essential aspect. It is, however, important also to consider where the pull towards life and sanity is. I believe that this part of the patient is located in the analyst, which in part, accounts for the patient's apparent extreme passivity and indifference to progress. This I shall return to later.

It will be seen that much that I have outlined in this introduction has already been described in the analytic literature. For example, Freud (1924) discusses the working of the death instinct in masochism and distinguishes the nature of the inner conflict in a negative therapeutic reaction from that seen in moral masochism. He adds at the end of the paper 'even the subject's destruction of himself cannot take place without libidinal satisfaction'. In the patients that I am describing it seems to me that the near destruction of the self takes place with considerable libidinal satisfaction, however much the concomitant pain. The main additional aspects, however, that I want to discuss are: the way in which these problems make themselves felt in the transference, and in the patient's internal relationships and his thinking; and the deeply addictive nature of this type of masochistic constellation and the fascination and hold on them that it has. Later I want to add a note on some possible aspects of the infantile history of these patients. I shall start by getting into the middle of the problem by bringing a dream.

This dream comes from a patient who is typical of this group. He started analysis many years ago, and was then cold, rather cruel, loveless, highly competent, intelligent, articulate and successful in his work – but basically very unhappy. During the treatment he had become much warmer, was struggling to build real relationships and had become deeply but ambivalently emotionally involved with a gifted but probably disturbed young woman. This was a very important experience for him. He was also now deeply attached to the analysis although he did not speak of it, did not acknowledge it, was often late and seemed not to notice or be aware of almost anything about me as a human being. He often had sudden feelings of great hatred towards me. I am going to bring a dream from a Wednesday. On the Monday he had consolidated the work we had been doing on a particular type of provocation and cruelty silently achieved. By the end of the session he had seemed relieved and in good contact. But on the Tuesday he phoned just at the time of the end of his session and said that he had only just woken up. He sounded very distressed, but said that he had hardly slept in the night and would be here the following day. When he arrived on Wednesday he spoke about the Monday, how surprised he was that following the better feeling in the session he had felt so terrible and tense physically, in his stomach and in every way on the Monday night. He had felt much warmer towards K, the girl friend, and really wanted to see her, but she was out for the evening. She said she would phone him when she got back, but she didn't, so he must have been lying awake getting into a bad state. He also knew that he very much wanted to get to analysis and he expressed a strong positive feeling that he felt was emerging since the last session. He had found the work we had done during the Monday session very convincing and a real culmination of the work of the last period of analysis. He altogether sounded unusually appreciative and absolutely puzzled about the complete sense of breakdown, sleeplessness and the missing of the Tuesday session.

When he was describing the pain and misery of the Monday night, he said that he was reminded of the feeling that he had expressed at the beginning of the Monday session, the feeling that perhaps he was too far into this awful state ever to be helped out by me or to get out himself. At the same time during and immediately after the session there had been feelings of insight and more hope.

He then told a dream: he was in a long kind of cave, almost a cavern. It was dark and smoky and it was as if he and other people had been taken captive by brigands. There was a feeling of confusion, as if they had been drinking. They, the captives, were lined up along a wall and he was sitting next to a young man. This man was subsequently described as looking gentle, in the mid-twenties, with a small moustache. The man suddenly turned towards him, grabbed at him and at his genitals, as if he were homosexual, and was about to knife my patient, who was completely terrified. He knew that if he tried to resist the man would knife him and there was tremendous pain.

After telling the dream, he went on to describe some of the happenings of the last two days. He particularly spoke first about K. He then spoke about a meeting he had been to, in which a business acquaintance had said that a colleague told him that he, the colleague, was so frightened of my patient, A, that he positively trembled when on the phone to him. My patient was amazed, but linked this with something that I had shown him on the Monday, when I had commented on a very cold, cruel way in which he dealt with me when I queried a point about another dream. This association was connected with the idea of the man in the dream looking so gentle but acting in this violent way, and so he felt that the man must somehow be connected with himself, but what about the moustache? Then suddenly he had the notion of D. H. Lawrence – he had been reading a new biography of Lawrence and remembered that he was enormously attracted to him in his adolescence and felt identified with him. Lawrence was a bit homosexual and clearly a strange and violent man.

I worked out with him that it seemed therefore that this long, dark cavern stood for the place where he had felt he was too far in to be pulled out by himself or by me; as if it was his mind, but perhaps also part of his body. But the too-far-in seems to be linked with the notion that he was completely captured and captivated, possibly, by the brigands. But the brigands are manifestly associated with himself, the little man linked with Lawrence, who is experienced as part of himself. We can also see that the giving-in to this brigand is absolutely terrifying, it is a complete nightmare, and yet sexually exciting. The man grabs his genitals.

Here I need to interpose – I had been impressed for some time about the pull of despair and self-destructiveness in this man and one or two other patients with similar difficulties, and was driven to conclude that the actual despair, or the describing of it in the session, contained real masochistic excitement, concretely experienced. We can see it in the way these patients go over and over their unhappinesses, failures, things they feel they ought to feel guilty about. They talk as if they are attempting unconsciously to pull the analyst into concurring with the misery or with the descriptions or they unconsciously try to make the analyst give critical or disturbing interpretations. This becomes a very important pattern in the way that they speak. It is familiar to us and has been well described in the literature (Meltzer 1973; Rosenfeld 1971; Steiner 1982) that such patients feel in thrall to a part of the self that dominates and imprisons them and will not let them escape, even though they see life beckoning outside, as expressed in my patient's dream, outside the cavern. The point I want to add here is that the patient's experience of sexual gratification in being in such pain, in being dominated, is one of the major reasons for the grip that the drive towards death has on him. These patients are literally 'enthralled' by it. In this patient A, for example, no ordinary pleasure, genital, sexual or other, offered such delight as this type of terrible and exciting self-annihilation which annihilates also the object and is basic to his important relationships to a greater or less extent.

So, I think the dream is clearly a response, not just to the girl friend K being out on the Monday night and A lying in bed getting more and more disturbed about it, of which he was conscious, but to the fact that he had felt better, knew he had and could not allow himself to get out of his misery and self-destruction – the long cavern – or allow me to help him out. He was forced back by a part of himself, essentially sado-masochistic, which operated also as a negative therapeutic reaction, and which used the distress about the girl friend as fuel. I also stressed here, and shall return to, his triumph over me when our work and the hope of the last weeks are knocked down and he and I go under.

I am discussing here, therefore, that it is not only that he is dominated by an aggressive part of himself, which attempts to control and destroy my work, but that this part is actively sadistic towards another part of the self which is masochistically caught up in this process, and that this has become an addiction. This process has always, I believe, an internal counterpart and in patients really dedicated to self-destructiveness, this internal situation has a very strong hold over their thinking and their quiet moments, their capacity for mulling things over or the lack of it. The kind of thing that one sees is this. These patients pick up very readily something that has been going on in their minds or in an external relationship and start to use it over and over again in some circular type of mental activity, in which they get completely caught up, so that they go over and over with very little variation the same actual or anticipated issue. This mental activity, which I think is best described by the word 'chuntering', is very important. The *Oxford English Dictionary* describes chuntering as 'mutter, murmur, grumble, find fault, complain'. To give an example, A, in the period when I was trying to explore in him this dedication to masochism, described one day how he had been upset the previous evening because K had been going out with somebody else. He realized that on the previous evening he had, in his mind, been rehearsing what he might say to K about this. For example, he would talk about how he could not go on like this with her, while she was going around with another man; how he would have to give up the whole relationship; he could not go on like this, and so on. As he went on speaking about what he was planning to say to K, I got the feeling, not only from the ideas, but from his whole tone, that he was not just thinking what he might say to K, but was caught up in some kind of active cruel dialogue with her. Slowly then he clarified the ideas that he had had, and how he had been going over things in his mind. On this occasion and indeed on others, he realized that he would be saying something cruel, for example, and that K in the phantasy would reply or cry or plead or cling, she would become provocative, he would get cruel back, etc. In other words, what he then called 'thinking about what he would say' is actually actively being caught up in his mind in a provocative sado-masochistic phantasy, in which he both hurts and is hurt, verbally repeats and is humiliated, until the phantasy activity has such a grip on him that it almost has a life of its own and the content becomes secondary. In such cases, unless I could begin to be aware of the problem of their being caught up in these phantasies and start to draw my patients' attention to them, these phantasies would not come into the analysis, although in some way or another they are conscious. Patients, who get so caught up in these activities, chuntering, tend to believe that they are thinking at such times, but of course they are living out experiences which becomes the complete antithesis of thought.

Another patient, when we had finally managed to open up very clearly the enormous importance and sadistic grip that such going over and over in his mind had on him, told me that he felt that he probably spent two-thirds of his free time absorbed in such activities; then in the period when he was trying to give them up he felt that he had almost too much free time on his hands, and had a vague feeling of let-down or disillusionment as he began to do without them; the sense of let-down coming from the relinquishing of the exciting pain of this internal dialogue.

My point about the circular mental activities being the antithesis of thought is, of course, important in the analytic situation. I am stressing that the internal dialogue, the chuntering, is lived out in the analytic dialogue as well as in these patients' lives. Such patients use a great deal of analytic time apparently bringing material to be analysed and understood, but actually unconsciously for other purposes. We are all familiar with the kind of patient who talks in such a way as, they hope unconsciously, to provoke the analyst to be disturbed, repetitive, reproachful or actually critical. This can then be used by the silently watchful masochistic part of the patient to beat himself with, and an external 'difficulty' can be established in the analysis and perpetuated internally, during the session, with the patient silent and apparently hurt; or outside in an internal dialogue. We can then see that it is not 'understanding' that the patient wants, though the words are presented as if it were so. These self-destructive patients appear very often to be passive in their lives, as on one level did A, and a very important step is taken when they can see how active they are, by projective identification, for example through the kind of provocation that I am describing or in their thinking and phantasy. But there are other ways of expressing this type of self-destructiveness in the analysis. For example, some patients present 'real' situations, but in such a way as silently and extremely convincingly to make the analyst feel quite hopeless and despairing. The patient appears to feel the same. I think we have here a type of projective identification in which despair is so effectively loaded into the analyst that he seems crushed by it and can see no way out. The analyst is then internalized in this form by the patient, who becomes caught up in this internal crushing and crushed situation, and paralysis and deep gratification ensue.

Two issues arise from all this. First, that this type of patient usually finds it very difficult to see and to acknowledge the awful pleasure that is achieved in this way; and, second, I believe it is technically extremely important to be clear as to whether the patient is telling us about and communicating to us real despair, depression or fear and persecution, which he wants us to understand and to help him with, or whether he is communicating it in such a way as primarily to create a masochistic situation in which he can become caught up. If this distinction is not clearly made in the analysis from moment to moment, one cannot analyse adequately the underlying deep anxieties because of the whole masochistic overlay and the use that is being made of this. Further, I think that one needs to distinguish very clearly between the masochistic use of anxieties that I am discussing and dramatization. I am here describing something much more malignant and much more desperate to the personality than dramatization.

I want now to bring an example to illustrate further this connection between actual anxieties and the exploitation of anxieties for masochistic purposes: and the connection between genuinely persecuted feelings and the building up of a kind of pseudo-paranoia for masochistic purposes. I shall bring material from the patient A in a period when he was in great distress. It had been indicated to him that he would be likely to be promoted to a very senior position in the firm where he worked, but he got into a bad relationship with a principal man – himself probably a difficult and tormenting person. For a period of about two years things quietly deteriorated until there was a major reorganization in which he was to be demoted. He was deeply disturbed and decided he would almost certainly have to leave rather than be put in an inferior position. It should, however, be remembered that in his position there would be no likelihood of his having difficulty in finding other high-grade and financially rewarding work.

I bring a session from a Monday at this time. The patient came in most distressed, then remembered he had not brought his cheque, but would bring it the following day; then described the happenings of the weekend and his talk with his principal on Friday and how worried he felt about his job. K, his girl friend, had been helpful and kind, but he felt sexually dead and as if she was wanting sex from him, which became rather horrifying. Then he queried, 'was he trying to be cruel to her?' – already that question has something a bit suspect about it, as if I was supposed to agree that he was trying to be cruel to her and get caught up in some kind of reproaching of him, so that the question became in itself masochistic rather than thoughtful. He then brought a dream. In the dream, he was in an old-fashioned shop at a counter, but he was small, about the height of the counter. There was someone behind it, a shop assistant. She was by a ledger but was holding his hand. He was asking her, 'was she a witch?' as if wanting a reply, persistently asking, almost as if he wanted to hear from her that she was a witch. He felt she was getting fed up with him and would withdraw her hand. There were rows of people somewhere in the dream and a vague feeling of being blamed for something he had done. In the shop a horse was being shod but with a piece of white plastic-looking material, about the shape and the size of the material one would put on the heel of a man's shoe.

In his associations he spoke about his anxiety about his relationship with K at the moment and his sexuality. He was the height of a child in the dream. He had tremendous feelings of panic and anxiety at night. What would he do? Would he really run out of money, and what would happen to his whole position? We spoke about the realities of this a bit more.

He had seen a lot of horses being shod as a child and well remembered the smell of the iron going into the horse's hoof. He spoke about his guilt about the situation that he felt he had helped to create at work and realized that he must actually have acted very arrogantly with his principal and that this had probably really helped to bring the ceiling down on him.

I linked the ledger with the forgotten cheque and his anxiety about finances. He is worried about his lack of sexual interest at the moment, but seems to want me to be nasty about the cheque, and K about his lack of libido. In the dream he wanted the woman to say that she was a witch and this attitude appears to be an old story, since he is the height of a child. The guilt, I believe, is not just about his faulty handling of his work situation, his arrogance and harsh attitude, which has really led to serious work problems, but this is used both in his mind and actively in the transference in an attempt to draw me into agreement with his despair, to criticize his arrogance in his relationship with K and shatter him and create utter despair and a sense of uselessness in both of us. This is the masochistic use of anxiety in his mind and in the session. We can then see something about the sexualized excitement, of a very cruel kind, that he gets in this attitude by looking at the associations to the shoeing of the horse. There is a picture of a burning iron being put into the horse's foot and the fascination and horror of this as a child, feeling that it is bound to hurt, though in fact one subsequently knows it doesn't. So, I could then show him the indulgence in a tremendously masochistic attitude that was going on visibly in the dream, currently in the session, as misery, despair and pseudo-paranoia were being built up. There is almost a fragment of insight in this dream, as when he demands that the woman tells him if she is a witch and vaguely he knows that he hopes that she will agree that she is. As we went over this he began to see it again very clearly and his whole attitude became more thoughtful and quiet, as opposed to desperate and hopeless. He slowly added that, of course, there is the problem that this kind of sexual excitement and horror seems so great that nothing else can be so important and exciting to him. Now, when he said this, at first there was clearly a sense of insight and truth about, but then there began to be a different feeling in the session as if he really meant there was nothing one could do about it. Even the insight began to contain a different message. So I showed him that there was not only insight, not only anxiety and despair about being so much caught up in this kind of masturbatory excitement, but now there was also a triumph and a kind of sadistic jab at me, as if he were digging a burning iron into my heart to make me feel that nothing we were achieving was really worth anything and nothing could be done. Once again he could see this and so it was possible to link the desperate sexualized masochistic excitement with the triumphant doing down of his object, external and internal.

I have tried to show in this example how this masochistic excitement was covering up at that time deep anxieties stirred up by his work situation, connected with feelings of rejection, being unwanted, failure and guilt. But it is only possible to get through to them if the masochistic use, exploitation, is first dealt with. If one does not do this then one gets a situation which is so common with these patients that interpretations may appear to be listened to, but some part of the patient's personality will treat the analyst with contempt, with sneering and with mockery, though the mockery and contempt will be silent.

But we are still left with a major problem as to why this type of masochistic self-destruction is so self-perpetuating; why it has such a grip on this type of patient. One reason which I have discussed in this paper – the sheer unequalled sexual delight of the grim masochism – is undeniable, yet it is usually very difficult for a long time for such patients to see that they are suffering from an addiction, that they are 'hooked' to this kind of self-destruction. With A, by the time we reached the dream about the sexual assault in the cavern, we had worked through a lot of this, and he felt consciously that he was in the grip of an addiction from which he believed he would like to be free. But he felt that the part of him that would like to be freed was nothing like as powerful nor were the possible results as attractive as was the pull of his addiction. And this he could not understand.

This problem needs considering from the angle of these patients' passivity that I mentioned at the beginning of the paper when I described how the pull towards life and sanity seems to be split off and projected into the analyst. One can see this in the transference, in severe cases going on sometimes over years, roughly like this. The patient comes, talks, dreams, etc. but one gets the impression of very little real active interest in changing, improving, remembering, getting anywhere with the treatment. Slowly the picture builds up. The analyst seems to be the only person in the room who is actively concerned about change, about progress, about development, as if all the active parts of the patient have been projected into the analyst. If the analyst is not aware of this and therefore does not concentrate his interpretations round this process, a collusion can arise in which the analyst carefully, maybe tactfully, pushes, tries to get the patient's interest or to alert him. The patient briefly responds only quietly to withdraw again and leave the next move to the analyst, and a major piece of psychopathology is acted out in the transference. The patient constantly is pulling back towards the silent kind of deadly paralysis and near complete passivity. When these lively parts of the patient remain so constantly split off it means that his whole capacity for wanting and appreciating, missing, feeling disturbed at losing, etc., the very stuff that makes for real whole object relating is projected and the patient remains with his addiction and without the psychological means of combating this. To me, therefore, the understanding of the nature of this apparent passivity is technically of primary importance with these patients. Moreover, it means that with such splitting-off of the life and instincts and of loving, ambivalence and guilt is largely evaded. As these patients improve and begin to become more integrated and relationships become more real, they begin to feel acute pain sometimes experienced as almost physical – undifferentiated but extremely intense.

I think it is often at these periods of analysis, when concern and pain near to guilt begin to be experienced, that one can see a quick regression to earlier masochistic methods of avoiding pain linked essentially with infantile and childhood behaviour. To give a very brief example – A, following a good analytic experience had a dream in which his mother, dead or near dead, was lying on a slab or couch, and he, to his horror, was pulling off bits of sunburnt skin from one side of her face and eating them. I think that instead of becoming aware of, and guilty about, the spoiling of the good experience, he is showing her how he again becomes identified with his damaged object by eating it up, and it is also important to see the link between the painful exciting physical horror and his earlier nail-biting and skin-tearing, familiar to us.

Freud, of course, describes this process of identification in 'Mourning and melancholia' (1917) and he also adds 'the self tormenting in melancholia . . . is without doubt enjoyable . . .' Despite certain important similarities the patients that I am describing

321

are not 'melancholic' – their guilt and self-reproach being so much evaded or swallowed up by their masochism.

My impression is that these patients as infants, because of their pathology, have not just turned away from frustrations or jealousies or envies into a withdrawn state, nor have they been able to rage and yell at their objects. I think they have withdrawn into a secret world of violence, where part of the self has been turned against another part, parts of the body being identified with parts of the offending object, and that this violence has been highly sexualized, masturbatory in nature, and often physically expressed. One sees it, for example, in head-banging, digging nails into fists, pulling at one's own hair and twisting and splitting it until it hurts, and this is what we are still seeing in the verbal chuntering that goes on and on. As one gets into this area and these patients are able to recognize, usually at first with great difficulty and resentment, the excitement and pleasure they get from these apparent self-attacks, they can usually show us their own particular personal predeliction. One of my young male patients of this group was still pulling at and splitting his hair when he was well into his analysis. Another, an older man, who spoke of the amount of time used up by his chuntering, used, in times of great disturbance, to lie on the floor drinking and putting on his radio as loud as possible, as if caught up in a wild orgy of rhythmical bodily experience. It seems to me that instead of moving forward and using real relationships, contact with people or bodies as infants, they retreated apparently into themselves and lived out their relationships in this sexualized way, in phantasy or phantasy expressed in violent bodily activity. This deep masochistic state, then, has a hold on the patient, that is much stronger than the pull towards human relationships. Sometimes this is to be seen as an aspect of an actual perversion, in others it is part of a character perversion.

It will be seen that in this paper I have not attempted to discuss the defensive value of the addiction, but there is one aspect of this problem that I would like to mention before ending. It has something to do with torture and survival. None of the patients whom I have in mind as particularly belonging to this addictive group have really very seriously bad childhood histories, though psychologically in a sense they almost certainly have – as, for example, a lack of warm contact and real understanding, and sometimes a very violent parent. Yet in the transference one gets the feeling of being driven up to the edge of things, as I indicated, and both patient and analyst feel tortured. I get the impression from the difficulty these patients experience in waiting and being aware of gaps and aware of even the simplest type of guilt that such potentially depressive experiences have been felt by them in infancy, as terrible pain that goes over into torment, and that they have tried to obviate this by taking over the torment, the inflicting of mental pain on to themselves and building it into a world of perverse excitement, and this necessarily militates against any real progress towards the depressive position.

It is very hard for our patients to find it possible to abandon such terrible delights for the uncertain pleasures of real relationships.

Summary

This paper describes a very malignant type of self-destructiveness seen in a small group of patients. It is active in the way that they run their lives and it emerges in a deadly way in the transference. This type of self-destructiveness is, I suggest, in the nature of an addiction of a particular sado-masochistic type, which these patients feel unable to resist. It seems to be like a constant pull towards despair and near-death, so that the patient is fascinated and unconsciously excited by the whole process. Examples are given to show how such addictions dominate the way in which the patient communicates with the analyst and internally, with himself, and thus how they affect his thinking processes. It is clearly extremely difficult for such patients to move towards more real and object-related enjoyments, which would mean giving up the all-consuming addictive gratifications.

References

Freud, S. (1917) 'Mourning and melancholia', *SE* 14.
—— (1924) 'The economic problem of masochism', *SE* 19.
Meltzer, D. (1973) *Sexual States of Mind*, Perthshire: Clunie Press.
Oxford English Dictionary, Compact Edition (1979) London: Oxford University Press.
Rosenfeld, H. (1971) 'A clinical approach to the psychoanalytic theory of the life and death instincts: an investigation into the aggressive aspects of narcissism', *International Journal of Psycho-Analysis*, 52, 169–78.
Steiner, J. (1982) 'Perverse relationships between parts of the self: a clinical illustration', *International Journal of Psycho-Analysis*, 63, 241–52.

The interplay between pathological organizations and the paranoid–schizoid and depressive positions

JOHN STEINER

This article was originally a paper read to a scientific meeting of the British Psycho-Analytical Society on 20 February 1985 and first published in 1987 in the *International Journal of Psycho-Analysis*, 68, 69–80.

In this paper I shall discuss some of the ways defences may be assembled into pathological organizations which have a profound effect on the personality and can lead to states of mind which become fixed so that the patient in analysis shows a characteristic lack of insight and resistance to change. I will emphasize the clinical importance of these organizations and try to show how they exist in an equilibrium with the paranoid-schizoid and depressive positions. I shall only briefly describe the characteristics of these positions since they are now well known, but I will emphasize transitions within them which are easy to overlook and which I believe are points at which the patient is particularly vulnerable to the influence of a pathological organization.

Melanie Klein's differentiation of two major groupings of anxieties and defences, the paranoid-schizoid and depressive, has proved to be a major conceptual tool which has made it easier to examine the way mental structures are organized at different levels of development (Klein 1952; Segal 1964). This is an important technical aid since it helps us to orient ourselves to clinical material by enabling us to assess the level at which the patient is functioning. We can learn to evaluate whether his anxieties, mental mechanisms and object relations are primarily depressive or primarily paranoid-schizoid, and this will determine the way we interpret.

A continuous movement between the two positions takes place so that neither dominates with any degree of completeness or permanence. Indeed it is these fluctuations which we try to follow clinically as we observe periods of integration leading to depressive position functioning or disintegration and fragmentation resulting in a paranoid-schizoid state. Such fluctuations can take place over months and years as an analysis develops but can also be seen in the fine grain of a session, as moment to moment changes. If the patient makes meaningful progress a gradual shift towards depressive position function is observed, while if he deteriorates we see a reversion to paranoid-schizoid functioning such as occurs in negative therapeutic reactions. These observations led Bion (1963) to suggest that the two positions were in an equilibrium with each other and hence joined schematically with a bi-directional arrow, i.e. P/S↔D. This way of putting it emphasizes the dynamic quality and focuses attention on the factors which lead to a shift in one direction or another.

As a brief summary: in the paranoid-schizoid position anxieties of a primitive nature threaten the immature ego and lead to the mobilization of primitive defences. Splitting, idealization, and projective identification operate to create rudimentary structures made up of idealized good objects kept far apart from persecuting bad ones. The individual's own impulses are similarly split and he directs all his love towards the good object and all his hatred against the bad one. As a consequence of the projection, the leading anxiety is paranoid, and the preoccupation is with survival of the self. Thinking is concrete because of the confusion between self and object which is one of the consequences of projective identification (Segal 1957).

The depressive position represents an important developmental advance in which whole objects begin to be recognized and ambivalent impulses become directed towards the primary object. These changes result from an increased capacity to integrate experiences and lead to a shift in primary concern from the survival of the self to a concern for the object upon which the individual depends. Destructive impulses lead to feelings of loss and guilt which can be more fully experienced and which consequently enable mourning to take place. The consequences include a development of symbolic function and the emergence of reparative capacities which become possible when thinking no longer has to remain concrete.

The distinction between the two positions has an impressive clarity but does sometimes make us forget that, within the positions, mental states with very different qualities exist. In the paranoid-schizoid position the type of splitting described above can be considered as normal and distinguished from states of fragmentation which result from disintegrative splitting. Projective identification of a violent kind may then lead to both the object and the projected part of the ego being splintered into minute fragments creating persecutory states often with depersonalization and extreme anxiety. Such states may result when hostility predominates and especially if envy stimulates attacks on good objects. When this happens the normal split between good and bad is likely to break down, leading to a confusional state (Rosenfeld 1950; Klein 1957) and these states seem to be particularly difficult to bear and may lead to disintegrative splitting. As I will try to show later, the break-down of normal splitting may make the patient vulnerable to the influence of a pathological organization which offers a kind of pseudo-structure to help deal with the confused and chaotic state of mind (Meltzer 1968).

Another important differentiation exists within the depressive position where it is easy to forget that splitting also plays an important role. Klein (1935) emphasizes how splitting is resorted to again when the good object has been internalized as a whole object and ambivalent impulses towards it lead to depressive states in which the object is felt to be damaged, dying or dead and 'casts its shadow on the ego'. Attempts to possess and preserve the good object are part of the depressive position and lead to a renewal of splitting, this time to prevent the loss of the good object and to protect it from attacks. The aim in this phase of the depressive position is to deny the reality of the loss of the object by concretely internalizing it, possessing it and identifying with it. This is the situation of the bereaved person in the early stages of mourning and appears to be a normal stage which needs to be passed through before the subsequent experience of acknowledgement of the loss can take place.

A critical point in the depressive position arises when the task of relinquishing control over the object has to be faced. The earlier trend, which aims at possessing the object and denying reality, has to be reversed if the depressive position is to be worked through, and the object is to be allowed its independence. In unconscious phantasy this means that the individual has to face his inability to protect the object. His psychic reality includes the realization of the internal disaster created by his sadism and the awareness that his love and reparative wishes are insufficient to preserve his object which must be allowed to die with the consequent desolation, despair, and guilt. These processes involve intense conflict which we associate with the work of mourning and which seem to result in anxiety and mental pain. A central theme in my paper will be that this is another critical point for the patient and, if these experiences cannot be faced, a pathological organization may again be called into play to deal with the conflict.

It is therefore at the transitions which take place within both the paranoid–schizoid and the depressive positions that the individual seems to be most vulnerable to the influence of a pathological organization.

The characteristics of pathological organizations

These organizations have been described by a number of different authors who stress different aspects. Riviere (1936), Segal (1972), Riesenberg-Malcolm (1981), and O'Shaughnessy (1981) give clinical descriptions which illustrate the defensive nature and the variety of forms of expression, while Rosenfeld (1964, 1971) Meltzer (1968) and Sohn (1985) emphasize the narcissistic nature of the object relations, the organization into a gang or mafia and the perverse nature of the relationships involved.

The nature of the defences which become organized into a pathological organization varies in different patients and may, for example, be predominantly obsessional, manic, perverse, or even psychotic. The variety of form does, however, conceal common elements which reflect the underlying organization of the defences. This organization is basically narcissistic in all these conditions and reflects the preponderance of projective identification which creates objects which are controlled by parts of the self projected into them. Splitting tends to create multiple objects which are then assembled into a highly organized structure. Within this common structure the clinical manifestations vary considerably. For example, the organization may be held together by obsessional mechanisms where control is paramount, erotization may play a role giving a hysterical flavour, or manic mechanisms may result from an identification with a powerful figure, sometimes the leader of the gang, which results in triumph and excitement.

In psychotic states the personality may be taken over by a psychotic structure which imposes a delusional order. What these different conditions have in common is a stability and resistance to change which derives from the common underlying structure. The main features of this are first that objects are controlled and identified with by projective identification, and second that the object is split and projected into a group and that this group is assembled into an organized structure by complex and often perverse means. It is particularly when defences become organized into such complex systems that they seem to give rise to lasting pathological states, which are extremely damaging to development and which can be very resistant to change.

The interplay with the paranoid–schizoid and depressive positions

To take account of these states and to facilitate their recognition, I have found it conceptually helpful to consider these pathological organizations to have characteristics distinct from both the paranoid–schizoid and the depressive positions and to exist in an equilibrium with them. We can construct a triangular equilibrium diagram as follows:

Pathological Organization

Paranoid–schizoid Position ⟷ Depressive Position

which I believe can help us to orient ourselves more precisely to the patient's material. We can then attempt to assess whether the patient is functioning at a paranoid–schizoid, or a depressive level or whether we are in the presence of a pathological organization; we can also try to follow the shifts between the pathological organization and the other two positions.

When we do this it becomes clear that the pathological organization functions as a defence, not only against fragmentation and confusion, but also against the mental pain and anxiety of the depressive position. It acts as a borderline area between the other two positions, where the patient believes he can retreat if either paranoid or depressive anxieties become unbearable. It is common to observe that a patient will make contact with depressive position experiences and then retreat again to the paranoid–schizoid position as if he could not tolerate the mental pain he encountered (Joseph 1981; Steiner 1979). He then meets the disintegration, fragmentation, confusion, and persecutory anxiety of the paranoid–schizoid position and if these too become unbearable the patient has nowhere where he feels safe unless he can find or construct a defence against both positions.

To do this, omnipotent phantasies and primitive mental mechanisms are brought into play, and these have usually been considered as paranoid–schizoid position activities. What I am suggesting is that when these take the form of a complex organization of defences they have special properties which make it helpful to consider them separately as a pathological organization. They provide a kind of pseudo-integration under the dominance of narcissistic structures which can masquerade as the true integration of the depressive position, and which can provide, or give the illusion of providing a degree of structure and stability for the patient and a relative freedom from anxiety and pain.

The balance between the pathological organization and the other two positions will vary in different patients and in the same patient at different times. All patients, however, seem at times to come under the sway of a pathological organization especially in periods when the analysis is stuck and the patient seems to retreat from contact. This is true even in patients who can function at a relatively mature level in other settings. In other patients the pathological organization seems to dominate a whole analysis and produces formidable obstacles to progress. Even in these patients however it is often possible to trace movements between the organization and the other two positions. This may enable the analyst to identify those minute shifts towards the depressive position which can be so important clinically.

Clinical material

I will try to examine the value of this approach by considering some material from a patient who was often difficult to understand, and who presented problems of technique which seemed to be linked to the difficulty I had of orienting myself to her material by assessing the level correctly.

She was an attractive, recently married woman in her twenties who had dropped out of university and who tended to develop withdrawn states when she would take to her bed and do nothing except read novels endlessly. When still a baby, her family had escaped from a country where they experienced political persecution. They were occasionally able to return to visit her grandmother and these visits and the border crossings they entailed were especially anxious times for her.

She sought treatment because of attacks of incapacitating anxiety, at first associated with major decisions such as whether she should stay in England, or whether she should let her future husband move into her flat when, at that time, he didn't intend to marry her. They would also occur when she got involved in long discussions on existential themes which resulted in panic when she realized that she saw no meaning in life. She would find herself trembling, would feel her surroundings recede and become distant, and found that she could not make contact with people because a diffuse barrier came between them. When her husband agreed to marry her the anxiety lessened but would reappear periodically, for example once, when she lost a locket containing a piece of his hair. In addition, she suffered from a specifc fear of being poisoned from tinned food which she would become convinced had been contaminated. Even between anxiety attacks she was preoccupied with pollution and poisoning and had terrifying dreams in which, for example, radio-activity produced a kind of living death and people became automata. A fascination with deadness and aridity was linked to a preoccupation with the Sahara Desert which she had visited and to which she planned to return in an expedition when her treatment was over.

A central feature of the analysis was the fact that she was a silent patient, in fact often silent for the greater part of the session for months on end. She would begin with a long silence or a comment such as, 'Nothing has happened', or 'It is going to be another silent session'. Occasionally she would give an explanation and, for example, say, 'I sort things out into what I could say and what I couldn't say, and the things I could say are not worth saying.' Very often there was a mocking, teasing quality, usually accompanied by a sulky little girl voice. 'I felt totally misunderstood yesterday and I am not going to say anything today, so there!' Or she might admit that she said to herself, 'Don't show anything to him unless you have thought it all out so he cannot find fault with it', or 'Don't say anything to him unless you are sure you can win the argument.' The silence might turn into a game in which she would alternate between starting a session herself or making me start, or she might gamble on how long she would have to wait before I spoke. During the silence she often thought of herself as sunbathing on a desert island, and she acknowledged that she enjoyed these games and their accompanying fantasies. The most prominent mood was of a smiling indifference, a kind of nonchalance and a playful lack of concern in which the difficulties of the analysis and indeed the realities of life going on around her were *my* problem. This sometimes made me feel exploited and put upon as if I had colluded with the notion that I should care more about her analysis that she did. At other times I seemed to be provoked to interpret her lack of concern in a critical way, as if I was trying to persuade her to become more caring because I was unwilling to take on the responsibility.

At the same time there was a deadly seriousness about her analysis, and she was rarely late and almost never missed a session. On one occasion, when I had let a silence go on for longer than usual, she began to weep silently and when I asked her what she was thinking I was told a tragic story about a girl who had taken an overdose and was left to die because nobody came until it was too late.

As she lay on the couch, the patient would move her hands restlessly and incessantly. She would pick at her finger-nails in a jerky and irritating way, or pull threads out of a bandage or out of her clothing or play with her sleeve or her buttons. For a time she found it hard to resist picking at the wallpaper next to the couch, where there was a small raised piece at an edge which she longed to pull off. Most often she played with her long hair, pulling down a bunch as if milking it, teasing out individual hairs, making patterns with them, twisting them and then milking them free again. I was reminded of Freud's statement in the Dora case that, 'no mortal can keep a secret. If his lips are silent, he chatters with his finger tips . . .' (1905, p. 78), but for the most part I could not understand the factors behind her silence or the meaning of the hand movements.

She would say that she had a large number of thoughts which she could not string together, and this suggested a fragmentation such as that seen in the paranoid-schizoid position. However it was clear that something more active, teasing and pleasurable was going on, which resulted in long periods of deadness and aridity in which no development was discernible. This state seemed to protect her from anxiety, both paranoid-schizoid anxiety represented by her panic attacks and depressive anxiety if she inadvertently allowed herself to acknowledge a capacity to care about herself and the treatment. The evident gratification which her games provided suggested a perverse element.

She began a session two years into the analysis, by hunting in her bag for her cheque which she eventually gave me, and which I noticed had been incompletely filled in. She then spoke after only a short silence to tell me a dream. In it she had invited a young couple for a meal and then realized that she had run out of something, probably wine or food. Her husband and the friends went out to get the provisions while she waited at home. When they returned they brought the girl back on a stretcher and explained that she had been cut through at the waist and had no lower half. The girl did not seem upset but smiled and later went off on crutches. The patient asked her husband to take her to show her where it had happened. He did this and explained how a car had hit her from behind and cut her in two.

It was a relief to have a dream instead of the silence, and I interpreted that the dream itself might represent provisions for the analysis, as if she realized that we had run out of material to work with. The girl in the dream had been violently attacked when she went out for the provisions and I suggested that she might be afraid that something similar would happen to her if she brought material for analysis. Perhaps, I added, she was less afraid of being attacked now and could express a wish to understand these fears, represented in the dream by the request to find out how the accident had happened.

She was attentive and nodded as if she understood what I meant and this led me to go a little later and try to link the dream with her experience at the beginning of the session when she was hunting for her cheque. I suggested that she might be divided in her feelings about paying me, having brought the cheque and then losing it in her handbag, and also by filling it in incompletely.

There was a sharp change of mood and the patient became flippant saying that if that was the case she could put it right immediately because she had a pen with her, and she didn't want me to have anything I could use in evidence against her. It felt as if the contact with her had been abruptly cut off. She now seemed to feel that I had caught her out and was making a fuss, using her mistake with the cheque to put pressure on her to admit her ambivalence and to talk about her feelings. A mistake which she hadn't noticed left her feeling dangerously out of control and she had to attack the mood of co-operation and correct the mistake as quickly as possible. The mood in the earlier part of the session had, however, given a feeling of contact, and I think it did represent a move towards the depressive position in which she could show some concern for herself and her objects. This however, stimulated a violent attack when it seems I went too far or too fast, to link it up with something actual which had happened in the session.

In retrospect I think I got the level of this interpretation wrong and that I did not realize that she was unable to sustain the integration which would enable her to hold on to me as an analyst she could work with and at the same time admit negative feelings towards me. Instead she reverted to a state of mind in which she was cut off from her feelings just as the girl had been in the dream. The fact that the girl smiled and did not mind being cut in two seemed precisely to reflect the patient's smiling, flippant lack of concern. There was also an innuendo that I was more concerned with my cheque than with her needs so that she acted as if she had to satisfy me. Coming from behind, the attack seemed to come from me and to be directed against the relationship with me and against any part of her which had a desire to co-operate with the analytic work by bringing material and to acknowledge her ambivalence and understand it. Subsequently all the desire to understand resided in the analyst and she directed her endeavours to keeping me at bay. I think we can see how I became part of the pathological organization and played an essential role in maintaining it by acting out these attacks for her. In fact I may even have been set up to attack her over the cheque and I suspect that I could not avoid being party to a shift in mood which she then dealt with by retreating out of contact.

I think envy played a part in provoking these attacks and perhaps it was to avoid them that she seldom acknowledged any improvement in our working relationship or indeed in her life in general. It was only in passing that I heard, over the next few months, that she had applied to an art school for which she was preparing a portfolio, and that she was taking driving lessons. She did, however, mention that her husband was installing central heating, and that although she was reluctant to leave her art work, she had somewhat grudgingly agreed to help him. She had become quite involved and interested in this work and had admitted that when she did bring herself to help she found it satisfying. This seemed to correspond to a warmer atmosphere which had begun to develop in her sessions, although she remained somewhat grudging, sulky and sensitive.

She then failed to turn up for three sessions, and because this was so unusual I telephoned her to enquire what had happened. She explained that while working on the central heating she had dropped a radiator on her toe and that she had in fact tried to ring me at her session time, but I had failed to answer, in fact because my telephone bell had inadvertently been turned off. On her return she could admit that not only her toe but her feelings had been hurt by my failure to be available, and she had once more taken to her bed and her novels. She then described a dream in which a girl had died of a mysterious illness and she had been summoned by the girl's parents to talk to them. She did not know what to say, and was told that it did not matter, as if they saw that she was upset and were being careful not to make her cry. She then added, 'You can say, "How nice" when something good happens but . . .' and she trailed off. In the dream the room to which she had been summoned contained bookshelves and a coal stove which she was able to link to bookshelves in a children's home where she had been left as an infant. She idealized her memories of this home; in particular the beautiful dolls there, but in fact said that she had been left there while the family went on holiday with her younger brother and on their return she refused to recognize her mother and became so ill that she was unable to leave the home for a further two weeks.

A further association then emerged to a waiting room on the frontier when the family had been stopped after a visit to her grandmother. Her mother had on this occasion been taken off the train by border guards to have some irregularity in her passport checked, and the family waited for her in a room with bookshelves and a coal stove.

I was able to interpret that elements in the dream reflected her feeling that when I did not answer the telephone, a tragic event like a death from a mysterious illness had occurred, and that when I had telephoned her, it felt as if I had summoned her back to the analysis to ask her to explain her reaction. I think the analytic work represented by the installing of central heating had put her more in touch with her feelings, and the associations to the dream seemed to confirm that horrific memories were revived of times when she feared she might lose her mother.

We can conceptualize the movement in this fragment of the analysis to reflect a shift from a pathological organization towards the depressive position where contact of a meaningful kind took place and analytic work was possible. The patient, however, also shows how narcissistic defences are redeployed to pull her back into a pathological organization when depressive feelings become intolerable.

The pathological organization seems to offer the patient an idealized haven from the terrifying situations around her. The perverse flavour was connected with the apparent lack of concern on the part of the patient, and the evident pleasure and power she derived from the self-sufficiency of the borderline state. The analyst by contrast feels extremely uncomfortable, being asked to carry the concern and yet knowing from his experience with the patient that whatever he does will be unsatisfactory. If I had not telephoned the patient I had the impression she would not have been able to make the move towards me and we might have had a very long absence or even a breakdown in the analysis. On the other hand, I was also left feeling that telephoning her was a serious error in technique and I had an uneasy sense of doing something improper as if I had been seduced or was seducing *her* to make her feel she was coming back to the analysis for my benefit and at my summons. It is interesting to observe that it is sometimes the analyst's shortcomings which are exploited to justify a return to the pathological organization. Here the patient could argue that my failure to answer her telephone call meant that I had let her down and this justified a retreat to her bed and her novels, which could again be idealized as safe and warm. This makes the analyst feel that any lapse on his part can become a stimulus for a perverse orgy.

Precisely the same kind of issue seemed to be a factor in her silence which also seemed to be a retreat to an idealized state which she could call her desert island where she could sunbathe. I thought she had some insight into the way she created these states of mind, and that the safety she found there was illusionary while the deadness and aridity she created was real and extremely disabling. She therefore had a true desire to make progress in the analysis and to find creative capacities within her, which could lead to development professionally and to the satisfaction of a long-hidden wish to have a family.

Such developments however depended on her capacity to withstand destructive attacks which were regularly mounted whenever she approached the depressive position and got in touch with her need of objects and her reparative impulses towards them. In fact some progress gradually became apparent and she began her art course and passed her driving test. She also made better contact with her parents whom she was able to invite and even appreciate. Her silence remained a problem throughout the analysis however, and periods of productive work continued to be interspersed by long periods of deadness and aridity.

I think it is possible to see how the pathological organization protected the patient from both paranoid-schizoid and depressive anxieties. It offered the comforts of withdrawal to a state which was neither fully alive nor quite dead, and yet something close to death, and relatively free of pain and anxiety. This state was idealized even though the patient knew she was cut off and out of touch with her feelings. I think perverse sources of gratification were prominent and that these helped to keep her addicted to this borderline state of mind. The panic attacks seemed to represent a breakdown of the defensive organization and a consequent return to the persecutory fragmentation of the paranoid-schizoid position. At other times it was possible to observe a change of attitude which seemed to represent a move towards the depressive position, and these could be recognized as constituting analytically meaningful change. She seemed able, at least temporarily, to relinquish her dependence on the pathological organization and establish a relationship with me as her analyst. It was evident, however, how precarious this contact was and how rapidly it could be cut off as for example happened when I interpreted her ambivalence regarding the cheque.

Discussion

There are several excellent descriptions of pathological organizations (Riviere 1936; Meltzer 1968; Rosenfeld 1971; Segal 1972; O'Shaughnessy 1981; Riesenberg-Malcolm 1981; Spillius 1983; Sohn 1985) and I will here only mention a few features which were prominent in the patient I have described. I will then briefly discuss some of the possible reasons for the tenacious hold which these organizations have on the personality and describe the way they interfere with development. Finally I will emphasize the clinical relevance of recognizing the equilibrium between the organization and the two basic positions.

In phantasy the organization can be represented in a variety of ways, most vividly as a gang or mafia in the manner described by Rosenfeld (1971). He showed how splitting and projective identification lead to the disowning of destructive parts of the self and destructive internal objects which are distributed in the members of the gang. The group is idealized and the cohesion of the defensive system is represented by the cohesion of the gang which depends on perverse methods to ensure dependence and loyalty. The gang or its leader will persuade, seduce and if necessary threaten, to obtain obedience from its members including the patient, who often seems to be an unwilling member but too weak to escape.

I have previously suggested (Steiner 1982), that the patient's attitude to the organization is not always as innocent as he pretends and that a perverse collusion develops involving complex relationships between parts of the self in which good and bad parts become inextricably entangled. This often makes it difficult for the analyst to find a trustworthy patient he can address, and interpretations which imply that the patient is a victim who needs to be rescued by the analyst may be experienced as a collusion.

At other times the organization has a predominantly spatial representation, sometimes in the form of an idealized place such as a desert island, or a cave or building within which the patient can take refuge. In my patient, for example, the room on the border seemed to have become an idealized haven and the terrifying experiences associated with it were denied. The patient may then find it very difficult to emerge from this haven to face the real world where pain and anxiety threaten.

This spatial aspect of the organization may be why several writers have used the term 'position' in connexion with it. Melanie Klein herself (1935) spoke of the manic position as a defence against both paranoid–schizoid and depressive anxieties, Segal speaks of a narcissistic position (1983) and I have thought of it in terms of a borderline position (Steiner 1979). This helps us to visualize the equilibrium diagram in spatial terms but can be misleading because the organization is actually making use of paranoid–schizoid mechanisms. Unlike the situation in the other positions I believe these organizations are always pathological and always interfere with development. Indeed I think most analysts see in them an expression of the death instinct and a manifestation of envy as well as a defence against it (Spillius 1983). It may allow a restricted type of life and even at times prevent or postpone an acute breakdown, but it must be relinquished for a true contact with reality to be achieved.

The organization consequently seems to offer a solution to what Rey (1979) has called the claustro-agoraphobic dilemma. If the patient attempts to emerge from it and move towards his objects he will often retreat and argue that he cannot afford to experience the emotional contact which closer relationships entail. In many cases this is experienced as a claustrophobic anxiety and the object is felt to threaten the ego by imprisoning it, by suffocating it, or by making too many demands on it. On the other hand there is also a fear that a relinquishing of the defences will plunge the patient into schizoid anxieties, especially confusion, and fragmentation which are often experienced as agoraphobia. If he moves towards his objects he becomes claustrophobic, while if he moves away from them he is agoraphobic. The pathological organization often appears to be the only way out since in it objects are bound in an organized structure where the emotional distance to them can be controlled.

At times the anxieties of relinquishing the protection of the pathological organization seem very real and the patient will vividly convey the horrors he would have to face if it were to be abandoned. At other times however, the need for it is less convincing and the impression develops that the organization is turned to not so much of necessity but because the dependence on it has become a kind of addiction. The patient may then show that he has insight into the essentially self-destructive character of the organization and that he is at least partly aware that the equilibrium provides only an illusion of safety. Nevertheless the organization is adhered to, and this seems partly at least to be due to the perverse gratification which it provides. Sado-masochistic elements have been described by most of the authors writing about organizations and I think were clear in the way my patient teased and tormented me in her silences.

Sometimes the perverse flavour arises primarily from the way truth is twisted and distorted, which leads to a peculiar borderline relationship to reality which is similar to that which has been described in perversions (Chasseguet–Smirgel 1974). Freud (1927) first drew attention to these mechanisms in his study of fetishism in which the female penis is recognized and yet disavowed often with the help of an ingenious rationalization. I think they are characteristic of pathological organizations and are at the root of the perverse atmosphere.

It is these distortions which evade the internal reality of the depressive position so that the catastrophic state of the inner world is not faced and there is consequently no acknowledgement of a need to mourn and no reparation to be done. The patient seems not so much to destroy his insight but rather *turns a blind eye to it* and may then become involved in a complex cover up of the truth (Steiner 1985). This often misleads the analyst and provokes interpretations at the wrong level, as in my patient for example, where I was often persuaded that she had the capacity to understand only to find that she was unable or unwilling to sustain it. It is also, I suspect, one of the reasons for the paradoxical impression which the patient conveys of a serious and honest wish to have analysis combined with a continuing need to distort and misrepresent reality.

The aim of the organization seems to be to retain the status quo, namely the situation where narcissistic object relations persist and projective identification leads to self and object being confounded. The situation bears a similarity to that seen in the early phases of the depressive position, and the object is possessed, controlled and identified with through projective identification. It is the organized character of the defences which serves to cement the objects and projected parts of the self together, and consequently to prevent the latter from being withdrawn and returned to the ego.

This means that the next phase of the depressive position, in which the object has to be relinquished and mourned, does not proceed and the patient is stuck with concretely internalized objects each containing parts of the self of which he cannot let go. To do so would involve not only facing the loss of the object but the loss of the self which is contained in it. Mourning which would normally allow the gradual separation of self from object does not proceed and the consequent advantages such as the enrichment of the ego derived from the return of projections and especially the resultant capacity to think symbolically does not ensue.

Pathological organizations clearly have an important theoretical interest but it is in particular as a clinical tool that I believe the concept is most helpful. If the triangular equilibrium diagram is kept in mind it helps us to identify the leading anxiety of the session which is often connected with a transition or a threatened transition between two of the three states. For example, the transition:

Paranoid-schizoid Position ←   → Pathological Organization

is often the area of maximum tension in disturbed patients, especially early in an analysis. The patient may in fact have sought analysis as a result of a breakdown in a defensive organization which may lead to the development of symptoms. In analysis he may then try to re-establish the organization in order to get relief and will often use the analyst as part of the defensive system (Riviere 1936; Joseph 1983). The analyst needs to understand that in this phase there is no question of interesting the patient in understanding in the usual analytic sense since his priority is to find his equilibrium. Sometimes, the anxiety quite rapidly improves only to usher in a long stuck period in which the patient manages reasonably well as long as the analysis is there and as long as no development proceeds. The fear of a return to fragmentation and confusion is such that no development is allowed. For long periods my patient seemed to be afraid of such disintegrative states as were represented by her panic attacks, and the equilibrium she achieved in the analysis kept her relatively free of anxiety, and quite unable to develop.

Sometimes it is possible to observe patients operating in less pathological ways in which defences operate in isolation without being caught up in an organization and this can be considered as an expression of the equilibrium:

Paranoid-schizoid   Depressive
Position   ————————————————————→ Position.

Even in relatively well-adjusted patients, however, situations arise when pathological organizations take over, and the patient will become stuck, sometimes only in a restricted area of his mental life because he is unable to negotiate a particular conflict. The situation here is a less malignant version of that seen in the patients whose whole analysis is dominated by the organization. If the analysis is trying to deal with the difficult area of conflict the analytic work in both types of patient takes place in the equilibrium:

Pathological
Organization ←   Depressive
                                                   → Position

Even those patients who are very stuck will usually be seen to make occasional movements towards the depressive position and I believe it is important to recognize and interpret these. It is of course common to find that a move towards contact with depressive anxieties is followed by a retreat back to a pathological organization as if the patient argues that he cannot afford to experience the emotional contact which a closer relationship with objects entails. Sometimes this seems to be connected with an intolerance of experiences such as guilt and despair which characterize the depressive position and sometimes in addition, with the development of an unbearable quality to the psychic pain associated with the relinquishing of the protective organization (Joseph 1981). Much of an analysis may be occupied with following these shifts to and fro and in some cases progress and development do occur and the patient manages to emerge from the pathological organization into a more real object relationship (Segal 1983).

Summary

I have presented clinical material to illustrate how a pathological organization can be considered to exist in an equilibrium with the paranoid–schizoid and depressive positions. While making use of paranoid–schizoid mechanisms such as primitive splitting and projective identification, the defensive structure is highly organized and held together by narcissistic intrapsychic relationships in which perverse gratification plays an important role. This organization of defences seems to be designed to produce a place of real or illusionary safety from the anxieties experienced in the other two positions. All individuals fluctuate in the defences they employ and hence can be thought of as moving between these organizations and the other two positions. They consequently demonstrate some evidence of paranoid–schizoid level function and also of the existence of pathological organizations even if they may function in a relatively mature way at other times and in other settings. In some patients however the pathological organization dominates the personality and leads to analyses which become fixed and stuck.

It is argued that a recognition of these organizations of defences enables the analyst to orient himself more accurately to the clinical material and hence to address himself to the patient at a level he can understand.

References

Bion, W. R. (1963) *Elements of Psycho-Analysis*, London: Heinemann; paperback Maresfield Reprints, London: H. Karnac Books (1984).

Chasseguet-Smirgel, J. (1974) 'Perversion, idealization and sublimation', *International Journal of Psycho-Analysis*, 55, 349–57.

Freud, S. (1905) 'Fragment of an analysis of a case of hysteria', *SE* 7.

——(1927) 'Fetishism', *SE* 21.

Joseph, B. (1981) 'Toward the experiencing of psychic pain' in J. S. Grotstein (ed.) *Do I Dare Disturb the Universe?*, Beverly Hills: Caesura Press, 93–102.

——(1983) 'On understanding and not understanding: some technical issues', *International Journal of Psycho-Analysis*, 64, 291–8.

Klein, M. (1935) 'A contribution to the psychogenesis of manic depressive states' in *The Writings of Melanie Klein*, vol. 1, London: Hogarth Press, 262–89; paperback New York: Dell Publishing Co. (1977).

——(1952) 'Some theoretical conclusions regarding the emotional life of the infant' in *The Writings of Melanie Klein*, vol. 3, London: Hogarth Press (1975) 61–93.

——(1957) *Envy and Gratitude* in *The Writings of Melanie Klein*, vol. 3, London: Hogarth Press (1975) 176–235.

Meltzer, D. (1968) 'Terror, persecution, dread', *International Journal of Psycho-Analysis*, 49, 396–401; reprinted in *Sexual States of Mind*, Perthshire: Clunie Press (1973).

O'Shaughnessy, E. (1981) 'A clinical study of a defensive organization', *International Journal of Psycho-Analysis*, 62, 359–69.

Rey, J. H. (1979) 'Schizoid phenomena in the borderline', in J. LeBoit & A. Capponi (eds.) *Advances in the Psychotherapy of the Borderline Patient*, New York: Jason Aronson.

Riesenberg-Malcolm, R. (1981) 'Expiation as a defence', *International Journal of Psychoanalytic Psychotherapy*, 8, 549–70.

Riviere, J. (1936) 'A contribution to the analysis of the negative therapeutic reaction', *International Journal of Psycho-Analysis*, 17, 304–20.

Rosenfeld, H. A. (1950) 'Notes on the psychopathology of confusional states in chronic schizophrenia', *International Journal of Psycho-Analysis*, 31, 132–7; also in *Psychotic States*, London: Hogarth Press (1965).

——(1964) 'On the psychopathology of narcissism: a clinical approach', *International Journal of Psycho-Analysis*, 45, 332–7; also in *Psychotic States*.

——(1971) 'A clinical approach to the psychoanalytic theory of the life and death instincts: an investigation into the aggressive aspects of narcissism', *International Journal of Psycho-Analysis*, 52, 169–78 (also reprinted in this volume, pp. 239–55).

Segal, H. (1957) 'Notes on symbol formation', *International Journal of Psycho-Analysis*, 38, 391–7; also in *The Work of Hanna Segal*, New York: Jason Aronson (1981) 49–65.

——(1964) *Introduction to the Work of Melanie Klein*, London: Heinemann; also New York: Basic Books (1964).

——(1972) 'A delusional system as a defence against the re-emergence of a catastrophic situation', *International Journal of Psycho-Analysis*, 53, 393–401.

——(1983) 'Some clinical implications of Melanie Klein's work: the emergence from narcissism', *International Journal of Psycho-Analysis*, 64, 269–76.

Sohn, L. (1985) 'Narcissistic organization, projective identification and the formation of the identificate', *International Journal of Psycho-Analysis*, 66, 201–13.

Spillius, E. (1983) 'Some developments from the work of Melanie Klein', *International Journal of Psycho-Analysis*, 64, 321–32.

Steiner, J. (1979) 'The border between the paranoid-schizoid and the depressive positions in the borderline patient', *British Journal of Medical Psychology*, 52, 385–91.

——(1982) 'Perverse relationships between parts of the self: a clinical illustration', *International Journal of Psycho-Analysis*, 63, 241–51.

——(1985) 'Turning a blind eye; the cover-up for Oedipus', *International Review of Psycho-Analysis*, 12, 161–72.

References to general introduction and other introductory material

Abraham, K. (1919) 'A particular form of neurotic resistance against the psycho-analytic method', in *Seleected Papers on Psycho-Analysis*, trans. D. Bryan and A. Strachey, London: Hogarth Press (1942).

Bick, E. (1968) 'The experience of the skin in early object relations', *International Journal of Psycho-Analysis*, 49: 484–6.

Bion, W. R. (1950) 'The imaginary twin', paper read to the British Psycho-Analytic Society, November 1950, in *Second Thoughts*, London: Heinemann (1967), 3–22; reprinted in paperback, Maresfield Reprints, London: H. Karnac Books (1984).

—— (1952) 'Group dynamics: a re-view', *International Journal of Psycho-Analysis*, 33: 235–47; also in M. Klein, P. Heimann, and R. E. Money-Kyrle (eds.) *New Directions in Psycho-Analysis*, London: Tavistock Publications (1955) 440–77; paperback, Tavistock Publications (1971); also reprinted by Maresfield Reprints, London: H. Karnac books (1985).

—— (1954) 'Notes on the theory of schizophrenia', *International Journal of Psycho-Analysis*, 35: 113–18; also in *Second Thoughts*, 23–35.

—— (1955) 'Language and the schizophrenic', in *New Directions in Psycho-Analysis*, 220–39.

—— (1956) 'Development of schizophrenic thought', *International Journal of Psycho-Analysis*, 37: 344–6; also in *Second Thoughts*, 36–42.

—— (1957) 'Differentiation of the psychotic from the non-psychotic personalities', *International Journal of Psycho-Analysis*, 38: 266–75; also in *Second Thoughts*. 43–64.

—— (1958a) 'On arrogance', *International Journal of Psycho-Analysis*, 39: 144–6; also in *Second Thoughts*, 86–92.

—— (1958b) 'On hallucination', *International Journal of Psycho-Analysis*, 39: 341–9; also in *Second Thoughts*, 65–85.

—— (1959) 'Attacks on linking', *International Journal of Psycho-Analysis*, 40: 308–15; also in *Second Thoughts*, 93–109.

—— (1962a) 'A theory of thinking', *International Journal of Psycho-Analysis*, 43: 306–10; also in *Second Thoughts*, 110–19.

—— (1962b) *Learning from Experience*, London: Heinemann; reprinted in paperback, Maresfield Reprints, London: H. Karnac Books (1984).

—— (1963) *Elements of Psycho-Analysis*, London: Heinemann; reprinted in paperback, Maresfield Reprints, London: H. Karnac Books (1984).

—— (1965) *Transformations*, London: Heinemann; reprinted in paperback, Maresfield Reprints, London: H. Karnac Books (1984).

—— (1967) 'Notes on memory and desire', *The Psychoanalytic Forum*, 2: 272–3 and 279–80.

—— (1970) *Attention and Interpretation*, London: Tavistock Publications; reprinted in paperback, Maresfield Reprints, London: H. Karnac Books (1984).

Brenman, E. (1982) 'Separation: a clinical problem', *International Journal of Psycho-Analysis*, 63: 303–10.

—— (1985a) 'Cruelty and narrowmindedness', *International Journal of Psycho-Analysis*, 66: 273–82.

—— (1985b) 'Hysteria', *International Journal of Psycho-Analysis*, 66: 423–32.

Eigen, M. (1985) 'Towards Bion's starting point: between catastrophe and death', *International Journal of Psycho-Analysis*, 66: 321–30.

Freud, S. (1916) 'Some character types met with in psycho–analytic work', (see especially 'II – Those wrecked by success', *SE* 14, 316–31) *Standard Edition of the Complete Psychological Works of Sigmund Freud*), London: Hogarth Press (1950–74).

—— (1923) *The Ego and the Id*, *SE* 19, 3–66.

—— (1924) 'The economic problem of masochism', *SE* 19, 157–70.

—— (1937) 'Analysis terminable and interminable', *SE* 23, 209–53.

Gallwey, P. (1985) 'The psychodynamics of borderline personality', in D. P. Farrington and J. Gunn (eds.) *Aggression and Dangerousness*, London: John Wylie, 127–52.

—— (in press) 'The psychopathology of neurosis and offending', in P. Bowden and R. Bluglass (eds.), *Principles and Practice of Forensic Psychiatry*, London: Churchill Livingstone.

Grinberg, L. (1962) 'On a specific aspect of countertransference due to the patient's projective identification', *International Journal of Psycho-Analysis*, 43: 436–40.

Grotstein, J. S. (1981) *Splitting and Projective Identification*, New York: Jason Aronson.

Heimann, P. (1950) 'On countertransference', *International Journal of Psycho-Analysis*, 31: 81–4.

Hughes, A., Furgiuele, P., and Bianco, M. (1985) 'Aspects of anorexia nervosa in the therapy of two adolescents', *Journal of Child Psychotherapy*, 11: 17–32.

Isaacs, S. (1948) 'The nature and function of phantasy', *International Journal of Psycho-Analysis*, 29: 73–97; also in M. Klein, P. Heimann, S. Isaacs, and J. Riviere, *Developments in Psycho-Analysis*, London: Hogarth Press (1952) 67–121.

Jackson, M. (1978) 'The mind-body frontier: the problem of the "mysterious leap"', paper read to the Psychiatric Section of the Royal Society of Medicine in March, 1978.

Joseph, B. (1981) 'Defence mechanisms and phantasy in the psychological process', *Bulletin of the European Psycho-Analytical Federation*, 17: 11–24.

—— (1982) 'Addiction to near-death', *International Journal of Psycho-Analysis*, 63: 449–56.

—— (1986) 'Envy in everyday life', *Psychoanalytic Psychotherapy*, 2: 13–22.

—— (1987) 'Projective identification: some clinical aspects', in *Projection, Identification, Projective Identification*, J. Sandler (ed.), New York International Universities Press.

Klein M. (1921) 'The development of a child', in *The Writings of Melanie Klein*, vol. 1: *Love, Guilt and Reparation*, London: Hogarth Press (1975), 1–53; in paperback, New York: Dell Publishing Co. (1977).

—— (1923) 'The role of the school in libidinal development', in *The Writings of Melanie Klein*, vol 1, 59–76.

—— (1928) 'Early stages of the Oedipus conflict', in *The Writings of Melanie Klein*, vol. 1, 186–98.

—— (1930) 'The importance of symbol formation in the development of the ego', in *The Writings of Melanie Klein*, vol. 1, 219–32.

—— (1932) *The Psycho-Analysis of Children*, in *The Writings of Melanie Klein*, vol. 2, London: Hogarth Press, (1975); in paperback, New York, Dell Publishing Co. (1977).

—— (1935) 'A contribution to the psychogenesis of manic depressive states', in *The Writings of Melanie Klein*, vol. 1, 262–89.

—— (1940) 'Mourning and its relation to manic depressive states', in *The Writings of Melanie Klein*, vol. 1, 344–69.

—— (1942) 'Some psychological considerations: a comment, in *The Writings of Melanie Klein*, vol. 3, *Envy and Gratitude and Other Works*, London: Hogarth Press (1975), 320–3, in paperback, New York: Dell Publishing Co. (1977).

—— (1946) 'Notes on some schizoid mechanisms', in *The Writings of Melanie Klein*, vol. 3, 1–24.

—— (1952a) 'Notes on some schizoid mechanisms', in M. Klein, P. Heimann, S. Isaacs, and J. Riviere *Developments in Psycho-Analysis*, London: Hogarth Press, (1952) 292–320.

—— (1952b) 'The origins of transference', in *The Writings of Melanie Klein*, vol. 3, 48–56.

—— (1957) *Envy and Gratitude*, in *The Writings of Melanie Klein*, vol. 3, 176–235.

—— (1975) *The Writings of Melanie Klein*, in four volumes, London: Hogarth Press; in paperback, New York: Dell Publishing Co. (1977).

Klein, M., Heimann, P., and Money-Kyrle, R. E. (eds.) (1955) *New Directions in Psycho-Analysis*, London: Tavistock Publications; in paperback, Tavistock Publications (1971).

Klein, S. (1965) 'Notes on a case of ulcerative colitis', *International Journal of Psycho-Analysis*, 46: 342–51.

—— (1974) 'Transference and defence in manic states', *International Journal of Psycho-Analysis*, 55: 261–8.

—— (1980) 'Autistic phenomena in neurotic patients', *International Journal of Psycho-Analysis*, 61: 395–402.

—— (1984) 'Delinquent perversion: problems of assimilation: a clinical study', *International Journal of Psycho-Analysis*, 65: 307–14.

Langs, R. (1978) 'Some communicative properties of the bipersonal field', *International Journal of Psychoanalytic Psychotherapy*, 7: 87–135.

Malin, A. and Grotstein, J. S. (1966) 'Projective identification in the therapeutic process', *International Journal of Psycho-Analysis*, 47: 26–31.

Meissner, W. W. (1980) 'A note on projective identification', *Journal of the American Psycho-Analytic Association*, 28: 43–67.

Meltzer, D. (1964) 'The differentiation of somatic delusions from hypochondria', *International Journal of Psycho-Analysis*, 45: 246–53.

—— (1966) 'The relation of anal masturbation to projective identification', *International Journal of Psycho-Analysis*, 47: 335–42.

—— (1968) 'Terror, persecution, dread – a dissection of paranoid anxieties, *International Journal of Psycho-Analysis*, 49: 396–400; also in *Sexual States of Mind*, Strathtay, Perthshire: Clunie Press (1973), 99–106.

—— (1973) *Sexual States of Mind*, Strathtay, Perthshire: Clunie Press (1973), 90–8 and 143–50.

—— (1975) 'Adhesive identification', *Contemporary Psychoanalysis*, 11: 289–310.

—— (1978) *The Kleinian Development*, Strathtay, Perthshire: Clunie Press.

Meltzer, D., Bremner, J., Hoxter, S., Weddell, D., and Wittenberg, I. (1975) *Explorations in Autism*, Strathtay, Perthshire: Clunie Press.

Mitchell, J. (1986) *The Selected Melanie Klein*, Harmondsworth: Penguin.

Money-Kyrle, R. E. (1956) 'Normal countertransference and some of its deviations', *International Journal of Psycho-Analysis*, 37: 360–6; reprinted in *The Collected Papers of Roger Money-Kyrle* (ed. D. Meltzer with the assistance of E. O'Shaughnessy), Strathtay, Perthshire: Clunie Press, 1978, 330–42.

—— (1969) 'On the fear of insanity', *The Collected Papers of Roger Money-Kyrle*, 434–41.

Ogden, T. (1979) 'On projective identification', *International Journal of Psycho-Analysis*, 60: 357–73.

—— (1982) *Projective Identification and Psychotherapeutic Technique*, New York: Jason Aronson.

Ornston, D. (1978) 'Projective identification and maternal impingement', *International Journal of Psychoanalytic Psychotherapy*, 7: 508–28.

O'Shaughnessy, E. (1981a) 'A clinical study of a defensive organization', *International Journal of Psycho-Analysis*, 62: 359–69.

—— (1981b) 'A commemorative essay on W. R. Bion's theory of thinking', *Journal of Child Psychotherapy*, 7: 181–92.

Rey, J. H. (1979) 'Schizoid phenomena in the borderline', in J. LeBoit and A. Capponi (ed.) *Advances in the Psychotherapy of the Borderline Patient*. New York: Jason Aronson, 449–84.

Riesenberg-Malcolm, R. (1981a) 'Expiation as a defence', *International Journal of Psychoanalytic Psychotherapy*, 8: 549–70.

—— (1981b) 'Melanie Klein: achievements and problems (reflections on Klein's conception of object-relationship)', published in Spanish as 'Melanie Klein: logros y problemos', *Revista Chilena de Psicoanalisis*, 3: 52–63: also published in English in R. Langs (ed.) *The Yearbook of Psychoanalysis and Psychotherapy*, vol. 2, New York: Gardner Press (1986).

Rivière, J. (1936) 'A contribution to the analysis of the negative therapeutic reaction', *International Journal of Psycho-Analysis*, 17: 304–20.

Rosenfeld, H. (1947) 'Analysis of a schizophrenic state with depersonalization', *International Journal of Psycho-Analysis*, 28: 130–9; also in *Psychotic States*, London: Hogarth Press (1965), 13–33; also published in New York: International Universities Press (1966) and reprinted in paperback, Maresfield Reprints, London: H. Karnac Books (1982).

—— (1949) 'Remarks on the relation of male homosexuality to paranoia, paranoid anxiety, and narcissism', *International Journal of Psycho-Analysis*, 30: 36–47; also in *Psychotic States*, 34–51.

—— (1950) 'Notes on the psychopathology of confusional states in chronic schizophrenias', *International Journal of Psycho-Analysis*, 31: 132–7; also in *Psychotic States*, 52–62.

—— (1952) 'Notes on the psycho-analysis of the superego conflict of an acute schizophrenic patient', *International Journal of Psycho-Analysis*, 33: 111–31. Also in M. Klein, P. Heimann, and R. E. Money-Kryle (eds.) *New Directions in Psycho-Analysis*, London: Tavistock (1955), 180–219; also in H. Rosenfeld, *Psychotic States*, 63–103.

—— (1954) 'Considerations regarding the psycho-analytic approach to acute and chronic schizophrenia', *International Journal of Psycho-Analysis*, 35: 135–40. Also in *Psychotic States*, 117–27.

—— (1963) 'Notes on the psychopathology and psycho-analytic treatment of schizophrenia', *Psychiatric Research Report, no. 17*, American Psychiatric Association; also in *Psychotic States*, 155–68.

—— (1964) 'On the psychopathology of narcissism: a clinical approach', *International Journal of Psycho-Analysis*, 45: 332–7; also in *Psychotic States* 169–79.

—— (1971a) 'Contribution to the psychopathology of psychotic states: the importance of projective identification in the ego structure and object relations of the psychotic patient', in P. Doucet and C. Laurin (eds.), *Problems of Psychosis*, vol. 1, The Hague: *Excerpta Medica*, 115–28.

—— (1971b) 'A clinical approach to the psychoanalytical theory of the life and death instincts: an investigation into the aggressive aspects of narcissism', *International Journal of Psycho-Analysis*, 52: 169–78.

—— (1978a) 'Notes on the psychopathology and psycho-analytic treatment of some borderline patients', *International Journal of Psycho-Analysis*, 59: 215–21.

—— (1978b) 'The relationship between psychosomatic symptoms and latent psychotic states', paper given at a scientific meeting of the British Psycho-Analytical Society on 3 May 1978.

—— (1986) 'Transference – countertransference distortions and other problems in the analysis of traumatized patients', unpublished talk given to the Kleinian analysts of the British Psycho-Analytical Society, 30 April 1986.

—— (1987) *Impasse and Interpretation*, London, Tavistock Publications.

Sandler, J. (1987) 'The concept of projective identification', in J. Sandler (ed.) *Projection, Identification, Projective Identification*, New York: International Universities Press. Paperback, London: H. Karnak Books.

Scott, W. C. M. (1948) 'Notes on the psychopathology of anorexia nervosa', *British Journal of Medical Psychology*, 21: 241–7.

Segal, H. (1950) 'Some aspects of the analysis of a schizophrenic', *International Journal of Psycho-Analysis*, 31: 268–78; also in *The Work of Hanna Segal* (including a postscript), New York: Jason Aronson (1981), 101–20; reprinted in paperback, London: Free Association Books (1986).

—— (1952) 'A psycho-analytical approach to aesthetics', *International Journal of Psycho-Analysis*, 33: 196–207; also in *The Work of Hanna Segal*, 185–206.

—— (1956) 'Depression in the schizophrenic', *International Journal of Psycho-Analysis*, 37: 339–43; also in *The Work of Hanna Segal*, 121–9.

—— (1957) 'Notes on symbol formation', *International Journal of Psycho-Analysis*, 38: 391–7; also in *The Work of Hanna Segal*, 49–65.

—— (1964a) *Introduction to the Work of Melanie Klein*, London: Heinemann; also published New York: Basic Books (1964).

—— (1964b) 'Phantasy and other mental processes', *International Journal of Psycho-Analysis*, 45: 191–4; also in *The Work of Hanna Segal*, 41–7.

—— (1967) 'Melanie Klein's technique', in B. B. Wolman (ed.) *Psycho-analytic Techniques*, New York: Basic Books (1967); also in *The Work of Hanna Segal*, 3–24.

—— (1972) 'A delusional system as a defence against the re-emergence of a catastrophic situation', *International Journal of Psycho-Analysis*, 53 393–401.

—— (1973) *Introduction to the Work of Melanie Klein*, 2nd edition, London: Hogarth Press.

—— (1974) 'Delusion and artistic creativity', *International Review of Psycho-analysis*, 1: 135–41; also in *The Work of Hanna Segal*, 207–16.

—— (1982) 'Mrs Klein as I knew her', unpublished paper read to the Tavistock Clinic meeting to celebrate the centenary of the birth of Melanie Klein, July 1982.

—— (1983) 'Some clinical implications of Melanie Klein's work: emergence from narcissism', *International Journal of Psycho-Analysis*, 64: 269–76.

Sohn, L. (1985a) 'Narcissistic organization, projective identification, and the formation of the identificate', *International Journal of Psycho-Analysis*, 66: 201–13.

—— (1985b) 'Anorexic and bulimic states of mind in the psycho-analytic treatment of anorexic/bulimic patients and psychotic patients', *Psycho-analytic psychotherapy*, vol. 1, no. 2, 49–56.

—— (in press) chapter on 'Treatment' in a book on forensic psychiatry to be edited by J. Gunn and P. Taylor.

Steiner, J. (1982) 'Perverse relationships between parts of the self: a clinical illustration', *International Journal of Psycho-Analysis*, 63: 241–51.

—— (1987) The interplay between pathological organizations and the paranoid-schizoid and depressive positions', *International Journal of Psycho-Analysis*, 68: 69–80.

Thorner, H. (1970) 'On compulsive eating', *Journal of Psychosomatic Research*, 14: 321–5.

—— (1981a) 'Notes on the desire for knowledge', *International Journal of Psycho-Analysis*, 62: 73–80.

—— (1981b) 'Either/or: a contribution to the problem of symbolization and sublimation', *International Journal of Psycho-Analysis*, 62: 455–63.

Williams, A. Hyatt (1960) 'A psycho-analytic approach to the treatment of the murderer', *International Journal of Psycho-Analysis*, 41: 532–9.

—— (1964) 'The psychopathology and treatment of sexual murderers', in I. Rosen (ed.) *The Pathology and Treatment of Sexual Deviation*, London: Oxford University Press, 351–77.

—— (1969) 'Murderousness', in L. Blom Cooper (ed.) *The Hanging Question*, London: Duckworth, 91–9.

—— (1978) 'Depression, deviation and acting out in adolescence', *Journal of Adolescence*, 1: 309–17.

—— (1982) Adolescents, violence and crime, *Journal of Adolescence*, 5: 125–34.

Williams, A. Hyatt and Coltart, N. (1975) 'The psychology of sexual development' in S. Jacobson (ed.) *Sexual Problems*, London: Paul Elek, 33–44.

Name Index

Abraham, K. 41, 102, 103, 106, 107, 196, 242–3, 267
Alexander, F. 17
Aristotle 180
Aronson, J. 172
Barros, E. DaRocha 141
Bick, E. 158, 187–91
Bion, W. 11, 61–78; on bizarre objects 174, 207; on communication 139–40; on container and contained 172; on dread 230; on envy 202; on equilibrium between paranoid-schizoid position and depressive position 325; on linking 87–101; on parasitism 126; on pathological organizations 196; on projective identification 13, 83–5, 121; on thinking 5, 12, 154–7, 159, 178–86, 197; on transformation and representation 212
Bleuler, E. 206
Brenman, E. 6, 199, 256–70
British Psycho-Analytical Society 4

Coltart, N. 6

Deutsch, H. 103

Eigen, M. 157
Eissler, K.R. 15, 24, 47–8n.
Eliot, T.S. 226

Federn, P. 15
Freud, S. 76, 164, 216, 280, 331; on anality 102–3; on concreteness 211; on consciousness 182–3; on death instinct 4, 167, 239–40, 242–5, 247, 249, 254, 312; on ego 63–4, 271–2; on fetishism 338; on identification 273, 321; on narcissism 197, 241–2, 276, 278; on negative therapeutic reaction 196; on object relationships 206, 250, 267; on pleasure principle 70; on projection 82; on psychoanalysis 94; on reality principle 61, 63, 65, 93, 180; and restitution 214; on splitting processes 304; on sublimation 167; on superego 18; on thinking 66–7, 220; on transference 272; on unconscious phantasy 3; on works of art 162
Fromm-Reichmann, F. 15, 48n.

Gallwey, P. 6
Garmes, H. 49n.
Grinberg, L. 84
Grotstein, J.S. 82
Guntrip, H. 205

Hartmann, H. 211, 241, 245
Hayward, M.L. 18
Heimann, P. 48n., 84, 102
Hitler, A. 257

351

Subject Index

354

ALSO IN THIS SERIES